FOREST

PRAIRIE

EDGE

FOREST PRAIRIE EDGE

PLACE HISTORY IN SASKATCHEWAN

MERLE MASSIE

UMP
University of Manitoba Press

University of Manitoba Press
Winnipeg, Manitoba
Canada R3T 2M5
uofmpress.ca

Printed in Canada
Text printed on chlorine-free, 100% post-consumer recycled paper

18 17 16 15 14   1 2 3 4 5

Cover design: Marvin Harder
Interior design: Jessica Koroscil

Library and Archives Canada Cataloguing in Publication

Massie, Merle, 1971–, author
Forest prairie edge : place history in Saskatchewan / Merle Massie.

Includes bibliographical references and index.
Issued in print and electronic formats.
ISBN 978-0-88755-763-7 (pbk.)
ISBN 978-0-88755-452-0 (PDF e-book)
ISBN 978-0-88755-454-4 (epub e-book)

1. Human ecology—Saskatchewan—Prince Albert Region.
2. Ecotones—Saskatchewan—Prince Albert Region. 3. Prince Albert
Region (Sask.)—History. 4. Prince Albert Region (Sask.)—Economic
conditions. I. Title.

GF512.S3M38 2014   304.2'30971242   C2013-908508-4
                                               C2013-908509-2

The University of Manitoba Press gratefully acknowledges the financial
support for its publication program provided by the Government of Canada
through the Canada Book Fund, the Canada Council for the Arts, the Manitoba
Department of Culture, Heritage, Tourism, the Manitoba Arts Council,
and the Manitoba Book Publishing Tax Credit.

FSC
www.fsc.org
MIX
Paper from
responsible sources
FSC® C016245

For Sargent Ernest McGowan and
David Sargent McGowan,
always in my thoughts.

And for Dave De Brou,
because I promised.

CONTENTS

ACKNOWLEDGEMENTS

Special thanks, first and foremost, to my grandparents, who made the move to the forest fringe many years ago and set the stage for the story that follows. Thanks and appreciation also to the men and women from the north Prince Albert region who spoke with me about my project, both formally (through interviews) and informally (at the coffee shop, Remembrance Day ceremonies, funerals, and auction sales). Their perspective and wisdom helped to shape my work.

Financial support came from the University of Saskatchewan, Dean's Scholarship Fund, the Social Sciences and Humanities Research Council Doctoral Fellowship, and the Department of History through both a doctoral scholarship and travel funds to pursue archival and oral research. I thank Jean Wilson at University of Manitoba Press for her initial enthusiasm and David Carr and the editorial and marketing teams for their astute suggestions and sympathetic e-mails. Two anonymous reviewers of the manuscript gave excellent feedback and tremendous encouragement.

Erika Dyck, Maureen Reed, Geoff Cunfer, Jim Miller, and George Colpitts: academic reviewers, colleagues, critics (in the best sense), and mentors (depending on the day). My thanks to you all. Andrew Dunlop scanned several maps and photographs using the facilities provided by the Historical GIS lab at the University of Saskatchewan. I am grateful.

Bill Waiser, role model *extraordinaire:* he not only kept me organized but also continually pushed me to speak clearly, say what I mean, and mean what I say. His productivity, commitment to others, and public presence as a professional historian continue to set the bar high.

Aspects of this book were published as "When You're Not from the Prairie: Place History in the Forest Fringe of Saskatchewan," *Journal of Canadian Studies* 44, 2 (2010): 171–93. My thanks to the editors and peer review readers for their feedback and support. Public response to parts of this book, through radio, newspaper, and *Canada's History* magazine, has been tremendous.

Family sustained the project from beginning to end. My in-laws—Ron and Joyce, Glenn and Lesley, Ryan and Jenn, and their families—cheered from the sidelines. My brothers and their families—Jamie and Jodie, Kerry and Melanie—offered a warm bed, hot meals, and babysitting services on innumerable research trips. My mother, Mary McGowan, accompanied me on research and conference trips, participated in oral history research, borrowed books for me, and kept me on track with stories from her childhood. My children, Bronwyn and Alric, have followed the family trend toward reading books, books, and more books. They are, as always, exceptional kids. My husband, Garth, is a star.

FIGURES

MAPS

FOREST

PRAIRIE

EDGE

EDGE, PLACE, AND HISTORY

I am from Saskatchewan, but I am not from the prairie.

How can that be? Saskatchewan is *the* "prairie" province. The description travels hand in hand with the provincial name. A Saskatchewan girl carries the prairie in her blood. She is weighted down by the sky, blown by its winds. Books declare it so.

It is not so.

I grew up on the edge, where the open plains surrender to the dark uprightness of the forest. When I look out from between the trunks of aspen and pine, I see where the dappled forest floor, the damp moss, and the willow-rimmed muskeg pools open out to a dry and tilled sunny field, soil nurturing wheat, barley, canola. I twist direction, now north and now south, viewing across the divide that separates and connects. I hardly move at all; I shatter sightlines and shadows.

The place where I stand is the transitional landscape between the Canadian south and the Canadian north. It is the divide between the two solitudes of Saskatchewan. The Saskatchewan flag bears colourful witness: the green stripe over the yellow is the heraldry symbolism of the two main Saskatchewan ecosystems. The lower half is burnished yellow, where classic fields of wheat wave across the prairie; the upper half is forest green, a boreal expanse reaching across the nation, "draped like a green scarf across the shoulders of North America."[1] The boreal scarf settles and shifts, cloaking the prairie from above.

I began to know Canada from the viewpoint of our "stumpranch" farm, as my parents called it, which sits at this ecological divide. The farm was cut tree by tree by tree and pulled painstakingly root by root, created through the sweat and

Figure 1. Saskatchewan flag.

muscle of post–Great War soldier Arthur Bridge and his brother, Cyril. They left lots of trees behind, and through the years the stumpranch that will always be my home defined my perspective of Saskatchewan. But my dad put it best: "I love Canada so much, especially the transfer area, where we leave field and farm and enter the forest area. I was born on the 'fringe' and just loved it—to be able to make hay one day and go blueberry picking the next is right up my alley. Drop the manure fork and in minutes ... have a fishing rod in your hand, is my idea of heaven."[2]

At the nexus between farm and forest, my family blended agriculture with forest-based activities. From a practical, child's eye view, my brothers and I built our "treehouses" on the ground. What was the use of going ten feet up? We would have a great view of ... yet more poplar trees. So what? And the treehouses would break apart in the next big wind. On the ground, we could build larger treehouses, big enough to camp out in, while hoping that the skunks and raccoons would not invade. Our family house was heated with wood; we learned how to chop and haul trees, cut, split, and pile the firewood, and build and maintain fires from an early age. With the Garden River running through our farm and copious large sloughs within easy reach, my dad and brothers were prolific trappers of beaver and muskrat. I became adept at fleshing. Hunting was a regular activity, with forest stretching almost from our doorstep. Ducks and geese, jumpers (deer), moose, and elk regularly flew or wandered by, unwittingly to grace our supper table, along with homegrown beef, pork, and poultry. Fishing was an evening activity in the summer on any number of nearby lakes, canoe paddle dipping along. While we casted, Mom would toss a jig over the side and read—and she caught as many fish as the rest of us. It was nothing to take a daylong excursion on Christmas Day, or at the warm end of February or March, by snowmobile or truck, onto the frozen crust of Bittern or Montreal or Anglin Lake. A five-gallon pail can carry a dipper, a spoon lure tied to a spool of line, a sandwich and a couple of chocolate bars, and a book. It does triple duty as a seat while you fish and a carrier for your catch at the end of the day. Nothing tastes better than pickerel (walleye) fried over a campfire. Forgot your frying pan? My brother's improvisational skills proved that hubcaps pried off the truck would substitute, and switching beer for the classic butter gave a lovely malty flavour.

I have great sympathy for those travellers who look out their windows on the Trans-Canada Highway and think *This is Saskatchewan? That's it?* I read a Twitter description of that highway in 2012: "Give me a ladder, and I can see Manitoba." The *Corner Gas* song plays on this stereotype: *first you tell me that your dog ran away/ then you tell me that it took three days.* The *Betty* cartoon, written and illustrated by Gary Delainey and Gerry Rasmussen, ran a series in March 2010 on the idea of taking a tourist trip to Saskatchewan. In an attempt to dissuade Betty from this plan, her husband suggested she take a 'virtual' trip to the province using Google's Street View. On finding her asleep at the computer, the son asked, "So are we going to Saskatchewan?" "I doubt it." The flat-equals-boring conception is common, but there is a physical aspect, a human reaction to immensity. As a child, I endured visits to relatives in Weyburn (not far from where *Corner Gas* was filmed) as a trial of the first magnitude: "all that sky, it's so *hot,* grasshoppers are yucky, I would like some shade, I have a headache, can we go home?"

While I admit solidarity with those who, like me, have found the prairie at times too much, my purpose is to shift your thinking about what Saskatchewan is and what it looks like. While working on the research that became this book, my desk and digital files were populated with classic northern Saskatchewan logging images. An office mate looked over my shoulder and asked, "Why do you have pictures of BC?" When I replied that these were from Saskatchewan, she gasped in shock. "You don't think of Saskatchewan as having trees." It is precisely those stereotypical assumptions that, I believe, need to be challenged.

This book is, first and foremost, a local or "place" history. It tells the story of my hometown region north of the city of Prince Albert, Saskatchewan, reaching back into the archaeological past and moving forward to 1940. As such, the first audience for this book is the neighbours and friends and relatives who populated my world when I was growing up and who continue to live in the area today. This place sits at the transition between the prairie and the boreal forest, which introduces a second important theme in this book: edge. Much can be learned by changing the point of view for writing history. In this book, I tell the story from the perspective of a community that sits on the edge *between* the two most iconic Canadian regions: Canada's north and Canada's south. The identity and history of my home community belong fully with neither one nor the other. I hope that this book will challenge conceptions of Saskatchewan, how people have lived here, and how those stereotypes have shaped the ways in which we tell our stories. So, as part of that challenge, my second audience is the historians and geographers who take on the task of telling Canada's story. (My first audience, friends and neighbours, may wish to skip straight to Chapter 1.)

REGIONALISM

Most Canadians have a mental image of Saskatchewan that is serviceable if rather boring. Calendar pictures of classic "Canadian" landscapes include lighthouses, brightly coloured houses, covered bridges, and Peggy's Cove for the Maritimes and fields of wheat gleaming burnished yellow under a wide blue sky for Saskatchewan. Indeed, following this stereotype, the Saskatchewan flag should be yellow and blue, like the calendar pictures. There are accompanying background stories that create this typical vision of Saskatchewan: open plains filled with bison and First Nations on horseback, then the transition to wheat fields. Treaty making and rebellion, the railway, intense immigration, sod shacks and pioneers, political and social experiments leading to innovations such as medicare, and industrial extraction of uranium, potash, and oil. Stories of the fur trade fade away as soon as settlers hit the stage. Certain plots, such as the dust and despair of the Great Depression of the 1930s, have gained the aura of legend, scripted virtually in stone. Saskatchewan is the have-not province that everyone left, but now the people are once again returning, or arriving, in droves.

There is truth to these stories. But so much is missing.

The Canadian habit of dividing Canada into regions has left the Canadian story deeply divided along arbitrary and artificial divisions. It is usual, almost automatic, to assume that Canada as a country can and should be divided politically, ecologically, or culturally. Cultural shorthand has standardized these chunks: the Prairies or the west (with or without British Columbia), the Maritimes or the east, central Canada or Ontario and Quebec, the north or the Far North, and the south. These regions (however defined) remain the most common method of controlling and discovering, comparing and contrasting the Canadian story. Substituting direction for space can mean "somewhere else" or "not here" or even "here," depending on your point of view or purpose. Historian Gerald Friesen suggests that the old "prairie" distinction was a political or social construct that was not necessarily natural and has lost most of its power. It has been replaced by the modern concept of "the West."[3] I agree. But the word *prairie* retains enormous strength when considering the environment or landscape. It is the cultural shorthand most synonymous with "Saskatchewan."

Regional divisions cause tensions on many levels. The boundaries have no political basis and shift according to the needs of those doing the arguing. Imagined boundaries have created both unity and serious internal strife—mention the National Energy Policy of Trudeau in Alberta and you will immediately note a strong negative reaction. Mention the Saskatchewan Roughriders and you will find every Canadian's second favourite football team—unless, of course, you're in Saskatchewan, where blood runs green and the 2013 Grey Cup win at home in Regina took Rider Nation pride to dizzying heights. Historians, in attempting to chronicle, analyze, and interpret the Canadian story, are prone to extended conversations, even fights, over the "best" way to write Canadian history. Despite eloquent calls for a unifying national story, regionalism remains. In part, it comes down to the purpose of the story. Manageable chunks allow for finer detail, comparisons, and the ability to draw attention to certain areas that are underrepresented in the larger national story. From the academic perspective, historian Ramsay Cook stated that Canada's story is already one of "limited identities" or stories told from the perspective of race, class, gender, or region. Gerald Friesen argued that, in Britain, class is the dominant national language or "framing"; in the United States, race takes precedence; in Canada, region reigns.[4]

Regionalism is a useful tool if used with caution. But I think that it has become too established, to the point of myopic assumptions and narrow-minded storytelling. It is all too easy to ascribe common cultural and physical characteristics to large areas that, on closer scrutiny, are not homogeneous. What implications has regionalization had for the Canadian story, both in the ways in which it has unfolded and in the ways in which historians (of all types, from the academic to the coffee shop) have framed the story? Which decisions and policy choices have been made using regional stereotypes? Which underlying assumptions have pushed the path of history? How has regionalism shaped interpretations of characters, settings, or plots? Geographer David Wishart warned that dividing space into regions, similar to dividing time into periods (such as "the roar of the twenties"), brings about a high degree of inertia, which will "inhibit new ways of understanding." It stops us from thinking fresh even before we start. We cannot approach a story in a new way, and we risk skewing our storylines, if we start from iconic and potentially incorrect assumptions. Wishart suggested a way out: "Reflection on what we take for granted ... can yield fresh insights, opening up new possibilities for new narratives."[5]

What have we, as Canadians, taken for granted? One thing is the iconic mental image of Saskatchewan. That image, and its scripted storyline, will come under scrutiny, even attack, in this book as I reflect on the difference between the Saskatchewan of the Canadian public imagination and my own lived experience. The prairie biome, the expanse simply of land and sky, has been appropriated as if representative of the entire province. Prairie ecology, history, and economy have become the essence of Saskatchewan. I will not simply rail against the stereotypical view of my province or regale you with northern stories. I will show that over-simplifying our understanding of Saskatchewan, reducing it to "prairie," has limited and actually skewed historical investigation and interpretation and influenced policy and decision making from the personal level to the federal level. Two problems have arisen: non-prairie spaces, and non-prairie stories, have been virtually invisible; moreover, in approaching Saskatchewan history with a host of assumptions, certain stories have been mistold. Venerable historian G.F.G. Stanley justified static "prairie" stories by claiming that historians of western Canada should only be concerned with the treeless prairie and the adjoining parkland: "My terms of reference do not include the forest area ... because those regions have their own distinctive geographical features, their own problems and their own future."[6] Separating the history of the prairie from that of the forest as Stanley wanted, or south from north, skews the Saskatchewan—and the Canadian—story in important ways.

The overwhelming cultural force of the prairie mystique has overshadowed the history of what historians Ken Coates and William Morrison term "the forgotten north," the provincial Norths of the subarctic boreal forest. "Long-ignored, politically weak, economically unstable, home to substantial aboriginal populations, these areas have played a significant, if relatively unknown, role in Canada's history," they contend. Scholarship is divided between the agricultural South and the "true north" or "Far North," the Yukon, Northwest Territories, and Nunavut in the arctic region "north of 60." This division skips right over the provincial Norths, slicing the fabric of both the provincial stories and the pan-Canadian story.[7] Coates and Morrison showcase the problem of regionalization: breaking Canada into geographically defined chunks, such as "the Prairies" and "the Far North," has fractionalized Canadian history. As a result, not only can it come apart at the seams, but sometimes, those seams do not meet at all.

Tied to the growing interest in Aboriginal history, work on the provincial norths has recovered forgotten history as a balance to the decades of scholarly work on the Prairies and the Arctic.[8] One key work that focussed on Saskatchewan's north, from a northern perspective, was historian David Quiring's lyrically titled *CCF Colonialism in Northern Saskatchewan: Battling Parish Priests, Bootleggers, and Fur Sharks.* Colonialism has been an important theme in Aboriginal history, and Quiring pointed to the twenty-year reign of the Co-operative Commonwealth Federation (CCF) as a time of overt colonization and exploitation of northern Saskatchewan. Focussed on policy history during the CCF period in Saskatchewan (1944–64), Quiring ably followed Coates and Morrison's suggestion that the Saskatchewan provincial north (like other provincial norths) was little more than a colony of the south, a tabula rasa where the CCF wanted to experiment with socialism.[9]

Although Quiring's work, and others like it, has provided important pieces of the Saskatchewan and northern story, it reinforced Stanley's arbitrary dividing line. Splitting the province in two allows a better view of certain stories, such as southern colonialism over northern inhabitants and landscape. To achieve this richly detailed and well-documented history, however, Quiring argued that the CCF was the first government to include the "previously ignored" north as a major priority suggesting that, from a policy and political perspective, there was little government interest in the Saskatchewan north prior to 1944. In an even more damning, and incorrect, assertion, northern specialist R.M. Bone claims that, "indeed, the North was ignored by Euro-Canadians until its forest and mineral wealth caught their attention in the post-World War II period."[10] Both statements, when measured against the historical record, are clearly misleading, even wrong. The northern boundary was a moving line, drawn more in the imagination than on geographical, or administrative space. It was an arbitrary division that loosely gathered up spaces with trees as "northern" and spaces without trees as "southern." The "north" of Bone and Quiring was not the same in the nineteenth century and early twentieth century as it became in the second half of the twentieth. Northern places, however defined, captured a large amount of energy and interest prior to 1944. To be fair, northern development on the scale and context to which Bone and Quiring referred was only possible with modern mechanization, such as airplanes and caterpillar tractors, more readily available after the Second World War.[11]

The movement to write northern history, from an Aboriginal or industrial/ development perspective, is laudable but still falls short: recovering the history of the provincial norths might add depth to the northern story but continues to create a false separation, reinforcing the contrasts and power imbalances but ignoring the connections. A recent book by environmental historian Liza Piper crosses provincial boundaries and redefines western Canada using the historical term "northwest." I applaud this move. Her work reflects a unique narrative that combines environmental history and Aboriginal and development history in the large lake region of the boreal forest. It reimagines both the north and the west, linking their stories in fascinating new ways.[12] Despite Piper's example, the Canadian story in both the public imagination and through books still splits along seams drawn from perceptions of landscape. Assumptions and stereotypes abound.

A second critical assumption that has skewed western Canadian history—and Canadian and regional public policy—is the concept of an "ideal" wheat farm. Historian R.W. Sandwell argues that there is now a growing understanding that the wheat monoculture was perhaps *not* the norm for the majority of agricultural endeavours, at least in nineteenth-century Canada.[13] That understanding, though, has not yet penetrated deeply into western Canadian history, where wheat remains king. A fascination with wheat has meant that other kinds of farms, such as subsistence and mixed, have been, to say the least, under-studied. A similar point, that "the single job, single wage norm ... may come to be seen as a historical aberration," is found in the work of researchers Rosemary E. Ommer and Nancy J. Turner. They argued that pre-industrial social exchange and trading practices have not disappeared but become the rural informal economy. Occupational pluralism, or making a living by more than one job on a seasonal, barter, or other basis, was often found at sites of ecological pluralism or landscapes with rich local diversity—like the forest fringe. Such pluralism was pragmatic and flexible, a localized response to place, landscape, and economic need.[14]

Emphasizing contrasts and connections, this book investigates the artificial dividing line between the north and the south. That dividing line emerges instead as a place of contact and exchange rather than a line from which histories have diverged. In Saskatchewan, the two ecosystems and cultures have drawn from and responded to each other. Like a clamshell, the two halves form a whole. The iconic mental image of flat prairie is still much in evidence, but I will recast it through the lens of contrast. Ironically, provincial citizens used the iconic images of flat and treeless prairie to market and sell northern spaces or experiences. While keeping—even shading more clearly—the stereotypical starting points of prairie and forest, I explore the *connections* (instead of an arbitrary separation) between the Saskatchewan provincial north and south before the Second World War.

ECOLOGICAL AND CULTURAL EDGES

The point of contact between the two major ecosystems of Saskatchewan is often called the "forest fringe."[15] Where two ecosystems meet is known as an *ecotone,* the place of transition or ecological edge. In Canada, the "fringe" is found across the continent at the boreal forest edge.

Ecotones present high levels of biodiversity or species richness.[16] They tend to display soils, plants, and animals drawn from both parent ecosystems as well as unique features or species, and as a result they are even more diverse than their parent ecosystems. The ecotone, though, is *not* the "parkland." This is a common assumption, but I consider it incorrect (see Chapter 1). Forest fringe areas that have seen extensive fires, forestry, or agricultural settlement "look" more like the parkland, and some researchers have been known to confuse the two and point to parkland as a kind of transition zone between the prairie and the forest. It is not. Humans are drawn to ecotones, and a higher incidence of archaeological sites has been found in these places.[17] There are three possible reasons. One, an ecotone displays "edge effect" of species richness, a diverse landscape upon which to draw. Two, humans living within and across an ecotone enjoy easier exploitation of nearby parent ecosystems. Nearby exploitation helps to access greater diversity not just within but also adjacent to the ecotone. Three, if the dominant ecosystems support unique cultures (in this case cultures adapted to the prairie or the boreal forest), then those cultures will meet and interact at the ecotone, leading to exchange among and increasing flexibility for each cultural group. Ecotones, by their nature, are rather narrow in depth, though they have exceptional linear extent. The Canadian forest fringe ecotone spreads from the mountain cordillera to Quebec. Despite its breadth, the narrow depth of the forest edge means that it is less likely to support a social system or human society solely within the transition zone. For the forest fringe region, fire, logging, and productive farming, as well as conservation and reforestation, shift and re-create the forest/prairie interface. It has moved, expanded, and contracted over time. The forest edge provided a relatively diverse base *in* which to live, *from* which to access the two main parent ecosystems of boreal forest and open plains, and *to* which humans would go to access different cultural, social, economic, and ecological knowledge and experience. The ecotone offered human occupants a measure of resilience and adaptive capacity, through both local diversity and nearness to other ecosystems.

The forest fringe is a dividing line between one way of life and another. Ethnobotanist Nancy Turner, ethnoecologist Iain Davidson-Hunt, and anthropologist Michael O'Flaherty have suggested that ecological edge zones display characteristics of cultural edge zones, where separate cultures converge. Their work is based primarily on examples drawn from Indigenous peoples. At the point of convergence, the resulting cultural edge was "rich and diverse in cultural traits, exhibiting cultural and linguistic features of each of the contributing peoples. This results in an increase in cultural capital and resilience ... especially in times of stress and change."[18] In other words, at cultural edges, there was not only an exchange of material goods (trade patterns) but also the ability to learn from one another and adapt ideas from the other culture (many of which were drawn from long experience with the parent ecological system).[19] I define the cultural characteristics of a forest-based society as resource exploitation: fur, fish, game, berries, timber, and medicinal products, to cite a few examples. The methods of extraction and use became embedded in the culture—firing the forest to encourage blueberry growth or trapping certain species at certain times of the year. In the prairie ecosystem, pastoral (bison husbanding/hunting and livestock) and agricultural grain-growing characteristics have defined human life. I consider cultures supported by bison as pastoral in a general sense. Such cultures did not follow the bison blindly but knew and manipulated bison patterns, building jumps and pounds and firing the prairie to encourage and control feed and pasturage. Where these two systems meet, trading and knowledge sharing were important components. Knowledge gained in these interchanges would allow a measure of success and adaptation should a culture need to cross an ecotone and enter the other.

Plains and Woods Cree converged at the forest fringe, using the ecotone during certain times of the year and exchanging cultural knowledge and practices. Records show Aboriginal elders in times past reflecting on the cultural and embedded differences between bison hunting on the plains and tracking moose and elk in the boreal forest. A hunter good at one might not have been good at the other. The best interpretative understanding of the significance of this ecological and cultural edge comes from historical geographer Arthur J. Ray, whose book *Indians in the Fur Trade* showed how both boreal forest bands and plains bands used the forest edge as an integral part of yearly economic exploitation cycles. "The ability to exploit all of these zones," Ray maintained, "gave these groups a great deal of ecological flexibility" and "permitted them to make rapid adjustments to changing economic conditions."[20] Ray used early journals and diaries written by some of the first white traders in the West to support these claims. For instance, the famous French fur trader, La Verendrye, wrote how "many of the tribal bands moved to the parklands or lived in the outer fringes of the forest [in winter]. In these settings they had access to the bison ... and the relatively sizeable moose population of the forest."[21]

When Ray published *Indians in the Fur Trade* in 1974, it would have been hard to imagine the dynamic and ongoing importance of this work. It has been a catalyst leading generations of scholars to study First Nations history and explore a variety of research ideas, methods, and sources. This variety has included First Nations people as active participants and "middlemen" in the fur trade; research on fur-trade journals to study fur-trade life; in-depth examination and analysis of trade goods and economics; First Nations environmental history; gender and mixed-blood dynamics; interdisciplinary work mixing archaeology and anthropology with history and geography; demographic and epidemic studies; and First Nations migration. Although Ray's work has been cited as seminal by countless researchers in First Nations and fur-trade history in the past forty years, most have concentrated on how his work placed First Nations groups at centre stage in the fur trade. Few have picked up on his place-based exploration and explanation of ecological and cultural edges.[22] I will pick up the dropped thread and use it to "sew" the split seam of the two ecological and cultural regions of prairie and boreal back together.

Societies living at edge zones benefit from diversity and resilience, whether the diversity is ecological or cultural. Resilience refers to "flexibility and adaptive capacity" and is used in particular to describe what happens to a community following a disaster or setback.[23] I interpret resilience at an edge ecotone as creating a society based upon several possible and intertwining pursuits. As a result, human life might look different from one year to the next—flexibility is central. Fishing might be good one year but not the next, while hunting or farming is better. Seasonality is important: the turning of the seasons presents different opportunities and problems. Resilience, as demonstrated by Aboriginal life at this particular ecotone in Saskatchewan, is an excellent viewpoint to think about successive examples of human occupation. Edge becomes a theoretical tool that allows me to consider, contrast, and compare the different cultures that have lived in and used the forest edge from pre-contact to the end of the Great Depression.

THE "PIONEER FRINGE" AND THE "FRONTIER"

There is a great term, well used by geographers, for the outer edge of human habitation: "ecumene." Within this line, you find human society. Past this line, human society has no influence. A similar term, and one that is more familiar, is "the frontier," a North American cultural symbol found in books, movies, and media. Nineteenth-century cultural historian Frederick Jackson Turner interpreted the frontier myth in two ways: first, the frontier is a place, a "thinly-settled ... line where civilization ends, an area where man meets the wilderness"; second, the frontier is a process whereby humans (in Turner's work, Europeans) became stripped of European sensibilities and were reborn and renewed by the vigorous and dangerous life of the pioneer. Pioneers, in turn, built a new civilization crafted on individual values and democracy.[24]

Numerous books have referred to human societies built at the forest edge as frontier and pioneer societies, at the place where civilization meets wilderness. The enduring description is the "pioneer fringe" of human settlement.[25] The term was crafted by geographer Isaiah Bowman of the American Geographical Society in the 1920s and 1930s. Bowman was deeply intrigued by the social and economic problems presented by "pioneer settlement": that is, human settlement in completely new, uncultivated places at the ecumene. Following the Great War, Bowman was part of a committee to study geographical and mapmaking information (in preparation for the Paris Peace Conference) to reconstruct or redraw firm national boundaries in Europe. This experience led to his ongoing interest in internal agricultural settlement, efficient planning, and the ability to push the boundaries *within* a country and turn land at the pioneer fringe into productive farmland.[26]

He advocated intensive study of such new settlements in pioneer fringe areas around the world in an attempt to determine which conditions, and problems, could benefit from support and solutions to ease successful human adaptation at fringe zones. Bowman called these studies the "science of settlement."

The twentieth century was marked by intense human migration into "new" regions worldwide, from the Canadian West to the Andes, from southern Africa to Siberia. Bowman supported governments anxious to solve the problems dogging successful human settlement in "pioneer" regions. His work made the term "pioneer fringe" part of the geographical and historical lexicon.[27] Pioneer fringe studies were published in two volumes in the United States, *The Pioneer Fringe,* by Bowman, and *Pioneer Settlement: Co-operative Studies,* from contributing authors studying pioneer belt regions around the world, including Canada, Rhodesia, Mongolia, South Africa, Tasmania, Siberia, and Argentina.

The concepts of frontier, pioneer fringe, and ecumene suggest that cultures move in only one direction, that an expanding culture reshapes the landscape, economy, and society in its own image. Success or failure is measured against the ideals of the parent culture. That a culture adapts to or changes in the new environment, or infringes on a society already resident there, is rarely part of the story. In the case of the forest fringe in Canada, the story has consistently been told as agricultural society moving north. Typical storylines suggest that settlement beyond the eaves of the forest was driven by fear that the free and easily-farmed agricultural land was all gone. Success was defined, therefore, as the ability of a pioneer fringe farm to support a farm family without accessing off-farm sources of income—an ideal built on a prairie wheat model that actually never existed. Prairie homesteaders often took off-farm jobs (on the railway, in town building civic buildings, or with other farmers). Measuring success by drawing comparisons with the parent culture causes real problems in how the story is told. The significant drawbacks of boreal agriculture, including a higher incidence of frost, poor soil quality, and severe transportation impediments, have been well studied, while the non-agricultural advantages of the boreal forest have been downplayed and ultimately misunderstood.

The story of the forest fringe has been told in one of two ways. The first story portrays the familiar homesteader bravely facing the elements to carve a new life out of the forest in Denis Patrick Fitzgerald's 1966 geography dissertation, "Pioneer Settlement in Northern Saskatchewan." Fitzgerald's work, though never published for a broader audience, redefined human life at the pioneer fringe not just as a repeat of the southern pioneer story but also as something more: forest fringe pioneers "gird themselves for battle in a land ... thrice cursed by Thor."[28] The physical landscape was more demanding, Fitzgerald argued, with trees, rocks, muskeg, mosquitoes, and fires. The pioneers, therefore, had to be something special: super-pioneers. Fitzgerald shaped a classic battle between a harsh landscape and indomitable human will, a process through which human life was expected to emerge strong and victorious. Acknowledging the boreal and non-prairie landscape, he documented non-farm activities and resources found in a forest environment and showed how pioneers adapted to and used these resources. The lens remained focussed, however, on farmers, the "forest invaders" looking to develop "new and moderately expensive farm homes, modern equipment, purebred cattle, full rich heads of grain on thick sturdy stocks, painted barns, oiled highways and other outward signs [of] ... victory."[29] Ultimately, by the early 1960s, it had become "difficult to distinguish the oldest areas of settlement, along the southern margins of the pioneer region, from those in the adjacent parklands."[30] The physical landscape, the economy, and the culture of the pioneer fringe had blended with that of the adjacent parent culture, Fitzgerald noted with obvious pride and delight. What was once northern and different had changed to become indistinguishable from its southern parent ecosystem.

The second story is told best by retired geographer J. David Wood in *Places of Last Resort: The Expansion of the Farm Frontier into the Boreal Forest of Canada, c. 1910–1940*. Wood tells a story of decline in which those who attempted forest fringe agriculture were deliberately misled and deluded, either by their own desire for a farm anywhere at any cost or by politicians and religious groups who strongly believed in the importance of a continuing farm frontier. Where Fitzgerald's thesis recognized the influence of the landscape on pioneer fringe life and culture (ultimately celebrating a landscape vanquished), Wood's narrative was much more narrowly defined. Wood emphasized the line of farm frontier moving ever farther north, beyond the edge of where it should have been. Interested in the limits of traditional farming and farming practices "that had been perfected over the centuries in northwestern Europe and eastern North America," Wood's narrative was built around a supposed universality of farm practices and their subsequent failure on boreal farms.[31] His work was pan-Canadian in focus, both worthy of praise and extremely problematic. The experience of boreal forest agriculture in the Clay Belt region in northern Ontario, and the abandonment of those areas (with which Wood was most familiar), were not necessarily the experience of the Clay Belt region of Quebec, or the forest fringe regions of the West, particularly the Peace River region of Alberta, which has continued its agricultural expansion into the twenty-first century.[32]

In trying to force a national narrative, Wood missed important regional nuances. In essence, he assumed that the story he knew best applied everywhere—regionalism carried to its absurd degree. He also did not delineate among various migrations to the farm frontier, such as soldier settlement or Depression resettlement, which happened at different times for widely different reasons. As a result, the book tried to compare frontier experiences from 1910 in northern Ontario with those from 1935 in northern Saskatchewan without also comparing the economic, social, and political backgrounds. Wood worked too hard to present a declensionist narrative—describing "places of last resort" in which poor men were duped into trying to create a life on poor farms, with tragic social and environmental results. The lack of investigation of the boreal landscape or culture meant that Wood did not give adequate recognition to the "pull" factors at work that drew people to the forest fringe, either non-agricultural economic opportunities through lumbering, fishing, trapping, hunting, mining, or freighting, or non-economic factors such as a desire to live among the beauty of the trees. It should not simply be a story of what people were running from; it is also imperative to consider what they were running to.

THE NEXUS OF SASKATCHEWAN

The *nexus* is the centre; it is also the point of connection, linkage, exchange, and association between two or more people, places, or things. A nexus is both centre and edge—exactly how I will reorient the story that follows. I will use four key concepts to explore the edge: edge as hinge (connection, linkage, and exchange), edge as imagination (wilderness versus civilization), edge as refuge (place of safety), and edge as nexus (centre, place of pluralism, mixing, and resilience). Each had a role in shaping the cultural conception of the forest fringe and ultimately in shaping nature and setting out terms for human uses of the environment.

The edge is, first, the point of linkage connecting Saskatchewan's boreal north and prairie south. The cultural construction of north/south has had a profound impact on the physical, economic, and social formation of the province, as it has on much of the rest of Canada. I will show how those contrasts have been used to create particular economic and cultural landscapes. The extensive bison hunting and pemmican industry built across the Great Plains had a particular purpose and customer: to feed the canoe and York boat supply lines strung across the boreal north. The treeless prairie could be filled with settlers because the boreal forest was full of wood, ready to be processed for the prairie market. It is in the *contrasts* between the two ecosystems and cultures that certain characteristics of each landscape can be most clearly understood. Obvious comparisons include resources versus agriculture, bison versus moose, wet versus dry, treeless versus tree-full. Human descriptions of and uses of these environments have been shaped and reinforced by an acute understanding and exploitation of these contrasts.

Edge is also a place of imagination—where, on a medieval map, you fell off the edge of the known world into the mouths of hungry dragons. As in the concept of ecumene, edge becomes a rather frightening place beyond which humans have little knowledge or influence. In the Canadian context, writer Margaret Atwood explores Canada's north in both *Survival: A Thematic Guide to Canadian Literature* and *Strange Things: The Malevolent North in Canadian Fiction* as a way to expose the artificial but intrinsic divide between the south as civilization and the north as perilous wilderness.[33] Grey Owl, the shapeshifter Archibald (Archie) Belaney, worked to preserve the wilderness and its inhabitants as the last Canadian natural space. The civilization/wilderness divide found traction at the forest edge.

The forest edge was a place of refuge, of shelter and protection, where the edge environment became a place of safety or sanctuary from threatening, harmful, or unpleasant situations or places elsewhere. A refuge must be considered through two lenses: geography and time. The forest edge became a place *to which humans would go* to find refuge *for a short period of time*. Using the forest edge on an occasional or seasonal basis sustained both boreal and prairie-adapted cultures.

The final concept is edge as nexus or centre. The forest edge was the transition zone between prairie and forest, a space where both farming and forest were evident. From this viewpoint, the edge becomes a place of pluralism where the two parent cultures intertwine. I argue that pluralism was a hallmark of human life at the forest edge, where cultures sought resilience through mixing. Resilience refers to the ability to recover, to adapt, and to be flexible. The focus is not on place as temporary destination to relieve a particular problem but on place as home. Resilience is a long-term concept, encompassing a broader time frame than refuge. The term "resilience" has been applied to both ecotones, with their diversity of resources, and to the cultural intentions of the human occupants of that edge environment. Human society would seek out or use edge places in order to create a more adaptable and resilient way of life. The focus is on the way in which the landscape is used and integrated over time. Those who have studied ecological and cultural edges in an Aboriginal context note that First Nations actively created and maintained ecological edges, whether by fire or other means, over successive generations. Edges were tools to maintain diversity as part of adaptive strategies. Newcomers such as forest edge farmers also sought to use or manipulate the forest edge to promote diversity.

All of these concepts—edge as hinge between two different landscapes, edge as imagination, edge as refuge, and edge as nexus—shape and inform this book. Often more than one concept can be found within a particular storyline. For example, three concepts were strongly found in the south-to-north Depression migration: migrants were physically moving from one environment to the other; some were seeking a short-term refuge from the prairie disaster; others were looking for a long-term solution to the drawbacks of one-crop farming through resilience and the mixed-farming movement. Similarly, though the creation of Prince Albert National Park and the north Prince Albert "Lakeland" area found cultural strength in the contrast between prairie and forest, tourists heading to those places were looking for a short-term "refuge," a time of rejuvenation and relaxation within a green and humid landscape. Tourism literature strongly promoted "accessible wilderness" at the edge of civilization. These concepts offer a new language drawn from ecological and cultural edges that moves beyond the rigid terms of "frontier" and "pioneer fringe" and suggests that the forest edge is the point of connection, exchange, contrast, and transition in the Saskatchewan—and by extension Canadian—landscape.

PLACE HISTORY AND THE LURE OF THE LOCAL

It is important to remember that neither the landscapes nor the cultures that live in them are static; in other words, neither humans nor ecological systems stay the

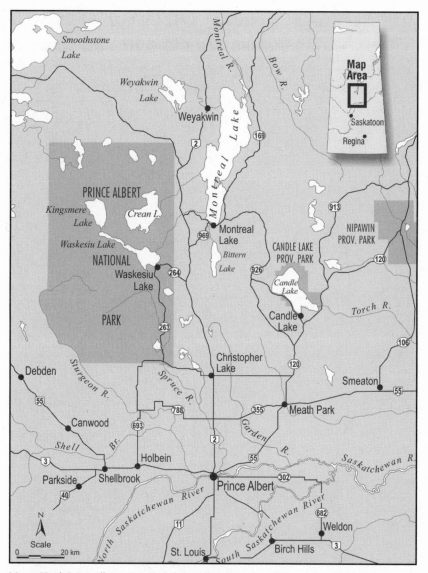

Map 1. North Prince Albert region (including research focus region). Source: Modified from *Prince Albert and Northern Lake Country* 1, 1 (2008): 5.

same for long. Place history allows for a deep-time historical investigation that layers, contrasts, and compares different occupations of the same place or sometimes the same occupation but at different times or for different purposes.

The general area of study in this book extends north from the city of Prince Albert. Bounded by the communities of Shellbrook to the west and Meath Park

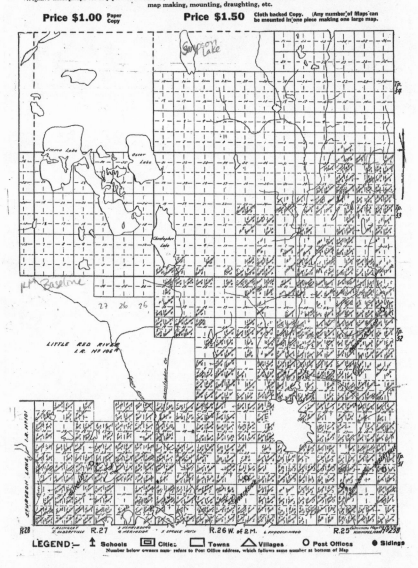

Map 2. Cummins Map 258. The community names reflect existing postal services as of 1922.
Source: SAB, Cummins files.

to the east, the region reaches to the resort community of Waskesiu and the south shore of Montreal Lake at the Montreal Lake Cree Nation Reserve (Map 1). The focus study region is somewhat smaller, corresponding roughly to Cummins Rural Directory Map 258 (Map 2). It includes the farming community of Alingly; the Little Red River First Nation and its sister community at Sturgeon Lake; the village of Christopher Lake; the community of Tweedsmuir at the south entrance to Prince Albert National Park; the resort communities and cabins surrounding Anglin, Christopher, Emma, and Candle Lakes (commonly known as Lakeland); the communities of Spruce Home, Henribourg, Albertville, Paddockwood, and Northside; and the old postal district known as Forest Gate. The region is about 18 miles (29 kilometres) in width and 24 miles (34.5 kilometres) in depth, or just over 400 square miles (1,120 square kilometres) of physical space. It offers a variety of landscapes used in a variety of ways: active farmland, rangeland, and pasture; First Nations reserves; resort communities; Northern Provincial Forest; recreational forest; and, along its border, Prince Albert National Park.

Studying a small region over a long period of time is a common historical tool.[34] Historian Dan Flores referred to such investigations as "deep time" history, a specific effort to examine environmental change across sequential cultures. My book responds to his call for what he terms "bioregional" histories of place. Over time, a region is physically remade by both natural and human changes and is a place of flux and transition from one to the other and back again. Much of what began as boreal forest was remade into parkland—a form of prairie—through intensive logging, forest fires, and agriculture. As parks were created, fires were suppressed, and some agricultural land was abandoned, there was a long ecological succession back to boreal forest. Throughout its history, human and natural manipulation of the landscape has resonated through cultural and economic adaptations in the local region. As well, humans developed north-south trails to move through the landscape, crossing the transition zone and tying Saskatchewan together on a north-south, rather than east-west, axis.

Flores believes that history can be effectively studied in terms of bioregion: "natural geographic systems ... [are] appropriate settings for insightful environmental history."[35] Sometimes, though, as another historian, Shannon Stunden Bower, points out, bioregions have no respect for human-created boundary lines, such as provincial boundaries or international borders.[36] Although it might make sense on some levels to define a study by a particular landscape, that is exactly the problem I am trying to combat. Studying western Canadian history through the lens of either "prairie" or "boreal forest," without considering the connections between the two, has created flawed interpretations and a tendency to start with basic (and incorrect) assumptions. Following the strict interpretation of Flores, this book would not work. He might prefer the traditional method of looking at Saskatchewan history as either prairie history or boreal history, as if the two have no points of connection, exchange, or shared history. This book's study area is not a bioregion but the transition zone between two bioregions. Luckily, Flores notes that, "given the natural human preference for ecotone edges, interesting settings for human history won't necessarily be bounded [by] ecoregions."[37] I take that comment as a challenge and an invitation.

The secret to doing place-based history is to think laterally: what activities, businesses, pastimes, transportation routes, or trysts have occurred in the dance between humans and landscape in this place? Published scientific research in archaeology and anthropology, climatology and soils, forestry, forest fires, and ecology gave voice to the landscape and its original inhabitants. Parliamentary debates, speeches, newspapers, and records of the railways and the Department of the Interior offer the Canadian national and Saskatchewan provincial agendas for the expansion of settlement and resource extraction in both the prairie and boreal environment of the western interior. The local story was found in the Department of Indian Affairs RG 10 files concerning Little Red River Reserve, the 1930 Saskatchewan Commission on Immigration and Settlement, Soldier Settlement Board files, Department of Northern Resources files, the 1955 Royal Commission on Agriculture and Rural Life, and regional newspapers (particularly the *Prince Albert Daily Herald* and other Prince Albert–based newspapers). Community history books gave excellent genealogical, ethnic, and social history and were an important reference for migration information, and they made me think about how people migrate in chains of friends, neighbours, and relations to keep their social safety nets secure. Newspapers and local histories were the two most important sources, for they offered the best assessment of the *perception* of the locale. Photographs from regional, provincial, local, and private collections added an important visual component to the story, complemented by historical and contemporary maps. Oral history was an integral part of this study, and local residents provided sketches and stories of life at the forest fringe. This book is not a policy history, so I used government sources specifically to provide information and commentary that related directly to the study area or to the broader themes that emerged.

University colleagues worried that my research area was too small. People who lived in my research region worried that the research region was far too large. How could I possibly tell the stories of all the small communities within the area? The local perception and commentary was based firmly on the way in which local history has been written in western Canada: a community-based voluntary project in which the outcome is a book that contains as many family biographies as possible.[38] I remain fascinated by the power of these community history books to inform, entertain, and elicit feelings of belonging and pride. The discipline, drive, economics, and sheer determination involved in organizing and producing a community history book by a group of volunteers deserve applause. A visit to the Prairie History Room of the Regina Public Library is an eye-opening event. Thousands of history books, published by various communities across western Canada, weigh down the shelves. Several such books from the local study region were important sources for this book.

At the same time, there is a subtle but important difference between cooperatively written community histories and what has been termed "local" history. Community histories sought family, corporate, church, and school histories and photographs defined by locale. Editing was minimal, contributions were voluntary, and results depended on the response and writing ability of each author. A local history, in contrast, is generally written by a single author with a more narrative style. Although also focussed by locale, local histories have only occasionally been written by academics. Historian Paul Voisey wrote a damning review of community history production and a manifesto to create better local history in his essay "Rural Local History and the Prairie West." Voisey argued that the best local history, if compared with an international standard, has "limited and definite purposes, shuns events and individuals in favour of structures and groups, and is interdisciplinary in theme and method." He also argued that "the best local histories tackle themes of property, agricultural production, demographic change, family structure, social class, class relations, social mobility, geographic mobility, social order, community conflict, community development and disintegration, and the impact of urban growth on nearby rural areas."[39] His list bears no relation to the issues of concern for community history groups trying to collect family stories. While Voisey's style might indeed produce a fine local history, it is not the only way that it can or should be done.

If there is a general rule that professional historians are better off not writing local histories, exceptions to this rule are "case studies." Such studies, different from local histories, are interested in big picture themes and theories, which are "tested" against the local story to see which ideas work and which do not. Such a study would satisfy Voisey's list of themes. An excellent example of the case study approach is historian Joy Parr's groundbreaking *The Gender of Breadwinners: Women, Men, and Change in Two Industrial Towns, 1880–1950.*[40] The book compares the industrialization of two towns in Ontario through the lens of gender. It shows that concepts of "women's work" and "men's work," combined with traditional gender-related responsibilities of childrearing, cooking, cleaning, and shopping, shaped two industrial towns in terms of their social attitudes and merchant and other occupations. One town was clearly a women's town, the other just as clearly a men's industrial town. Case studies flip the lens: the research questions, not the place, become paramount.

In general, local history has been dismissed by academic historians as too narrow in focus, narcissistic and limited, of little use to any audience beyond the local.[41] But historian William Baker found this narrow-minded view of local history to be wrong: "local history is not the poor brother of Canadian history." Local history, he argued, is about "vantage point," and none is superior to or more significant than any other.[42] His point rings true. Some academics struggled to justify their decisions to write local histories. This struggle was clear in the introduction of historian Kerry Abel's award-winning *Changing Places: History, Community, and Identity in Northeastern Ontario.*[43] Abel's work provided an important precedent for place histories, both for its success and its layered approach to history. Abel met head-on the expected criticism: "Why look at a place that is completely unknown to many Canadians, a place with fewer residents than the city of Lethbridge, Alberta?" She answered that question in three ways. One, her chosen place (which she sometimes called a "subregion") "deserves to be better known, for its history has always been directly connected to events that made Canada what it is today" (mining dynasties, newspaper magnates, and Shania Twain). Two, it "provides a sort of laboratory in which the big, abstract questions can be answered on a smaller, more manageable scale" (similar to a case study). Three, it was "a worthy object simply in its own terms. 'National' history, or 'big' history, or even 'total' history is not the only legitimate undertaking for our generation of historians."[44] According to Abel, small, local place histories are legitimate undertakings too. Flores noted that local history, as something more than a case study, is gaining ground in historical circles. Indeed, he reported with cautious optimism that "histories of place have already made strides in eroding [the] sniffing condescension [of academic historians]."[45] I hope that this book will not only shatter perceptions of Saskatchewan, but will stand as an example of what place history can be, for both academic and public audiences.

Finally, this book is rooted in the personal. I grew up in the north Prince Albert region, as did my mother and my father. All of my grandparents fled to the forest fringe: my dad's parents in 1934, abandoning the dust and despair of the east Weyburn area during the dirty thirties; my mom's parents in 1939, running from the Poland-Ukraine border to the forested spaces of Canada, with four sons and a daughter in tow, to save the boys from the horror of the war about to descend on Europe. Place researcher Cliff Hague notes that, though place identities are ultimately personal, they are formed in relation to other people, other places, and other identities and so are filtered, fostered, and formulated through socialization. The concept of the forest fringe, and the place identity of the north Prince Albert region as presented, are ultimately mine but have been shaped by my association with others, particularly my parents and grandparents and their experiences and choices. I was born and raised at Paddockwood, and to a certain extent what follows is an investigation of my own past. As an "insider" to the region, I have an insider's knowledge of its stories; its roads, rivers, lakes, and trees; its sights, sounds, and smells; its people and identity. This book, through place history, explains how a person can be from Saskatchewan but decidedly *not* from the prairie.

Despite the limited physical map of the north Prince Albert region, writing a place history from the forest fringe has proven to be an immense project. Chapter 1 presents a physical description of the landscape, drawing on botany, climatology, topography, and soil patterns. Following and overlaying the physical description is an analysis in Chapter 2 of First Nations perceptions and uses of the forest edge. I move beyond accepted models of First Nations use of the forest edge as a winter refuge to suggest that both boreal and plains bands used and modified the edge landscape in all seasons. From the edge, I show the intensification of plains bison hunting and processing (the pemmican trade) as the economic alignment of south-north with the northern boreal fur trade. Resource extraction, in turn, forced the dominion government to respond to repeated demands of the Montreal Lake and Lac La Ronge Woods Cree Nations for adhesion to Treaty 6. From the perspective of the dominion, treaty adhesion was unnecessary at first since the land was not considered fit for agriculture. But as resource interest grew and industrial exploitation spread north from Prince Albert, a treaty for resource purposes became imperative. From the perspective of the First Nations, however, a treaty simply reinforced long-held practices of local bands accustomed to living within and traversing across the ecotone. The subsequent creation of Little Red River Reserve for farming in the north Prince Albert region marked legal physical ownership of a landscape that was an important part of traditional cultural usage. Moving through the late nineteenth century, I add new layers of occupation, including the permanent founding of a community at Prince Albert. From that point on, resource exploitation flipped the south/north ecological duality. Chapter 3 describes how the dominion government and local entrepreneurs articulated a narrative of trees and lumber to contrast and supply a treeless but growing prairie society. Whereas in the pemmican trade the south supplied the north, codification of the north Prince Albert region as a place of timber wealth created a supply of northern goods for the south. The absence of trees in the prairie landscape, combined with a steady stream of prairie settlement, created a ready market.

In practice, the north Prince Albert region remained the stronghold of foresters until the devastating winter of 1906–07. The subsequent fuel crisis forced the dominion government to survey large tracts of forested land for homesteading purposes, a new departure in dominion policy. The north Prince Albert region became a popular homestead destination. Chapter 4 outlines the quest for long-term resilience tied to the mixed-farming movement, an idea deeply rooted in landscape. An ideal mixed farm contained both arable farmland and scrub land for hay or fuel. As such, a mixed farm was situated within, and deliberately became, an ecological edge landscape. Mixed farms offered agricultural diversity and resilience since a farmer's assets and liabilities were spread over several marketable crops, livestock, and farm products. Prince Albert promoters (particularly the Board of Trade) along with dominion land surveyors and newspaper editors declared the forest edge landscape as ideal for the development of a successful mixed farm. In considering the role of mixed farming, Chapter 4 breaks open the classic prairie wheat narrative.

Chapter 5 discusses the deep cultural shift in dominion homestead policies after the Great War, which radically changed to include extensive hands-on guidance for settlers. The mixed-farm concept appealed strongly to returned Great War soldiers and influenced those who developed Soldier Settlement Board policies. A devastating regional drought on the prairie worsened in 1919 just as the soldiers were returning home. That led to an environmentally driven south-to-north migration of both soldiers and others looking to escape drought-prone regions. Soldier settlement and later land settlement schemes encouraged and supported south-to-north migration.

In practice, the concept of mixed farming changed within the forest edge environment. Not only were the farms a mix of grain and livestock—the typical description of a mixed farm—but forest edge farmers also actively participated in the non-farm economy available at the ecotone, such as the lumber and cordwood industries, fishing, freighting, and trapping. The forest edge as a landscape of economic resilience took mixed farming to a different level: the informal rural economy was built on occupational pluralism that deliberately combined a mixed farm with off-farm opportunities. Unlike J. David Wood, who measured boreal farming against an unrealistic southern farming model, I argue that the forest edge environment offered economic diversification beyond the mixed-farm model. Chapter 6 looks into those off-farm opportunities in the forest edge landscape.

The north/south duality, and its imprint on the cultural landscape of Saskatchewan, is discussed again in Chapter 7. The north Prince Albert area was rebranded as a place of recreation, a landscape of lakes known as "Lakeland" or "vacationland," anchored by Emma, Christopher, Anglin, and Candle Lakes as well as Prince Albert National Park. Much of the cultural push behind the creation of the national park can be found in the contrast between the treeless, arid prairie south and the green, forested, and well-watered landscape of the north. Improved roads, camping facilities, and the relative simplicity and inexpensive demands of car tourism brought the north Prince Albert region within reach of prairie residents. It became the "Playground of the Prairies," and the Prince Albert Board of Trade, in conjunction with the dominion government, began a marketing campaign about duality and contrast. Two figures stand out in the historical record as part of the edge-ness of this place. Archie Belaney, or Grey Owl, lived in Prince Albert National Park. His books extolled wilderness preservation and reinforced the divide between the civilized prairies and the last vestiges of wilderness in the forest. Painter Augustus Kenderdine used the contrast between the dried-out prairies and the northern woods to reinforce, dramatize, and advertise his Emma Lake Artist Camp, which began in 1936. In addition, a visit to the green forest and cool lake region was portrayed as a healthful interlude, an oasis, a refuge from the demands of daily life, not so much from the cities (the usual cultural model) as from hot, dusty, prairie farms.

All eyes converged on the forest fringe during the Great Depression, when tens of thousands of refugees from the dual prongs of drought and economic devastation retreated from the prairie to take refuge under the forest canopy. Chapter 8 details this Great Trek, one of the most important movements of people in Canadian history. The Great Trek story has generally been told from the perspective of the "pioneer fringe," where frantic settlers relocated to marginal boreal forest farms as a "place of last resort." Consistently, the Depression migration has been evaluated primarily in terms of agricultural success and thus has been found wanting. I argue that the economic and cultural landscape of the forest fringe prior to the Depression—Woods and Plains Cree ecotone exploitation, the rise of the resource industry, the mixed-farming movement, occupational pluralism derived from the non-farm economy, previous in-migration from the prairie, the growth of tourism—played a significant part in the Great Trek. The forest fringe was a landscape of hope and resilience, drawing trekkers *to* the forest edge ecotone as much as they were moving *away from* the devastation of the prairie. For the trekkers, hope and resilience re-created the forest fringe as a refuge, and they were the refugees. The economy at the forest edge *boomed* during the Great Depression in astonishing contrast to the iconoclastic stories of dust and despair that Canadians recognize from the classic prairie narrative. Northern resources—cordwood, fish, furs—were in demand despite the general economic depression, and forest fringe residents participated in a booming off-farm economy that mitigated many of the worst effects of that dismal decade.

Storytelling is at the heart of what historians do. As pointed out so eloquently and simply by environmental historian William Cronon, how a historian chooses to tell a story matters.[46] The story of the forest fringe, as seen through events and cultures in the north Prince Albert region, is more than just "marginal" farming carried too far past the forest edge. When viewed a little differently, taking into account deep-time history, a new narrative of cultural and ecological edges, resilience, refuge, and nexus offers a broader and deeper perspective. Significant historical events are viewed from a fresh perspective. New methodological ideas such as edge theory and place history offer a critical approach to bridge the artificial and culturally constructed gap *between* isolated regions that plagues the Canadian historical record. The Canadian habit of reducing this country into regions has shaped conceptions of nature and region, promoted inertia, and skewed analysis. It is time to break open stereotypical narratives to find new ways of telling the Canadian story. Reinterpreting the Saskatchewan story will, I hope, offer a new narrative arc. The edge is important: I challenge you not to ignore the edges between Canadian regions but to actively look into them as sites of new meaning in Canadian history. Instead of writing history from the centre, write it from the edge, looking out in all directions. As William Baker said, it's all about vantage point.

CHAPTER ONE

ECOTONES AND ECOLOGY

The connection between the land and the society that develops on that land is complex and crucial, giving new meaning to the old saying "history from the ground up" or "history from below." To understand the human history of the north Prince Albert region, it is first necessary to understand the land itself: land is "at the root of human existence."[1] Soil, topography, ecology, and foods and other commodities (from a human perspective) that can be coaxed or harvested from the land differ greatly from one area to another, and as a consequence the communities that develop also differ. Communities, in turn, are influenced by population, methods of resource extraction, agriculture, political regimes, economic drivers, and cultural and religious thought. Yet the human-ecological dance must stand on something. What does the ecological edge between the prairie and the boreal forest look like at and near the forks of the North and South Saskatchewan Rivers? How has that landscape changed over time?

First, a note about terminology. The Saskatchewan landscape covers a breadth of ecological diversity. It is too simple to say that there are only two major ecological areas, but despite obvious variations scholars argue that two effective ecosystems exist in the central Saskatchewan interior: boreal forest and grassland, commonly referred to as prairie. Where the two meet is often called the "parkland," the aspen grove section characterized by black soil, trembling aspen, balsam poplar, and willow that lie in groves surrounded by medium and tall grasses.[2] But the parkland is not the ecotone. In the late 1940s and early 1950s, researchers in the Department of Plant Ecology at the University of Saskatchewan, Robert Coupland and

T. Christopher Brayshaw, argued that the ecotone is in fact the place where parkland and boreal forest meet.[3] Ecologist Ralph Bird, whose 1961 book *Ecology of the Aspen Parkland in Western Canada* remains a major source of information on the flora and fauna of the middle parts of the western interior, reinforced Coupland and Brayshaw's assertions. Bird argued that the effective ecotone was the "point of contact" between the parkland and the boreal forest and called it "an area of stress," constantly in flux from one state to another.[4]

Archaeologist David Meyer, after extensive work in the parkland and boreal forest regions of Saskatchewan, suggested that from an archaeological perspective the "grassland communities within the parklands are a northern extension of the plains grassland ecosystem" and that grassland and parkland were occupied as a unit by human inhabitants.[5] The parkland has been misinterpreted to be the ecotone between the forest and the prairie, and its "importance ... has become exaggerated," Meyer declared.[6] The parkland showed a variation and extension of grassland cultures; the meeting place between forest-adapted and prairie-adapted cultures was the forest fringe.

I take the view that the ecotone is the boreal forest edge. Not only are there two major effective ecosystems, but also they are quite different from each other. The prairie has been consistently defined as treeless and arid, the boreal forest as well-treed and moist. It is in the *contrast* between the two that much of the tension and interplay of history has evolved.

PREHISTORY

The western interior of North America was covered in glaciers during the last ice age. During their retreat, glacial lakes formed at the receding edge. For about 400 years, from 11,300 to 10,900 BP, one of these lakes, glacial Lake Saskatchewan, covered what archaeologists call the Greater Forks region or what became the confluence of the North and South Saskatchewan Rivers. As the lake receded, the forks acted as a delta. The region would have looked rather like a shrub/tundra steppe, with large grazing animals. By 10,300 BP, white spruce advanced throughout the western interior, and the climate remained brisk because of the receding glaciers. In general, the cultural traces (spearpoints and other archaeological findings) point to the influence of southern culture on the local landscape.[7] Over time, the boreal forest edge receded north. During the Altithermal period (6000 BP), a time of excessive dryness, the grassland pushed the forest edge to its northern apex at approximate latitude 59° north, almost to the northern boundary of current-day Saskatchewan. The cooling period following the Altithermal period allowed the boreal forest to advance southward to more or less contemporary conditions by about 4000 BP.[8] Although this information might seem little more than archaic background, it does show that landscape changes on a grand scale can have significant local effects. The area under study has changed from glacier covered, to lakebed, to delta, to steppe, to spruce forest, to prairie, and back to boreal forest. It is important to contest the assumption that this place has always looked the way it does today.

FOREST COMPOSITION, SUCCESSION, AND FIRE

At the north bank of the North Saskatchewan River west of the forks prior to settler and logging encroachment, dark pines and white spruce stood tall. Their near-impenetrable canopy presented a formidable wall of green stretching hundreds of miles toward the Canadian Shield. It was the southern edge of the Boreal Plain ecozone, which today accounts for nearly all of the commercial forest zone of Saskatchewan.[9] The vegetation is officially classified as Mixedwood Boreal Forest. A mixedwood forest contains a mix of coniferous trees from white spruce to balsam fir on well-drained soils. When burned or logged, the mixedwood forest regenerates with trembling aspen and poplar. Jack pine trees are found in sandy soil zones, and black spruce, mosses, sedges, and tamaracks live on poorly drained areas known as muskegs (bogs).[10] The kind of tree that inhabits a particular area corresponds directly to physiographic position (hillside, valley, north or south facing), soil texture (fine to coarse), and drainage. Black spruce, for example, grow best in peaty and wet places, white spruce prefer uplands and hillsides that are well drained, and jack pine are suited to sandy soils.[11]

Scientist Henry Youle Hind visited the Saskatchewan forks region in 1858. Sent to the western interior to determine its suitability for farming, Hind recorded evidence of excellent soil and timber in the North Saskatchewan River valley. "Much of the timber," he noted with dismay, "has been burnt, and the country is fast becoming an open prairie land."[12] According to the scientific thought of his time, successive fires would change a forested landscape to open prairie. Those who had travelled over the vast open prairie supposed that its treeless state was due not to aridity but to frequent fires. As renowned fire historian Stephen Pyne explained, fire was "often annual, nearly everywhere, [and] the flames were among the prairies' defining feature. No other Canadian biota had so many fires so often and so widely cast." As Pyne went on to question, "were those fires merely a property of the prairies ... or, more boldly, were they a generative agent without which the grasslands could not exist, a flaming axe that hewed back the original forest?"[13] The treeless state of the prairie, scientists suggested, was due to centuries of man-made burning, a cultural landscape as much as a physical one. There was no doubt, as observers at the time noted, that suppressing and stopping prairie fires resulted in a southward surge of the forest.[14] It stood to reason, then, that fire was indeed a "flaming axe" that hewed down or altered a wooded landscape.

Ecological geographer Celina Campbell has suggested that the story of fire as the major factor in prairie creation/forest exclusion is incomplete. The plains region contained bison. Huge herds of animals browsed, ate, wallowed, trampled, and toppled aspen growth and churned the grassland to mud and dust. Using pollen analysis, Campbell and her colleagues argued that removal of the bison led to the expansion of aspen growth in the northern prairie, creating what is now known as the "parkland," rather than the limited fire suppression practised by European and Canadian homesteaders toward the turn of the twentieth century.[15] Campbell argued that three factors—drought (aridity), fire, and bison—had roles in creating and maintaining the extent of the open plains and that "the removal of any one of these limiting factors could have allowed aspen populations to expand."[16] The removal of two factors, bison and fire, in the past century and a half has allowed for a dramatic increase in aspen parkland. Ralph Bird also noted that there were "major fluctuations of the forest and grassland before the white man broke the land for agriculture." Bird suggested that wet and dry periods were primarily responsible for the advance or retreat of aspen forest on a local or regional level. In general, the aspen forest would expand during a wet season and contract during a dry one, but at the micro level of sloughs the opposite would be true, as previously slough areas drying up would lead to aspen expansion, but excessive rain accumulation would lead to drowned and killed tree vegetation.[17] Ultimately, I argue that (1) the parkland is part of the grassland ecosystem and (2) the parkland probably expanded following the removal of bison and fire from the prairie. It is possible that the problematic interpretation of the importance of the parkland region reflects the current physical, not historic, extent of the parkland.

Just as fire has been an integral part of the grassland biome, so too the boreal forest is a fire-based ecological regime. Pyne, in his book on fire in Canada, claims that the breadth, size, and intensity of boreal fires "define Canada as a fire nation. Its boreal forest is to Canada what the arid Outback is to Australia.... With that flaming landscape, Canada becomes a global presence for earthly fire ecology."[18] Fire is one of three principal causes of boreal landscape fragmentation and regeneration, the other two lumbering and farming. The boreal forest, generally a green, cool, and wet biome, builds its reserves of biomass into juggernaut proportions. When a dry season hits, the boreal forest contains a magnitude of flammable timber and debris, peat and moss, shrubs and grasses. Factors that contribute to boreal fires include amount of available surface material, combustion properties, atmosphere, wind, moisture, lightning, anthropogenic interference, and fire frequency.[19] The result is that boreal forest landscapes are almost always "mosaics of different ages resulting from the overburning of past fires."[20] These mosaic landscapes encourage and support different ages, stages, and types of biota, a pattern called *succession*. Within the boreal forest region north of Prince Albert, there are various succession patterns. In general, fire hazard is highest in jack pine stands, intermediate in spruce or fir stands, and low in hardwood (primarily trembling aspen) stands, except in a dry spring, when forest floor debris is particularly flammable.[21]

A mixedwood boreal forest, consisting of both hardwood and softwood, can regenerate in several ways following a fire, depending on the intensity and length of the burn and the state and mixture of the parent stand. A hot burn, especially one that exposes mineral soil and retains access to an adjacent seed source, will seed in with conifers, both white and black spruce and jack pine. White spruce seeds well into the low canopy provided by young hardwood trees, which often overseed and crowd, resulting in a natural thinning process. In this instance, fire succession a few years after a burn shows a dense cover of aspen with white spruce seedlings. Jack pine, the most flammable of conifers, is adapted to fire and will regenerate densely. A lower intensity burn leads to aspen seedlings and poplar sprouts. Conifers grow more quickly than aspen, and by the time the forest reaches about sixty years following a burn the trees are co-dominant in the canopy, after which the aspen start to die out, and the stand reverts to conifers, though conifers suffer damage from being "whipped" by nearby deciduous trees.

Consider also the age of a stand that burns. If a stand of trees that is not yet mature burns again, then the probability of conifer regeneration is limited, though aspen and poplar are less affected. If an area is repeatedly burned, then tree cover might revert to shrubland and grasses, with damaged or stunted hardwoods. If a mixedwood stand is burned and regenerates to aspen without any conifer source, then the stand might eventually reach its life span and degenerate into shrubs and brush (such as hazelnut, speckled alder, or willow in wet areas). To the eye, this landscape would most resemble parkland (bluffs separated by open, grassy fields). Thus, boreal forest fires, in particular cases, might encourage a reversion to parkland and eventually grassland—a phenomenon noted by early explorers and scientists such as Henry Youle Hind, proving that their assumptions were not far from the mark.[22]

Human activity also changes boreal forest composition. Extensive logging creates an effect similar to low-intensity burns, which regenerate with aspen seedlings and, in time, conifer re-establishment (if a mature seed source remains). Logging, however, does not encourage rejuvenation of shrubs and plants on the forest floor. Extensive agricultural intervention re-creates the landscape more dramatically than logging or fire. In general, conifers are completely eliminated, used as firewood and building material. Poplar and aspen remain almost as weeds, repopulating themselves with ease at pond and river edges, in rockpiles, or in fields whenever agricultural pressure ceases. The overall effect of human intervention, either logging or agriculture, is a gradual physical change from a mixedwood boreal forest to a parkland/prairie resemblance.[23] The parent boreal forest becomes physically and culturally subsumed.

Fire is not always a natural process. In the boreal forest of the western interior of North America, First Nations cultures burned "corridors" or trails as well as "yards" or meadows.[24] Burning a meadow encouraged fresh growth of grasses and sedges to entice moose, elk, or deer or to create fresh hay for horses. The young grass would also sustain mice and rabbits, which would bring predatory animals such as fox, lynx, and marten. One Beaver Indian woman from northern Alberta claimed that burning around sloughs was good for the muskrat population, which loved the tender new shoots.[25] Moose and beaver browse new aspen growth. A burn in a sandy Jack pine forest would encourage a new growth of blueberries, a favourite crop for humans (and bears) in the north.

Aboriginal forest inhabitants would not deliberately burn an organically rich, peaty, or mossy forest, for such fires tended to burn for a long period of time and were difficult to control. The majority of burns would be initiated in the early spring, when there were still pockets of snow on the ground, which would act as natural breaks. Burning in summer, with the risk of hot weather, high winds, and destructive crown fires, was not a part of traditional First Nations practice.[26] Natural fires, lit by lightning when conditions were ripe, were in general the most destructive and out of control. Anthropogenic fires, unless carelessly lit or by accident, were generally more domestic, intended to groom the forest for certain purposes, particularly to encourage new plant growth for human or animal consumption. Large, destructive fires, however, had their human uses: for example, the young, straight pines found growing thickly a few years after a destructive burn could be harvested for teepee poles. Deliberate anthropogenic fires and harvest practices shaped the tenor of the forest and created commodities for human purposes.[27] Between anthropogenic and natural fires, a forest would be a mosaic of many burns of different ages and scales. No matter how "wild" it might appear, the boreal forest developed as a human-shaped cultural landscape.

SOILS

Soil creation is a complex process between the parent rock (or bedrock) and the vegetation that grows on that rock. This process is in constant flux and can change both from year to year and over centuries. A barren rocky area can be colonized by lichen and moss, which (over time) will decompose to form pockets of soil from which more complex plants, such as grasses and eventually trees, can take root. The parent rock within the north Prince Albert region is glacial till, a mixture of boulders, sand, silt, and clay deposited by glacial ice. In places such as the Sand Hills (now known as the Nisbet Provincial Forest), just north of Prince Albert, the parent rock is glaciofluvial, with coarse-textured deposits of sand and gravel. Archaeologists note that these sandbeds were laid down by water, both as part of the wind scouring of glacial Lake Saskatchewan and as the river formed a delta into that lake.[28] Glaciolacustrine soils are stratified, their layers easily identifiable, with silt, clay, and sand. Formed at the bottom of glacial lakes, this parent rock can encourage soils more suited for agriculture. A wide pocket of glaciolacustrine soils can be found in the Shellbrook-Meath Park plain running in an east-west band just north of the Sand Hills.

The Nisbet Provincial Forest shows the back-and-forth process between rock and colonizing vegetation. An area colonized by coniferous trees tends to have acidic soil, well leached by the trees. Conifers are evergreen trees, which do not shed their needles and so give little humus back to the soil. Deciduous trees such as trembling aspen and poplar, conversely, prefer a soil high in organic material. They contribute to the soil's high organic content by dropping their leaves in fall. Across an area of a few hundred metres, soils can change over time, depending on both the parent rock and whether it has been colonized by one vegetation or another.

Soil taxonomies common to the mixedwood boreal forest[29] include brunisolic soils associated with jack pine forest; dark grey chernozemic soils that have a "salt and pepper" appearance of both light grey and black, common to the boreal transition zone; black chernozemic soils found in "pockets"; gleysolic soils found in regions of prolonged water saturation, such as sloughs; organic soils, where deep layers of peat are present; and luvisolic soils, the classic forest soil that looks grey when disturbed or cultivated, leading to the common term "grey soil zone." In general, the north Prince Albert region has three somewhat distinct bands of soil: brunisolic (sandy) soils just north of the city in the jack pine Nisbet Forest Reserve; chernozemic (dark grey and black agricultural soil) in the Shellbrook-Meath Park plain north of the pines; and the grey luvisolic or leached forest soil at the edge of cultivated land at the Northern Provincial Forest, stretching from Emma Lake in the west to Candle Lake in the east. The soil bands show a transition from sand to dark grey/black to, finally, leached grey luvisolic soil, generally considered unsuitable for agriculture.

PHYSIOGRAPHY AND HYDROLOGY

The physiography of the research region belongs to the Saskatchewan River Plain. The ground in the southern portion of the research area (the Nisbet Provincial Forest and the agricultural belt) is gently undulating to rolling. North and west toward Christopher and Emma Lakes and Prince Albert National Park, steeper slopes and well-drained soils of the Waskesiu Upland promote tree growth that has been particularly well suited to forestry exploitation. The majority of upland forest land is still owned by the Crown as part of the Northern Provincial Forest or the federal government as Prince Albert National Park.[30]

The entire region is part of the North Saskatchewan River catchment basin, an area crossed by three smaller river systems. The first is the Sturgeon River, at the outer western edge of the area. At the mouth of the Sturgeon (known on fur-trade maps as the Net-Setting or Setting River), where it empties into the North Saskatchewan, Peter Pond once operated a fur-trading post.

The second drainage body is the Spruce River system, now known as the Little Red River, which originates in Prince Albert National Park and moves south to empty into the North Saskatchewan River near Prince Albert. These two rivers, Sturgeon and Little Red, have been important historically for their access to prime lumber forests, and they were used and developed extensively to run logs to the mills at Prince Albert.

The third river is the Garden River, once known as Sucker or Carp Creek prior to agricultural settlement. This river drains from the swamp and muskeg land north of Paddockwood and passes almost straight south before curving east to enter the North Saskatchewan east of Prince Albert near the forks. Its drainage, far

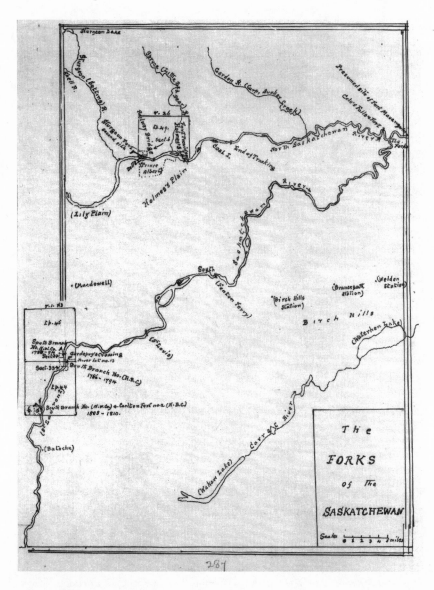

Map 3. The forks of the Saskatchewan.
Source: SAB, Morton Manuscript Collection (files of Professor A.S. Morton), S-A32, Vol. 9.

upstream from Prince Albert and separated from the city by a series of shoals and rapids, hampered its potential use for the timber drive. The catchment of the Garden River, however, drains some of the best agricultural land on the north side of the Saskatchewan River, hence its name. All three rivers are south of the Continental Divide and flow into the North Saskatchewan and out through Hudson Bay.[31]

The river systems are tied to the regional lakes. Recreational lakes in "Lakeland" developed for commercial purposes include Round, Sturgeon, Christopher, Emma, Anglin, and Candle Lakes, as well as those found within the borders of Prince Albert National Park. Other local lakes of importance, known for their good fishing, include Bittern and Montreal Lakes. Smaller lakes, with no commercial development and difficult access, include Oscar Lake (a large slough between Christopher and Anglin Lakes), McConechy Lake, and Clearsand Lake. Several other large water bodies, essentially large sloughs, abound throughout the region, including Egg Lake, near Spruce Home and Henribourg (see Map 2). These large sloughs contribute to local hydrology and provide important habitat for waterfowl. Summer temperatures and evapo-transpiration rates affect considerable seasonal and annual changes in water level. In some years, these lakes and water bodies are very low; in other years, they overflow onto surrounding lands.[32]

The number and extent of water bodies increase sharply going north from Prince Albert, from small rivers and sloughs to lakes, then to extensive muskegs deeper into the forest, such as Boundary Bog in Prince Albert National Park. Bogs develop on low-lying land over thousands of years, and their presence is considered an indication of the age of a boreal forest. The northern part of the research region is also within or near the southern limit of permafrost—small pockets of permafrost can be found as far south as Prince Albert National Park and might well be present at or near what became the northern limit of agriculture. The presence of permafrost is the standard by which many scientific groups classify the beginning of the Canadian "north."[33] Permafrost presents a significant limitation on agricultural capability but is hard to detect by inexperienced homesteaders with no botanical training. The isotherm of 0°C, marking the southern boundary of discontinuous soil permafrost and the northern extent of agriculture, dissects the research region.[34]

FLORA AND FAUNA

Trees and water have been the primary defining characteristics of the boreal forest, but First Nations bands also exploited boreal flora and fauna. Perhaps the most important non-human inhabitant of the boreal forest—in terms of its ability to re-create its surroundings—is the beaver. With an insatiable appetite for young aspen and poplar trees and a penchant for building dams that flood acres of forest, the beaver is second only to humans for environmental manipulation. Bison were once a major component of the region, particularly (according to historical documents) in the winter months when the beasts would break into smaller groups and spread throughout the southern edge of the forest, taking shelter from the bitter blizzards on the prairie.[35] Farmers who moved into the region often found bison skulls while plowing the land. Extermination of the plains bison led to several ecological changes in both the prairie and the boreal forest, where bison were known to graze heavily on both grasses and shrubs and to damage and kill fully grown trees. Their disappearance led to gradual but pervasive forest regrowth.

Other key boreal species include large ungulates, from moose, elk, and deer to the occasional caribou. Large carnivores, such as the timber wolf, black or brown bear, fox, wolverine, marten, and lynx, thrive. Aquatic animals such as otter, beaver, and muskrat make their homes in streams and ponds, and small land animals, including mice and rabbits, abound. Birds are also abundant, particularly at the forest edge or lake edge where insect populations are at their largest. Woodpeckers, grey jays, chickadees, spruce grouse, hawks and eagles are common, as are aquatic birds such as herons, cranes, Canada geese, ducks, loons, and pelicans. Water bodies have their own vegetation, from cattails to bulrushes, reed grasses, sedges, and mosses, and support a plethora of tiny aquatic animals. Minnows and fish species are abundant, and in some of the larger lakes fish can grow to a tremendous size. Northern pike (commonly called jackfish), walleye (pickerel), perch, whitefish, and trout (brook, rainbow, and lake) can all be found, as well as a type of ugly catfish commonly called mariah. In the woods, aside from the trees, can be found many plant varieties, including dogwood, low-bush cranberry, ostrich fern, horsetail, fireweed, blueberry, and Labrador tea. All of these animal, plant, bird, and fish species have, at one time or another, been harvested for food, shelter, clothing, utensils, or medicine by humans.

CLIMATE

Saskatchewan has a continental climate with long, cold winters and short, relatively hot summers. It is a dry climate, with the southern prairie classed as semi-arid and the northern region as sub-humid. There are considerable climatic differences between southern and northern Saskatchewan that contribute to its two main ecosystems of boreal forest and prairie. The mixedwood forest at the ecological edge is typical of the sub-humid, or more northern, boreal environment. Although rainfall is not extensive—the yearly average is about forty centimetres, some of which is from winter snowfall—it does not evaporate as quickly as that in the semi-arid regions of the prairie.[36] The growing season for all plants is about 160 days, though there is a higher possibility of late spring or early fall frosts at the forest edge, which can hamper plant growth.[37] The area receives on average 2,100 hours of bright sunshine but is protected from major surface winds by its extensive tree cover. Extreme variations, as on the open plains, can occur but with less frequency. A tornado and accompanying plow winds, with hail and rain, ripped through the research region in the fall of 2008, pulling up trees by the roots, flattening crops, and smashing buildings.[38] Older residents of the area claimed that these kinds of storms were non-existent when the region was first settled and have become more frequent as the land has been opened for agriculture.[39] Opening forest land for agricultural purposes has been proven to have effects on local climate, temperature, and soil organic content.[40]

CONCLUSION

The north Prince Albert region sits on the ecological edge between the boreal forest and the open plains. Before extensive human interference through logging and farming, the research region most resembled a classic mixedwood boreal forest, but through fire succession, soil composition, and climate it also showed some prairie characteristics. As an ecotone between two dominant landscapes, the area promoted species richness and diversity. The mixedwood boreal forest hosted a wide variety of flora and fauna on a transitional land base that offered both poor and good soil, extensive water resources, and timber. Climate variations and weather events, as well as forest cover change from mixedwood boreal to almost exclusively aspen, have contributed to the sometimes erroneous assertion that the north Prince Albert region is a parkland environment. I agree with the scientific researchers, ecologists, and archaeologists who have argued that the north Prince Albert region straddles the ecotone, the place where the two parent ecological systems of forest and prairie meet. But I also recognize that, at the edge, change is the only constant. The long-term history of this particular landscape is one of flux. Nonetheless, over the past few hundred years, this landscape has witnessed a history of ecological and cultural exchange that reinforces my ecotone/edge interpretation. A similar edge can be found at the boreal forest fringe across Canada—both a line and a place of flux and transition.

CHAPTER TWO

THE GOOD WINTERING PLACE

It was "the Good Wintering Place."[1] Scientist and explorer Captain John Palliser recorded in 1863 that the Plains Cree customarily spent the winter at or near traditional wintering grounds on the North Saskatchewan River. Today "the Good Wintering Place" hosts the city of Prince Albert. There, Palliser claimed, "the buffalo in winter approach the edge of the woods, and so also do the Indians, seeking fuel and thick-wood animals, in case of the buffalo failing them during the winter."[2] Clearly, that tradition had a long history. Hudson's Bay Company (HBC) employee Matthew Cocking went into the western interior in the fall of 1772 to convince the Blackfoot Nation to travel to the forts at Hudson Bay to trade with the English. He commented on the Saskatchewan valley region: "Indians tell me that in Winter buffalo are plenty here, which is confirmed by the quantity of Dung on the ground."[3] The north Prince Albert region was a refuge for the Cree from a brutal prairie winter, offering shelter from storms and game to tide bands through until spring should come again.

The Prince Albert region also had a slightly different name, noted by long-time Prince Albert resident John Smith. He claimed that "the Indian tribes, both the Plains Indians and those from the Bush ... called it 'The Meeting Place,' which in Indian was 'Kestapinik.'"[4] Smith explained that here the northern bands would meet the southern bands to exchange goods, engage in ritual dances and religious rites, make treaties and war pacts. These meetings were typically held in summer, allowing access overland or via canoe. Where Palliser described a place of winter refuge and resilience, Smith identified a summer cultural exchange. Both interpretations acknowledged the region as an edge place, where fundamentally different cultures based on unique ecosystems came together. Seasonality, however, is less well understood.

WINTER'S EDGE

Traditional interpretations of human use of the parkland and boreal forest edge argue that it was a *winter* environment: "One thing was certain; the yearly cycle of humans following bison herds from the grasslands in summer to sheltered areas in the parklands or wooded areas from the fall to the spring was essentially an unchanging and unchangeable phenomenon."[5] In this "Parkland Convergence" model, presented most eloquently by Arthur J. Ray in his seminal work *Indians in the Fur Trade,* the bison would retreat from the plains to the forest edge in winter. First Nations groups from both the plains and the forest would converge at the forest edge, following the bison, and spend winters in the relative shelter of the forest.[6] The Parkland Convergence model suggests that between December and February of each year the bison would break into smaller groups and migrate to take shelter along the edge of the trees during the coldest and stormiest winter months. First Nations bands would mimic the bison pattern, breaking into smaller and more mobile units to winter at the forest edge, within reach of the bison. The earliest part of this season, from November into December, was the time of bison pounding. Pounding, or building "pounds" into which bison were herded before being killed, required trees, found at the forest edge, parkland, and on the open plains in isolated groves or near rivers. The meat was then frozen or dried for use during the rest of the winter.

The forest edge as winter refuge anchored the Aboriginal seasonal cycle. Most researchers, including Ray, have operated from the assumption that the parkland is a relatively stable zone that has been in its current position back through the historic and prehistoric past. Modern maps showing the current extent of the parkland are used. Researchers trace the travels of First Nations, voyageurs, fur traders, explorers, and scientists, "mapping" their location relative to the current position of prairie, parkland, or forest. This leads to controversy, for historic records do not coincide well with current conditions; nor do the arguments account for year-to-year variations in severity—a mild winter might mean neither the bison nor the bands would migrate north. Ceasing First Nations anthropogenic burning practices, demise of the bison, logging, and the introduction of large-scale farming methods have substantially altered or possibly created the so-called parkland landscape and certainly moved the edge of the forest.[7]

Geographers and historians have accepted, for the most part, the Parkland Convergence model.[8] But anthropologists M. Malainey and B. Sherriff suggest that the model is wrong.[9] Historical documents and archaeological findings offer ample evidence suggesting that plains tribes lived on the open prairie year round. Bison stayed on the prairie when snow cover was minimal and warm Chinook winds kept temperatures moderate; in the parkland, deep snow covered the grass, and the animals had trouble finding food.[10] Malainey and Sherriff document a prairie-adapted seasonal round in which the Cree entered the forest only to travel north and east to Hudson Bay by canoe when the ice broke up on the rivers. They would travel back (an arduous trip involving tracking and portaging) to meet their families who waited for the trippers at or near the rivers and streams. By then, it would be middle summer to early fall. From there, they would abandon their canoes and travel overland, generally in a southerly and westerly direction, heading for bison country. Winter was spent on the prairie, trapping wolves and taking bison (often using pounds) until it was time to move once again north and east, toward stands of birch to make canoes, when the cycle would begin again. Malainey and Sherriff argue that bison hunting—and, therefore, the Plains Cree culture—were prairie phenomena.[11]

Yet the use of pounds indicated at least a partial forested setting—extensive bluffs or possibly the forest edge. Malainey and Sherriff suggest that the outlines of the "fertile belt" provided by Palliser and Hind in the late 1850s serve as the best contemporary outline of the parkland zone. What none of these archaeological researchers has noted is that the parkland zone, as noted by ecologists, is difficult to define or proscribe on a map for the simple reason that it blends so easily into the prairie. Ralph Bird insisted that "in the northern part of the parkland the forest cover is broken by only occasional patches of grassland on the drier locations. As one approaches the great plains, the percentage of forest cover diminishes until it occupies only small, isolated groves and is finally restricted."[12] If bison moved to the more southern portions of the parkland zone, then it would become a matter of debate and interpretation to a casual observer (such as fur traders or other itiner-ants) as to whether it was indeed "forest," "parkland," or "prairie." A second piece of this puzzle is semantics: both prairie and parkland, when flat, were often termed "prairie" until the turn of the twentieth century.

Archaeologists J. Rod Vickers and Trevor Peck agree with Malainey and Sher-riff's statement that there has been a wide variety of interpretations regarding plains bison movements. All have been supported to a greater or lesser extent by both historical and archaeological findings and scientific evaluation.[13] Knowing that bison movements varied so greatly from year to year (depending on snow cover, vegetation, and climate), Vickers and Peck contend that it is impossible to construct a single model that accounts for all variables. Researchers are unable to forge a consensus. Instead, counter Vickers and Peck, winter occupation should be approached "through a consideration of the limited distribution of non-mobile critical resources such as water and wood."[14] Wood was the one resource that the plains lacked in any large capacity except in particular locations (along riverbeds or in certain upland regions, such as the Cypress Hills). Bison dung, though adequate for cooking fires in the summer, could not produce sufficient heat in the winter—moreover, it was hard to find under snow.[15] Coal and wood were the only two fuels that could produce sufficient heat in the winter, and of the two coal was rarely mentioned as a fuel source by anthropologists or archaeologists of North America.

It is possible that coal was taboo for some First Nations. Peter Fidler, during his journey from Buckingham House west across the plains, added some coal that he had found to the fire in the tent that he shared with his local hosts. This, apparently, was a "heinous offence" for which the chief, "much affronted," punished Fidler by not visiting the tent for two nights. Was it the coal smell? Perhaps the quality of the smoke? Fidler was unsure. Wood was the primary fuel, particularly in winter, for domestic use. If wood, rather than bison, was the critical resource, then the forest edge remained a strategically important place of shelter and refuge for Plains Cree. Travellers tended to plan their winter movements "from island to island" of bush and forest throughout the "sea" of grass or snow.[16]

Debate regarding bison migration patterns focusses on Plains Native experiences and perceptions. Forest-adapted bands followed a different model. Traders Joseph Waggoner and Joseph Smith journeyed inland from York Factory in 1756 to winter in the homeland of the Cree Indians who occupied the region surrounding Cedar Lake and the north end of Lake Winnipeg. Their journals explained the boreal forest cycle. The Cree band moved slowly through the region, fishing and hunting moose.[17] By December, they reached the most southern point of their journey, still well within wooded lands. There they found and killed "buffeloo."[18] From this point, they journeyed back north and east, living once again on moose meat until they camped at Swan River, where there was a stand of birch trees. They camped for two months, making canoes and waiting for spring breakup, when the men travelled upriver to Hudson Bay to trade. The women and children spent the spring and summer fishing and hunting small game and waterfowl along the shores of the lakes and rivers until the men returned.[19]

The journals of Waggoner and Smith depict three separate but similar journeys that cycled south and west and then back north and east toward Hudson Bay. When the boreal bands were at their most southerly point, they accessed the buffalo, at or near the forest edge. It was at the same time as plains bands were moving to the forest edge regions in pursuit of the retreating herds of bison.[20] The two would have occupied the forest edge at the same time, in early to mid-winter.

SUMMER'S EDGE

In Christopher Creek near the south shore of Christopher Lake in 1931, two brothers—Tom and Joe Johnson—were knee deep in sand and silt digging a trench. The two property owners were widening the creek channel to allow the lake to drain down the creek. Despite the increasing hold of drought on the open plains to the south, Christopher Lake had burst its banks that year, overflowing into the trees and washing over its normally generous sandy beaches. The Johnson brothers, looking to alleviate the situation and encourage summer bathing beach and camping customers, were busy digging when they came across a remarkable artifact. From the depths of the channel, they pulled up what at first they must have assumed was a rotted tree trunk, partially fossilized. On closer inspection, they realized that it was a tree that had been deliberately modified. It was a dugout canoe, designed by First Nations people and used on the local lake, probably for foraging, trapping, or fishing purposes. They cleaned the sand and mud from their find and loaded it up on their wagon, bound for Prince Albert, where they gave it to the local historical society.[21]

The canoe is considered to be a unique artifact in North America. The craft was built with a full bow, but no stern, which allowed one paddler to sit far forward while the back end rose up out of the water but could be used for stowing gear, hauling a catch, or holding collected items. Holes, either bored or naturally occurring knotholes, on either side of the bow were likely used for transportation. A sturdy stick could be placed through the holes as a convenient handle for moving the craft between nearby water bodies and over beaver dams.

Although it is well known that First Nations groups on both the Atlantic and the Pacific coasts made and used dugout canoes, this practice was little known in the interior.[22] The common mode of travel was the conventional birchbark canoe, known for its lightness, versatility, and ease of repair. From the Algonquin to the Woods Cree, and adapted by the fur traders and voyageurs for their trade, the birchbark canoe plied the inland waters for thousands of years.[23] The find at Christopher Creek shattered previous assumptions, proving that the boreal forest people had developed a yearly exploitation cycle rooted in place. A dugout canoe, meant for strength and endurance but not speed or lightness, could be used year after year on the same body of water. A birchbark canoe, exposed to the harsh winter snows, had to be remade each spring. The presence of a dugout canoe, which would have required many hours to build, suggests a deeper commitment to place and perhaps less inclination or need for mobility. The waterways in and around Christopher and Emma Lakes, and the fens of nearby Oscar Lake, provided freshwater fish, game birds, furs (particularly muskrat and beaver), and a variety of green plants for food, baskets, and medicine.

Why is the canoe an important find? How can its existence change the interpretation of the forest edge? Archaeologist David Meyer, a specialist in parkland and forest edge cultures, has pondered Ray's thesis of winter co-occupation of the parkland. According to Meyer, this interpretation does not fit the archaeological record.[24] Between AD 500 and AD 1000, the northern forests were occupied by the "Laurel" complex, while the plains were inhabited by the "Avonlea" phase. Laurel people moved to the forest edge in spring to access spring fishing in the spawning grounds of rivers and streams. They stayed well within the northern forests in winter. Avonlea people also occupied the parkland and southern boreal forest in the spring but spent their winters mainly on the grassland. Archaeologists have used the evidence to hypothesize that southern plains Avonlea people would retreat to the forested regions during the winter only if weather on the grasslands was particularly severe. Any co-occupation was during the spring, to access the spawning fish or travel using the opening waterways.

During the Old Woman's phase on the open plains (AD 1000 to AD 1450), there was no indication of any north-south interaction in the archaeological record. The archaeological record for the central boreal forest of Saskatchewan is sketchy for the Old Woman's phase, in part because of the problematic nature of boreal forest excavations, which offer a sparse database. Sites would probably match the Blackduck, common across northern Manitoba in this time period. Such interaction might yet be found, when more sites are discovered throughout the boreal forest.[25] Between AD 1450 and AD 1700, or pre-contact phase in the western interior, the suite of archaeological sites from the plains are called the Mortlach Aggregate. No Mortlach site has been found at the forest edge and only a few have been found in the parkland. Their northern binary, the Selkirk occupation, was common throughout the boreal forest to the southern edge of the forest and into the parkland. These sites bear evidence of spring and early summer occupation, but no winter site has been found. These people, Meyer suggested, moved into the boreal forest proper in the winter, subsisting on hunting moose and caribou and ice fishing. Meyer points out that the archaeological record paints a picture in opposition to Ray's model: the two major groups of inhabitants in the western interior, particularly in central Saskatchewan, would have been farthest away from each other in winter. In the Selkirk phase (which extends roughly to the beginning of the fur trade), the boreal forest bands extended south, indicating increasing strength and influence, possibly coinciding with the beginning of the fur trade, for which the boreal landscape offered an abundance of fur.

By the historic period, as recorded in fur-trade journals and diaries, forest-adapted hunter-gatherers exploited diverse resources throughout the year. Their hunting and fishing grounds extended to the forest edge and into the parkland.[26] Archaeological investigation along major river systems points to spring and summer fishing exploitation as a major component of life in the western interior. Malainey's research on fat/lipid residues on pottery sherds shows that, though forest-adapted bands utilized the spring spawning grounds, plains-adapted people could not. They would get sick if they switched from a lean bison meat diet to a fat-rich fish diet in spring. Rather, plains bands adapted fetal and newborn bison into their diet instead of fish. Yet, when the men canoed to Hudson Bay, the women stayed behind in camps usually near the rivers or lakes, indicating a gender-oriented aquatic exploitation. Perhaps women and children could transition to the fat-rich aquatic diet more easily, or by summer their bodies were more adapted to a fatty diet.[27]

The Waggoner and Smith journals outlining the boreal cycle mirror Malainey and Sherriff's depiction of a plains yearly cycle split not only by season but also by hydrology and gender. Men would make the arduous trip to the bay, while women, elderly band members, and children would create encampments within strategically rich aquatic environments, usually at streams and lakeshores near the forest edge. The canoe find at Christopher Creek indicated a deep sense of place and a tool for gathering fish, birds, and plants. Summer encampments fell within a distinctly feminine and domestic sphere. Considering the past through the lens of gender might reveal nuances that have so far been overlooked. Fishing was generally within the feminine sphere. Women traded isinglass (dried air bladder from sturgeon, a natural gelatin used to clarify beer) at fur-trade posts.[28] It is possible that the movement to and from the fur-trade posts along the waterways was an innovation that shattered and changed older adaptations along gender lines, changing the use of the forest edge.

If the transition zone between prairie and forest came to prominence during the early days of the fur trade, then one point becomes clear: water, in addition to trees, was an important component of the edge landscape. The dugout canoe discovered in Christopher Creek represents seasonal exploitation geared toward summer. Even so, Ray's original model of winter exploitation should not be forgotten—in severe weather, the forest edge would provide critical fuel resources and shelter. Despite the ongoing debate over which season saw the highest use, the forest fringe was an ecological edge of critical importance for the human occupants of the western interior. It offered diverse resources, from fuel and teepee poles to large ungulates such as bison, moose, deer, and elk. Extensive water sources provided habitat for fish and wildfowl. Berries and mosses grew in abundance, and other plants—used for medical or edible purposes—not found elsewhere could be harvested. Exploiting the resources found within and across the forest edge allowed for greater ecological adaptation and resilience for all bands living in the western interior.

CULTURAL EDGE

Kestapinik, the "Meeting Place," was a point of contact for First Nations bands in the western interior for thousands of years. Prehistoric archaeological research on human cultures consistently shows lines of separation at or near this place, suggesting that bands defined their areas of influence and adaptive strategies to coincide roughly with the forest boundary. The forest edge marked more than a mere physiographic description, argued geographer G. Malcolm Lewis, a specialist in First Nations mapmaking. Lewis studied early maps of the North American interior, the majority of which were made by or with the extensive help of First Nations residents. The forest edge represented a cultural as well as an ecological edge, necessitating a different mode of life. "In the absence of mountains, sea coasts, and major lakes, [the treeline was] the main landmark," Lewis noted. First Nations groups "anticipated, planned for, and even feared" moving from the forest to the plains:

> in the absence of trees, kindling wood and tent poles had to be carried; in order to guarantee fresh water at nightly camp sites, circuitous routes had to be followed, such that a day's journey could be considerably longer or shorter than an ideal march; to afford shelter against sudden blizzards, the ideal route in winter was never far from the shelter of a valley or a clump of trees; in a dry season it was necessary to be wary of grass fires to windward and in a wet season, when

naturally induced fires were rare, it was essential to conceal camp fires, which at night would announce the existence of a camp to other Indians within a radius of several tens of miles.[29]

The need to move with some stealth and care throughout the prairie landscape was mitigated, at least in part, by the strength in numbers of plains bands. The adaptive strategies of plains bands versus woods bands were particular cultural responses to the landscape within which they spent the majority of their time. Plains bands were defined by the bison hunt, which in good years could support large, healthy encampments of 100 tents or more. The boreal environment supported significantly smaller band units, adapted to smaller animal populations, and diversified hunting and gathering strategies.

The historic occupants of the north Prince Albert region were Cree, but the historical record also notes an extensive co-occupation of the area by a northern group of Assinboine.[30] Three specific Cree groups used the region: the Pegogamaw, who inhabited the forks region and area between the branches to the west and south, along the South Saskatchewan (which took in a parkland gradient leading into grassland or Plains Cree orientation); the Keskachewan or Beaver Cree, who inhabited the North Saskatchewan and Beaver River regions, which combined boreal and parkland settings; and the boreal forest or Western Woods Cree, who lived on the north side of the North Saskatchewan basin and along the Churchill River system.[31]

The territories of influence of these three bands overlapped in the north Prince Albert region. The Pegogamaw Cree probably migrated southward during the early years of the fur trade to dominate the strategic inland water "highway" of the North and South Saskatchewan Rivers near the forks and forcing the Gros Ventre, the region's previous occupants, out.[32] The migration represented a period of great transition for the group, as not only did their territorial range shift significantly, but likely they restructured their economic orientation to learn bison hunting (particularly pounding) from the northern Assiniboine and took on a marked involvement with the European fur trade. As fur-trade posts moved into the western interior, the Pegogamaw Cree were oriented more to the south and west of the north Prince Albert region but probably retained their occupation of the Sturgeon, Little Red, and Garden River systems, firmly within the transition zone.[33] Continued occupation of the north Prince Albert region would have allowed access to better moose hunting and excellent beaver and muskrat hunting grounds, fishing in the lakes, sphagnum mosses for diapers, and blueberries and cranberries in addition to the prairie saskatoons and bison.

The Beaver Cree operated to the west of the Sturgeon River, but records indicate that they sometimes used that river as an inland highway, and certainly both the Beaver and the Pegogamaw were known to trade with the Canadian "pedlars" who had established a fort at the mouth of the Sturgeon River called Sturgeon Fort, just to the west of modern-day Prince Albert on the north side of the river.[34] These bands also developed an overland road that started near the forks of the

Map 4. Pegogamaw lands. Note the absence of bands north of the Pegogamaw, in what became the north Prince Albert region. Source: Meyer and Russell, "Lands and Lives of the Pegogamaw Cree," 227. Used with permission.

Saskatchewan and went west, parallel to the river, providing an overland route into their home territory. This road was described by HBC inland fur trader and explorer William Pink, who made four trips to the Prince Albert region from 1766 to 1769. According to Pink, the group would abandon their canoes at the forks, put away a large cache of dried meat and other supplies, then travel overland. They would spend the winter trapping and hunting wolves and marten for the fur trade as well as beaver and muskrat. At some point—it differed from year to year in his journal, sometimes as early as December, sometimes as late as March—they would travel south to participate in bison pounding. As spring approached, the band would travel back east to a canoe-building site to get ready for the spring trip to the bay. [35]

There is little clear indication in the fur trader's journals that the Western Woods Cree of the Churchill region came so far south, as they would likely have entered into HBC trade using the Churchill River system. The archaeological record does show that the north Prince Albert region was well used by both Plains and Woods Cree. Ethnohistorical interpretation, drawn from fur-trader records, suggests that all three groups (Pegogamaw, Beaver, and Woods Cree) used the area to a greater or lesser extent, depending on the year and circumstances. Of these groups, the Beaver and Pegogamaw were devastated by the smallpox epidemic of 1781–82. Local fur traders retained some hope for the eventual recovery of these two bands. Indeed, in the summer following the epidemic, the master of Hudson House, William Walker, decided to stay in the region during the summer of 1782 instead of travelling back to Cumberland House and the bay forts, as was the usual practice: "There is a good few Indians alive up here yet, Some not over the Pox, and a great many young fellows gone to bring their own and the furrs of their deceased relations, who had laid them up when they took the Distemper, a great way off, they have most of them promis'd to come here with their furrs, So I thought that it would be of more Benefit to our Honble. Masters to stay up here without Orders, than to Carry the Goods down to Cumberland House, where there is hardly an Indian man alive."[36]

The loss of so many people from the smallpox epidemic presented a serious blow to the fur trade in the north Prince Albert region and across the western interior, since the Hudson's Bay Company relied on the inland Indians to trade both furs and provisions and to make canoes and paddle the canoe brigades up and down the Saskatchewan River system.[37] Even the short-term contraction in numbers in the region made it likely that the Woods Cree, less affected by the epidemic, expanded their territory south to take advantage of what might have been a large supply of wildlife and subsistence necessities in the region. The word *Pegogamaw*, in reference to a specific band or group, disappeared from the fur-trade journals after the epidemic.[38]

In general, there is a gap in the historical record relating to the area between the Saskatchewan and Churchill systems. This gap is due, in large part, to geography. First Nations and fur traders primarily used water routes as roads: from Cumberland House, canoe routes could go north to the Churchill or west and south down the Saskatchewan. As a variant, they could travel up the Sturgeon River to its source, then cross overland to Beaver River and from there north to La Loche, Île-à-la-Crosse, and Methye Portage. This route was accessible only in high water, and was not reliable, hence the overland variation west from the forks. Interestingly, Prince Albert resident John Smith commented on the difference between southern and northern bands and their primary modes of transportation: "Indians from the South were not equipped to travel by water, while those from the North knew of no other way of travelling than by water. The plains Indians used ponies," he noted, while northern bands either canoed in summer or used dogs and snowshoes in winter over the frozen waterways.[39] Smith's comments reinforce a somewhat arbitrary distinction between prairie and boreal bands where plains bands used overland transport, while boreal bands preferred water.[40] At the confluence of cultures within the north Prince Albert region, all transportation options—horses, dogs, snowshoes, birchbark canoes, and dugout canoes—were evident.

In the north Prince Albert region, local subsistence and settlement patterns were much more diverse and diffuse than those of their southern, bison-adapted neighbours. This diversity meant two things: first, their diet shifted according to seasonal needs, allowing an omnivarian repertoire that included fish, fowl, both small and large fauna (from snowshoe hares to moose and bear, along with the occasional bison), and a variety of flora, including blueberries, Labrador tea, and wild parsnips. Second, if one resource was scarce, another was usually plentiful, allowing both seasonal change and a certain measure of resilience over time. Peter Erasmus, the Cree guide and interpreter present at the signing of Treaty 6 at Fort Carlton, lived in such an environment.

> It was an ideal life of abundance and good health these northern In-
> dians enjoyed. They were not as the other tribes solely dependent on
> the buffalo for a living. Their hunting excursions to the prairies gave
> them additional security and provided a good reason to get together
> in the social band life that they all loved. They shared the proceeds of
> these trips with the less-fortunate people at home. ... I make these
> statements as dealing with the times leading to and prior to the settle-
> ment of white people in the country. There were plenty of wild fruits:
> strawberries, raspberries, blueberries, black and red currants, goose-
> berries and three different kinds of cranberries. ... Buffalo meat from
> the prairies was used as a supplement to deer, moose, and bird game
> in those days. ... Fish were numerous in the lakes. In the spring, I
> have seen rough fish, such as jacks, actually push each other out on
> the shores by the masses that drove up the creeks. I believe that the
> variety of food was a leading factor in the health and energy enjoyed
> by the people.[41]

Even though these resources were diverse, this description is probably overly romantic. Forest resources were not as plentiful as the plains bison. Forest-adapted people were consequently never as numerous as those on the prairie. Bison-adapted groups enjoyed a flourishing culture not seen in the forest and sustained several economically independent and powerful nation-states. They had, though, as historical geographer A.J. Ray noted, "one fatal flaw": bison-adapted culture "was based on the exploitation of a single renewable resource [that was depleted] at a rate that exceeded the level required for a sustained yield harvest."[42] If the bison could not be found, plains bands starved. Meanwhile, forest-adapted bands "were able to continue to support themselves by hunting, fishing, and trapping."[43]

First Nations bands that lived at or near the ecotone acquired a level of strength and resilience—but not numbers—greater than those of their plains counterparts. Aboriginal people chose to live near—or to create—ecological edges in order to exploit the resources of more than one biome and promote economic resilience (and good health, if Erasmus was correct). Those who resided at or near ecological edges usually exhibited high levels of cultural interaction that "promote the exchange of knowledge, technologies, and resources in such a way as to increase the adaptive repertoire available to any one social group."[44] The Pegogamaw incursion south and west, where they interacted with the northern Assiniboine and learned how to hunt bison through pounding, is an example of such an interaction.

The resilience of Cree bands living at or near the north Prince Albert region, despite the devastation of the smallpox epidemic, suggests that the ecological and cultural forest edge presented a landscape that could offer livelihood flexibility and resilience and a wider array of possible adaptive responses.[45] Ten years after the smallpox epidemic, fur trader Duncan McGillivray entered the old Pegogamaw lands in 1794 and wrote that the people there appeared to be "the most powerful clan in this quarter," in part because of rich local resources.[46] Following the small-pox epidemic of 1781–82, which reduced the inland First Nations population severely, there were other, smaller epidemics of smallpox, measles, and whoop-ing cough that put further pressure on the First Nations population (in particu-lar 1819–20 and 1837–38). It seems probable that, with a reduction in hunting, gathering, and fishing pressure, there was a corresponding resurgence and richness in local resources.

What became the north Prince Albert region, north of the Saskatchewan River at the edge of more than one First Nations home territory, might also have oper-ated as a "neutral zone" or "borderland." Such places became ecologically rich, particularly in larger ungulates, because they were on the edge of traditional lands and might even have served as "buffer zones" between hostile groups. The story of a fierce battle between the Cree and Chipeweyan at "The Lake of the Hanging Hearts," or the Hanging Heart Lakes in Prince Albert National Park, suggests that, at least at one point, the north Prince Albert region was a "buffer zone" between the Chipeweyan or Dene, whose territory usually extended north of the Churchill River, and the Cree of the Saskatchewan River. Northern bands centred on the Churchill River traded at the Churchill posts. With bands pulled south and north, the north Prince Albert region found itself rather lightly touched by human oc-cupation or the demands of the fur trade through the mid-1800s, though certainly nearby traders encouraged bands to harvest local fur populations. The Hudson's Bay Company established Carlton Post in 1795 on the North Saskatchewan River down from the old Hudson House post. Posts on the Churchill River, such as Île-à-la-Crosse and Stanley, were also in operation for parts of this period, as well as Green Lake, an important inland distribution point for pemmican, connected to Carlton Post by an overland trail. There is little indication, though, in either the written historical sources or the oral tradition, that these posts drew heavily from the north Prince Albert region. [47]

EDGE AS HOME: THE LOBSTICK TREE

In 1911, settlers Percy Carter and Pat O'Hea pushed north from Prince Albert following an "old Indian trail." When they arrived in Township 52, they found a remarkable cultural artifact: a large white spruce remade into a lobstick tree, standing in lonely splendour in a small open meadow. According to the Paddockwood history book, Carter located his homestead on the quarter containing the meadow and lobstick: "It is remembered that in the vicinity of that tree, Indians traveling north to hunt and fish, would pitch their camp and rest for a while." Presumably, those travelling from north to south, or east to west, would also use the site.[48]

Culturally modified trees were common in Nordic countries, among them the lobstick tree of the Canadian boreal forest. For the Cree of the western interior, a lobstick was created by shaping a tall and conspicuous white spruce or pine tree by "lopping" most of its branches off. The top would then bush out in a tuft, becoming easy to spot. These trees were used in many ways, both practical and symbolic. They were signposts, chosen and designed to mark trails, portages, and pathways through the boreal forest, berry patches, or hunting grounds. They were also cultural markers, used to designate meeting places, burial grounds, ceremonial sites, and even personal totems or to honour a guest or visitor.[49]

European explorer Alexander Mackenzie was one of the first Europeans to comment on lobstick trees, and in his assessment they "denoted the immediate abode of the natives and probably served for signals to direct each other to their respective winter quarters."[50] Warburton Pike, an Englishmen who travelled into the far northern tundra in search of big game, also commented on these markers: "Many an appointment has been kept at [lobsticks]," suggesting their role as convenient meeting points that everyone could find.[51]

Caroline Podruchny documents in her book *Making the Voyageur World: Travelers and Traders in the North American Fur Trade* the physical creation and the symbolic meaning of the lobstick tree within the voyageur world. In that version, all of the branches except the topmost would be removed, leaving a tall tree often called a "maypole." Sometimes the bark would be removed, leaving a smooth surface on which to cut names, dates, or symbols, or simply to shoot patterns into the tree with gunshots. A particularly cheerful version was created for Frances Simpson, wife of the HBC governor, with feathers and streamers for decoration. A lobstick, according to Podruchny, was created to honour a new leader, particularly if it was his first trip into the northland. To repay the voyageurs for the honour of making a maypole/lobstick tree, the leader was expected to offer presents or at least a generous measure of rum. It seems clear that in the voyageur world the trees were created for their symbolic meaning—and, of course, to have a party.

Cree groups from both the forest and the plains would meet at selected places throughout the western interior to engage in economic, social, and cultural exchange. Archaeologist David Meyer called them "ingathering centres" and identified several along the Saskatchewan River, including the forks.[52] The lobstick tree would have been easy to spot for anyone who travelled overland from the forks

Figure 2. Lobstick tree. Original drawing by Merle Massie.

using the trail identified by William Pink in the 1700s. If the lobstick tree was indeed the site of an Aboriginal ingathering centre, then it made sense that the tree stood in lonely splendour in a meadow. Any surrounding bush and scrub would have long been used for teepee poles and firewood. The meadow might have been kept open through the First Nations traditional practice of burning to encourage new growth around the lobstick, attracting deer, moose, elk, and bison.[53]

The lobstick tree was in a meadow not far from Bigelow Lake and just a few miles from Cheal (Egg) Lake, both well known as nesting grounds for ducks and geese. In addition, the Garden River was nearby. These small watercourses were home to a variety of waterfowl much prized by the Cree, who might have used the site to participate in water-related ceremonial celebrations. The Goose Dance, for example, was popular among the Swampy Cree who lived to the east, from Fort à la Corne to Cumberland House.[54] It would have been a good place for Cree from Candle, Sturgeon, Christopher, and Emma Lakes, the North Saskatchewan River, and Fort à la Corne to meet. A water-based culture would explain the amazing dugout canoe find at Christopher Creek.[55] The fact that the lobstick was still in existence in 1911 shows the remarkable cultural depth of the north Prince Albert Aboriginal presence. The life span of a white spruce is well over 200 and up to 300 years. The trees are considered mature at between seventy-five and 100 years. In photographs in the Paddockwood history book, the tree was fully mature and very large by the time homesteaders pushed north. It is possible that the lobstick tree might have been created as many as 100 years or more before Euro-Canadian settlement in 1911, indicating a deep-time use of the north Prince Albert region as home, meeting place, and ceremonial site.[56] The lobstick tree was an important symbolic marker of "home."[57]

Traditional Cree ethnographers believed that the Cree migrated westward with the fur trade, using their middleman status, guns, and technology to push out previous inhabitants. This view has been questioned, even completely rejected, situating the Cree as traditional inhabitants.[58] The Cree at Sturgeon Lake have enjoyed a deep history within the North Saskatchewan River landscape. Their aquatic and terrestrial harvesting territory extended north from Sturgeon Lake to include Emma, Christopher, Oscar, and Anglin Lakes, as far north as the Narrows of Red Deer (Waskesiu) Lake, as well as south to what they called "Moon Lake" and the North Saskatchewan.[59] By the 1860s, the Sturgeon band was well established in their home territory.

Sometime in the mid-1800s, an influx of Cree people arrived. Che We Che Chap or Crooked Finger, whose anglicized name was James Bird, brought his family from Grand Rapids, at the northwest corner of Lake Winnipeg, west following the fur-trade river routes to La Ronge. It was not uncommon for small pockets of Cree bands to move west, following the fur trade and searching for fresh resources. Their motivations and movements mirror many later Canadian internal migrations. From La Ronge, Bird and his family turned south, finding the Thunder Hills and the expanse of Montreal Lake.[60] This region was rich in game and resources and seemingly empty, and Cree elders remembered their first years there as some

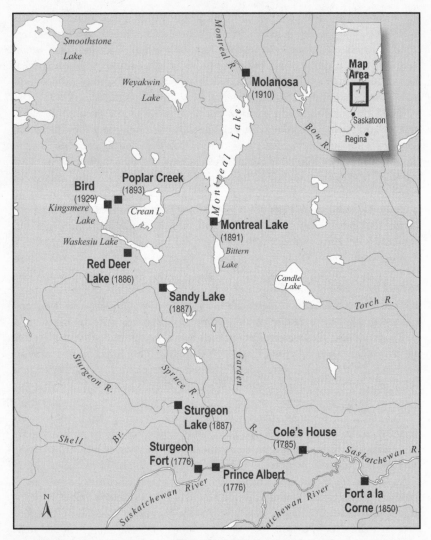

Map 5. Trading posts in the north Prince Albert region. Note that the majority of posts between Prince Albert and La Ronge were established between 1870 and 1930.
Source: Adapted from "Trading Posts Pre-1789–Post 1930," *Atlas of Saskatchewan*, 34.

of the happiest years of their lives.[61] The small, family-based band units lived "a seasonal pattern of movement that took them to camping spots at Candle Lake, Bittern Lake, Red Deer (Waskesiu) Lake, Trout (Crean) Lake, and the north and south ends of Montreal Lake."[62] Their territory included much of the northern watered landscape of the north Prince Albert region. The local population, a combination of recent immigrants and traditional inhabitants, was still relatively small, numbering a few hundred people.[63] Their lifestyle followed a boreal pattern centred on hunting and fishing, with incursions south to take bison or trade.

Fur trading within the region mushroomed throughout the nineteenth century in response to the increased First Nations occupation. By 1851, the Hudson's Bay Company re-established the post at Fort à la Corne, east of the forks. This post was in operation until well into the 1900s and for a time operated a satellite post at Candle Lake.[64] Smaller outposts and regional distribution centres were established along Sturgeon Lake, the Narrows area of Waskesiu, and the south end of Montreal Lake, particularly in the late 1800s.[65]

These groups shared an identifiable territory, interests, and similar lifeways. The people became more and more of a community through interaction at local fur-trade posts at the Narrows and Montreal Lake. Although few records exist, it is reasonable to assume that berry-picking expeditions, weddings, and other community celebrations were held to which many were invited and attended. Those who considered the area their home created a seasonal round based for the most part on the riches of the boreal forest and less so on the bison hunt of the prairie. As Peter Erasmus noted, Cree groups from the forest would use bison as a supplement to their diet but did not rely on it.

PEMMICAN EMPIRE

From the late 1700s, when trading posts were established along the Saskatchewan Rivers, through to the mid-1800s, the southern bison-hunting economy exploded. Bands were drawn to the plains in response to the intense and profitable pemmican and provisioning trade and the richness of the horse and gun bison economy and culture.[66] The bison (pemmican) provisioning trade rose to prominence as fur-trade forts spread into the western interior, and major canoe brigades operated each year from the Athabasca region to Hudson Bay or Montreal.

The pemmican trade, or what historian George Colpitts calls the "pemmican empire," was, in essence, a major economic, ecological, and social force.[67] What made it fascinating, from the perspective of ecological and cultural edges, is that it drew the two major ecological zones of the western interior into a major business and marketing relationship: the bison of the plains were harvested and processed by both First Nations and the new Métis communities to provision the fur-trade brigades that operated in the fur-rich northern boreal forest. This binary relationship was not new. Northern boreal bands had met southern prairie bands at or near Kestapinik (Prince Albert) for thousands of years to participate in trade. The pemmican empire accelerated these traditional trading relationships from a small, inter-band scale to a much larger scale that led to the growth of new social and cultural groups, particularly the Métis.

The fur brigades required small and easily portable food supplies that could be eaten while canoeing. The Canadian winter environment, so necessary to create the lush fur coats on animals, meant that water was in its frozen state for several months of the year. Canoe brigades could operate only between May and September—a short window of opportunity that dictated long days and short stops. The brigades would leave their forts, loaded heavily with furs, and head east as soon as the river ice broke enough for travel. The trips, depending on the origin and destination, could take several weeks. After furs were unloaded at their destination posts, the canoes were filled with goods to resupply the interior forts. The brigades would then face the upstream trek back to the forts, all before the snow flew and the ice closed rivers. Time was precious; little time could be spent in hunting, fishing, or even stopping to cook along the way.

Pemmican was a portable source of protein that could sustain the brigades over their treks. Bison meat was pounded to a fine texture and mixed with rendered bison fat. Some pemmican—depending on what was available, the recipe maker, and likely the band's own preferences—was also mixed with dried berries to add texture, extra flavour, and nutrients. Sewn into large bags, pemmican became a major trade item for bands and individuals at each interior post, especially along the South Saskatchewan and other posts within traditional bison-hunting territory. "Beat meat" was a trade staple at Hudson House, "the house in buffalo country."[68] Traders, with strict instructions from Montreal and London to use their wits and goods to live off the land, traded for food items such as fresh, dried, and beat meat almost as much as they traded for furs. Interior posts, such as Hudson House, were created as cache points for pemmican. It was stored and then shipped with the fur brigades to other distributing posts such as Cumberland House, where the canoe brigades could access the precious portable protein supply.[69]

Buffalo-hide trade rose to prominence in the nineteenth century as industrialization and the need for bison leather to make industrial belts created a market in the cities along the eastern seashore of North America. Even so, pemmican, not furs, drove trade on the prairie, creating an economic and ecological window through which to view the contrast between the boreal north and the prairie south.

David Mandelbaum, the eminent Plains Cree ethnographer, noted that there were important differences between hunting bison and hunting moose or elk. Bison hunting, particularly pounding, jumping, or on horseback, was a communal activity suited to the larger plains encampments of several hundred people. Moose and elk required tracking and stalking, methods that suited lone and highly experienced hunters or small hunting parties.[70] Cree warrior Fine Day told Mandelbaum that "anyone could kill a buffalo but it took a good hunter to get moose or elk," another way of saying that bison hunting was an easier life.[71] Mandelbaum suggested that "the lavish supply of buffalo made for a neglect of forest hunting techniques," an indication that some of the plains tribes might have been unable to move back into a forest-adapted economy or even access forest-edge animals other than bison.[72] Forest resources, sufficient for small bands, likely would never have been able to accommodate the hunting pressure required by the much larger plains bands on an extensive or intensive basis. Plains bands used forest resources only when necessary as a refuge or to alleviate food shortages on the open plains.

TREATY 6: BISON TO AGRICULTURE

When the Presbyterian mission at Prince Albert was established in the 1860s, bison could still be hunted nearby, but not for long.[73] As the decade passed, it was becoming clear that the bison were in decline, and by the 1870s plains bands looking to trade in the pemmican empire or simply to feed themselves had to travel south far beyond their traditional hunting grounds to access this precious resource in any substantial capacity.[74] Boreal forest-adapted bands also would have missed this resource, though perhaps to a smaller degree. Decimation of the bison, combined with violent plains warfare, alcohol, and another extensive smallpox epidemic in the late 1860s and early 1870s had tremendous effects on the Plains Cree. Cree leader Mistawasis declared, in a heated session with other band leaders during the 1876 Treaty 6 negotiations, that "we are few in numbers compared to former times, by wars and the terrible ravages of smallpox."[75] Nowhere in this speech did Mistawasis claim that the bison had been killed by white people. It was the First Nations, weakened by whiskey and energized by horse stealing and thoughts of pride and bravery, who had engaged in the fur and pemmican trade so heavily to procure guns and ammunition with which to carry out their wars with the Blackfoot nations. Star Blanket concurred with this assessment: "If we had been friends we might now be a host of people of all nations and together have power to demand the things some of you foolishly think you can get and insist on now demanding. No, that is not the road we took, but killed each other in continuous wars and horse-stealing, all for the glory we all speak of so freely." Starvation and decline drove plains bands to sign several of the numbered treaties in western Canada.[76]

Treaty 6, signed at Fort Carlton and Fort Pitt in 1876, is generally interpreted as a convergence of interest between the Crown and First Nations bands of the region. Although the treaty is referred to as a "Plains Cree" treaty,[77] it was in fact signed between "Her Majesty the Queen and the Plain and Wood Cree Indians and Other Tribes of Indians."[78] "Plain and Wood Cree" might well be a reference not so much to the differences between individual bands as to the fact that bands living around Fort Carlton and Fort Pitt would have originated from both ecosystems and followed the pattern of traversing across the ecotone, drawing their living from both.

The Crown advocated a transition to permanent agrarian settlement. First Nations bands, fearing the end of their way of life through the bison hunt, asked for help to transition to farm settlements. Both Mistawasis and Ahtakakup, considered by historians (citing Cree interpreter Peter Erasmus) to be the most important figures at the treaty signing, pushed hard to establish good terms in the treaty. They wanted help for their people to "learn to gain their livelihood from the earth in a new way."[79]

The treaty terms specifically referred not only to those to whom farming would be a new experience but also to those already involved in it: "It is further agreed between Her Majesty and the said Indians, that the following articles shall be supplied to any Band of the said Indians who are now cultivating the soil, or who shall hereafter commence to cultivate the land."[80] Clearly, at the time of treaty, some bands were already cultivating the soil, adding to their subsistence base through agriculture. Those bands requested further agricultural help, as promised in the treaties, and worked to ensure that cultivated fields were included in their reserve land entitlements.

Reverend James Nisbet, the Presbyterian missionary at Prince Albert, wrote about the beginning of Native agriculture in the Prince Albert district. He claimed in 1869 that several families "cultivate small pieces of land both here and at a lake twenty miles distant."[81] Less than ten years later, Chief Ah-yah-tus-kum-ik-im-am (whose anglicized name was William Twatt) signed Treaty 6 in 1876. Twatt and his councillors came to the treaty signing from their home at Sturgeon Lake, twenty miles from the Prince Albert settlement. They immediately requested that their reserve be established on the north side of the lake. E. Stewart, the dominion land surveyor, later claimed that the best farming land was to be found on the north side.[82] As well, the acting Indian agent reported houses and a garden, with potatoes and barley already sown, without any help from outside agents.[83] The Sturgeon Lake band was already farming by 1876 and had chosen the best land in their home region. The terms of Treaty 6 clearly acknowledged contemporary First Nations farming practices, which quickly became an important aspect of First Nations land usage in the north Prince Albert region.

Treaty 6 sought to extinguish Aboriginal title to a vast region of western Canada. The northern boundary ceded in the original treaty passed in a straight line running east-west through the boreal forest, north of the boreal edge. In today's terms, the line would run west just north of latitude 54° north from the source of Mossy River and Macdougall Creek near Nipawin Provincial Park to the south end of Green Lake. This tract would have included land used by Woods Cree living around Candle Lake, Bittern Lake, Red Deer (Waskesiu) Lake, and the smaller lakes to the south, such as present-day Christopher and Emma Lakes. These families were not signatories to Treaty 6. The official treaty statement read thus: "Commencing at the mouth of the river emptying into the north-west angle of Cumberland Lake; thence westerly up the said river to its source; thence on a straight line in a westerly direction to the head of Green Lake." Historian Bob Beal suggested in the 2005 *Encyclopedia of Saskatchewan* that there was a serious disconnect between the written treaty terms and their meanings, as understood by the assembled chiefs: "There was no indication that land rights surrender was even discussed or explained. Erasmus read the written treaty, including the legally worded surrender clause, to the assembled First Nations; but the semantic differences between the languages and cultures may well have been too vast for even the best translator to bridge." Beal also noted that the territorial description of exactly *which* land was being surrendered might have been omitted in negotiations and added later. In the years following 1876, more bands who lived within the Treaty 6 region came forward to sign what are called "internal" adhesions.[84]

Adhesions caused tremendous angst in Ottawa, where Indian Department costs, particularly "annuity" or yearly treaty payments per person, were skyrocket-

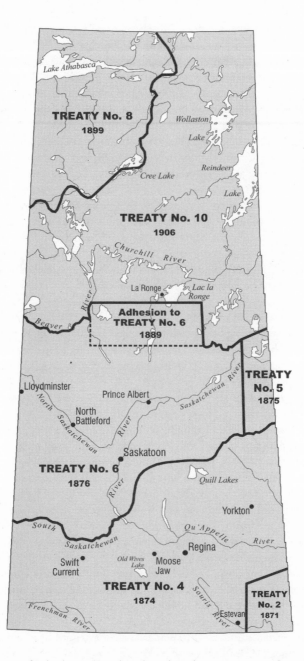

Map 6. Treaty map of Saskatchewan. Treaty boundaries shown here are approximate lines, for visual reference.
Source: Based on maps from Office of the Treaty Commissioner, Saskatchewan, and Aboriginal Affairs and Northern Development Canada, http://www.aadnc-aandc.gc.ca/eng/1100100032297/1100100032309.

ing. Ottawa responded with "shock and alarm," noted historian A.J. Ray, primarily because "no one in government had any idea of how many Indians lived in the surrendered territories." Furthermore, the agreements were clear: First Nations groups could wait to sign their adhesions while they decided where to settle on reserves; when they did, they could expect not just yearly annuities but also those in arrears, back to the signing of the treaty. Ottawa MPs roared: "How many more 'stragglers' could be expected"?[85]

According to a contemporary observer, John Sinclair of the Anglican mission at Stanley, several people from the region "presented themselves at Carlton during the time Treaty was being made with those Indians and asked to be paid but they were told that their part of the country was not fit for agricultural purposes and therefore could not get anything."[86] According to reports, they presented themselves again when treaty payments were being made the next year at Sturgeon Lake but were once again refused. Their firm demands would soon push Ottawa to action. As industrial exploitation, particularly lumbering and commercial fishing in the region north of Prince Albert, began to take hold throughout the decade following the treaty, the issue became more important. The bands that clearly occupied the region but were refused treaty adhesion and annuity payments complained directly to the surveyor who had come into the region to define timber limits. He replied that the bands were occupying territory that had been ceded in 1876.[87] If so, the bands argued, then compensation was due. These bands continuously petitioned the Crown throughout the 1880s amid growing discontent, starvation, and unrest among their plains brethren.[88]

The comment "not fit for agricultural purposes" was telling, particularly compared with the experiences of the Sturgeon Lake band members who had already made some transition toward including farming as part of their forest edge lifestyle. The intent of all signatories to Treaty 6 was to replace the bison lifestyle with a mix of grain and cattle farming. For those Woods Cree bands for whom bison was not central but merely one aspect of a mixed boreal way of life, loss of the bison was perhaps not as traumatic as it was for some of the Plains Cree bands. Indeed, other forest lifeways—fishing, trapping, and hunting—were virtually unaffected. The kind of agriculture practised by (and expected of) the north Prince Albert bands was small scale, transitional, and supplementary to other ways of making a living. They pursued a highly diversified way of life that moved seasonally throughout the region, accessing game, fish, and birds and trapping fur-bearing animals. Adding agriculture in some ways substituted for the bison hunt. Loss of the bison hunt confined the Plains Cree to their reserves, where, as they made the transition to agriculture on a large enough scale to supply food to their people, they required extensive government assistance. The Woods Cree of the north Prince Albert region largely continued a diversified way of life drawn from the forest edge environment.

TREATY 6 ADHESION: BOREAL AGRICULTURE

On a cold day in February 1889, at the north end of Montreal Lake, Woods Cree and Rocky Cree families from Lac La Ronge and Montreal Lake met with representatives of the Crown to sign an external adhesion to Treaty 6.[89] After years of agitation and repeated requests from the boreal bands in the north Prince Albert region, the Crown finally agreed to offer treaty. The difference between an internal adhesion and an external adhesion was crucial: an internal adhesion added people to existing treaty stipulations; an external adhesion added both new people and new lands to an existing treaty. In the latter, treaty terms were at least somewhat negotiable.

The external adhesion attempted to sort out a dual problem. On the one hand, there were bands with homes in the north Prince Albert region, within the boundaries of Treaty 6, that had not been offered treaty. Securing an external adhesion, which acted essentially as a new treaty, clarified the uncertainty of who was, and who was not, in treaty relationship with the Crown. Although there is nothing in the official records to act as confirmation, an external adhesion could negate continuing calls for arrears in treaty annuity payments. The government did not want news of the new treaty to spread: "Mr. Dewdney was anxious that the business should be kept quiet in order that outside Indians might not be attracted to the District."[90] Meeting in winter, and sending runners ahead to alert people to attend the meeting, also limited attendance.

The second problem came from the commercial interests of investors in Prince Albert. Surveyors, scouting and marking out timber berths, realized that the boundaries of Treaty 6 did not entirely cover the potential area of forest resources that the Prince Albert community believed was within their economic sphere. In short, the land ceded by Treaty 6 did not correspond to the boundaries of the Saskatchewan District of the North-West Territories[91] or Prince Albert's intended commercial empire of northern boreal resources. Officials at Indian Affairs explained: "The object in getting the surrender just now is in order that the Govt might legally dispose of the lumber in that Section permits to cut which have in some cases already been issued."[92] It was a somewhat frantic and belated effort to legally rectify a serious error—the government was issuing timber permits on land that had possibly not yet been ceded by treaty.

Adhesion to Treaty 6 kept the major original terms of the treaty but ceded additional land. Treaty 6, designed primarily to promote agricultural development, has generally been described as incompatible with boreal forest bands. The overtly agricultural terms of Treaty 6 included grants of agricultural implements, stock, harness, and instruction in their use. As historical consultant Joan Champ noted, "these provisions hardly recognized the reality of the Woodland Cree's environment and lifestyle," tied to the hunting, fishing, and trapping cycle.[93] Yet recorded negotiations between the treaty party and the First Nations at Montreal Lake showed a keen understanding of the specific agricultural components that *would* work well in their boreal lifestyle.

Boreal forest bands also had farming experience. The Sturgeon Lake band had land under cultivation at the time of the original treaty in 1876. By 1889, when the northerly bands signed the adhesion, agricultural pursuits were common. Reverend John A. Mackay, a mixed-blood Anglican missionary who held several roles in the Prince Albert diocese, including acting as the missionary in charge of Stanley Mission in the mid-1800s, travelled back and forth through the region from Stanley Mission to Prince Albert. Fluent in Cree, Mackay was an important figure in the region and knew many of the people intimately. As Bill Waiser writes, "he ran a 15-acre agricultural operation, including a mill that made the mission almost self-sufficient. He also used a small printing press to begin to produce Cree translations of the Scriptures and religious services. In fact, there was little that the priest could not turn his hand to, a talent that was surpassed only by his capacity for northern travel. He was an imposing figure. With his flashing eyes, bushy eyebrows, and long clerical garb, he looked every part the prophet and reportedly feared no one but God." Mackay's fifteen-acre farm was an experiment in northern farming and gardening that had a significant impact on local bands.[94]

In his travels to and from Prince Albert and his northern mission post at Stanley, Mackay noted extensive potato and garden plots cultivated by boreal forest families, often on lakeshores or islands where good land could be found. Agricultural pursuits resonate through First Nations oral histories from the region, which speak of a long history of gardening, particularly at the sites of winter trapping camps. Potatoes and other root vegetables would be planted in the spring, just as families were packing up to take their furs to market, to fish, and to engage in summer work.[95] These plots would be ready for harvest in the fall when the families returned to their trapping camps and would supplement the family's food requirements over the winter.[96] Nonetheless, agricultural pursuits at La Ronge, through both the mission and the more traditional gardens grown at the trading post and by many locals on their trapping grounds, showed a widespread, though not intensive, integration of agriculture as one facet of the boreal landscape. The northern bands, though centred on and adapted to a boreal environment based on resource harvesting, incorporated agricultural pursuits in their seasonal lifestyle and cultural worldview.

To a certain extent, the boreal bands of the region went through a fairly rapid sea change in 1889–90, moving from a mixed boreal-based lifestyle to one that anticipated greater importance for agriculture. This sea change was expressed in the adhesion and annuity documents. During the 1889 negotiations, the chiefs of both bands at first rejected the agricultural components of Treaty 6. Chief James Roberts of La Ronge commented that "there are some things offered to them by the Government, such as cattle, which would be no use to them, and they would like to get something instead." The adhesion documents also reported that "William Charles [of Montreal Lake] would not like to receive any cattle just now, as they have no means of looking after them at present."[97] A boreal lifestyle built on seasonal movements for hunting, fishing, and trapping was not compatible with the sedentary occupation required for raising cattle. In addition, wolves abounded in the boreal forest; keeping cattle safe was not an easy task. Benjamin Bird, a senior councillor with the Montreal Lake band, was clearly not afraid to contradict his chief. He stated that the Montreal Lake band "would like to have an Instructor to look after them and teach them the mode of farming," but the document does not state which *kind* of farming Bird was thinking about.[98] The men retired to their tents to discuss the treaty terms and come to a compromise regarding the agricultural components of the treaty.

When they came back, James Roberts revised his requests. Probably recognizing the success of Mackay's Stanley Mission farm (which had some livestock), the band asked for a bull, three cows, an ox, and pigs. They also requested "three ploughs for the whole Band, (small light ones that can be carried in canoes)," along with a few scythes to cut hay for the animals. In lieu of what the government would still owe them, they requested the balance in ammunition and twine for nets. The chief went on to note that, "in regard to a horse, harness, and wagon, which would be of no use to him, he would like to get something as an equivalent ... 1 tent, 1 stove, and 4 sets of dog harness." Roberts presented an interesting compromise between the needs of a boreal band and the agricultural promise held out in Treaty 6. He clearly believed (after some convincing) that agricultural implements had a place and could be used with some success. But some agricultural requirements were clear: "Next Spring they will plant their potatoes where they have been accustomed to. They want, next Spring, seed potatoes to plant; about twenty bushels would be sufficient to supply those who have none."[99] Whether planting potatoes is defined as simple gardening or a local boreal adaptation that showed a marked acceptance of agriculture, the point remains: First Nations understood the scale of agricultural possibility as one aspect of their boreal lifestyle. During negotiations, they created a fine balance between current needs, such as extra twine, ammunition, and dog harness, and future needs and possibilities, including scythes and plows and more seed potatoes to expand production.

William Charles of Montreal Lake refrained from making specific requests, pending further discussion with his band.[100] The horse, wagon, and harness due to him as chief, as per the treaty stipulations, were accepted. Charles knew that a rude cart trail existed between the settlement at Prince Albert and the south end of Red Deer (Waskesiu) Lake, forming an overland link between Prince Albert and the northern territory. A wagon (which could be outfitted with sleighs) could be a useful vehicle. In April, government agents tried to ship seed potatoes to reach the bands in time for spring seeding but were not successful. Both bands also requested timber implements such as pit saws, logging chains, axes, and assorted tools.[101] Given the forested boreal environment, the possibility of earning income from lumber, and the need to build permanent residences and a school on the reserve, these items were practical and necessary. Agents brought the first treaty payment in September, which included agricultural implements and supplies such as hay forks, grubbing hoes, and garden seeds.[102]

In the negotiations surrounding the Treaty 6 external adhesion, agriculture, particularly adapting agricultural promises to the boreal landscape, became the focus. Clearly, boreal bands had already adapted extensive gardening, but animal husbandry and large-scale grain growing using the European cultural model were different matters that required more knowledge and training, and more consideration, before the bands were ready to commit to them. It was not a case of outright rejection as if agriculture were a foreign, unknown, imposed, colonial idea. The concept of "ecological imperialism" in the Canadian north, or cultural colonization through imposing a foreign and unknown way of life, an idea put forward by historians such as Liza Piper and John Sandlos, does not recognize the depth of connection between First Nations groups living in boreal edge environments and agriculture.[103] The bands understood what would work, what perhaps could work, and what could not work in the boreal environment and within their cultural way of life.

In many ways, what happened in the north Prince Albert region was an extension of the phenomenon of Indian agriculture along the parkland and forest edge, as traced by historical geographers D. Wayne Moodie and Barry Kaye. Small-scale cultivation of Indian corn, potatoes, and other root crops in microclimatic conditions and pockets of good land in what became Manitoba was common throughout the late 1700s and 1800s: "If not entirely based on Indian cultigens, it was conducted on Indian terms."[104] Boreal microclimate agriculture was significantly different from the disastrous reintroduction of plains First Nations agriculture, a topic well studied as an example of government colonialism, control, incompetence, indifference, and hostility.[105] There are significant nuances to the term "agriculture" that need to be reconsidered: what a "farm" looks like, which kinds of activities happen there, and what "success" looks like should not be fixed concepts. There remains ample room to reconsider the complex character of Aboriginal agriculture, and the transition to industrial agriculture, from the perspective of the boreal edge, as a much-needed contrast to the plains story.

LITTLE RED RIVER RESERVE

The most effective way to capitalize on the large-scale agricultural promise of the treaty would be to develop a reserve on land capable of supporting more extensive cultivation, in the fertile Saskatchewan River basin. For boreal bands already well adapted to seasonal use of the edge environment, substituting farming for bison hunting changed only one component of the mixed boreal lifestyle. The adhesion brought the Lac La Ronge and Montreal Lake bands into close contact with Prince Albert through subsequent treaty payments and proximity.[106] In many ways, the adhesion carried on a traditional use of the north Prince Albert landscape as the southern edge of the boreal bands' territory.

After signing the Treaty 6 adhesion, the Lac La Ronge and Montreal Lake bands debated the location of their home reserves. After much discussion, the Montreal Lake band settled on a site at the southern end of Montreal Lake and proceeded to build a new settlement.[107] The Lac La Ronge band, however, consisted of multiple-site family-occupied units and had no clear consensus on where to build a single community reserve. Even the surveyor, A.W. Ponton, could not see the benefit of creating a single community. The band, Ponton noted, wanted to set aside all of the holdings that they occupied along the lake "on which they have their houses and buildings" as well as their garden plots, on the scattered bits and pockets of usable soil. If the government tried to force them to live on just one reserve, "they [would] probably have a strong inclination to return to their [scattered] holdings where they have been accustomed."[108]

If the La Ronge band was undecided about which of its northern occupations it wanted surveyed as the main reserve "in common," they did know one thing: "all agree that they would, looking to the future, like some of their land surveyed near the Saskatchewan."[109] Requesting legal rights not only to land at Lac La Ronge but also closer to the Saskatchewan River strongly reflected the traditional boreal band use of the ecological edge found near Prince Albert. Archdeacon Mackay, interpreter at the adhesion in 1889, was a steady force behind this request. Mackay spoke with the first chief, James Roberts, and argued, "someday, all this land will be taken, the fish and moose will disappear and you will be destitute. Farms will never disappear but will grow in value."[110] Mackay suggested that the band request some of their reserve land as agricultural land within the Saskatchewan River watershed, at the southern edge of their traditional territory. In addition to tending their traplines and home gardens, those who attended residential schools or Emmanuel College in Prince Albert (where Mackay worked for many years as a senior staff member, Cree catechist, translator, and teacher) worked on school farms and gardens. Residential schools used farms and gardens both to supply food and to give the students exposure to and experience in farm and garden practices. Historical opinion is divided on the role of garden and farm work in residential schools. Some researchers regard work on gardens and farms little different from child labour and slavery. An unexpected perspective comes from the oral histories of the Lac La Ronge Woods Cree, who declare that exposure to farming practices led to the call for and development of a farm reserve.[111]

After Archdeacon Mackay spoke with Chief James Roberts, "the Chief thought about this for a long time. One day he told his wife to make three pairs of moccasins for his long journey. His wife got the help of some other ladies and next morning she gave him his moccasins." Roberts began the long journey south by dog sled. Along the way, he spoke with Chief William Charles at Montreal Lake. The two of them went to Prince Albert, where "Archdeacon Mackay interpreted and the two chiefs gave their case to the government officials."[112]

The Indian Department, upon receiving the request, acted surprisingly quickly. Hayter Reed, Indian commissioner of the North-West Territories, wrote to the superintendent general at Ottawa: "The Indians of the Lac La Ronge Band desire to have the portion of their Reserve, asked for on the Saskatchewan, near the Sturgeon Lake Reserve, and subject to the Department's approval, I propose to select and define some land on the South side of some good lake, in that locality, which will act as a barrier against frost, and to afford protection to crops."[113] Reed asked surveyor Ponton to investigate if there was a large enough tract of suitable land available.

Ponton recommended a tract of land just north of the William Twatt (Sturgeon Lake) Reserve:

> The country is undulating and generally covered with a scattered growth of small poplar. Fire has passed over the country in the past, and left large quantities of dry wood, and open areas ready for the plough. A creek or small river flowing South would cross the Eastern portion, and it is said to be well stocked with jackfish and suckers. Small game such as rabbits, ducks, and prairie chicken are still numerous, and the Band would be located on the direct roads to such fishing lakes as Red Deer Lake, Bittern Lake and others, which they could easily visit at the proper seasons to lay in a supply of fish.[114]

Ponton's recommendation illuminated several important points. Although the agricultural capability of the land was paramount, other aspects of its landscape and location were significant. It was near the Sturgeon Lake band, for the boreal bands wanted to be near other Woods Cree, with whom they could "meet ... and make friends."[115] The location was also convenient for the Indian Department, which assumed that "proximity to the Sturgeon Lake reserve would enable instruction and oversight to be given comparatively easily."[116] Firewood supply, fish, and small game were important. Road access connected the boreal bands with their other seasonal hunting and fishing lands.[117] The location seemed ideally suited to all purposes.

Problems arose immediately. The Department of the Interior rejected the reserve selection since "the whole of these lands ... are timber berths, and are under license to Messrs. Moore and MacDowall, of Prince Albert, consequently they are not available."[118] Both the Department of the Interior and the Indian Department agreed and anticipated that the desired reserve would, or could, be good farming land. Its primary role, in the meantime, was to service the burgeoning lumber industry at Prince Albert. The Department of Indian Affairs was unable to overrule the Department of the Interior, and there the matter rested.

According to oral tradition, the chiefs of both Montreal Lake and La Ronge continued to press their case for a farming reserve during annual treaty annuity payments. They also made trips to Prince Albert to remind the Indian Department of the bands' continued interest in the lands in question. At no point did the bands try to acquire any other suitable lands.[119] In 1894, Indian Agent W. Sibbald reported that "the older men say that this farming land is for the rising generation to fall back upon when the hunt will no longer provide a living for them, which is a state they all believe is fast approaching."[120] The bands were essentially using the arguments of Archdeacon Mackay and cleverly playing into the ideals of the Indian Department, for which agriculture represented a clear road to civilization and settlement. The agricultural argument gave the bands leverage in their fight to own a southern reserve in addition to their northern territories. If the Indian Department wanted the boreal bands to embrace farming on a scale larger than the microclimate of soil pockets and root vegetable gardens, then it had to provide land with better soil and growing capability.

The continued and determined lobbying pushed the Indian Department to renew its efforts. Reed reviewed the whole situation in 1895. The Montreal Lake band, in particular, was suffering from reduced fishing and hunting resources, and some were inclined to move south. The farming instructor at Sturgeon Lake would be nearby to give advice, which the boreal bands specifically and repeatedly requested.[121] Reed once again asked the Department of the Interior if the timber berths on these lands had been renewed or if the lands were available. He even hoped that it might be "possible in the meantime to allow the Indians to occupy the lands in whole or in part, conditionally upon their respecting the right of Messrs. Moore and Macdowall to the timber covered in their license."[122] Confusion followed the request. At first it seemed that the land title was clear; then railway and timber interests interfered. Distance (and conflicting records) between Ottawa and the land office at Prince Albert held up the process.[123]

In March 1897, Reverend T. Clarke, minister serving at Montreal Lake, sent an alarming communication to Hayter Reed. He suggested that it was well known that the department was trying to secure a reserve around Little Red River. Some Métis were planning to move onto the land and demand squatter's rights, Clarke contended. He warned that no hay permits should be issued for the area for fear of leaving nothing for the incoming bands. He also recommended that a crop of potatoes and other vegetables be sown to be ready for band members planning to move.[124] The threat of squatters, real or imagined, seemed to galvanize the Indian Department to again ask the Department of the Interior to reserve these lands.[125] This time all outside interests were swept aside. A.W. Ponton completed the survey of Little Red River Indian Reserve No. 106A in the spring of 1897, and by 1900 an order-in-council officially created the reserve held in common for the bands at Montreal Lake and Lac La Ronge.[126]

Although the boreal bands requested this southern reserve, and the Indian Department approved and supported it, it was not universally lauded. J. Lestock Reid, a surveyor for the Indian Department, and Prince Albert's member of the legislative assembly of the North-West Territories, objected to the new reserve.[127] He sent a strongly worded letter to T.O. Davis, member of Parliament for Prince Albert, in 1897. After sheepishly admitting that the land in question was where he pastured his herd of cattle, Reid went on: "In the name of all that is holy why bring the Wood Indians from their hunting grounds where they are making a living to try and make farmers of them and starvation." Reid claimed it was better to give them reserve land "where they have been accustomed to live and have lived for generations. I know, no one better, that these Wood Indians will never make a living not even an attempt at farming. If they are brought down it becomes permanent starvation and perhaps worse and help to swell the catalogue of Almighty Voices."

The reference to Almighty Voice is significant. Almighty Voice shot a cow—considered to be government property—on his Cree home reserve of One Ar-row, south of Prince Albert, in 1895. Public records and oral history diverge at this point: was it to feed a hungry family, or to celebrate a wedding, or just for spite? While Almighty Voice was in captivity, the guards told him that he would be hanged. He escaped but was tracked down. He killed the officer and escaped, which set off a massive manhunt. For nearly two years, Almighty Voice roved at will across the ecotone, heading north into the bush and south to his home and neighbouring reserves, eluding police. In the spring of 1897, the police, with heavy weaponry, cornered Almighty Voice and two companions in a bluff south of Prince Albert. They were shot to death.[128]

By invoking Almighty Voice, Reid raised specific concerns about starvation policies, the "fitness" of First Nations for agriculture, the problematic history of government intervention in Aboriginal agriculture, and the possibility of wide-spread resistance, following Almighty Voice's lead. Reid was a treaty commissioner in 1876, sent to the Berens River and Norway House area of Manitoba to ac-cept adhesions to Treaty 5, so he had some experience of boreal lifeways. It is unlikely, however, that he had visited any traplines or homes to witness the kind of small-scale boreal agriculture common in Manitoba and Saskatchewan. More-over, Almighty Voice, in many ways, was a victim of prairie Aboriginal agricul-tural policies, which were underfunded, wrongheaded, and by the late 1890s being abandoned by many prairie First Nations.[129] Killing a "government" cow is one interpretation; the band, it could also be said, owned the cow as part of Treaty 6. What Reid did not fully appreciate was that Aboriginal boreal agriculture, always seasonal and designed to fit with other aspects of boreal life, had a different pur-pose. The boreal bands would continue to have their northern reserves. They were asking, in essence, for a legally recognized base of land in both boreal and forest edge environments. Ensuring access to a larger-scale land base for agriculture, the bands were essentially broadening their subsistence base and spreading their efforts to ensure a greater measure of resilience.

CONCLUSION

The ecotone found in the north Prince Albert region marked both a typical example of an ecological and cultural edge between prairie and boreal environments and a special place. From a larger perspective, First Nations' use of the western interior was not confined to only one or the other environment. Both plains- and forest-adapted bands used the forest edge as a place of refuge, diversification and resilience, and cultural adaptation and exchange. Resource exploitation and interaction involved all seasons of the year to access fish, waterfowl, large and small game, plants, medicine, and fuel. Before treaty and segregation on reserves, plains bands could access the forest as a temporary refuge from harsh winter conditions or spring and summer domestic exploitation. At the height of the pemmican empire, plains bands used the ecological differences between the boreal North and the prairie South to their advantage: they manufactured pemmican as a trade item to fuel the fur trade, and acted as seasonal employees of the fur trade paddling and portaging through the northern waterways. As the bison disappeared, the opportunities and lifestyles of boreal and plains bands moved in opposite directions. Confined to reserve lands on the open plains, and subjected to problematic and inappropriate government intervention that stymied, rather than helped, their transition to agriculture, plains bands often became dependent on assistance. They could no longer migrate to the boreal region to exploit its resources. It should be noted, though, that many plains bands sought a measure of ecological resilience through their choice of reserve land in forested or scrub environments where game, timber, and other forest resources could be found, even though such land was often less fit for agriculture. Boreal bands had a long history of using forest edge resources in a cycle that moved from deep within the forest to the forest edge and beyond. Although they also took up reserves, boreal bands experienced somewhat less disturbance, at least in the early years after treaty.

The Treaty 6 external adhesion offers a place-based perspective to reconsider key points in the western Canadian story. The significant differences between boreal microclimate agriculture and the types of farming adapted across the south show a potential new direction to rethink and re-evaluate Aboriginal agriculture in the post-treaty transition era. What did "farming" look like? Variations and complexity must be acknowledged.

The lobstick tree, as a marker of home, foreshadowed the formalization and entrenchment of reserve communities for northern bands within the north Prince Albert region—reserve lands chosen to provide bases in more than one ecological zone. The Indian Department considered environmental and agricultural capability of the landscape; it did not consider the long-held Aboriginal practice of using spaces across the ecotone. Nonetheless, the Indian Department supported the boreal bands' requests for a portion of treaty land entitlement to be ceded in the Saskatchewan River basin on land that could be used for agriculture. The adhesion and the farming reserve also reflected a longer history of life at the boreal forest edge, one that included not only the resources of the forest (game, fish, berries, plants, and wood) but also agriculture. With the demise of the bison and the continued call for a treaty, the seasonal routine and cultural interest shifted to include both an intensified microclimate agriculture and larger-scale farm practices tied to place, both stock raising and grain farming, to supplement the returns of the boreal forest. Only fifteen miles from the lobstick tree, Little Red River Reserve was not a new idea or a radical experiment but a continuation of long-held practices at the forest edge.

Ironically, the lobstick tree represented not only the symbolic home of the Cree but also the most enticing feature of the northern boreal landscape in the eyes of incoming resource extractors: white spruce, the new economic backbone of the north Prince Albert region.

CHAPTER THREE

WOOD IS SCARCE

Government explorer, botanist, and dominion field naturalist John Macoun published *Manitoba and the Great North-West: The Field for Investment; the Home of the Emigrant* in 1882. His intention—and his job—were to entice people to immigrate to the Canadian western interior. He was fighting an uphill battle. The western interior, many thought, was either a wasteland of endless prairie desert or a wilderness full of wild game and Indians. Western settlement had been disappointing. Macoun's publication set out to correct false assumptions. The most damning description of a cold-winter prairie country was the lack of timber for fuel and building supplies. On the contrary, Macoun countered, timber could be found across the west, though he admitted that "wood is scarce in the southern part of the prairie section." Settlers who chose to settle in northern districts, though, "will never experience a scarcity." Investors, too, were encouraged to migrate west. "North of Prince Albert," Macoun trumpeted, "are fine forests which are easy of access" and valuable to timber barons. Prophesying profits, Macoun urged reaping the boreal forest to serve the needs of prairie settlers.[1] His words signalled a significant acceleration of resource exploitation in the north Prince Albert region.

Resource exploitation on a commercial scale by non-Native newcomers was built on the belief that the treeless open plains could be filled with immigrants *because* there were significant timber resources in the forested regions, which curved over the prairie in an arc from Calgary, north through Edmonton, east through Prince Albert, and down to Winnipeg. Industrialization reinforced the binary conception of what would become Saskatchewan, contrasting the treeless south with the boreal north. Prince Albert was not alone; commercial exploitation along the forest edge was common as soon as the railways penetrated the west, and particularly following completion of the Great Northern Railway in 1906, which ran close to accessible timber.[2] The Saskatchewan lumber industry, the majority of which centred on Prince Albert and Big River, soon outstripped its prairie rivals. By 1908, Saskatchewan produced as much lumber as Alberta and Manitoba; in 1912–13, its production was *double* that of the other two provinces.[3] On the doorstep of an accessible and enormous commercial wood basket but at the edge of the prairie, Prince Albert leveraged its fortunes to become the pivot point between the resource north and the prairie south.

Despite its regional importance, the thriving timber industry did not penetrate the "prairie" stereotype of Saskatchewan. In 1910, Allan Kennedy, an Ontario lumberjack, came west on a harvest excursion. Threshing over, he and his brother looked for something else to do: "Then we heard that there was logging going on at Prince Albert which was a surprise to us because we did not know there was any logging in Saskatchewan."[4] The lumber industry, in fact, has been a major factor in provincial development. But wood could only be found, and commercially exploited, in certain places. The origin of the lumber industry in the north Prince Albert region provides a little-known and important counterpoint to the perception of Saskatchewan as prairie.

EARLY LUMBER INDUSTRY

In 1874, while on a hunting expedition in the western interior of Canada—the wilderness full of wild game—Captain William Moore saw a business opportunity. Snowbound, Moore headed for the Prince Albert settlement to secure flour and other supplies. Farmers in the area had successful crops, and grain was available. Flour, though, was scarce and prohibitively expensive. The wind-powered grist mill, dependent on the vagaries of nature, had not been in operation for some time. Moore immediately saw the potential for a steam-powered flour mill. The wealth of timber across the river led him to purchase a dual-purpose mill, both to grind wheat into flour and to cut logs into lumber. In 1875, Moore brought eight wagons and fifteen carts overland from Winnipeg to Prince Albert. Loaded with millstones, a steam boiler, saws, equipment, tools, and men skilled in their operation, the wagons and carts brought the commercial dream of mechanized milling to Prince Albert. Capable of both grinding grain and sawing logs into lumber, Moore's mill ushered in what writer and archivist Brock Silversides suggested has been the most enduring and identifiable business in the Prince Albert region—the commercial lumber industry.[5]

During the mill's first full year of operation in 1879, Moore took 9,000 logs out of the area where the Little Red River meets the North Saskatchewan River. By the time dominion field naturalist John Macoun cajoled investors to develop the resources north of Prince Albert in 1882, there was a growing movement to exploit the trees. Moore's lumber and grist mill was the opening gambit in what became several ambitious and expansive commercial enterprises that led early development of the north Prince Albert region.

Long known as "the Good Wintering Place," Prince Albert drew intensive and permanent immigration in the mid-nineteenth century. On the south bank of the river, fields of grain and potatoes could be found, planted by "les autres Métis" or English-Scotch half-breed farmers.[6] These English-speaking Presbyterian and Anglican settlers were drawn by ties of kinship and chain migration to build on the agricultural success of James Isbister, the first farmer in the Prince Albert region. Prince Albert historian Gary Abrams callously dismissed Isbister as merely a "half-breed trapper and former interpreter for the Hudson's Bay Company," who, with his Indian wife, "lived on" the land that later became River Lot 62.[7] Such a dismissal was unwarranted. Historian Paget Code's investigation of the English and Scotch Métis of the Prince Albert settlement revealed a more complex and interesting background. Isbister's settlement was not only deliberate but also anchored a nucleus of migration out of the Red River area following the transfer of Rupert's Land to Canada in 1870.[8] Within a few years, the population exceeded 300 English-speaking settlers "whose houses extended 14 miles along the south bank of the North Saskatchewan," Abrams admitted, in classic river-lot formation.[9] Moore embedded himself in this fledgling farming community and ground the local grain. Soon his commercial interest turned to exploiting the white spruce and jack pine forest on the north bank of the river.

Until Captain Moore brought in the steam-powered boiler and sawmill, the majority of timber in the Prince Albert region was cut for domestic use (fuelwood or building logs) or to power the steamboats travelling up and down the Saskatchewan River. The Hudson's Bay Company completely overhauled its transportation operations in 1871. Steamboats operating on the Saskatchewan represented "capital-intensive transportation technologies" intent on replacing the labour-intensive (and expensive) boat and cart brigades.[10] Historian Jim Mochoruk noted that increased local opportunities such as day labour, farming, and work in fishing, cordwood, and lumber camps were drawing Aboriginal and mixed-blood labourers away from traditional fur-trade employment opportunities. In response, the Hudson's Bay Company completely reinvented its inland water transportation system, constructing a railway portage at Grand Rapids (at the north end of Lake Winnipeg) and purchasing or building large-capacity steamboats to haul goods into the Saskatchewan interior.

When the Hudson's Bay Company sold its interests to the dominion in 1870, it retained one-twentieth of the arable land in the western interior. Without settlers, that land capital was useless. The new transportation policy reflected a shift in purpose for the company from primarily a fur-trading monopoly to a retail sales and land development company. Passengers, travellers, and settlers bound for the western interior would not only purchase passage on the steamboats but also possibly buy land for settlement from the company and provide a new market for HBC goods after they settled.[11]

Figure 3. Steamboat on the Saskatchewan River.
Source: SAB, R-A2116.

The steamboats required massive loads of fuel. Demand for cordwood escalated. A "cord" is a measure of wood four feet square by eight feet long. At a time
when all cooking and heating were done with either coal or wood, cordwood was
an important commodity, particularly on the open plains, where homesteads and
farms could not provide their own sources of fuel. Wood could also power steam
engines, such as those on steamboats or trains, if necessary. Wood to power engines
did not have to be merchantable timber. Any scrub wood, from jack pine to poplar, would do. Men with little capital could operate successful cordwood berths
(cheaper to lease than timber berths) on or near the Saskatchewan River to fill this
niche market. Or they could simply sell for profit the wood that had to be cut from
their homesteads to make land.[12] Extra loads of wood could easily be marketed as
household fuel for the growing commercial centre at Prince Albert.

Although steamboats created a burgeoning market for cordwood, the commercial timber industry in the Prince Albert region after Captain Moore arrived remained tied to local requirements. The Prince Albert settlement was growing: there
were 831 people recorded in the district by 1878, and three years later there were
four times that number.[13] From the start, Moore's mill was busy. The phenomenal local growth at Prince Albert showcased the transition from one way of life to another:
as the editor of the *Saskatchewan Herald* noted in 1878, "the buffalo hunter is rapidly
giving way to the farmer, and the Indian trader to the merchant."[14] Historian G.F.G.
Stanley explained that, until the rail line was finished across the southern plains in

1885, "there were [virtually] no settlements south of the North Saskatchewan valley. Not only were the northern settlements deemed more suitable for agriculture, but they were also more accessible," due to water transport.[15] Saskatoon did not exist, and Regina was Pile o' Bones; Prince Albert was the place to be. Agricultural settlers and industrial entrepreneurs from Manitoba, Ontario, and Britain began to join the mixed-blood community at Prince Albert in larger numbers.

This growing commercial centre experienced a land and real estate boom throughout the early 1880s. The Land Office opened in 1881, welcoming settlers travelling overland on the Carlton Trail or disembarking from steamboats. The railway boom, however, was taking hold. Residents of Prince Albert believed that it would soon be joined to all points east and south through this important technological advance. The original proposed route of the Canadian Pacific Railway went through the North Saskatchewan River valley, and Prince Albert was assured a bright future.[16] When the railway went west across the open plains, residents of Prince Albert were not worried at first. A major branch line had been proposed, and several railway charters had been issued to criss-cross through the region.[17]

For many, the Saskatchewan River valley was the logical hub of the western interior. In 1882, the North-West Territories were divided into the provisional districts of Assiniboia, Saskatchewan, Alberta, and Athabasca.[18] Prince Albert became the centre of a provisional district that stretched from the north shore of Lake Winnipeg in the east to the Districts of Alberta and Athabasca in the west, south to the District of Assiniboia, and north to latitude 55°.[19] Anchored by the Saskatchewan River and tied to Winnipeg by steamboat, much of the traffic into and out of the west passed through the district. Newspaper articles and pamphlets from local boosters presented the Saskatchewan identity in sharp contrast to the District of Assiniboia to the south, painting a scene comparing rich agricultural lands and the wealth of forest resources with flat, dry, treeless prairie. Encouraged to immigrate to Prince Albert, entrepreneurs engaged in commercial investments, such as the burgeoning timber industry. By 1883, though, the boom was over. Prince Albert faced the dual prospect of no railway in the near future combined with a national economic depression that pushed booster and boom activity to the wayside.[20]

Grievances in the District of Saskatchewan from First Nations, Métis, and white settlers grew throughout 1883 and 1884 until they reached a conflagration in the spring of 1885.[21] The 1885 rebellion took place primarily within Saskatchewan and further cemented a particular "Saskatchewan" identity.[22] Although no battles were fought in the vicinity, Prince Albert settlers and businessmen were caught up in the rebellion. Opposing sentiments ran high. In the aftermath, the town stagnated. Buffeted by a severe agricultural depression and struggling to deal with land grievances in the wake of the rebellion, the population dropped dramatically. To revive the fledgling community and jumpstart its economic potential for resource development (particularly timber), commercial interests pushed for a railway. The Qu'Appelle, Long Lake, and Saskatchewan Railway line, linking Prince Albert to the CPR at the fledgling community of Regina, was finished in late 1890.[23]

THE DOMINION LANDS ACT
AND THE LUMBER INDUSTRY

Following completion of the Qu'Appelle, Long Lake, and Saskatchewan rail link and its first season of operation in the winter of 1890–91, the settlement became the centre of a massive lumber industry that dominated the region and its economy for thirty years. Lumber interests expanded exponentially throughout the 1890s as prairie settlement surged. Dividing land into reserves for First Nations and quarter sections for farmers to be purchased or homesteaded and therefore "owned" was a sedentary transition. Tents were appropriate for First Nations groups accustomed to travelling through the landscape, using a broad definition of "home" that included many camping areas that provided seasonal and yearly needs. Reserve life dictated a move to permanent dwellings.[24] Euro-Canadian settlers, as soon as they could afford it, chose to build wood houses instead of the tents or sod dwellings hastily constructed on their homestead quarters. These houses—whether crude log cabins or clapboard shacks—represented a significant change in land use. Homestead rules required habitable, permanent dwellings before homesteaders could get their patent. As homesteads became farms, owners were expected (at least in a social and cultural sense) to upgrade or build new dwellings with commercial-grade sawn lumber.

Large-scale agricultural transition and redevelopment of the prairie sparked a massive demand for lumber to build houses, barns, fences, schools, churches, hospitals, and towns.[25] Between 1901 and 1911, Saskatchewan's population exploded, from just over 90,000 people in 1901 to nearly half a million in 1911.[26] To satisfy demand, the lumber industry grew dramatically. It was cheaper for new residents to purchase lumber from mills at Prince Albert than to have it shipped to the prairie from British Columbia, Ontario, or the Maritimes. The commercial lumber industry at Prince Albert marketed and sold its wood directly to growing prairie towns. Prior to the north-south railway link, Captain Moore and his partner had agents at Edmonton, Fort Saskatchewan, and Battleford selling their lumber. This lumber was shipped along the North Saskatchewan River. The Qu'Appelle, Long Lake, and Saskatchewan Railway did not commence full commercial operations until the winter of 1890–91. Despite exorbitantly high freight rates, rail led to the development of regional lumberyards in southern prairie towns. For instance, the Sanderson mill at Prince Albert operated lumberyards at Hague, Rosthern, and Vonda by the mid-1890s. As well, lumber continued to be shipped using the river. According to Prince Albert historian and archivist Bill Smiley, "each spring, Indian crews would arrive at the Sanderson Mill and construct scows twenty to thirty feet long, load them with lumber and move them. ... They would be further loaded with flour and other freight. The scows were floated down the river to their various destinations where they would be unloaded, dismantled and the timber used." There was a connection between commercial sawmills, regional markets, and transportation links, both the older waterways and the new rail lines: the water network of the Saskatchewan River reinforced the identity of the District of Saskatchewan, while the rail networks created a market with the Districts of Assiniboia, Manitoba, and Alberta. As railways continued to be built, water transportation stopped, and the industry found itself increasingly relying on the railways.[27]

Economic development of timber was regulated through the Dominion Lands Act.[28] The source of information on township surveys and homestead regulations, the Dominion Lands Policy was without a doubt primarily about homesteading, which affected thousands of people in the western interior over a sixty-year period of intense immigration, until the land was ceded to the three western provincial governments in 1930. For the Prince Albert region, however, timber policies were perhaps equally important. The Dominion Lands Act set out the rules and regulations surrounding timber limits and permits, swamp lands, grazing, mining, and water rights.

Farmers on the open plains required access not only to crop land through their homesteads but also to timber for much-needed fuel and building material. Economic historian Chester Martin argued that "the Canadian prairies have seldom been associated with forest growth of any form. The scarcity of forests by comparison with British Columbia or New Brunswick has made the limited reserves of timber correspondingly valuable for the lumbermen and the prairie settler."[29] Scarcity created value. The earliest dominion lands statute (amended on an almost yearly basis) stipulated that all timber lands—those capable of producing lumber—and all products of timber, including fuel and bark, were reserved against settlement. Forest lands of any kind were not to be opened for agricultural use. Perhaps this stipulation accounts for much of the push to put settlers onto prairie land—forest land in the western interior was considered too valuable to be parcelled out to individual settlers.

On the prairie, "islands" or "belts" of trees (islands were large copses or groves; belts were areas of continuous trees, as along a lakeshore or stream) were to be divided, according to the Dominion Lands Act, into ten- to twenty-acre woodlots, "as to benefit the greatest possible number of settlers and to prevent petty monopoly. ... As far as the extent of wood land in the township may permit, one wood lot to each quarter section farm" of this precious resource. Woodlots never materialized on a broad scale on the prairie. Settlers whose homesteads contained no timber or brush were allowed to cut, by permit, sufficient quantities for their needs on unoccupied Crown lands nearby, if there were any with wood. Settlers could cut extra for sale or barter for a nominal fee. Only those quarter sections that contained less than twenty-five acres of "merchantable" timber could be homesteaded.[30]

Of the "merchantable" timber, lumber barons targeted white spruce.[31] The north Prince Albert region contained some of the largest stands of white spruce in the western interior. Trees could range in size up to thirty inches—over two feet—in diameter at the base (stump—hence the term "stumpage fees"). The Dominion Lands Act of 1883 specified that all merchantable trees with an outside bark diameter of twenty-five centimetres (ten inches) or more at the stump *should* be harvested from a timber limit. Within these parameters, millions of board feet of lumber were harvested from timber berths north and east of Prince Albert between 1890 and 1919. One board foot is the volume of a one-foot length of a "standard" board, twelve inches wide by one inch thick. As a result, one board foot measures 144 cubic inches. In this way, the number of board feet could be figured if lumber was neatly stacked, no matter to which dimensions the wood was cut. The act maintained that no timber under these dimensions should be cut; in practice, many more trees were cut than merely those to be sold. Smaller trees were sacrificed for roads and trails (which were extensive), to open clearings, to build and heat bush camps, to make cant hooks and other poles, to open loading and docking areas, and to build dams and bridges.

Timber reserves were divided and leased. The dominion issued two kinds of licences to cut timber: timber licence berths (often called "limits") and timber permits. Timber permits covered small, generally one-square-mile, areas and were

Figure 4. Sturgeon Lake Lumber Company, north of Prince Albert, c. 1906.
Source: Glenbow Archives, NA-303-239.

issued to settlers who could use their own portable sawmills to cut lumber, shingles, and laths primarily for their own use. Any excess that they wished to sell was charged above the rental fee for the permit. Settlers could also apply for permits to cut cordwood, fence rails and posts, telegraph poles, and railway ties. With the exception of shingles (of which 96 percent were cut by small timber permit holders), the amount of timber cut for any purpose by permit was dwarfed by the output of the larger timber berths.[32]

Timber berths issued on a commercial scale had to follow certain rules. The Dominion Lands Office surveyed timber limits into blocks of up to twenty-five square miles.[33] These limits were offered for lease by public tender, with an upset price established by the minister of the interior. Those who leased timber berths had to offer a cash price for the berth, annual ground rent of between two and five dollars per square mile, plus dues on the cut timber, which ranged (depending on what the timber was made into) from fifty cents per thousand board feet for sawn lumber, to one and a half cents per railway tie, to fifteen cents per cord for cordwood. Each licence was negotiated individually, and few timber limits operated under exactly the same terms (and those terms changed from year to year as the Dominion Lands Act was reviewed and changed).[34] Licences were renewable each year at the end of April provided that there was merchantable timber still available on the berth and that all regulations and dues had been satisfactorily met and paid.

Licensees were required to erect one or more sawmills capable of cutting at least 1,000 board feet of lumber per day for every 2.5 miles of limit within their leases. Monthly returns of dues (which required accurate bookkeeping of everything made and sold) were lodged at the Dominion Lands Office. Preservation of seed trees and immature trees, disposal of slash and debris, and an agreement to fund half the cost of fire protection were other key provisions of the act and the timber berth contracts.[35] The lease holder had to comply with all of the above conditions, or the lease would be withdrawn. These rules, which still allowed a timber limit to operate at a hefty profit, were further strengthened by the easy terms accorded to the building of dams, slides, piers, or booms, and the free use of and access to rivers and lakes, for the purpose of moving the logs. Perhaps because of the easy terms, with no adequate provisions for reforestation and inadequate staff to enforce regulations, the north Prince Albert region experienced extensive forest exploitation to the point of degradation.

COMMERCIALIZATION OF THE LUMBER INDUSTRY

Between 1890 and 1913, the north Prince Albert lumber industry escalated, spreading through the landscape, economy, and society. Seasonal exploitation began in the early fall. An advance group of men would be sent in to cut the roads and build the camps, construct buildings, make repairs, and take in supplies. A full complement of men would arrive after freeze-up, generally in late November. Work in the lumber camp was divided. There were key people at each base camp, including cooks, a company storekeeper, a blacksmith, a handyman, the barn boss, and teamsters/freighters, along with various helpers. There were several men and horses employed on the tank crew, whose job was to spread water on the trails to make ice roads. Ice roads were an integral part of logging and the reason why logging was always a winter, not a summer, activity. Once an ice road was made, heavy

Figure 5. Cookshack on the Red Deer River, c. 1908.
Source: Prince Albert photographer T.H. Charmbury, SAB Photograph R-B333.

Figure 6. Prince Albert Lumber Company.
Source: Glenbow Archives, N-303-239.

loads could be hauled far more easily by regular teams of two or four horses. The majority of bush workers were those directly involved in cutting and moving the timber, including saw gangs, loading gangs, skidders (who pulled the logs out of the bush to loading areas), and sleigh drivers. The saw gang consisted of six men. An undercutter notched the trees to control direction of the fall, two men sawed, one cut off the limbs, and two swampers cut roads and piled the brush out of the way. From there, logs were skidded to a loading point and loaded onto sleighs, often twelve feet high and as much as seventeen feet wide at the top. A loading crew consisted of eight men. From there, sleighs were taken by teams to the collecting point, where they were piled in anticipation of the spring log drives. On any given day, there could be several crews of saw gangs, skidders, sleigh drivers, and loaders working in the limit. Logging would go on all winter, in all conditions but the worst of blizzards, though Sundays were always a day of rest, and Saturday night was the usual night for extra revelry, from dances to all-night card games to visits to nearby camps.[36]

After the turn of the century, the smaller mills—such as the Sanderson, Moore and McDowall, Telford Brothers, and Cowan mills—were dwarfed by two commercial enterprises. The Sturgeon Lake Lumber Company began operations in 1902, and the Prince Albert Lumber Company was opened by a syndicate of American businessmen in 1905. This company was able to purchase many of the timber berths owned by the Telford mill, which burned in the spring of 1905: "Saw-Mill Destroyed by Fire. Telford's Lumber Mill completely gutted. To the value of $100,000 buildings and machinery were totally ruined. Started in the sawdust carriers. Although partially covered by insurance they will not be able to take part in this season's work. Owing to the fire almost 100 men are thrown out of employment and the loss of one of the most complete and up-to-date saw mills in the North West will considerably reduce the output of the season's cut." [37]

With the coming of the second railway to Prince Albert, the Canadian Northern in 1906, the logging industry grew again. The peak year of the combined mill output at Prince Albert was 1909: over 50 million board feet of lumber worth over $1 million were exported.[38] The two larger, more commercialized firms led not only to intensification and expansion but also to industrialization. In the 1907 edition of *The Wheat Belt Review*, Prince Albert was described as the "lumber mart of the prairie provinces."[39]

At its height, between 1906 and 1913, as many as 2,000 men worked in various lumber camps north of the river. A large camp would house as many as 200 men.[40] Loggers required outfitting for extreme outdoor labour. General merchants and storekeepers in Prince Albert stocked up on mittens, moccasins, heavy shirts and pants, rubber overshoes, underwear, coats, and fur hats. Axes, saws, hammers, sleigh runners, cant hooks, pulleys, and other tools were also sold. Blacksmiths were hard at work shoeing horses for the heavy winter hauling, often with special spiked or sharpened shoes used on the ice roads. Hotels and bars, boarding houses, restaurants, and livery barns were full. Wholesalers were busy organizing bulk food supplies for the lumber camps. These retail and service trades experienced a direct economic spinoff that was an important part of the Prince Albert economy. Indeed, the *Prince Albert Times* noted that "we are a year-round town, not just busy in the fall when the harvest comes in," in contrast to the seasonal cycle of prairie towns tied to the wheat economy.[41] The same retailers experienced another surge when the camps broke up in the spring and the men came to town with money in their pockets. Novelist John Beames characterized the atmosphere in Prince Albert as raucous and rowdy the two times of the year—fall and spring—when lumberjacks congregated.[42]

Once spring arrived, work in the bush was finished. Most lumberjacks dispersed to their homesteads, but some would wait for the spring river drives in which they could earn money bringing the logs downriver to the mills. Transportation limitations to bringing the logs out of the bush and to the nearest mill meant that those stands closest to Prince Albert were logged first. Once the closest berths were logged, camps moved farther north. Owners soon learned that overland hauling by horse or ox was ineffective and inefficient. Timber berths were chosen for their proximity to rivers, particularly the Sturgeon River and Shell River systems, which empty into the North Saskatchewan just upstream from Prince Albert, and the Spruce or Little Red River system, just downstream from the main settlement. Logs were collected on the banks of these rivers. Come spring thaw, river drivers brought the logs down to Prince Albert.[43]Allan Kennedy, the Ontario-turned-Saskatchewan lumberjack, claimed that the goal, once the rivers opened, was to keep the logs moving twenty-four hours a day. They could run up to a million board feet per day, and a successful drive would run for about twenty to twenty-five days.[44]

Once the trees were cut and moved to the mill, the second stage of the lumber industry began. The Prince Albert Lumber Company, formed by a conglomerate of American businessmen, operated two mills in Prince Albert and was by far the largest local employer. The first mill was developed for its industrial capacity, with all the latest technology. A typical mill would have a sawing mill, a planing mill to finish the lumber, dry lumber storage, barns for horses, machine shops, and repair shops. Debris, including bark and sawdust, would be repurposed as fuel for the steam engines that ran the mills. Finished lumber could be loaded directly onto railcars from a siding that could accommodate twenty-five railcars at a time. Its output, including finished lumber and cordwood made from the odds and ends of unfinished logs, was shipped to the prairie. This mill was surrounded by what was virtually its own town, with married mill men's houses, bunkhouses, snooker shacks, laundries, its own water system, a library, and a store. The other company mill, at the other end of town, was the old Sanderson mill operated primarily for the local market. It had its own lumberyard for retail sales. For those who worked at the two mill sites, the lumberjacks, and the logdrivers, the Prince Albert Lumber Company had a payroll of between $30,000 and $50,000 per month, employing as many as 2,200 men each year.[45]

The Sturgeon Lake Lumber Company, a homegrown Prince Albert business built on the timber leases and experiences of local men Dan Shannon and A.J. Bell, was unique. Its mill was right at its timber limits, in the Sturgeon Lake district more than twenty miles from Prince Albert.[46] A virtual town—with log shacks, bunkhouses, and a company store—grew up around the mill. It also had its own post office, Omega, named by Bell, who thought that this timber limit was the far-thest place from Prince Albert anyone would move to.[47] The distance between the mill and Prince Albert meant that, instead of transporting raw logs, the company transported the finished product, lumber, to the railhead at Prince Albert. Begun in 1902, the company soon discovered that overland transportation was expensive. Water transport was not an option for finished lumber. Wood without its bark would become water-logged and warped if immersed, and edges banged and bro-ken. Finished lumber of high quality was worth more than logs, and companies could not afford risking damage. Moreover, while finished lumber could be moved on scows in larger rivers, the Little Red and Sturgeon Rivers were too small—as it was, logs often became jammed and hung up on edges, meandering corners, beaver houses, and low-water pools. Dynamite was often used to keep logs moving.

In a unique move, the Sturgeon Lake Lumber Company purchased a small steam caterpillar engine that was transported to Prince Albert during the brutal winter of 1906–07. Indeed, the train on which the engine was being transported became stuck in a snowdrift, and the manager of the company went with a crew to help dig out the train and retrieve his new engine. Calamity continued: "Upon its arrival here, the fell, headlight, oil cup and everything moveable was found to have been taken off the engine. It took all day Saturday to replace the missing parts and fix it up. A platform was erected and Saturday afternoon the engine was run off the car. Quite a crowd witnessed this." The newspaper went on to exclaim that "the steam engine for the Sturgeon Lake Lumber Co. arrived on Friday night. It is a good looking and powerful machine and is built to run on ice roads."[48] Using the caterpillar tractor, larger loads of lumber, up to 150,000 finished board feet at a time, could be moved from the mill to Prince Albert on an ice road thirty-five miles long.[49] This steam engine, known locally as "Dinky," became a fixture in local memory. Photographs of the engine at work can be found in several local history books, along with stories of working at the lumber mill and logging camps, driving on the ice road, or supplying feed and food to the camps. This engine proved so successful that more were purchased, both by the Sturgeon Lake Lumber Com-pany and by its main rival, the Prince Albert Lumber Company.

IMPACT OF LOGGING INDUSTRY ON LOCAL FIRST NATIONS

Both Sturgeon Lake Reserve (known at the time as William Twatt's band) and Little Red River Reserve (sometimes referred to as New Reserve or Billy Bear's Reserve) were embedded in the major wood "basket" of the north Prince Albert re-

Figure 7. "Dinky" engine hauling logs on ice road.
Source: *Footprints of Our Pioneers*, 814.

gion and straddled both the Sturgeon River and the Little Red River systems.[50] Extensive commercial lumbering in the region led to both opportunity and loss. First Nations men worked in the lumber camps, freighted supplies, cut and traded hay and oats, provided fresh meat, and worked on the river drives in spring.[51] Women found a ready market for moccasins and mittens, jackets and belts. Members living on these two reserves derived considerable income from the lumber camps, either through direct wage labour or in a supply capacity. Little Red River members in particular were closely tied to the lumber camps. The Indian Department noted in 1901 that residents of Little Red "derive their income from grain, potatoes, the sales of lumber, hay, freighting, and day labour (lumbering)."[52] Reports from the Indian Department until the end of the First World War reiterated these occupations, along with continued fishing and hunting.

The extensive lumber industry, however, had a negative ripple effect in the region. Trapping and fishing activities along the rivers were severely disrupted by the large log drives. Hundreds of men, strange sounds, and extensive environmental disturbance virtually eliminated local hunting opportunities, and hunters were forced to go farther and farther away from the reserves to find meat. Finally, the two reserves contained excellent saw timber. In particular, the Sturgeon Lake

Lumber Company and the Prince Albert Lumber Company desired those trees, and documents show that both companies culled valuable timber from Sturgeon Lake Reserve land without compensation or authority. In 2001, the Sturgeon Lake band succeeded in settling a major claim with the federal government for the loss of this wood revenue.[53]

The Little Red River band (as of 2013) is in the process of prosecuting a similar claim, but the economic and environmental impacts of lumbering on their reserve were more complicated. It was set aside as a farming reserve for the Montreal Lake and Lac La Ronge bands by 1897, but permanent farming was slow to take hold. In 1903, A.J. Bell, manager of the nearby Sturgeon Lake Lumber Company, requested disposal of the standing and fallen timber on the reserve.[54] The Indian agent went to Montreal Lake to consult with the chief and council there and came away with a signed deed of surrender, which initiated a series of problems. The Montreal Lake band expressed uncertainty over whether or not they should sell the timber and left it up to the Indian agent to make the final decision on their behalf. In effect, the band signed a *carte blanche*: "We have decided to leave the question of the sale of the standing and fallen timber in [the agent's] hands, if after he goes through the timber, he considers it best to leave it at present, we agree to that; if on the other hand he thinks it should be sold then we agree to that."[55] The agent decided that the timber should be sold for several reasons: it was at its maturity and thus at its economic height for merchantable timber; nearby timber limits were currently being logged, particularly the Shannon and Sanderson timber berths; the slash from those nearby limits heightened the fire potential of the area, and if a forest fire swept through before the timber could be logged it would be virtually worthless; the merchantable timber within the reserve was estimated at most to be 2.5 to 3 million board feet, considered a small cut. It would be better, the agent thought, to sell the timber when loggers were nearby and it was practical to cut it. A second surrender, this time from members of the band living on the reserve, was also taken.[56]

The fact that Little Red River Reserve was so far away from its two parent reserves created an administrative dilemma. It was difficult to decide whom to ask for a surrender, who had authority, and who had the right to make decisions. The timber was advertised and sold by tender in the summer of 1904 to I.G. Turpiff of Canada Territories Corporation Limited.[57] Almost immediately, a letter arrived from Reverend James Hines of Prince Albert at the Indian Commissioner's Office in Winnipeg. The letter indicated that the men living on the reserve in question, the New Reserve, "strongly object to all their timber being sold from them." Those who signed the timber surrender, the letter noted, "are living 60 miles north and have plenty of timber there." Those on the reserve did not object to selling *some* of the timber for cash, recognizing its proximity to the timber limits being worked all around the reserve, but they wanted to make sure that some of the bluffs were kept for their own use.[58]

The letter from Reverend Hines indicated the difficulty under which all parties were operating. By this point, there were two surrenders taken for this wood, one from Montreal Lake and one from men located on the New Reserve. Clearly, though, there were divisions within the New Reserve as well as between the two northern settlements and the one southern settlement. The Indian Department, however, was operating on the legal strength of the two surrenders, and the timber was sold. The sale led to the second major problem: the New Reserve was co-owned by both the Montreal Lake and the Lac La Ronge bands. In January 1905, a letter arrived from the Lac La Ronge band expressing their concern over how the wood surrender had been handled, since they were also owners of the New Reserve.[59] Although the response was that, indeed, the Lac La Ronge band was entirely correct in this assertion, "it was not deemed necessary to confer with them on the question of surrender of timber as they reside at a great distance from the Reserve…, although they are entitled to their equitable share of the proceeds of the timber and will receive it at the proper time."[60] The proceeds of the down payment on the timber berth were split between the two bands. The company that won the contract, however, was slow to hand over the capital. When it finally did, the sum was placed in trust solely for use of the Montreal Lake band. The trust amounted to over $5,000, and the interest was expended in purchasing supplies for the Montreal Lake band beyond those agreed to by treaty.[61] It was only in 1910, after a lengthy investigation into the surrender and sale of the timber and the disposal of funds, that the trust was redistributed to the credit of the Lac La Ronge band.[62]

The timber on Little Red River Reserve, because of its proximity to transportation, mills, and a market, was correspondingly much more valuable than any similar stands of timber found on the Montreal Lake home reserve or at La Ronge. Correspondence indicated, however, that only a portion of Little Red contained merchantable white spruce saw timber. The rest of the reserve, chosen for its agricultural capability, had open hay lands and stands of brush and aspen—it had been logged, in fact, long before it became a reserve.[63] The controversial timber limit on the New Reserve was neither large nor lucrative, at least according to official documents. The original bidder neglected to pay the rest of the tender price and never logged the timber. The Sturgeon Lake Lumber Company took over the contract. It tried unsuccessfully to renegotiate the original tender, arguing that it was unfair to pay ground rent on the whole reserve—56.8 square miles—when there was merchantable timber on only a small portion of that area, about three square miles. The company by this time was under considerable scrutiny from the Indian Department regarding its logging on Sturgeon Lake Reserve No. 101, for which it had not paid its dues or cut payments. The Indian Department was reluctant to renew the timber berth contract for Little Red when the company was obviously tardy in paying dues, rent, ground fees, and payment on the cut from Sturgeon Lake. The company protested, saying that it still had about a million board feet of timber to log out at Little Red. The company paid the remaining dues but only after many threatening letters from the Forestry Department. It soon rescinded the logging request. By 1909, the Sturgeon Lake Lumber Company had logged only a portion of the available timber. Of the original estimated 2.5 million board feet, it cut 1.5 million. Its timber licence was not renewed.[64]

In ensuing years, the men of Little Red River Reserve logged the area themselves and cut the logs using a mill owned by the Indian Department.[65] There was concern from the Forestry Department inspector that the band was leaving behind too much debris and slash and in general using wasteful practices. The Indian Department investigated and disputed these concerns, claiming that, since it was sponsoring the logging and milling, it would ask the band to oversee and minimize any potential fire hazard or other problem. The Forestry Department reminded the Indian Department that "no lumbering operations have been authorized by the Department since April 30th 1909 when the license of the Sturgeon Lake Lumber Co expired. You should report fully as to who actually cut timber since that time, for what purpose, whether for sale or building, to whom it was sold and the kinds and quantities of timber removed. You should particularly investigate any evidence that would tend to place the onus of these operations on trespassers." The reply from Silas Milligan, the Indian agent for the band, said that "none of this timber was cut by tresspassers, as the Montreal Lake overseer, Engineer, and Sawyer superintended the whole of the operations, none of the material has been sold, as it was cut simply for the use and benefit of the Montreal Lake Band." Milligan had written to the mill operators, giving instructions about debris and danger, "but the heavy snow experienced during the early part of the winter put a stop to the work. No doubt when the Spring arrives a further effort will be made by this Band to safeguard the Government Lands in the vicinity of the reserve." Little more exists in the file, but this perspective contradicts the oral memory of Little Red residents, who record extensive non–First Nations timber cutting that was never paid.[66]

The timber dispute, and the subsequent fight over the trust funds, set the stage for division. Little Red River Reserve was informally split. The Lac La Ronge band was accorded a much larger share of the reserve since they had not yet chosen all their treaty land entitlement in and around La Ronge; moreover, at the time of the treaty in 1889, they were a much larger band and had a larger treaty land en-.titlement. The Montreal Lake band was accorded nine out of the roughly fifty-six square miles, the Lac La Ronge band the remaining forty-seven.[67] Confusion over who owned what proportion of the timber (until the land was informally split), investigation of how much timber was actually logged and paid for when and by whom, and the debate over which band (Montreal Lake or Lac La Ronge) owned which parts of the reserve will complicate the current court case. The situation on Little Red River Reserve was not the same as that on Sturgeon Lake Reserve, even though the two reserves were situated in or near the same wood basket. Landscape and tree cover, regional logging prior to creating the reserve, ownership, payment, and actual logging are subject to conflicting interpretations.

Regardless of current court disputes, both the oral history and the contemporary documentation pointed to a mixed use of Little Red River Reserve. Although set aside as a farming reserve, its situation in and near the merchantable timber basket of the north Prince Albert region led primarily to continuing timber resource exploitation by both non-band and band members. Local residents of the reserve took cash employment in the nearby lumber industry. They also began to cultivate grains and gardens, raise cattle, and exploit the reserve's hay meadows, thereby taking economic advantage of local opportunities at the lumber camps.

LOGGING AND THE ENVIRONMENT

There was an almost wanton disregard for the environmental impacts of the logging industry. Cutting trees and bringing them to market abused and reshaped the entire north Prince Albert landscape. The Spruce/Little Red River was small and could not reliably handle log volumes. To compensate, the Prince Albert Lumber Company cut all the trees along the riverbank and built a series of dams to control water flow. This intervention culminated in damming Beartrap Lake (now in Prince Albert National Park) and building a canal southward to move its water into the Spruce/Little Red River system to flow south to the mills at Prince Albert—an environmental intervention with major implications for the local landscape.[68]

Millions of board feet of logs caused extensive damage to each river, from killing fish to altering its course. The dams changed not only the ebb and flow of the rivers but also their ability to handle rain and runoff. Extensive environmental intervention had a local effect on drainage throughout the region. Cutting trees on either side of a river led to slumping and excessive mud, actually exacerbating the problems of river drivers as well as those who had taken up homesteads along the rivers. Homesteaders in the Alingly district, opened for settlement during the height of the lumber industry after 1906, struggled to bridge the river effectively to allow travel within the district and kids to attend school. A 1916 newspaper report expressed local concerns: "J. Andrist has voluntarily built about 100 yards of trestle foot bridging over the back water on either side of the Little Red River. He did this to allow nine children on the west side of the river to get to school. Violet Smith, aged 6 years, however, fell off the trestling into the water on Monday last, but was rescued by the elder children. Mr. Andrist reports that the Centreville bridge is not safe and will require immediate attention after the log driving is over and the water goes down on either side of the bridge."[69]

There was correspondingly less logging along the Garden River (then known as Sucker Creek). The mouth of this river emptied several miles downstream from the mills at Prince Albert. Logs sent down this small river had to be collected in a "boom" and towed by steamboat up the river against the current and through a long stretch of rough water, rocks, and shoals to the sawmills. Often rocks or stray logs or other debris floating downriver would strike the boom. If it broke, logs would quickly float downstream past the forks and become irretrievable. As a result, the Garden River never suffered the environmental damage of the other two rivers.

While responsible for producing large-scale changes to the local environment, the lumber industry was also at the mercy of local environmental conditions. The size and situation of a timber limit, spring water levels in rivers, winter snowfall, droughts, and forest fires all had varying effects, some of them significant. The severe cold and snowstorms of 1906–07 had an impact on the winter cut since conditions were too dangerous for horses and men to operate in the bush. As a consequence, 1907 saw reduced mill throughput and a shorter milling season. Lumber camps had to be moved farther away from town as berths were logged out, necessitating more expense in freighting goods to the camps and finding efficient transportation (horse, steam engine, or river) to bring the logs or finished products back to Prince Albert.

The two most important environmental conditions that had severe impacts on the local lumber industry were water and fire. Lumberjack Allan Kennedy recalled that through the years several lumber companies got into serious financial trouble when they could not bring their logs down. In 1910, a very dry winter meant low water levels in the spring. The log drive was unsuccessful since the logs became "hung up" and would not come down the river. When the logs got hung up, some could be salvaged and brought to town with horses, but salvage freighting was a labour-intensive activity and depended on both the state of trails/roads and the capacity of bridges to take large loads. In most cases, the summer road system could not handle this kind of capacity.[70] As a result, logs were left to rot, though locals were happy to salvage them for their own purposes.[71]

White spruce is an old-growth tree that requires specific conditions to flourish. Unless a large area of fully mature white spruce was left unlogged, to offer a seed source for new growth, the species could not regenerate efficiently. The debris left from extensive logging, combined with the flammable nature of forest litter in aspen stands, led to forest fires within the area. Homesteaders placed increased pressure on the landscape. Escaped fires from brush clearing on the homesteads raged through the region. The combination of logging, agricultural settlement, and fire was nearly catastrophic: white spruce was virtually eliminated from the forest canopy.[72] Although the boreal forest is a fire-dependent regime and fire is a necessary part of the forest regeneration cycle, extensive forestry intensified the effects of fires. Logging virtually eliminated mature white spruce capable of producing cones, and the extensive tree litter prohibited cone regeneration. The impacts of fierce ground and canopy fires resulted in a local transition from primarily mixedwood forest to a canopy dominated by aspen, burnt brush, and open meadows.

The changeover to aspen/poplar in the north Prince Albert region encouraged both the rise of mixed farming after 1906 and the growth of the cordwood industry in the 1920s. As agricultural settlers moved north of the river, following the logging roads first to the area near the Shell River (Shellbrook) and later into the Buckland, Alingly, Deer Ridge, and Henribourg districts north of the Sand Hills, they found less mixedwood forest and more rank aspen growth and extensive brush on the cut-over and burned-over lands. Those who took land in the Garden River region, which experienced little commercial logging but some forest fires, found somewhat more mixedwood forest, which included both white and black spruce and pine on sandy soils in addition to aspen and birch on burnt-over land. The Paddockwood history book records that the first settlers in the region found that "the country was heavily wooded, mostly white and black poplar with the odd spruce bluff, all green timber."[73] However, it seems likely that the region had experienced forest fire activity, owing to the predominance of poplar (aspen), but those burns might have been as many as thirty years or more before major settlement. Of course, forest fires are erratic and do not burn evenly or absolutely, resulting in a forest mix between complete devastation and substantial green areas.

THE STURGEON RIVER FOREST RESERVE

The federal government regulated the lumber industry through its Dominion Lands Act, but in 1914 it added a new layer of administrative control in the north Prince Albert region. As homesteaders agitated for more surveyed land, increased political and economic pressure from the agricultural sector led to heated debates among settlers, Prince Albert businessmen, and the dominion government regarding land in the region. Was it best suited to the timber industry or farming? Intensive homestead pressure sent the Department of the Interior scrambling to find arable farmland. Reports regarding extensive environmental damage from the lumber industry were also disconcerting. Dominion land surveyor C.H. Morse was sent in 1912 to assess the landscape and the logging industry and to make a report. His commission was to view the region with an eye to creating a national forestry reserve, which would divide the landscape.[74] Land with timber suitable for the lumber industry or soil not suitable for farming was withdrawn from settlement. The Sturgeon River Forest Reserve, on land west of the third meridian and east of the Sturgeon River, between Townships 53 and 57, was set aside.[75]

Designation as a forest reserve had little impact on the ongoing lumber industry—there were *fourteen* timber berths operating within its borders, all but one controlled by the Prince Albert Lumber Company. In fact, historian Bill Waiser suggested that the lumber company "acted as if the region was now its own special preserve."[76] Wartime demand doubled the annual cut. At the same time, though, the dominion government, through its forestry reserve inspectors, increased its control. The dominion conducted audits and issued orders for restitution if the number of logs reported cut did not match the number reported at the millsite (with shrinkage allowed for fires or logs lost on the river drive). Overall, creating the Sturgeon River Forest Reserve signalled a significant change toward resource management and fire control. For homesteaders, it placed legal limitations on the landscape and narrowed agricultural expansion.[77]

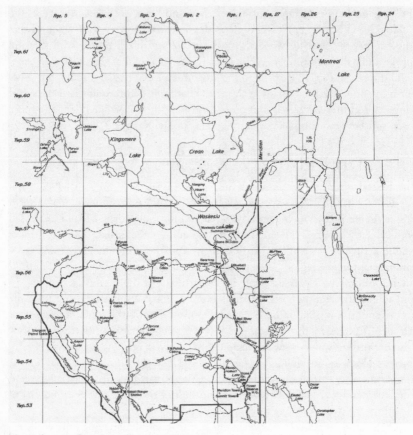

Map 7. Sturgeon River Forest Reserve, c. 1925.
Source: Waiser, *Saskatchewan's Playground*, 23. Used with permission.

END OF THE EARLY
COMMERCIAL LOGGING INDUSTRY

Prince Albert's logging industry continued through the First World War despite supply and manpower shortages. Lumber was considered essential to the war effort. In the spring of 1916, as the lumber camps were breaking up for the season, the federal government created the 224th Canadian Forestry Battalion. It actively recruited in Prince Albert to take experienced loggers and lumbermen overseas to Britain and France to help cut timber and saw lumber for the war effort. This was a volunteer effort and was ultimately successful. Men could volunteer for duty but not at the front; their work was considered specialized.[78] Prince Albert National Park historian James Shortt commented that the Great War gave the Prince Albert Lumber Company its most productive years, when it logged 124.47 square miles within what became park area, with a series of camps near Shoal Creek and Stump

Lake.[79] Toward war's end, however, demand for lumber slackened. Constrained by the wartime slump in residential and commercial building, the lumber companies faced a combination of problems: rising transportation costs, manpower shortages, and falling prices. Although an astonishing 520,000 logs were sent downriver from the Prince Albert Lumber Company's logging camps in the Sturgeon River Forest Reserve in the spring of 1917–18, over 25,000 logs were never removed. The company suspended local operations in October 1918. Those logs, along with the slash and debris from the entire cut, were left to rot or be salvaged by local homesteaders.[80]

HADES IS LOOSE

Almost thirty years of active logging in the north Prince Albert region had changed the aspect of the countryside dramatically. Extensive logging, with its rotting slash, change in forest canopy, and new rank growth of leaf-producing aspen, set the stage for a disaster of near-epic proportions in the spring of 1919. The *Prince Albert Daily Herald* reported that the spring arrived warm and soon became hot. By the end of April, all of Saskatchewan and eastern Alberta north of the North Saskatchewan River was tinder dry. Bush fires were breaking out.[81] By May, the region was devastated by wildfires. The *Daily Herald* observed that, "once the blaze develops into a conflagration, Hades is loose and little can be done to check it."[82] Serious blazes extended all across the forest edge, burning farms, killing livestock, and devastating local homesteads. "The Great Fire" raged from Lac la Biche in Alberta, Green Lake, and Île-à-la-Crosse east across much of the boreal plain, far beyond either agricultural settlements or timber berths. In all, 2.8 million hectares burned, and 300 people were left homeless. Fires endangered settlements at Lac la Biche, Big River, and Montreal Lake.[83]

Bishop J.A. Newnham of Prince Albert made a special trip north to check on the inhabitants of Montreal Lake and gave the *Daily Herald* the following harrowing report:

> For about a week thirty of the Indians were working practically day and night fighting fire under the guidance of the forest rangers. At one point on the trail, in the midst of a spruce bluff the bishop and his travelling companion, Mr. Barker of the Hudson's Bay Company had to swing their team around and rush back, for the flames came leaping over the treetops, twenty to thirty feet high and sweeping onward in a rush of flame. Three hundred yards back the team was halted for there was the edge of the fire zone and the bishop and Mr. Barker turned and watched the conflagration surge and crackle past. Five minutes later, the green bluff just a blackened patch with charred stumps, was recrossed and the journey resumed.[84]

The bishop had motored by car to Little Red River Reserve. From there, he and Barker went by team and wagon, following the overland cart trail through "ruined forests." Bishop Newnham was aghast at the ecological devastation: "On the way up the whole country seemed to have been burned over by the recent fires, and only blackened tree trunks, which had fallen or will fall within a year or so, remain in the once well-timbered area. The soil also has been deeply burned and even the muskeg had been on fire. The game suffered heavily, young birds and eggs being destroyed." The roads suffered as well, he added. "In general all bridges over the Little Red and Sturgeon rivers have been burned and a number of the Prince Albert Lumber Company's dams. The forest rangers are now [making] temporary repairs to the bridges and clearing the trails of fallen trees."[85] The devastation seemed complete.

Scientists and historians have pinned these fires to increasing agricultural expansion into the forest edge, where homesteaders and settlers, eager to clear land for farming, employed extensive brush burning.[86] The *Daily Herald*, however, suggested that the 1919 fires had started in the forest reserves.[87] Regardless of the origins, the devastation of the massive fire, aided and abetted by years of accumulated debris from logging and combined with a severe drought in 1919, put an effective end to the large-scale lumber industry at Prince Albert. The large companies abandoned their timber berths. The Prince Albert Lumber Company reorganized and became the Ladder Lake Lumber Company, moving its operations to eastern Saskatchewan and Manitoba, near Hudson Bay and The Pas. Local residents north of Prince Albert culled the fire-killed trees for firewood, posts, and telephone poles, and small logging permits continued to be issued for those areas untouched by the blazes, but on a large scale Prince Albert's early commercial timber industry was finished.[88]

CONCLUSION

The importance of the lumber industry to the early development of Prince Albert cannot be overstated. Not only was it the major commercial industry in the region, but also its exponential growth—supported by the policies of the dominion government through its Dominion Lands Act and forest reserves—went hand-in-hand with the population explosion on the open prairie. As settlers poured into the prairie south to build an agricultural utopia, they required lumber in tremendous quantities to build houses, barns, schools, churches, businesses, and bridges. Although mills in British Columbia could provide longer and larger pieces of lumber and continued to ship products into the prairie region, local mills at the forest edge found a strong niche market. Saskatchewan's Department of Agriculture noted in 1909 that "the lumbermen of Northern Saskatchewan are conveniently situated; as they have right at their door a market capable of consuming all that they can produce."[89] The edge provided the advantage: at the edge of the prairie, they were nearest to their largest market; at the edge of the forest, they could cheaply exploit the accessible timber. Yet, as Allan Kennedy's remarks proved, that there *was* a lumber industry in Saskatchewan was not well known. Despite the size, scope, and success of the commercial lumber industry, its existence was and remains overshadowed by the power and presence of the prairie agricultural story. There have not been, to date, sufficient publications that tell the story of Saskatchewan's colourful, dynamic, and dramatic early forest industry.

The lumber industry provided both small- and large-scale entrepreneurs with investment opportunities and profits. At the ecotone, several levels of edge use were clear: it was the commercial point at which the resources of the forest were funnelled to serve the prairie market, the hinge between boreal north and prairie South—the pemmican empire flipped. Yet those who lived at the ecotone built an economic and cultural landscape pulling from both forest and farm, a landscape of resilience and flexibility. Local First Nations combined forest edge pursuits of hunting and fishing with farming, logging, and providing goods and services. They were active participants in a diverse economic cycle that continued traditional seasonal exploitation. The surge of homesteaders on the heels of—and in contention with—the lumber industry brought the prairie/boreal cultural divide into question. Homesteaders moving north from Prince Albert looked to develop the cut-over forests into agricultural farms. But the assumption that these farms were developed on a "prairie" model is wrong. Northern homesteaders merged farming practices with contract work as freighters, lumberjacks, or fishers, as local suppliers of these industries, and as small-scale forest entrepreneurs. As dominion field naturalist John Macoun originally prophesied, the north Prince Albert region could encompass both the "field for investment" (the commercial timber industry) and "the home of the emigrant." Homesteaders, like their First Nations counterparts, recreated the north Prince Albert landscape as home, bringing resilience through mixed farming and forest exploitation to create a unique forest edge culture.

CHAPTER FOUR

A PLEASANT AND PLENTYFUL COUNTRY

Hudson's Bay Company explorer Anthony Henday travelled into the western interior of North America on a scouting and reconnaissance trip in 1754. When he arrived west of the forks of the Saskatchewan River, he described "fine level land and tall woods. ... I am now in a pleasant and plentyful country."[1] Henday's description combined both an aesthetic comment ("pleasant") and a practical one ("plentyful"). Both scenery and sustenance made their marks. Wood and good soil—"fine level land and tall woods"—filled the requirements of human occupation.

Henday's description in some ways predicted an agricultural ideal built on a landscape prized for both its park-like beauty and its ability to support diversified agriculture. That ideal was mixed farming.[2] A specific term, "mixed farming" referred to a farm that both grew grain and raised stock—dairy cattle, beef cattle, sheep, chickens, and pigs, for example—both for domestic consumption and, when possible, the off-farm market. By operating a mixed farm, rather than a monoculture (wheat) farm, a farmer could diversify the farm's holdings and spread assets over a broad base. Diversification as a risk management strategy offered better resilience over time than other farming operations, particularly the classic boom-and-bust cycle of wheat farming. A mixed farm was situated within (and became in and of itself) an ecologically mixed landscape that contained crop land, hay land, water, and timber. Continuing First Nations traditional cultural practices within an agricultural context, mixed farms—built at rich ecological/forest edge landscapes—were promoted as places of diversity and resilience.

The vast majority of studies on western Canadian agriculture focus on the wheat economy that became synonymous with the open plains.[3] The economic, social, and cultural importance of the wheat boom—which drew thousands of immigrants to the prairie west—deserves much of the analytical attention that it has received. Its importance, though, has been overplayed. The monolithic wheat narrative has marginalized and distorted the role of mixed farming in developing the western interior of Canada and the relationship between farming practices and landscapes. The mixed farm versus wheat farm debate was central to the agricultural history of the western interior. Mixed farming was swiftly tied to landscape in Saskatchewan: while wheat farming typified prairie agriculture, mixed farming was pursued in parkland and forest edge environments. The ideological debate symbolized the contrast between opening the Palliser Triangle in southwestern Saskatchewan for agricultural settlement with the opening of the "new north" of the forest edge. Mixed farming also became entrenched in soldier and other forms of assisted settlement in the post–Great War period.

Migration to the western interior might have been drawn by the wheat boom, but Prince Albert promoters advertised the northern edge landscape as a resilient, prosperous, healthy, fertile, and beautiful alternative to the bleak, dry, open plains. When the two Districts of Saskatchewan and Assiniboia were (essentially) amalgamated to form one province, the concept of "Saskatchewan" came to include, and soon to be taken over by, the prairie/wheat identity typical of Assiniboia. Until that point (particularly in the promotional material of the Prince Albert Board of Trade and local newspapers), the District of Saskatchewan was routinely cast as a rich, lush river valley in contrast to the dry, open plains landscape of the District of Assiniboia. The words *prairie* and *plain* were not interchangeable prior to 1900. In a pamphlet issued by the Lorne Agricultural Society of Prince Albert in 1890, the prairie was defined as the "fertile belt" and described as "probably at one time a dense forest. It naturally inclines to produce timber; and where a prairie escapes the yearly fires for any length of time it speedily becomes overgrown with vigorous young aspens and willows." This description became, sometime after 1900, the definition of parkland. The plain, on the other hand, "has doubtless been destitute of timber from the first," and its meaning was tied directly to terms such as "desert" or the classic flat, treeless landscape of the south.[4]

As drought and other natural calamities hit the drier regions, migration within the Canadian west was based on two points: moving from treeless and dry land to forested and humid regions, and the difference between monoculture (wheat) and mixed farming. Dominion land surveyors and other government explorers characterized the north Prince Albert landscape as a mixed-farming region. Prince Albert promoters capitalized on the grain versus mixed-farming debate to exploit an identity that was decidedly not the prairie. Internal migration from one biome to another changed the face of farming in the western interior.

WHEAT FARMING VERSUS MIXED FARMING IN HISTORICAL PERSPECTIVE

Agricultural historians have understood, in general, that prairie farms operated differently from farms at the parkland/forest edge. Land classification correlated directly to the type of agriculture that surveyors believed could be successful there. Sociologist R.W. Murchie, who wrote *Agricultural Progress on the Prairie Frontier,* explained that "it has been customary ... to speak as though only two types of land existed ... 'good wheat land' or 'excellent grain land,' while all other land which was available for settlement was characterized as 'good mixed farming land.'"[5] The Saskatchewan Department of Agriculture followed this general classification. A promotional booklet on Saskatchewan issued in 1909 divided the province into four distinct "zones": the open rolling prairie, the mixed prairie and forest, the great northern forest, and the Far North. The prairie, in this delineation, was "the Domain of King Wheat," but the mixed prairie and forest region (also called the park belt) was "splendidly adapted for mixed farming and for stock raising."[6] The pamphlet explained that "here the land is less easily broken up and the temptation to risk all in a wheat crop is thereby somewhat reduced."[7] The agricultural difference between prairie/wheat farming and parkland/mixed farming was reinforced in the *Atlas of Canada* map of 1950 (see Map 8), reflecting a continued cultural understanding of the connection between landscape and farm pursuits. The black soil of the parkland and the grey soil of the forest edge were known for their mixed farms. These landscapes usually contained water, hay land, and shelter in addition to crop land.[8]

The ability to grow wheat successfully, however, remained the primary criterion for agricultural land.[9] As a result, economists and historians have been drawn to the wheat story, and agricultural success or failure has been defined by the landscape's ability to support the wheat economy. Was wheat still important on a mixed farm? Of course, and even the most ardent mixed-farming literature or the boosterism of the Prince Albert promoters acknowledged that fact. The most common method of proving the worth of the local soil was to point to local farmers who had won regional, national, and international prizes for wheat. The Board of Trade averred that "the Prince Albert district is noted for the quality of wheat it produces and has not only gained the sweepstakes at the Columbus, Ohio exhibition this year and the first prize at Brandon from all the rest of Western Canada, but more recently an exhibit from this district won the $1000 prize offered by Sir Thos. Shaughnessy at the land show in New York."[10] This was a reference, of course, to Seager Wheeler of the Rosthern area south of Prince Albert. The Minneapolis newspaper the *Northwestern Miner* extolled Prince Albert's wheat-growing potential in 1908. A front-page story gave a glowing account of the quality of the local grain for the Minneapolis flour mills, where the hardness of the wheat made for better-quality flour.[11]

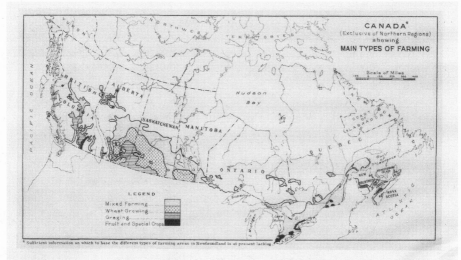

Map 8. Canada, main types of farming.
Souce: *Canada Year Book,* 1950.

Hard red spring wheat, particularly new strains that had a shorter growing sea-son, opened up new wheat lands in the western Canadian interior. Historian S.D. Clark, writing in 1931, examined the growth of the wheat boom. He argued that the scientific investigation of dryland farming techniques, including the develop-ment of earlier-maturing varieties of wheat, railway expansion, and the discovery of agricultural techniques and tools—such as summerfallow cultivation and the self-binding reaper—encouraged prairie wheat farms.[12] Prince Albert boosters were quick to reassure their audiences that the northern regions could indeed success-fully grow this key crop. Their messianic message, though, was that farmers at Prince Albert—with all the local advantages of water, shelter, and fodder—were capable of producing so much more than just wheat. Mixed-farming boosters were fighting an uphill battle, though: the astounding ability of the open plains to grow hard red spring wheat not only drew thousands of immigrants but also has been the central narrative for analysts of prairie history.

Agricultural historians John Herd Thompson and Ian MacPherson lamented the "over-generalizations many of us [historians] have indulged in in depicting an al-most-monolithic prairie agriculture," one that emphasized wheat, wheat, and more wheat on the open plains. "Future local studies, it is to be hoped, will look beyond our obsession with grain growing to the mixed farms of the park belt."[13] Historian Peter Russell agreed. By investigating the differences between farming practices on the semi-arid plains and those in parkland/forest edge environments, Russell, like Thompson and MacPherson, challenged historians and economists who categorized Saskatchewan's agriculture as a wheat monoculture. He argued that "*some* farmers did rely heavily on their cash [wheat] crop to supply their subsistence needs, but that turns out to depend much more on *where* their farm was located."[14]

Analyzing the agricultural census between 1911 and 1926, Russell showed that, "while wheat was the most commonly grown cash crop in most parts of the province in most periods, it alone did not determine 'the standard of living of the great majority of Saskatchewan farmers.'"[15] He provided an in-depth economic investigation of the connection between mixed farming and the more northern, parkland and forest edge, areas. Farms that contained forest land were more likely to have secondary field crops, particularly oats and barley (sometimes that acreage would be more than the wheat acreage), more stock, and more garden produce. Farms in the semi-arid regions were unable to diversify; in many cases, they were unable to grow even gardens, fodder, hay, or other subsistence crops because of low rainfall and poor soil. The landscape, devoid of wood for building or heating fuel, meant that plains farmers had to devote a much greater portion of available cash to buy it.[16] Economist G.E. Britnell showed that open plains farmers spent between 10 and 15 percent of their cash on heating and lighting; in the parkland and forest edge, the number dropped to 3 percent. The ecological advantages (and limitations) of the forest edge environment encouraged the development of mixed farming.[17]

What was even more shocking was that the practice of leaving land fallow (to allow it to rest every other year or every third year)—advice advocated vociferously in pamphlets, letters, public speeches, and newspaper articles—was heeded *least* in the area that needed it *most*: "At the southwestern extreme of the province most farms only began to use fallow as extensively as the rest of the prairies as a consequence of the post-war drought."[18] Russell's work corroborates the charge found in much of the agricultural literature of the period, that wheat farmers were "miners." Wheat mining was described by University of Toronto economist James Mavor in 1911 as follows:

> The specialist wheat farmer finds that by cultivating his land to
> the fullest extent he may in many cases obtain so high a return as
> entirely to recoup the cost of his land [and implements] by the sale
> of two or three crops. Although the land is exhausted by this suc-
> cessive cropping, and its productive value seriously diminished, the
> farmer finds himself in possession of from 160 to 640 acres of land
> which have cost him almost nothing, in a country in which the price
> of land is rising rapidly. ... So long as it is possible for the farmer to
> make a considerable sum of money in a few years and then to sell the
> partially exhausted land at a good price, recommendations of summer
> fallowing have little practical effect.[19]

Wheat mining, as an economic and cultural practice, exhausted and pulverized some of the most delicate prairie land.

THE MIXED-FARMING MOVEMENT

Mixed farming was typically practised on small to medium-sized farm holdings in eastern North America, Britain, France, and eastern Europe. Mixed farming had many fans, so many that historian Paul Voisey likened its boosterism to a crusade.[20] Agricultural scientists and newspapers, and various levels of government, consistently advocated a mixed-farming practice in contrast to a straight grain farm. The cliché, used time and again by mixed-farming promoters, was that farmers would do well to not "put all your eggs into one basket." It is ironic that mixed-farm promoters used a mixed-farm metaphor—eggs—to refer to straight wheat farming. Diversity was the key to a successful farm. To withstand the volatility of environment and market, farmers would find a high degree of stability and resilience through mixed-farming practices.

In Ontario, the wheat staple dominated agriculture throughout the mid-nineteenth century, but by Confederation it had been largely replaced by mixed farming, emphasizing meat and dairy products in addition to wheat and other grains.[21] It was, economist Marvin McInnis argued, an "interlude between two wheat staple periods," because the rise of the western Canadian wheat economy after 1896 initiated another wheat boom.[22] Mixed farming gained scientific credibility when it was taught at the Agricultural College at Guelph, which set important precedents. Vocal proponents of mixed farming in western Canada were fostered in Ontario during the mixed-farming push and came to prominence on the national stage: John G. Rutherford, the dominion livestock commissioner, and W.R. Motherwell, who became Saskatchewan's minister of agriculture.[23] Future farmers who either grew up or otherwise participated in the Ontario mixed-farming economy immigrated to the western interior of Canada. Many of these settlers, Voisey commented, agonized over the question of what kind of farm to create in the west. Settlers in the Vulcan area of Alberta, many of whom came from mixed-farming backgrounds in sub-humid environments either in Ontario or east of the 100th meridian in the United States, were "tormented" by self-doubt over wheat monoculture.[24]

Mixed-farming advocates developed a two-pronged approach to promote their ideas: farm economics and moral integrity. A mixed farm, it was believed, offered diversity and protection for farmers. If one crop or product should fail (for either environmental or market reasons), the farmer had other crops or products to tide the family through. Mixed farming was described primarily as a long-term investment. Year-over-year gains were smaller than those of wheat farms, it was usually admitted,[25] but generally came out ahead over several years or a lifetime.[26] Indeed, dominion scientist John Macoun noted the difference between wheat and bush farms in 1882. In his book *Manitoba and the Great North-West*, a series of illustrations graphically outlined the differences between bush farming and prairie farming. In the short term, the prairie looked like the quicker and easier path to a developed farm. Over the long term, however, the bush farm showed significant and comfortable prosperity. Overall, mixed farming was believed to hold appeal for farmers concerned about long-term resilience, stability, and risk management.

Figure 8. First year in the bush.
Source: Macoun, *Manitoba and the Great Northwest,* 48.

Figure 9. Fifteen years in the bush.
Source: Macoun, *Manitoba and the Great North-West,* 181.

Figure 10. Thirty years in the bush.
Macoun, *Manitoba and the Great North-West*, 211.

Advocates of mixed farming stressed environmental considerations. Soil depletion from continuous wheat monocropping was a serious concern. Mixed farming
would add leguminous crops to the rotation to bolster soil nitrogen content. Manure from farm animals could be put back into the soil profile. Soil husbandry was
an essential aspect of farm management, particularly intensive farm management
over a long period of time. Farmers interested in developing a stable, resilient, and
profitable farm could not afford to deplete their primary resource. In addition, animals found on a mixed farm could convert legumes, grasses, weeds, and frozen or
otherwise poor crops to cash simply by eating them. A mixed farm offered a more
balanced approach to a sufficient and reliable living.

Moral suasion was also an integral aspect of the mixed-farming literature.
In Ontario, a prosperous mixed farmer enjoyed a prominent social status, with
enough wealth to send his children for higher education.[27] Social status derived not
only from wealth but also from a mixed farmer's interest in and knowledge of many
aspects of agriculture. Expertise in everything from the causes of ear mites in sheep
to the best feed to produce high-quality butterfat in dairy cattle enhanced a mixed
farmer's reputation for intelligence in local and regional circles. Another factor
in promoting social status was independence. As Laura Ingalls Wilder explained
in her semi-biographical book *Farmer Boy* (based on her husband's experiences
growing up on a mixed farm in New York State), a successful mixed farmer was
beholden to no one else. Such a farmer "depends on himself, and the land and the

weather. If you're a farmer, you raise what you eat, you raise what you wear, and you keep warm with wood out of your own timber. You work hard, but you work as you please, and no man can tell you to go or come. You'll be free and independent ... on a farm."[28] Within the dry-farming ecology of the western Canadian interior, promoters suggested that mixed farmers added to their social stature as keepers of the soil. Crop rotation and soil fertility husbandry contrasted with the "wheat miners," who mined, stripped, and otherwise abused the soil for short-term economic gains at the expense of long-term conservation practices.[29] Mixed farming took the moral high ground of environmental stewardship, independence, intelligence, and long-term, stable wealth generation.

The idealism of the mixed-farming movement and its correlation to social status did not transplant successfully west of Ontario. Mixed farming in the western interior, despite its proponents and their persuasive arguments, did not sway everyone.[30] S.D. Clark, in his 1931 investigation of Saskatchewan settlement, argued that mixed farming was "regarded with a feeling more or less of repugnance" due, in part, to the much heavier workload of a mixed farm. Clark suggested that "interminable chores, hard work during the whole twelve months of the year, [and] cleaning out stables" turned many farmers away from mixed farming to the easier load of wheat farming. In addition to less arduous work, wheat farming meant the possibility of immediate wealth generation, with "big returns, extensive operations, [and] the opportunity to play the role of farm manager with a certain amount of leisure," Clark contended.[31] Wealth was an important social characteristic, and a huge wheat crop, sold at a high price, could achieve that. A wheat grower who obtained this golden ticket could spend his winters in leisure, perhaps in town, back east, in Europe, or in sunny California. There was nothing to hold him to the farm in the cold winter months, unlike the mixed farmer with stock to feed and look after every day.[32] The life of a rich man at leisure conjured up images of a wealthy magnate, a patron of the arts and letters, a philanthropist, and possibly a politician. Clark went on to claim that a mixed farmer was looked upon with "general disfavour ... by his more pretentious but frequently less substantial wheat growing brother."[33] Although advocates worked hard to present mixed farming as profitable, better for the soil, and more substantial in the long run, "wheat mining" continued to be a popular choice.

In some cases, the "pretentiousness" of the wheat farmer toward the mixed farmer was reflected in ethnic slurs. It was almost an axiom that certain settlers who had come *en masse* to the western interior of Canada from Germany, Ukraine, and Russia had a cultural preference for forested mixed farms.[34] Saskatchewan provincial historian John Hawkes, writing in 1924, argued that immigrants from eastern Europe "would not settle on the open sections, preferring those which contained some wood and hay, although they had to contend with a good deal of scrub."[35] Cultural preference for farms away from the open plains filtered back through the division between the straight grain farmer and the mixed farmer. The "men in sheepskin coats," smelling of garlic and pigs, were the mixed farmers; the grain farmers were clean, English-speaking men in suits organizing grain growers' societies and taking prizes for wheat at agricultural fairs.

An intriguing gendered perception of the primacy of wheat farming over mixed farming was put forward by the monthly magazine *Saskatchewan Farmer* in 1911. The magazine, produced in Moose Jaw, actively advocated the mixed-farming ideal. Straight grain farming, it reported, retarded agricultural development. It made no sense, the editors claimed, for butter, canned milk, and other products to be shipped into western Canada or feed grain shipped out of it when a thriving mixed-farming community could use local feed to create milk, butter, eggs, bacon, and cheese to feed the burgeoning cities and general population. What stood in the way of creating more mixed farms was the unequal gender population. With over 90,000 more men than women, the article declared, bachelor farmers were skewing western agricultural development to favour wheat over mixed farms. Bachelors did not bother with cows or pigs or chickens. Saddled with animals, a bachelor mixed farmer would not be able to adapt and move to access seasonal off-farm job opportunities or take trips for business or leisure. The six-month wheat farm suited him best.[36] The subtext of this contention, of course, was that women (and possibly children) were central to a successful mixed farm. The amount of work required on a mixed farm meant that it needed at least two people to manage the workload successfully.[37]

Despite reasoned and even impassioned advocacy of mixed farming, cereal crop monoculture and the wheat boom predominated on the open plains. Historian David Spector speculated that mixed farming did not achieve its celebrated potential on the plains for a variety of reasons. Wheat was a farmer's "path to profit" since it required little outlay for equipment and only six months of labour (or slightly less) per year. The introduction of Red Fife and later Marquis wheat varieties (which matured much more quickly and could reliably be harvested at good quality) led to an expansion of wheat acreage. Animal husbandry of any sort required large cash investments at startup to purchase stock, build barns and silos, find an adequate water source, build fences, and invest land in non-cash forage crops for feed. The semi-arid landscape of the plains, devoid of trees and prone to droughts, placed an unusually complicated burden on farmers who might have wanted to diversify their holdings. Adequate water, either from a well to supply stock or as rain to raise fodder crops, was not reliable, and many farms had difficulty finding potable water. In a drought year, everything suffered: water quality and quantity for both humans and animals declined, and both commercial cash crops and hay/fodder crops burned from lack of moisture. The double whammy left both the farmer and the stock in a precarious position. Any land not put to commercial (wheat) production meant less cash in hand; a drought year, with no cash production and no hay or fodder, could bring devastation. Building a stock herd took time, money, and good fortune before there could be much expectation of return on investment. Finally, the homesteading system, geared to grain farming, did not consider land to be "improved" unless it was cultivated and growing crops. Special permission was necessary to obtain patent on land that was left as pasture or hay land for the purpose of stockraising, and often permission was not given.[38] Many farmers on the plains, despite the advantages offered by mixed farming, either could not afford the original investment or make the switch down the road, even if that was the original intention.

The solution to the mixed-farming dilemma on the plains was location: those who wished to engage in so-called morally superior, environmentally responsible, and independent mixed farming were encouraged to locate their farms on lands suited to this endeavour. The mixed-farming ideal was specifically tied to landscape, a practical solution that meant building a successful farm on a piece of land that contained an ecological mix. Good soil would be used to grow cereal crops, and scrub land (such as marshy areas and forest glades) could be used for hay land, pasture, and fuel and lumber. Such a farm was described as efficient, for all land within the quarter section could be brought into productive commercial, domestic, or simply scenic use.[39]

A farm with such an ecological mix could be found or created. In a completely forested landscape, fields for cereal and rough grain crops could be cut, cleared, and grubbed—albeit only with a tremendous amount of work. The opposite—growing trees on the open plains—proved to be almost as difficult.[40] Tipping the scales in favour of forest landscapes was their ability to usually provide an adequate water source. In the Prince Albert region, land south of the North Saskatchewan River was typically described as parkland or a natural ecological mix of open fields and bluffs of trees. North of the river, farmers could create mixed farms by opening fields via axe and fire.

OPENING THE NORTH PRINCE ALBERT REGION

James Isbister's fledgling farming settlement on the fertile flats at what became known as Prince Albert alternatively thrived and languished in the decades between its founding and completion of the railway in 1890.[41] The absence of a rail link limited the export potential of local farms, which—like the lumber industry—remained closely tied to the local market. The rail link south to access prairie and international markets, the acceleration of the local lumber industry, as well as the overland supply link to Montreal Lake and Lac La Ronge stimulated the local economy after 1890.[42]

In the 1890s, promotional pamphlets from the Prince Albert district were designed for a general British and Ontarian audience who had likely heard of the "valley of the Saskatchewan." As early as 1872, the London Times began printing stories about the Saskatchewan country. Numerous writers, including Captain John Palliser, the Earl of Southesk, Henry Youle Hind, William Francis Butler, and other adventurers in the western interior of Canada, had written lengthy descriptions of the mighty Saskatchewan River and its environs, and their books were hugely popular. From 1882, when the four provisional districts of the North-West

Territories were formed, to 1905, when the provincial boundaries were decided, Prince Albert was the seat of the District of Saskatchewan, with an identity built on the local landscape of the Saskatchewan River valley. The 1885 rebellion took the word *Saskatchewan* to the world. The events of that year were reported with breathless intrigue in newspapers and later books drawn from first-hand accounts. Novels depicting the North West Mounted Police and extolling the valley of the Saskatchewan delighted readers.[43]

Prince Albert boosters began promoting the region as a natural fit for mixed farming. The 1890 Lorne Agricultural Society pamphlet claimed that "there is no line, either of production or speculation, that ensures a satisfactory return equal to mixed farming when undertaken by practical men." And mixed farming, the pamphlet was clear, would be most successful in the local mixed ecological landscape: "No country under the sun offers greater natural advantages for this independent occupation than the district of Prince Albert."[44] In that year, in addition to external migrants from Britain, Ontario, and the Red River region of Manitoba, the first internal migrants from the prairie began to trickle in. Families from the Estevan area abandoned their holdings to try their luck at Prince Albert.[45] Completion of the railway link, while a major factor in the ensuing explosion of the Prince Albert lumber industry, also initiated an increased influx of both first-stop and inter-regional migrants for agricultural settlement.

Prince Albert's agricultural development, despite the boosterism of the Lorne Agricultural Society and the promotion of mixed farming, enjoyed gradually increasing success but never exploded. Throughout the 1890s, local markets grew in response to the rise of the lumber industry, but in-migration was minimal until 1896–97, when three conditions merged to support extensive western migration. First, Minister of the Interior Clifford Sifton initiated a massive advertising campaign designed to draw immigration into the western interior. Second, a worldwide recession/depression ended, allowing capital and people to move more freely. Third, the Yukon Gold Rush drew migrants from around the world overland through the western interior. Retailers in the fledgling urban centres turned their focus to outfitting gold seekers as well as homesteaders, hundreds of whom were passing through the west every day. Routes to the gold rush regions were advertised. Communities such as Prince Albert and Edmonton placed themselves firmly on the gold rush route.[46] Boards of trade and territorial government officials were anxious to capture the interest of gold rushers, hoping that they would either stay or come back to build homesteads in the western interior.[47] Many did.

At the turn of the twentieth century, the prairie south witnessed intensive immigration and the rise of the wheat boom—a different kind of yellow gold. A cute story appeared in the *Prince Albert Times* regarding the astounding growth of prairie towns:

Apropos of the mushroom growth of new towns in the West, a locomotive engineer relates the following: "One day I was driving my engine across the prairie when suddenly a considerable town loomed up ahead where nothing had showed up the day before. 'What town is this?' says I to my fireman. 'Blames if I know,' says Bill. 'It wasn't here when we went over the road yesterday.' Well, I slowed down, and directly we pulled into the station, where over five hundred people were waiting on the platform to see the first train come in. The conductor came along up front and says to me, 'Jim, first we know we'll be running by some important place. Get this town down on your list and I'll put a brakeman on the rear platform to watch for towns that spring up after the trains get by!'"[48]

As agricultural development took off on the prairie, Prince Albert developed a two-pronged approach: exploit prairie popularity by marketing its timber, and develop the local agricultural landscape.

Agricultural settlement at Prince Albert, prior to 1904, was restricted to the land between the two branches of the Saskatchewan River. The exception was a pocket of settlement on the black soil found at Shellbrook, thirty miles west of Prince Albert on the north side of the river.[49] As surveyors moved through the north country, lining timber berths and Little Red River Reserve in 1897, land was surveyed for homestead development in what became the Shellbrook country. Although the land was forested, the soil in the area was exceptionally rich. Dominion lands regulations regarding farming in forested landscapes were overruled. In time, the success of the Shellbrook settlement proved that the forested land north of the river could eventually become good farmland.

None of the land directly north of the city had been opened for homesteading at the turn of the century. Except for the three First Nations land reserves (Sturgeon Lake Reserve No. 101, established in 1876; Wahpeton Dakota First Nation, set aside in 1894; and Little Red River Reserve, co-owned by the Montreal Lake and Lac La Ronge bands, set aside in 1897),[50] north Prince Albert was designated as dominion forest land, carved into extensive timber berths surveyed primarily by township and range. In response to the explosion of prairie settlement, Prince Albert's economic elite (along with the dominion government) had focussed their attention on lumber exploitation to serve the prairie market. Vying for the valuable wood basket around the Sturgeon and Little Red valleys, the lumber interests were intent on ensuring that potential timber regions were cruised, surveyed, and leased as timber berths—not homesteads. Land that had already been logged, however, could be opened for homestead settlement.

As the timber berths retreated ever farther north and away from the immediate environs of the city, agricultural settlers, eager to try their hand at mixed farming in the aspen scrub, began agitating for homesteads in the north Prince Albert district. In 1904, the Prince Albert Board of Trade, in response to an increasing number of requests at the Land Office and to the board, began a determined campaign to open land north of the river for settlement.

A letter from local MP T.O. Davis to Clifford Sifton, minister of the interior, suggested that railway lands north of the city should be opened up for Galician and Hungarian settlement. The arrival of Galician settlers sparked ethnic controversy in Prince Albert and district newspapers, evoking the ire of those who promoted British settlement. Eventually, the group chose land along the Garden River, between ten and twenty miles north of the city. Upon hearing news of the colony, the *Melfort Moon* wrote that, "if this is the same class that figures so prominently in the Winnipeg court records lately, we extend Prince Albert our heartfelt sympathy. We would advise our friends there to petition to government to increase the force of Mounted Police at that point, and see to it that a detail is on duty both day and night. Forewarned is forearmed."[51] Despite the ethnic controversy, the Board of Trade continued to push the dominion government to survey the land north of the river into quarter sections in preparation for homestead applications.

SURRENDER OF LITTLE RED RIVER RESERVE

The Prince Albert Board of Trade turned its land request and attention to what seemed like the easiest target: securing a surrender of the already-surveyed agricultural land of Little Red River Reserve No. 106A. The board asked MP Davis to "press the government to have this reserve thrown open for homesteading."[52] Political pressure led Minister of the Interior Frank Oliver (Sifton's replacement) to order an investigation in 1906. Biased observers claimed that "the reserve is nearly all good land and that there is only one Indian living on it." If there was virtually no one there, the Board of Trade declared, then perhaps the Indian Department could negotiate a surrender and open the land for settlement.[53] In the meantime, the Dominion Lands Office and the Department of Indian Affairs were inundated with requests for information on the possible opening of the reserve.[54]

The Department of Indian Affairs investigated the claims but was blindsided by a shocking revelation of greed and misrepresentation. Acting Indian Agent T. Eastwood Jackson sent an indignant four-page letter to the Secretary of Indian Affairs outlining a scene of gross misconduct. The farming instructor at the reserve, J.G. Sanderson, had been approached by a local real estate company that had offered him $100 cash if he would obtain a signed land surrender document from those living on Little Red Reserve. When he refused, a previous farming instructor, Patrick Anderson, was approached, and he accepted the bribe. He, along with T. Parker from the real estate company, proceeded to dupe 106A residents into signing a land surrender. When questioned individually by Jackson, Little Red residents replied that they had been told that the government was going to take back the land and that their signatures were little more than a formality. The men claimed that Anderson had also told them that they would be forced to go back to Montreal Lake to live. Little Red River resident Joseph Hunt noted with alarm, "I visited Montreal Lake twice during the winter, but I found that they were nearly starving: that fish were scarce, and game was scarce; that the people did not have enough to eat, and I do not want to go there." Another resident, Samuel Charles, noted that Anderson told him that the northern bands did not need to see or sign the document; only the people on the New Reserve had to sign it.

Jackson was horrified by these underhanded proceedings. He said, "I admit that it is annoying to see good land locked up from settlement within 35 miles from Prince Albert and that I have felt disgusted myself with the families residing on the reserve for not making better use of it." On the other hand, "the utmost consideration is due to these aboriginal owners of this country. The influx of white settlers is bound to cause increasing scarcity. ... In my opinion they should not be allowed to give up their reserve." Jackson went on to defend both the rights of the northern bands and their astute ownership of Little Red:

> The search for timber and minerals and the needs of the fishing com-
> panies will cause the invasion of the North by railways which will take
> from the Indian his employment in the transport of goods and furs,
> and I would respectfully submit that our Northern Bands should not
> be robbed of the only chance their descendants will ever have when
> darker days come upon them of exchanging their precarious existence
> for the more certain and equally healthy livelihood of the farm. The
> greed for gain of a Real Estate concern should not be permitted to
> deprive them of the fruits of [their] forethought.[55]

Jackson's strong stand was supported by Archdeacon John Mackay. He pointed out that those arguing that the Indians were not making proper use of the land were totally wrong. Not only were there farming and subsistence activities on the reserve, but also, when the reserve was set aside, it was never intended for the current generation but for future generations.[56] The question of current land use, Mackay declared, was moot.

Unfortunately, Indian Affairs had already asked Thomas Borthwick, who later became Treaty 10 commissioner, to inquire into getting a surrender. He approached the reserve's owners, the Montreal Lake and Lac La Ronge bands, and succeeded. A handwritten surrender signed by the chiefs and councillors of both Lac La Ronge and Montreal Lake bands was sent to Ottawa. Borthwick, thinking ahead, also visited the band members actually living at Little Red and told Indian Affairs that he had promised that "the Indians residing on that reserve ... should be allowed to retain the homes they had erected and the land they had begun to cultivate should they desire to do so," under homestead quarter section surveys. He solicited "the distinct understanding that in the event of their subsequent abandonment of their location, the amount realized from the sale of their land should go to the credit of the band and only the value of their improvements to themselves."[57] Borthwick's clarifications and negotiations proved that there was agricultural development on the reserve, more than enough to warrant special attention. A formal deed of surrender—not just the handwritten deed—was drawn up, but in light of the stated objections of Archdeacon Mackay and Agent Jackson, and the obvious controversy surrounding the actions of the real estate company, the surrender was cancelled.[58]

Renewed interest from the younger members of the Montreal Lake and Lac La Ronge bands and a local scarcity of furs and game around Montreal Lake led to a planned exodus, particularly from the Montreal Lake region to the New Reserve. Those most interested in moving to Little Red Reserve had taken job contracts as freighters.[59] Used to moving back and forth between the shield and the agricultural regions on the road that ran through the New Reserve, these men typified long-standing First Nations practice across the ecological edge. With limited agricultural help from Indian Affairs, some families from both Montreal Lake and La Ronge began to trickle in to join the families already established. The wishes of the Board of Trade for agricultural settlers in the north Prince Albert region were met, if not in the way that the board had wished.

THE DOMINION LAND SURVEY

The second part of the campaign to open the north Prince Albert region to agriculture was to initiate a dominion land township survey. Homesteads could not be legally filed and registered until the land had been surveyed and marked by the quarter section. The process was expensive and time consuming, and the dominion was careful to initiate it only when there was strong interest.[60] In addition, the region had been designated as Crown timber land, held apart from homestead settlement. To allow both kinds of landscape use (farming and timber harvesting) in the same area at the same time required a change in dominion intentions. The Board of Trade sent a telegram to Ottawa in 1906: "Delegates here representing five hundred families. Would settle north of river. Not sufficient land available."[61] The turn-of-the-century surge in homestead entries at the Prince Albert Land Office no doubt supported the Board of Trade's demands. In 1900, only 300 homesteads were filed at the Prince Albert Land Office, for land between the North and South Saskatchewan Rivers and at Shellbrook. By 1903, almost 3,000 homestead entries had been filed, and further homestead land was scarce.[62] The surveyor general approved the survey. But he added wryly, "a radical change must have taken place in the conditions around Prince Albert if fifteen townships are required for settlement north of the Saskatchewan River."[63]

Since the area opened for survey had already been extensively logged, neither the dominion lands agent nor the lumber interests registered any particular concerns about the policy change from forest to farmland. Extensive logging did not preclude farming. In fact, the logging industry was inextricably tied to the local homestead culture and probably would not have survived so successfully without it. Nearby farms provided both much-needed supplies and seasonal labour. The north Prince Albert region was beginning to be modernized and divided by the state according to principles of best use of the landscape: kept as forest reserves or berths or opened for farming.

The timing was exquisite. A perfect storm of converging interests would play out in the north Prince Albert region after 1904. Prince Albert had shed its poor missionary post and frontier town image and was declared a city in 1904. The Board of Trade, looking to capitalize on the agricultural campaign (and continued resource development) north of the river, signalled its ambitions by hiring a full-time secretary to send the Prince Albert message to the world.[64] Economic development from the railways and lumber mills, natural disasters on the open plains, and increased interest from the federal government soon had all eyes looking at the north Prince Albert region.

THE KILLING WINTER

In the midst of the push to open homesteads across the river came the brutal winter of 1906–07.[65] A mid-November, three-day howler exploded across the northern Great Plains in 1906, stretching from the Great Lakes to the mountains. Blizzard followed blizzard, with only minor reprieves, wreaking havoc on both human and animal life.[66] The terrible winter came after a long summer of strike and protest in the southern Alberta coal mines, initiating a coal shortage that complicated the chilly weather.[67] With no chinook to soften the storms, the fuel situation escalated from a coal shortage to a coal famine. Freight trains were immobilized by the snow and extreme cold; the engines, already stressed by the cold, which cut their output by half, could not produce enough steam to power the locomotives through drifts, where they became hopelessly stuck.[68] As the winter dragged on, the paralyzed railways left towns, villages, and cities across the Prairies stranded with sometimes extreme shortages.

Although the impact of the coal shortage was noted with alarm by prairie newspapers as early as November,[69] the situation was not as clear in Prince Albert, where costly coal was a secondary fuel source. Cordwood, cut from small timber limits, was more popular. By January, the city newspaper complained of minor shortages as freight trains were continually delayed. The *Prince Albert Times* reported on 17 January 1907 that "there is plenty of flour, meat, potatoes, and other staple articles of food, but luxuries, such as sugar, tea, and pepper and such are getting scarce."[70] Not long after this account, more information poured out of the prairie declaring the extent of the fuel famine and its repercussions. In early February, the *Prince Albert Times* expressed concern:

> The more we hear about the suffering from lack of fuel to the south
> of us, the more we feel constrained to offer our assistance. But how
> can we do it? Here we have plenty of fuel to supply all our needy
> neighbours to the south but we are powerless to lend aid. When we
> find even the railroads running out of coal, then we begin to realize in

some degree the extent of the disaster that has overtaken some parts of the West. … There is talk of starting the old freighting system that antedated the railways. The freighters could take down fuel to the plains and bring back freight that is long overdue here. Meantime the CNR would do well perhaps to start burning wood in their engines on the Prince Albert branch.[71]

The paper offered specific information, telegraphed from the town of Craik: "The fuel situation is horrible. J. Cole, a farmer, cried today when he found no coal here to take home to keep the family from freezing. C.C. Phillips, a farmer, has been burning manure. [The village of] Shipman has burned wheat for over a month. Mr. Brunt, in town, tore down his barn and outhouses for fuel. Three families at Long Lake have bunched together and are burning the other two houses. Some have been in bed for three days."[72] Newspapers across the country picked up the stories, both true and untrue. One family near Weyburn became a local legend. The Mountie who pushed through four-foot-high drifts to their remote homestead shack was surprised to find them alive: rumours had circulated for weeks that they were frozen in their beds.

The consequences of that brutal winter played out in many directions. For the Prince Albert region, they invigorated advocates who believed that settlers would be better off taking homestead lands in an area where they could at least have access to fuel.[73] Homestead registrations continued to be strong. The fuel shortage reignited Archbishop Taché's cautionary warnings regarding extensive settlement on the open plains. Taché, a resident of the western interior during its formative years, wrote *Sketch of the North-West of North America* in 1870. In it, he recounted some rather frightening experiences crossing the open plains in winter. In contrast to those who supported extensive prairie settlement, Taché offered a stinging indictment of such a scheme. No one could build a successful farm on the open plains, he argued, unless the farm or settlement was built where "the prairie touches on wooded country."[74] The scarcity of fuel, not the agricultural potential of the land, would be the limiting factor determining settlement potential. Dominion and provincial governments, shocked by the conditions of that brutal winter, seem to have reached a similar conclusion. The dominion government acted with uncommon alacrity to temporarily release prairie homesteaders from key homestead duties that winter, particularly the restriction of living for six months on the homestead. The fuel shortage led a shocked government to allow homesteaders to abandon their holdings and seek other shelter. Within certain sub-agencies on the prairie, where there were reserves of forested Crown land, the government temporarily rescinded the need to apply or pay for permits to cut fuelwood, opening the forests to desperate prairie homesteaders.[75] Fuel, both levels of government agreed, was indeed a primary concern.

RAILWAYS AND BRIDGES

The Canadian Northern Railway brought its line to Prince Albert in January 1906, the year before the killing winter. The rail line doubled local export capacity.[76] The lumber industry was quick to take advantage of it, ramping up production and building new milling facilities, reinforcing the importance of the northern wood basket to continued prosperity. The railway brought competition and somewhat lower freight rates, and it was expected to bring opportunities to all aspects of Prince Albert's development, from industry to agriculture. With ongoing growth in the Shellbrook community, the lumber and freighting trade, and the push to open homesteads across the river, it became imperative to build a traffic bridge over the North Saskatchewan River. Local citizens fully expected and planned for further rail lines to penetrate the north, both to serve the recently surveyed homestead land and to exploit minerals, timber, fish, and other resources, including fuel for the prairie market. As it was, the north Prince Albert region was cut off during key times of the year, when the ice was too weak to use in the spring and when it was not sufficiently frozen in the fall. In the summer, the ferry could handle only small loads. The *Prince Albert Times* noted with disgust in 1907:

> Traffic Conditions Are a Disgrace. River Crossing Facilities Woefully Inadequate. Shellbrook Farmers Delayed in City for Weeks. The need of a traffic bridge was amply demonstrated this week. For nearly a week it was impossible to cross the river and residents of Shellbrook were cut off from the market. All day Tuesday, Wednesday, and Thursday the river bank on both sides was crowded with teams waiting to cross. It would have taken half a dozen ferries to have accommodated this traffic. The unfortunate part of the inadequate crossing facilities was that many Shellbrook farmers lost two days of this fine seeding weather. Just now a day lost is a serious blow. Unfortunately when the ferry was being launched on Thursday she struck a stone and stove a hole in her bottom. Tuesday night City Engineer Moon and ten men worked nearly all night making repairs.[77]

Calling for a traffic bridge, the city was caught in a double bind: should the city build a bridge to service the settlers at Shellbrook and offer all-weather access to the region across the river, or should it wait for the Canadian Northern Railway to build a railway bridge and convince it to add a traffic bridge? With alarm, the local newspaper pointed out the heart of the problem: "The absence of [a railway bridge] has done untold injury to this city. People come to Prince Albert and go away again. They say that 'the land across the river is not worth anything and nobody lives there because it has never been necessary to build a bridge and if the land was worth anything the bridge would have been built long ago.'"[78]

The call for a bridge over the North Saskatchewan River was part of a much larger push to build a railway to Hudson Bay. The Prince Albert mayor went to

Ottawa in 1907 to procure support for Prince Albert as the logical starting point of the railway, and he relayed a positive message back to the city: "The Mayor says that since the Dominion Government has made its decision in regard to the Hudson Bay Railroad that Prince Albert is 'IT' and all eyes are turned this way. Prince Albert will be the great point in the new railroad."[79] The Hudson Bay Railway scheme played an important role in the boosterism of Prince Albert: as late as 1926, the city was calling itself "The Gateway to Hudson Bay." Although optimism regarding the scheme continued to feed the new Prince Albert agricultural boom, hopes were continually delayed. The city continued to joust with the railway, putting off building its own bridge until 1909, when the Canadian Northern Railway completed a dual railway and traffic bridge. Rail and other traffic could finally move easily over the river. The Hudson Bay Railway—which did not go through Prince Albert—was finally finished in 1929.[80]

THE "NEW NORTHWEST"

On 24 January 1907, in the middle of the fuel shortage and brutal winter (and building on the momentum of enthusiasm generated by the second railway, the Prince Albert economy, the lumber interests, and the potential Hudson Bay Railway), Senator T.O. Davis of Prince Albert stood up in the Senate and issued a call for a special committee to investigate the land north of the North Saskatchewan River.[81] The *Prince Albert Times* reported that it was time to "Unfold the Riches of the North." Davis called for exploration parties to look into the region north of the Saskatchewan watershed to ascertain not only its agricultural potential but its other resources as well.[82] His call set in motion a firestorm of popular interest that lasted well beyond that brutal winter. The Senate committee's report, prepared on a meagre budget by interviewing and collecting statements from people who knew the region, was eventually published as *Canada's Fertile Northland: A Glimpse of the Enormous Resources of Part of the Unexplored Regions of the Dominion.* Copies of the report were sent to major newspapers across the country, a savvy media blitz that resulted in extensive coverage. The Department of the Interior reeled from the avalanche of over 10,000 requests for the report.[83]

The next step was to fund a detailed physical investigation of the region, starting with the area north and west of Prince Albert. Civil engineer Frank Crean led two expeditions, one in 1908 to Green Lake and Île-à-la-Crosse, the other in 1909 to the Alberta region north of the North Saskatchewan River, near Cold Lake and Lac la Biche. Crean reported that, for the most part, the region would support mixed farming as opposed to wheat farming. He asserted that about one-quarter of the 22 million acres of land in his study region could be farmed. Crean deliberately emphasized what he believed was the region's "potential" for mixed farming, a vague but hopeful term. The area's most serious drawback was not climate or soil, he argued, but transportation and access. His reports were published as *New Northwest Exploration,* and the area became known as the New Northwest.[84]

Crean's report reinforced the Prince Albert Board of Trade's insistence on the fitness and potential of the area for mixed farming, though the board was more interested in the outlying regions for resource development, not farming. Farming required at least some good land, and those who had travelled the northern trails were sceptical of the grandiose assertions of good land as far north as Crean indicated. The Saskatchewan minister of education, for example, believed that, "after a line forty miles north of Prince Albert is reached, the land is unfit for any purpose whatever." Prince Albert citizens disagreed. After all, there were lumber, fish, and possible mineral resources. Nonetheless, for farming purposes, many agreed that the limit of agricultural land north of Prince Albert likely did not exceed the forty-mile band.[85] Regardless, Crean's repeated correlation between the New Northwest and mixed farming was echoed by dominion surveyors. The wood basket that supported the lumber industry had become denuded within thirty miles of the city, and clearcut logging and fires opened up more of the country. Into this landscape, quickly being repopulated by a vigorous growth of aspen and willow, came surveyors. Their quarter section survey reports and maps for the north Prince Albert region consistently presented the land as suitable for mixed farming.

The whole of 1907 was devoted to opening up twenty townships north of the river. Surveying twenty townships, instead of the fifteen extravagantly demanded by the Board of Trade, reflected the impact of the killing winter and fuel shortage on the plains. Homesteads with their own fuel source were popular in the aftermath of the shortages of the extreme winter. Surveyors described each township in terms of its aspect, soil, topography, water sources, and potential for development. A township is six miles in length and six miles in width, with thirty-six sections and 144 quarter sections. Surveying twenty townships opened up almost 3,000 new homesteads. Within that space, there could be considerable variation in the quality and suitability of each quarter section. A typical description covered access trails, soil conditions, timber and fuel resources, hay land, and surface or well water potential. The surveyor's reports also assessed potential mineral resources, such as coal outcrops or stone quarries. Local game was always described, particularly if any could be used for human consumption.[86] The survey report noted that "already the newly surveyed townships north of this city, where until quite recently it was generally supposed no land existed fit for settlement, 130 homestead entries have been made within a radius of twenty miles."[87]

Climatic conditions were also noted, but they were generally descriptions of what the weather was like when the surveyor visited the area. The summer of 1907, following on the heels of the brutal winter, was particularly miserable. A note in the newspaper section known as "Satchel of the Satellite" quipped on 9 May 1907 that "the Indians tell us that once in every hundred years there is no summer. I can't tell as I wasn't here the last time, but I'm here now alright! The ice is still not out on the river!"[88] The 1907 survey reports were littered with references to the cold and even freezing temperatures, giving the impression that these conditions were normal for the region. Since the dominion surveyors were men brought into the

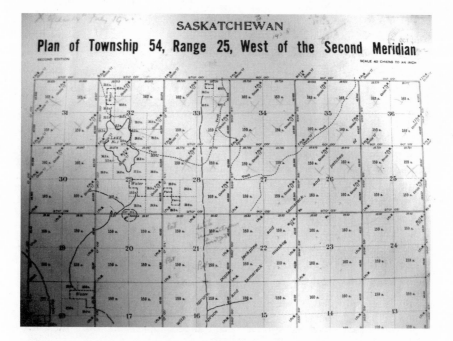

Map 9. Surveyor's map showing plan of Twp 54 R25 W2, 1918. "Gently rolling country covered with spruce, poplar, Jack pine and tamarack, willow swamps and spruce and tamarack muskeg." The trail shown in the centre by the long dotted line is the Montreal Lake Trail.
Source: Department of the Interior. Prince Albert Historical Society, Bill Smiley Archives. Photo by Merle Massie.

area from elsewhere in Canada, they might not have known typical local conditions. Their reports would plague development of the area for years to come. The dominion lands agent at Prince Albert, R.S. Cook, in an attempt to mitigate the effects of the survey reports, explained that "the year just closed has been the most unfavourable in the history of the country. The severe winter of 1906–1907 was followed by a late spring and a cold, wet summer." Crops were damaged all across the west, but at Prince Albert, Cook was quick to note, a fair or even a poor crop was enough for local farmers. The region "is essentially a mixed farming country and the light wheat crop does not seriously affect the condition of the farmer. The banking institutions and implement men inform me that collections are good, and that there is no serious falling off of business."[89] The survey of 1907 ended at the 14th baseline, from Townships 49 to 52, and Ranges 23 to 28, north of the river. These boundaries opened up the land west of the Indian reserves at Wahpeton, Sturgeon Lake, and Little Red River.[90]

MARKETING THE MIXED-FARMING MESSAGE

With homesteads available north of the river, and building on the recent fuel crisis, Prince Albert became a popular homestead destination. The Dominion Lands Agency at Prince Albert saw a rise of 500 homestead applications in 1908 over 1907.[91] The biggest competition for new homesteaders in the north Prince Albert region was the newly opened land in the Palliser Triangle of southwestern Saskatchewan and southeastern Alberta.

Originally closed to homestead settlement, the Palliser region had been reserved as Crown land for grazing purposes. The disastrous winter of 1906–07 crushed the ranching industry. Ranching historians have consistently pointed to the hand of nature in bringing about the end of the open plains ranching era. Writer Wallace Stegner, in his acclaimed classic *Wolf Willow: A History, a Story, and a Memory of the Last Plains Frontier,* noted the efforts of ranch hands to scrape snow from hillsides to help cows reach forage. These pitiful attempts were continually frustrated by the next blizzard. Cows, driven to bottom lands searching for shelter, ate willows and starved to death for lack of nutrition. Starving cattle also wandered into towns, searching desperately for food. Historian Joe Cherwinski noted cattle invading Lethbridge and Medicine Hat by the thousands. They had to be driven out by cowboys. Chinooks only made the situation worse, melting the top layer of snow, which then refroze and covered meagre forage supplies and froze cattle where they lay. Buried in ice and snow, their bodies served as burial platforms for other cattle, driven to seek shelter by the next storm and dying on top of the carcasses. By spring, dead animals lay three or four deep. Stegner called the spring of 1907 "carrion spring," in which stinking, bloated carcasses floated downstream with the spring breakup or hung in trees as the drifts melted away.

The killing winter spelled the end of the big, open-range cattle companies, many of which liquidated what cattle survived and abandoned their holdings.[92] Those who continued ranching began to practise a more forage/farming-oriented ranch style similar to mixed farming, in which some land was broken and seeded to provide sufficient fodder for the animals in winter. Following devastation of the cattle-ranching industry, the drylands were hastily surveyed and thrown open for settlement to the homesteaders who poured into the western interior.

The divergent push to develop land in two completely different biomes—the New Northwest and the Palliser Triangle—represented the difference between those who advocated mixed farming at forest edge landscapes and those who promoted dryland/wheat-farming techniques. Settlers in the dryland were allowed to file on both a homestead quarter and a purchased "pre-emption" homestead, thereby creating 320-acre or half-section farms. It was believed that, because the land was arid, it would be less productive. Twice as much land was necessary to operate a successful family farm. The opportunity to gain a half section of land proved irresistible: in 1908, this region drew over 18,000 entries; in 1909–10, a tremendous 26,000 homestead entries were filed, dwarfing interest in the northern forest edge.[93] Historian Curt McManus called the movement into the Palliser

Triangle "the Last Great Land Rush of modern times."[94] Scientific investigation of dryland-farming techniques such as summerfallowing and crop rotation bred enthusiasm that strategic farming would triumph over nature—as long as a farmer owned enough land to generate a living.[95]

Prince Albert boosters looked on the popularity of this southern region with envy and redoubled their efforts to promote mixed farming in the north as opposed to "wheat mining" in the south. The pre-emption, the dryland allowance for a second quarter, was remade as a detriment. Boosters contrasted the pre-emption region to the northern edge landscape: "So fertile is the land [in the Prince Albert area] and so favored by climatic conditions that the Dominion Government did not include it in the pre-emption area, knowing full well that 160 acres of this land was equal in production capacity to 320 acres in semi-arid ... south western Saskatchewan and southern Alberta."[96] These boosters connected permanence, resilience, and long-term prosperity to the forest edge landscape. Promoters admitted that "it is not surprising that the immigrants preferred the bare prairie, which could be easily broken up, to the richer but more bushy soil of the Prince Albert district." Such short-term gain, however, was not in a true farmer's best interest. Economic return on mixed farms, they stated, "if slow ... has been substantial and solid. The farmers not living on the prairie went in for the more sure occupation of mixed farming, and, never running risks of total loss from droughts, early frosts or hot winds, they have, almost without exception, built up a competence and in many cases much more than that."[97]

From the brutal winter of 1906 to the beginning of the First World War, the Prince Albert Board of Trade sold the north Prince Albert region as a mecca for those interested in the business of mixed farming in a forested landscape. The pamphlets trumpeted "Prince Albert—the Centre of Extensive Mixed Farming District" and "Prince Albert, Saskatchewan—Where Crops Are Sure." The pamphlets scorned the bleakness of the open plains and presented Prince Albert as a park-like paradise: "From a vantage on [Prince Albert's] wooded slope it is possible to get a birdseye view of the north country, as it lies spread out like a map stretching away to the farthermost horizon, a variegated mass, in the sunlight, of shaded green; changing as the woods merge from poplar into spruce, and from spruce into pine. For sheer picturesqueness of location there is no city in Western Canada that can compare with Prince Albert."[98] Typically, such effusive descriptions contrasted the idyllic, green landscape with "the bare, bleak isolation of the prairie town; the scorching winds as from Sahara; the blinding, death-dealing blizzards, which come as a terror by day in the bitter chill of winter."[99] Mixed farming and the beautiful, forested landscape were bound together.

The major disadvantage of mixed farming was that it required heavy capital investment, particularly for stock, buildings, and feed. Prince Albert promoters flipped those drawbacks into another advertising hook. The local landscape contained all "the essentials for settlers possessed of meager capital: cheap fuel, good water, and natural pasture. These [are] in abundance, without money and without price." A forest edge farm could also provide timber to construct barns and fences. As those who operated farms on the open plains knew, these resources "would cost a small income out of capital during the first years of development in a purely prairie country."[100] Prince Albert boosters promoted the region's natural advantages of wood, water, and hay land/pasture to those with little capital. Marketing to the low-income settler became a key feature in promotional literature, which became more and more important as internal migration came to rival external migration.

HOMESTEADING THE NORTH PRINCE ALBERT REGION

Between 1906 and 1914, over 15,000 homesteads were filed at the Prince Albert Land Office.[101] In the north Prince Albert region, homesteaders skipped over the scrub jack pine and sand in the Sand Hills (now Nisbet Forest Reserve) to move farther north in search of better land, settling the black and transition soils of the Shellbrook-Meath Park plain. Although the land was better, it meant travelling a greater distance over rather poor roads to the Prince Albert market. Profits and markets for northern homesteads were not necessarily tied to city markets or wheat exports. A jubilant article in the *Prince Albert Times* in the spring of 1907 declared that "these townships offer a splendid opportunity to settlers as they have a good market for all kinds of farm produce in close proximity and all winter they can have work in the lumber woods." The markets in "close proximity" were lumber camps, expected to soak up any excess supplies of eggs, butter, milk, meat, oats, and hay that the new homesteaders might have for sale—in fact, almost all farm produce *except* wheat. In addition, those lumber camps would provide work for the home-steaders to raise money to build up their farms.

The sprouting postal districts as well as the growing community at Little Red enthusiastically embraced the mixed-farming ideal. Shacks and houses were made with logs and locally sawn lumber. Soon community halls, churches, and schools were built using the same materials. The community hall at Paddockwood was built in the winter of 1915–1916; a rousing dance was held at its inauguration. Soon after, a school was proposed.[102] A cheese factory was built at Albertville and a creamery at Henribourg. These were local endeavours that offered a commer-cial outlet for the surplus milk and cream from the homesteads and injected cash into the mixed-farming economy. Garden produce, wild hay, fresh meat, eggs, and dressed game found a steady local market.

Although the mixed-farming ideal was theoretically based on an ecologically mixed landscape, and though promoters believed the north Prince Albert region eminently suitable, building a farm in the forest region rather than on the prairie meant solving a completely different set of problems. The landscape required new breaking and cultivation methods and equipment, different crops, livestock feed, and more time to change from a pioneer homestead to a settled and permanent farm. The Alingly oldtimers recalled in the 1950s that

The appearance of the landscape was very different at that time, with all the low spots and sloughs full of water. The abundance of water was a great attraction for all kinds of waterfowl [and] the mosquitos were very bad during June and July. As well as being too much water, there was also a great deal of poplar bush, spruce and willow. The clearing was done with an axe, and by burning. The breaking was done with four horse teams and fourteen inch brush breaking plows. The clearing was hard work, and slow, so if ten acres were done in a season it was considered a big job.[103]

Another major problem arising from the forest locale was swamp fever (infectious anemia), a viral infection thought to be water borne that killed valuable horses. The University of Saskatchewan College of Agriculture studied swamp fever in response to the needs of the forest-based mixed farmer. Heavy horses (such as Clydesdales or Percherons) noted for their strength on the open plains were of less use in the northern bush: the larger horses were "too clumsy, took too much feed, not as nimble in the bush for skidding logs, rather prone to swamp fever. The shorter, chunkier kind of horse was better." Such comments represent the trial-and-error nature of trying to bring prairie-based agriculture to the forest edge.[104]

Common methods of land preparation, before a plow ever came near the soil, were clearing the land by axe, grubbing out the roots, and burning the trash. Land clearing was a time-consuming process and a major deterrent to bush homesteading. Prairie land, free from scrub bush and endless roots, could be turned to profitable crops much more quickly, offering a faster return for the farmer. Fortunately, the government soon recognized that farming at the forest edge required a different set of rules. Homestead regulations designed for an open prairie environment, in particular the amount of land that the dominion expected to be broken up, plowed, and "improved" each year, could not be met. Homestead inspectors took local conditions into consideration and were known to allow patents on land where far fewer than thirty acres had been broken. Formal regulations justifying these decisions soon followed. The most common method of calculating the labour required to clear and break a bush homestead was the five dollars per acre rule. The dominion believed that open prairie land could be broken for five dollars per acre, for a total of $150 for thirty acres. If land was heavily forested, then it could cost as much as twenty dollars per acre to clear and break; therefore, some homesteads were allowed patent with ten acres or less in crop. The Buckland history claimed that

> The Homestead Inspector occasionally tried to check up on the clearing and breaking of settlers. He usually got lost or stuck in a mudhole with his buggy. He found it easier to waylay the settler at Prince Albert and take a statement from him about his improvements. In bush countries the required acreage was reduced and left to the discretion of the Inspector, so long as the man was a bona fide settler. An acre

looks a lot of land in the thick bush, and the term "homestead acres" was a standing joke. They were as much exaggerated in size as the fish some anglers catch.[105]

Roads were cut by hand with limited government subsidies along road allowances —a departure from the original trails that usually took the easiest route through the bush. Roads were critical to local politics. The Buckland municipal council pointed out that "many settlers who would have located in these townships had not done so on account of the bad condition of the roads." Road improvements, the council argued, would not only help the local population and encourage new im-migrants but also contribute to the city's finances and security. If settlers could get to and from the city more efficiently, then they could deliver wood and other goods more easily into town as well as build more efficient farms. "Transportation means everything in a new country," the council added, with a ring of both warning and promise.[106] Residents regularly called for municipal and provincial governments to improve transportation connections. They also took matters into their own hands at times, building roads and bridges to ease local traffic problems.[107] Settlers, for example, were interested in improving not only the roads into Prince Albert but also the trails that led east-west *between* communities. It was arduous and unnecessary, settlers thought, to have to go all the way to Prince Albert and back out on a different trail to reach a neighbour's house, school, community hall, post office, or village that was only a few miles away. The settlers and the rural municipality were effectively repeating what Frank Crean had noted in 1908 and 1909: the limits of the area north of the North Saskatchewan River (at least within the forty-mile band of supposed potential agricultural land) had less to do with the quality of the land for mixed agriculture and more to do with the limits of transportation.

In concert with the city of Prince Albert, homesteaders began agitating for a rail-way branch line north of the city. It was clear that, despite approval of the line in 1912, the Canadian Northern Railway was not building the expected line fast enough to suit local interests and conditions.[108] Although railways were important for all western farms, farmers in the forest landscape had particularly acute heavy railway transportation requirements. In a formal petition from the city of Prince Albert to the minister of railways, the mayor of Prince Albert, William Knox, argued that

> A good many of these people are struggling to make a living on land which has to be cleared of bush but without Railway facilities they can scarcely make a living and the authorities of this City are afraid that all the expense which has gone into advertising the district and the money which the Government has laid out in settling it will go for nothing.... In this particular section it is for the most part poplar bush some of it of very considerable size.... If a Railway were built in there would be a good business done for quite a number of years in shipping out cordwood, and this industry would enable the settlers to get their lands cleared.[109]

The cover letter to the petition noted that "if a railway could be commenced immediately the settlers in that part of the country would be able to find work, would be able to clear their lands of timber and ship [it], and from the revenue derived from this source would be able to bring the land under cultivation much more quickly than under present conditions." Although the local lumber and freighting industries offered off-farm work, the sheer number of homesteaders became more than these industries could support. A railway offered a different economic prospect, allowing homesteaders to capitalize on their poplar trees by turning them into cordwood. A local petition to go with Prince Albert's appeal was signed by sixty of the area's settlers. It emphasized the importance of this resource not only to the incomes of local homesteaders but also to meet the needs of prairie farmers: "The matter of fuel shortage has become a question of more than ordinary importance, not only to the people residing in the North, but also to those residents of the Prairie Sections."[110] Fuel shortages and the killing winter of 1906–07 were not far from anyone's mind, and settlers used those memories to support their request for a railway line.

In the meantime, despite transportation difficulties, those operating homestead farms in the north Prince Albert region were experiencing early prosperity, particularly during the war years. With wheat at or near two dollars per bushel, a phenomenal price, homesteaders had cash to put toward clearing and breaking new fields. Oats and hay were also in high demand, and the northern farms were well suited to providing these staples. War restrictions led to a surge in demand for farm produce, particularly meat, milk, eggs, and butter. The local lumber camps were in high production to serve the war effort, providing another excellent market. The newly established creamery at Henribourg had doubled its operation by the end of 1918, before the flood of soldier settlement. The cheese factory at Albertville swung into high gear.[111] As the fields grew, carving acreage from scrub aspen bluffs and heavy timber to create productive farmland, homesteaders could apply for patent. By 1919, the majority of land in the Alingly, White Star, Henribourg, and Albertville districts had been alienated from the public domain into private holdings. The 1955 jubilee history of the Buckland municipality noted that "the close of World War One marked the end of the first stage in the economic development of Buckland. Many of the homesteaders had left, and been replaced by men who bought their farms. ... Homesteads ... were beginning to be called farms."[112] Some of these farms, proved up and patented, were rented out to newcomers.[113] Homestead work in the Paddockwood district was also progressing well, though newcomers were limited when the area was reserved for soldier settlement.

The prices of farm commodities, particularly wheat but other crops as well, led to continued homestead registrations throughout the Great War. Over 5,000 homesteads were filed in the Prince Albert land office throughout the war years even though external immigration had effectively been halted. Homesteaders were either internal migrants or the offspring of previous settlers, with sons requesting permission to take on homesteads in response to wartime demands and prices (and perhaps to dodge war service).[114] Demand put pressure on local land resources: if the areas around Alingly, White Star, Henribourg, and Albertville were filled and transitioned to fully fledged farm operations, and Paddockwood was reserved for future soldier settlement, then where was that development to go?

As early as 1914, the Ratepayers' Association of Alingly, the community that considered itself "hemmed in" on the south by Wahpeton (Sioux), on the west by the Sturgeon Lake Cree Reserve, and on the north by Little Red River Reserve, began petitioning the Department of Indian Affairs, once again, to open Little Red for settlement. The petitioners argued that "outside of slough quarters there are no homesteads available in this Township and very few in the adjoining Townships." Predictably, the Alingly farmers targeted those living at Little Red, charging that "there are only eight families of Indians living on the North West corner of this reserve[;] it is unfortunate that this large tract of mixed farming country for which the Indians appear to have little or no use should be held up in this way." Not only were there merely a few families "holding up" the development of over fifty square miles of farmland, the petitioners declared, but also those living there were not pursuing agriculture. Little Red inhabitants were making their living choring for the lumber camps and operating stopping places for freighters, and the petitioners conveniently ignored the fact that many Alingly homesteaders were pursuing similar activities.[115] To add insult to perceived injury, they claimed, "there are three Indian Reserves in or adjacent to this Rural Municipality [Buckland,] and although the Indians use the public roads, they do not contribute to the making or the up-keep of them."[116] Roads and road building were already a point of contention for municipalities scrambling to fund such modern developments. The reserves, in the estimation of the Alingly ratepayers, were a serious drain on local resources.

The perceived "best use" debate over Little Red River Reserve dragged on for years in letters among the Department of Indian Affairs, Lands and Timber Branch; the Ratepayers' Association of Alingly; and the Prince Albert Board of Trade. Reserves could not be summarily opened for homesteading. The land had to be formally surrendered, and—as the previous attempt had shown—getting surrender for Little Red would be problematic at best and probably impossible given the different opinions of the parties in dispute.[117] The local Indian inspector dutifully wrote to Ottawa, stating calmly that, in his opinion, it was only a matter of time before "the northern bands interested in this reserve will begin to see the advantage of earning a livelihood from farming instead of depending on the hunt."[118] The reserve was steadfastly defended as the place where the northern bands would find their agricultural future.

In fact, settlers at Little Red were farming, though they were not bound by the restrictions and expectations of the Dominion Lands Act that set out rules defining homestead success: a minimal percentage of acreage opened and improved, a house, a barn, and other signs of "improvement" per quarter section. As a result, they had not expanded their operations or developed fields and crops to the extent that local farmers believed was the minimum. By 1914, there were at least sixteen heads of families on the New Reserve agitating for a local day school to serve more than twenty children. Local men, such as William (Billy) Bear, who operated a farm on the reserve as well as an extensive freighting business, stood his ground both in the matter of a land surrender and in pushing for local services, particularly a school.[119] The residents of Little Red derived their livelihood from both the local landscape (hunting, fishing, and farming) and local industries. Their way of life was entirely similar to that of the non-Native homesteaders surrounding the reserve—the difference lay in the emphasis. For the boreal families settled at Little Red, farming was just one aspect of a diversified economy drawn from products of the edge landscape. For incoming farmers, forest resources were a supplement to the more important business of developing a farm. The mixed base of hay crops, root vegetable crops, lumbering, and freighting income continued on Little Red River Reserve until the end of the war.[120]

CONCLUSION

The difference between mixed farming and grain farming became enmeshed in the contrast between the forested regions and the open plains. The forest edge offered resources such as trees for fuel, wild hay lands, and water sources. The shorter growing season with potentially damaging wheat frosts did not affect the oats crop needed for fodder. Wood was available to build houses, barns, and fences, an expensive undertaking on the open plains. Local lumber camps and freighters created strong demand for farm products and provided cash labour opportunities. As early as the 1890s, Prince Albert boosters promoted mixed farming at the edge landscape to both external and internal migrants. After 1906 and the opening of homestead land north of the river, this migration grew. Immigration to the north Prince Albert area was heavily influenced by the advertising campaigns of the Prince Albert Board of Trade, which emphasized highly coloured landscape differences between the bleak, isolated, dry open plains and the lush, green, forested northern landscape. Like HBC servant Anthony Henday, mixed-farming advocates and Prince Albert boosters believed that settlement required both "fine level land and tall trees" in a "pleasant and plentyful country." The ecotone in the north Prince Albert region was indeed a "plentyful" country where economic incomes or in-kind services from the landscape fulfilled a variety of needs and provided a mixed ecological and economic base. Extreme environmental conditions across the open plains, including devastating winters with extensive fuel shortages, also influenced migration. Proactive migration patterns brought settlers drawn to the mixed-farming promise of diversity and resilience and the beauty of the forested landscape.

Depicting the forest edge as a mixed-farming area is a significant but little understood aspect of Saskatchewan's agricultural history. The difference between the open plains and the forested region has often been described but not analyzed. The tremendous push by the Prince Albert Board of Trade to find a creative "hook" to entice settlers to the area became entangled in contemporary debate over the potential of mixed farming versus wheat farming. Mixed farming was depicted as an ideal farming method that shepherded and husbanded the land. It drew broadly on an ecological mix of resources, crops, and stock, thereby lowering farm risk. Such an enterprise, it was argued, offered perhaps a slower road to riches but a sure and steady one.[121]

The edge ecotone, along with the difference in the lifestyle, farming practices, and economic possibilities of the landscape, played a substantial role in soldier settlement, assisted land settlement schemes, and later aided Depression resettlement in the north Prince Albert region throughout the 1920s and 1930s.

CHAPTER FIVE

QUALITY OF PERMANENCY

Best friends David Dunn and James Stoddart, born in Scotland in 1885, were among the thousands of immigrants who came to western Canada in search of a new beginning. Taking harvest work in the Rosthern area of Saskatchewan, between Saskatoon and Prince Albert, they heard about the new homestead land opened up north of Prince Albert. Filing on adjoining pieces, the two continued their quest to build capital, working on farms and in cordwood camps, freighting, and construction to get a few dollars ahead. But the quest for capital threatened their long-term dreams: with no improvements on their homesteads, they were about to lose them. The men conferred. Homestead rules dictated a simple solution: they abandoned their two quarters, claiming that they were too stony to farm. Opting to abandon the land and lose the ten-dollar filing fee gained them time and retained their homestead rights. By 1914, they felt confident in their savings and together filed again, on two quarter sections next door to their originals, not far from the burgeoning village of Paddockwood. Erecting a log house, barn, and well, and breaking four acres on each property by 1915, the two were well on their way to fulfilling their homestead duties. But the war grew in strength and needed able men. Dunn and Stoddart signed on with the Prince Albert 44 Battery Royal Canadian Army.

While they were overseas, another fuel shortage due to extreme cold weather in the winter of 1916–17 led to a boom in cordwood production for homesteaders north of the city, who hauled the loads to town by sleigh while petitioning for a railway. Fuel shortages on the prairie led to increased business for, and interest in, northern homesteads.[1] With interest surging, and anticipating the needs of returned soldiers, dominion agents identified the Paddockwood area as suitable for soldier settlement, and the region was reserved against new claims, except from soldiers. Returning from the theatre of war in 1919, Dunn and Stoddart brought home English war brides and a posse of fellow soldiers ready for new lives at Paddockwood. A grateful government offered each a quarter section Soldier Grant in addition to a homestead, doubling potential acreage, plus loans to purchase new livestock and machinery. The men set about finding a "quality of permanency" in their lives.[2]

Early dominion immigration policies, such as those that filled the prairie with thousands of homesteaders, had an embedded "do or die" mentality. The homestead system under Clifford Sifton and Frank Oliver held out the carrot of 160 acres of cheap homestead land. For a ten-dollar filing fee, breaking, clearing, and building, a man (or a widowed, divorced, or deserted woman who was the head of a family[3]) could gain patent. Cheap land, a massive advertising campaign, and support from railways and steamships to move settlers drew immigrants to western Canada, but the homestead policies offered little else.[4] Once on a homestead, the settler had to succeed on the farm or choose to abandon it and go elsewhere.[5] Between the time that a homesteader registered his claim, through his application for homestead patent, dominion land agents had little to do. There were few or even no dominion programs in place that helped a homesteader to settle into farm life in western Canada, no matter where or what kind of farm it was. Other than a few drafty immigration sheds as temporary quarters for homesteaders en route to their land, or a bit of advice or help in locating their land, homesteaders "could expect minimal assistance."[6] Rugged individualism and a "pull yourself up by your bootstraps" mentality emanated from the dominion government, infecting the early homestead process.

Homestead registrations across the western interior were astounding, particularly in the dryland region after it was thrown open for settlement. Although homestead entries indicate the wild success of federal immigration policies, they do not reveal the whole tale. Homesteaders and their families would cancel (abandon) the lands on which they had filed their claims and leave. Free homesteads taken between 1870 and 1927 and subsequently cancelled, as calculated by economist Chester Martin, averaged 40 percent. Martin called cancellations "the silent but deadly attrition," "preventable wastage of human material," and "the real cost of the western Canadian frontiers of settlement."[7] Yet there remains ample room for investigation of abandoned homesteads. Dunn and Stoddart strategically abandoned their original quarter sections but soon took and later patented homesteads in the immediate vicinity. Their experiences fit both the "failure" and the "success" calculations.

Their choice of homesteads at the northern ecotone was equally strategic. Inadequate rainfall plagued farmers in the Palliser Triangle. A severe drought in 1914 marked the first serious warning that the decision to open the pre-emption region was fraught with difficulty. Farmers in the dry region had no crop. In desperate need of feed and fodder for stock, seed grain for the next planting season, and relief to tide families through until a successful crop should come, settlers appealed to the federal—not the fledgling provincial—government. Homesteading was a dominion-controlled process. At Saskatchewan's creation, Canada refused to grant the province the right to its own Crown land, retaining it for the dominion. As owner, the dominion was on the hook for aid when drought stalked the land. Society demanded support for hapless homesteaders shepherded onto land that, some contended, nature never meant to be farmed. In contrast to the "hands off" immigration policy, aid was reluctantly delivered on a scale "hundreds of times greater than the total advanced in all the years since 1886."[8] Dryland disaster refugees also searched for water, moving northward. On a national scale, the declaration of war overshadowed emerging problems in the dryland area, but local newspapers and homestead records pointed to a steadily growing number of new homesteaders coming to the Prince Albert region from southern areas of the province.[9]

The social outcry demanding government intervention and aid, based on the inadequacy of dominion homestead land policies, led during the Great War to a profound change. The federal government created new land policies that introduced intensive federal intervention, control, and support. The old "do or die" policy of minimal homestead assistance shattered. Assisted land settlement started first with Soldier Settlement Board policies, which later expanded to include other schemes. The Canadian National Railway (CNR) Colonization Department, as well as the dominion's Land Settlement Board and 3,000 British Families scheme, brought settlers to the north Prince Albert region in the postwar period. The *Prince Albert Daily Herald* lauded the idea, arguing that federal land settlement assistance would

> supply the necessary quality of permanency which has hitherto been
> absent from our land settlement policies. That the west is no more
> settled than it is, is not due to the fact that people have not gone into
> the western provinces, but that too many have not stayed there. They
> have simply gone through it like a sieve. Large numbers have gone
> out of the country because they had nothing to sustain them over a
> few bad years. The returned men taking up land under the soldier
> settlement scheme will be sustained in a way so that he may come
> through lean years.[10]

Soldier settlement policies moved distinctly toward promoting mixed farming as the most "sure" farming practice. As a result, the government recognized several important factors: the increased costs required to build a mixed farm; the amount of time required to set that farm on solid financial ground; farming experience as a major contributing factor in success; the importance of women in farming; and the need to build mixed farms in drought-resistant, ecologically mixed landscapes, such as the ecotone of the forest fringe.

Building on years of promotion as "The Home of Mixed Farming," the north Prince Albert region was ideally suited to the new experiment in sustained settlement and became a preferred destination.[11] Ongoing environmental disaster and drought on the open plains—which intensified during the spring and summer of 1919 when soldiers were arriving home and searching for land—also directed soldier settlement north, away from drought regions.[12] Prince Albert boosters found a receptive audience. Sustaining the new settlers, as opposed to merely registering them, became the new focus. In the postwar era, land settlement policies expanded to focus on building and sustaining farms, not just creating them.

THE DRYLAND DISASTER

With the ravages of the 1914 drought in the rearview mirror, an arid spectre stalked western Canada. The winter of 1918–19, famous for its Spanish influenza outbreak and soldier homecomings, was mild. By spring, what little snow there had been had melted, and it soon became hot. By May, Hades was loose in the northern boreal forest, and the massive spring conflagrations decimated the timber industry. As summer limped breathlessly on, the arid spectre returned with a vengeance: a severe drought took hold in the "drylands." Although the heart of the drylands was the old Palliser Triangle of southwestern Saskatchewan and southeastern Alberta (the pre-emption area that had been opened for homestead settlement only in 1908), aridity desiccated a much larger area. The *Prince Albert Daily Herald* outlined the extent: "The dry area may be defined as all that part of the provinces of Alberta, Saskatchewan and Manitoba lying roughly south and west from a line drawn from Wetaskiwin to Camrose, north to Chipman, east to Lloydminster, south to Chauvin, then to Elbow, Moose Jaw, Weyburn, Virden, Souris and south to the international boundary."[13] It was a huge region suffering.

Despite early enthusiasm and extensive in-migration, out-migration from the pre-emption region was astronomical. Year after year of dry conditions leading to poor grain and fodder crops, punctuated by a few spectacular crop years that did little more than extend the agony, initiated a disaster of epic proportions, appropriately termed the "Dryland Disaster." Thousands of families who had settled the arid pre-emption area in anticipation of years of wheat profits were defeated by the land and its harsh climate. Historian Curt McManus noted extreme cancellation rates—over 80 percent of those who had filed—within three years of opening the drylands for settlement.[14] Cancellations in the dryland region shattered the "normal" 40 percent and contributed to Saskatchewan's dismal record: between 1911 and 1931, cancellations were 57 percent. Almost from the start, disaster hit many farms, but by 1919 and throughout the 1920s at least 10,000 people—and probably a much higher number—abandoned the Saskatchewan drybelt region; a further 16,000 abandoned their lands in Alberta.[15] These numbers do not include the high rate of cancellations noted prior to 1917. The early cancellations were often dismissed as merely those of people who were not established or poor farmers in the first place.

The large-scale abandonment touched off a massive internal migration, noted in stories published in major community and agricultural newspapers. Not all of the migrants went north. Historian David Jones called the exodus somewhat "directionless." Those who had come to the drylands from the United States, for example, "slunk back into the States from whence they had come."[16] Others moved to cities, British Columbia, farms in the parkland, Washington State, or the forest edge. Chain migration, with several farmers from a region moving and relocating together, often applied. Clearly, though, those who stayed in the Canadian west deliberately moved either to irrigated farms or to ecologically mixed parkland and forest edge landscapes. These migrants typified the debate over wheat farming versus mixed farming. In the face of environmental disaster, many chose to abandon the prairie wheat monoculture to seek resilience and risk management through mixed farming at the ecotone.

As the drought intensified, the north received more and more attention. Letters poured into the Dominion Lands Office at Prince Albert asking for haying and grazing permits on Crown land to alleviate a major feed shortage in the drylands.[17] Interestingly, it was the drought that in fact helped to turn the north Prince Albert region into suitable haying and ranching country. The brutal and devastating fires in the north in the spring of 1919, which in effect decapitated the local lumber industry, recreated the landscape. The fires cleared the forest floor of years of accumulated slash and debris, leaving room for a lush growth of wild hay, pea vine, fireweed, and vetch. The dominion government stepped in to alleviate the feed shortage, either by supplying relief hay or subsidizing the movement of cattle north to graze and offering grazing permits in the forest reserves.[18]

Each week in the spring of 1919, the editor of the *Prince Albert Daily Herald* commented on the extent of the dryland disaster. He declared that the dominion government bore much of the responsibility for opening up that arid land to homestead settlement in the first place. For the first time, and long before the 1930s, Prince Albert newspapers began to use the term "trek" to refer to the incoming railcars and wagons of settlers moving in from the south. The *Daily Herald* noted, with a sense of satisfaction, that "the north-bound trek of the southern farmers continues, and daily four or five carloads of settlers effects arrive. These are permanent settlers who are taking up farms ... intending to carry on mixed farming."[19] The editor claimed that the movement "is most rational. It is almost inexplainable that men should continue to attempt farming in areas that have proven year after year that they are unsuitable."[20] It was inexcusable, the editor charged, that the government had opened up the lands in question in the first place. Such lands "might have filled the bill for grazing and ranching but once the prairie sod was destroyed by frequent cultivation the country was converted into a potential desert." These farmers were losing a battle against nature, insisted the editor, and it would be better for all if the government would "recognize this situation before further disaster is encountered and encourage the rapid removal of these people to the areas in the north where their sustenance is assured."[21] Prince Albert boosters viewed the coming of drought refugees with an attitude of "I told you so," reiterating their long-held views on the advantages of mixed farming and self-sufficiency over "wheat mining" monoculture.

Figure 11. Settlers from Vanguard trekking north, 1919.
Source: SAB, R-A-2727.

The Alberta government understood the nature of the disaster more clearly and instituted emergency measures to help settlers relocate to better land. Despite stark conditions, the Saskatchewan government remained reluctant to intervene. The dominion and Saskatchewan governments were embroiled in debate regarding who was responsible for the dryland disaster and who should bear the brunt of the cost involved in solving it. This debate was part of the ongoing fight between the province and the federal government over Crown land control. Provincial efforts concentrated instead on finding the proper crop rotation and farming techniques to farm the drylands successfully—a focus on farm practices rather than land assessment. Dryland was farmable, the government literature insisted, if done "properly." Efforts to find the proper techniques included continuing the Dry Farming Congress work through the Better Farming Congress of 1920, in an attempt to scientifically support farming the land.[22] Provincial reluctance to fully appreciate the extent of the dryland disaster meant that Saskatchewan experienced much higher migration and relief problems than did Alberta during the Great Depression.[23]

Despite ongoing drought issues, some soldier settlers took dominion land in the dryland region.[24] Many of these soldiers relocated to northern forested or parkland farms throughout the 1920s.[25] Overall, though, returning soldiers were acutely aware of the extent of the dryland disaster in the spring and summer of 1919, and for this reason they sought farms in parkland and forest edge regions northeast of Regina, east and north of Saskatoon, near North Battleford, and around Prince Albert. Soldier settlements sprang up across the parkland and forest edge region, including the augmented settlement at Paddockwood.

It is tempting to assess migration solely as an expression of vulnerability, degradation of resources, reactive response, and desperation. Such an appraisal is deficient. Migration as an adaptation strategy was also a proactive choice—assessing the situation, planning what to do, making it happen. The *Prince Albert Daily Herald* editors declared that internal migrants were seeking a more resilient and balanced mixed-farming lifestyle at the forest edge. To counteract the worst problems of wheat monoculture—the iconic picture of drought stalking the drylands—migrants would move to a landscape that could support a mixed farm. And, for the first time, the federal government changed its settlement policies to focus less on enticing homesteaders to choose Canada than on helping those who were here to succeed.

"GLAD TO BE AMONGST THE TREES ONCE MORE"

Another reason for moving north was a simple desire for better scenery: "Prairie Farmers Turning toward North Areas. They Want Sight of Tree Once in a While," headlines declared. The dominion lands agent reported that letters were "being daily received" from farmers in the southern part of the province, asking about the prospect of obtaining grazing lands for their stock or homesteads north of the city. "Many of the letters express themselves as weary of the monotonous life of the prairie and say they would be glad to be amongst the trees once more."[26] There is a simplicity to this story, one that resonated in local history books and memoirs written by people long after the move north. "No one minded leaving the prairie, we loved the forest and the lakes," one southern refugee remembered.[27] Greenery, growth, and beauty became a cultural draw beyond economic considerations.

Some of the settlers moving north, the newspapers suggested, had in fact been successful on the prairie. They were coming north deliberately with extensive capital to invest in a mixed-farming enterprise. "It is a noticeable fact," the *Daily Herald* declared, "that many of the new settlers are men who have made a success of farming on the prairie, but seemingly are tired of the monotony of straight grain growing." They sought the timber country, "with its wealth of fuel, plenty of wild hay and the availability of wild game at certain seasons of the year." Such a landscape would "appeal strongly to many men who are desirous to engage in farming of a mixed variety and to stock raising."[28] The prairie, in this interpretation, was a convenient stop for a short period to shore up some capital, but real farmers looking to create long-term, resilient, ecologically sustainable mixed-farming enterprises were heading north. In some ways, David Dunn and James Stoddart were typical examples. They worked on grain farms and found other opportunities to gather the necessary capital to build a farm at the ecotone. South-to-north migrations, newspapers asserted, were deliberate expressions of capability and choice rather than reactive responses to environmental vulnerability.

SOLDIER SETTLEMENT IN HISTORICAL PERSPECTIVE

The dominion government canvassed overseas soldiers fighting in France to find out what the men wanted the government to provide when they returned to Canada at the war's end to help them readjust to civilian life. One of the most popular ideas was that the dominion should provide loan support and land for ex-soldiers to become established farmers. A preliminary plan of action was put in place in 1917, creating the Soldier Settlement Board (SSB). Because of unprecedented and unexpected demand, an expanded version was passed in 1919.[29] The most important change between the Soldier Settlement Act of 1917 and that of 1919 was that the loan capacity of the SSB was expanded. As a result, soldiers could access loans to purchase title to farmland in any of the nine provinces. Soldiers could emigrate or return to Canada and take up farms wherever they chose or use the money to improve or expand farms already owned. They were not kept strictly to the remaining Crown land of the western interior. In fact, just one-sixth of the total number of soldiers who received land through the Soldier Settlement Board took the dominion homestead plus the soldier grant—and those men would have been spread across the western interior on any remaining Crown, school, or otherwise unalienated land.[30] Nonetheless, soldier settlement opened millions of acres of Crown land along the forest fringe.

Historical opinion on the soldier settlement scheme has been blunt: soldier settlement overall was a "disappointing failure."[31] It was expensive, many soldiers abandoned their holdings despite extensive and intensive support from the SSB, and conditions in places were harsh. Because soldier settlement was a national endeavour, and soldiers were placed on (or returned to) agricultural land in all of the provinces, historical analysis has favoured a national or even an international perspective. An exception is James Murton, whose detailed investigation of soldier settlement in British Columbia provides a distinct provincial focus and a varied assessment of "success." While stump farming at Merville on Vancouver Island is painted as rather unsuccessful, the orchard communities of the Okanagan Valley experienced more success. Frustratingly, Murton's work does not delineate between the federal Soldier Settlement Board schemes and the provincial manifestation through the Land Settlement Board in British Columbia, where Crown land was a provincial, not a federal, responsibility. Murton situates soldier settlement as an example of a "new liberal order framework," an activist form of government interested in providing for the general welfare of citizens, often through extensive social and environmental reform projects. Farmable land was scarce in British Columbia; the new liberal order framework allowed the government to push forward massive environmental engineering projects, such as draining Sumas Lake, stump farming at Merville, and various irrigation schemes in the Okanagan to create farmable land. In this work, tracing soldier settlement experiences across the BC landscape gave Murton a chance to reflect on the interwar period as an example of the turn to the new liberal order. Despite its breadth and depth, the disconnection between dominion and provincial soldier and land settlement policies makes comparison difficult.[32] Murton characterizes the 1919 changes to the SSB loans policy, which significantly expanded loan potential so that soldiers could create opportunities across the dominion, as "essentially just a bank."[33] Conversely, a national viewpoint without recognizing distinct provincial characteristics is equally problematic. The three western interior provinces of Manitoba, Saskatchewan, and Alberta fell directly under federal authority. Soldier land settlement in each of the other provinces had to be mediated between provincial and federal land agencies. Because Saskatchewan soldier settlement fell under federal jurisdiction, as did homesteading, federal policies had a direct impact.

Soldier settlement on agricultural land fired the imaginations of many across the country at the tail end of the war. Editorial pages, letters to the editor, and advertisements in newspapers heralded the scheme.[34] The 1919 Soldier Settlement Act provided for three land settlement options. If a soldier already owned agricultural land, he could obtain a loan to clear "encumbrances" (usually mortgages, liens, and taxes), to purchase livestock and implements, or to erect permanent buildings. A soldier could alternatively purchase land through the SSB, which acted as both realtor and bank, setting the land price and holding the mortgage and title until the loans were paid off. He would also qualify for a loan to purchase stock and erect buildings. Loans secured by the returned men were to be paid back over the course of twenty-five years.[35] During that time, the soldier settler would continue to be advised and supported by the SSB. Finally, a soldier could take free dominion land within the western provinces (usually a soldier grant and a homestead) and qualify for a smaller loan to purchase livestock and equipment or erect buildings.[36] The soldier settlement scheme was, as a result, both nimble and unwieldy. It could respond on an individual level to a soldier's needs, but it became difficult to manage its strengths and weaknesses at the aggregate level.

Historical analysis of soldier settlement, in large part because of the individual nature of the loans and land process, has been fundamentally flawed. To compare the experiences of a soldier who returned to his farm and took modest loans for improvements and pre-empted his "soldier grant" quarter to secure a larger land base, with those of another soldier who purchased expensive farmland and took large loans to buy stock and equipment, with those of another soldier who chose free dominion land and qualified only for smaller loans, is problematic at best. The differences among provinces, due to their differential rights over Crown land, are also important. Climates, soils, and agricultural capacities at the regional level also played major roles. Finally, it is critical to recognize that, in the western interior, soldier land settlement policies, in large part, were reactions to the shocking inadequacies of dominion homestead policies and marked a turn toward a different kind of land settlement. Soldier settlement, when viewed on a deep time scale, marked a critical transition point in dominion land policy direction.

Historical discussion of soldier settlement has produced a second problem. There has been an overall tendency to rely on negative stories, easily found in newspaper files or government records of those who needed help. Too often the most disastrous and unfortunate examples have been used to explain broader trends. For example, though the majority of returned soldiers across the dominion purchased or returned to developed farms (such as David Dunn and James Stoddart), historical analysis has favoured the study of block settlement schemes on remote, undeveloped, forested Crown lands. These remote forested settlements are easier to trace as distinct examples of soldier land settlement. For the most part, they are considered failures.[37] As a result, perception of the success of soldier settlement has been skewed.

Describing soldier settlement at the forest edge as settlement on "scrub" land, incapable of productive agricultural development, frames the story in a particular way. Men become "forced" to take off-farm employment in regional industries or to hunt, trap, or fish to help feed their families. The lure of mixed farming, the strong forest economy, and access to both a homestead and a soldier grant have been downplayed. Off-farm opportunities, however, were more of a draw than a detriment, as I discuss in the next chapter. Local history books from forest edge communities indicate that both on-farm and off-farm opportunities drew soldiers. Even government files show what soldiers were looking for and asking about. Canadian Expeditionary Force soldier Roger Picand, of the 67th Battery 52nd Artillery Regiment, wrote to the Saskatchewan Department of Agriculture from Angéloûme, France, on 30 September 1916. Picand requested information regarding settlement in northern Saskatchewan. Was the Saskatchewan River navigable, he wondered, and how long were the winters? Can wheat and oats be grown north of the North Saskatchewan River? And, finally, what were the game and fish like in these parts? His letter, anticipating land resettlement concessions, outlined questions typical of northern homestead development. Picand was interested in transportation, climate, potential agricultural crops, as well as off-farm products of the local landscape.

In contrast, academic studies have characterized soldiers as little more than pawns, tricked into taking poor land in a larger game orchestrated by federal and provincial governments. It was a game "designed to open up vast new areas of land," whether that land was fit for settlement or not—and the narrative consistently suggested that the Crown land available for settlement, particularly in western Canada after the war, was not fit for agriculture.[38] This storyline is problematic, in part because it fails at the local level.[39] In the north Prince Albert region, soldier settlement overall was a success and a critical aspect of regional development.

SOLDIER SETTLEMENT REGULATIONS

Soldier settlement ushered in a new era of assisted settlement on a scale not seen before in Canada. It was highly regulated. The soldier had to apply to the program and be approved. Between one-quarter and one-third of applicants were rejected.[40] The SSB required soldiers with no farming experience to undergo practical training through courses and/or with a farmer (as hired help) to learn the business of mixed farming. In contrast, dominion homestead regulations did not evaluate homesteaders. By 1921 in the Prince Albert district, over 1,300 soldier settlers had been placed on farms, forty had been recommended for training, and of those twenty-five had been placed "with the best farmers in the various districts, and the wages have been satisfactory to all the settlers in training."[41]

The land also had to be approved. Land assessment was the cornerstone of the soldier land scheme, according to the SSB: "If the first maxim is that the *man* must be 'fit to farm,' the second maxim is that the *land* must be 'fit to farm.' They were of equal importance."[42] To that end, the SSB hired inspectors to oversee land purchases and to evaluate and approve or reject improved farms or unimproved "wild" land.[43] One of the founding principles of the Soldier Settlement Act was that soldiers should not be asked to go to farms many miles from service centres or transportation facilities. The SSB literature insisted that "the board does not contemplate the settlement of soldiers as pioneers in remote locations or under isolated conditions, removed from markets, in virgin forest areas."[44] As a result, the SSB pushed itself to place soldiers primarily on land in established farming districts, within fifteen miles of a railway. Agricultural surveys conducted in western Canada throughout the latter part of the war years showed a relative scarcity of dominion land, particularly in contrast to the amount of land that had been available prior to and during the major settlement era between 1896 and 1910. What was left was either in the forested regions or in the Palliser Triangle. Any remaining productive prairie land had been alienated from the government, owned by the Hudson's Bay Company, railway and colonization companies, private speculators, school boards, or Indian bands. The monthly agricultural magazine, *The Saskatchewan Farmer*, deplored the fact that there were millions of acres of unoccupied land within easy reach of settlements and railways that were in the hands of speculators. "The Government has in the past commandeered part of our wheat crop. Why not commandeer this vacant land? ...Surely something can be done to compel the owners of our vacant lands to...sell it at a reasonable figure, so as to allow returned soldiers or other purchasers to cultivate it." A forced purchase scheme was infinitely better, the magazine noted, than offering homesteads in remote, northern, timbered districts without rail lines or established service centres.[45] To bring land back under the auspices of the federal government for the soldier settlement scheme, it had to be purchased. Prices were negotiated with farmers who decided to sell their holdings to the Soldier Settlement Board, such as the Gatskys, a Ukrainian family in the Paddockwood district who had proven their quarter by 1920, when they sold it to the SSB.[46] Companies, private individuals, or Indian bands were squeezed to find land for soldier settlement.

When demand still exceeded supply within these limitations, soldier settlement was promoted in places *likely* to get a railway soon or in "specially approved districts along projected lines where general settlement is well developed."[47] The restriction to land within fifteen miles of a railway did not match practice. Special allowances were made to settle in certain areas, including the Porcupine Forest Reserve in east-central Saskatchewan or the Merville region of British Columbia. These areas, contrary to the stated intent of the SSB, were "virgin forest areas." The north Prince Albert region, with the fledgling communities of Alingly, Henribourg, Albertville, and Paddockwood, and a promised branch railway line, was both "virgin forest area" and "special approved district." It offered a landscape of opportunity: an edge ecotone that, at the end of the war years, retained nearby lumber opportunities for fuel and building supplies and showed promise for mixed farming. Quarter section surveys, including soil assessments, were done on every piece of land bought through the SSB, in an attempt to direct soldiers onto land suitable for mixed farming.

MIXED FARMING AND SOLDIER SETTLEMENT

The first report of the SSB declared mixed farming as the soldier settler's route to established success. Using clichés typical of the most ardent mixed-farming advocates, the SSB declared that "settlers are not encouraged to embark on a scheme of farming in which 'their eggs are all in one basket.' ... The impulsive direction is towards mixed farming, because it is based on sound economic principles." Those principles showed that "where several important crops are grown and several classes of animals are kept they are not all likely to meet adverse conditions of climate or market in the one year."[48] Operating a mixed farm, with cows, pigs, poultry, and a good vegetable garden, soldier settlers would be assured of a "healthy livelihood."[49] Mixed farming promoted not only resilience and profit over time through diversification but also a large measure of self-sufficiency. Soldiers were encouraged, even outright directed, to engage in mixed-farming practices. The report continued that "different crops and different classes of animals make for better distribution of labour throughout the season. Waste is lessened because the product from one crop or animal is utilized by another class of animal. Fertility is conserved because manure rich in plant food is returned to the soil. Income is steadier and better distributed throughout the seasons; consequently there is less likelihood of contracting a great number of small debts." In response to years of promotion—and the advice of federal scientists and surveyors—the mixed-farming directive encouraged soldiers to file on homesteads and soldier grant lands (or purchase farms through the SSB) in parkland and forested areas suited to mixed farming. Although the SSB would never have admitted it, it seems reasonable to assume that the board was not interested in creating a wealthy class of successful wheat farmers who had time in

30,000,000 ACRES
OF FERTILE & IDLE
LAND
HELD BY GRABALL & CO.

160 ACRES
FREE LAND
ONLY 100 MILES
FROM CIVILIZATION

RETURNED
SOLDIER

DENIED ACCESS TO THE LAND WHICH HE BLED TO DEFEND

Figure 12. Thirty million acres of fertile and idle land. This political cartoon has done much to propagate the idea that soldier settlement on forest land (where the wolf was near to howl at the door) was a poor way to repay soldiers for their sacrifices. Many newspapers, including *The Saskatchewan Farmer*, lamented the amount of good land owned by speculators. Under the 1919 regulations, the SSB could purchase alienated land, mitigating somewhat the push onto forested and remote lands.
Source: SAB, R-A19420.

the winter to meet and agitate for change. It supported a scheme that kept soldiers busy—and the heavy demands of a mixed farm fit the bill.[50]

When the first trickle of soldiers began to arrive during the winter of 1918–19, Prince Albert advocates sprang into action. The soldier settlement scheme was popular, though there was disgruntlement in Prince Albert when Land Settlement

Boards were announced for Regina and Saskatoon. The Prince Albert Board of Trade angrily pointed out that "not one of the men selected to perform the vital duty of securing land for the returned soldiers was familiar with the northern part of the province where hundreds of the soldiers desire to locate."[51] There were real differences, both the Board of Trade and the *Daily Herald* editors cautioned, between wheat farming on the prairie and mixed farming in the north: "the principle of loaning money that applies on the prairies" simply would not apply. Local veterans met with SSB representatives to plead their case. They called for "a plan that will give the prospective mixed farmer of northern Saskatchewan an even break with his neighbour in wheat raising on the prairie."[52] Given the stated aims of the SSB in regard to mixed farming, the board had little choice but to give in. Soldier settlement policies, including the amount of money needed for loans, the kind of land required, and other issues were different in the local context. After several letters, meetings, and hot debates, the SSB relented and agreed to establish a local Land Settlement Board at Prince Albert. Saskatchewan was the only province to have three boards.[53]

As soldier settlers poured into the north Prince Albert region, calls for a railway north of the city were renewed. The influx of soldiers gave added regional pressure to the railway push. If Paddockwood was to be a preferred soldier settlement area, promoters argued, then it needed a railway. The *Prince Albert Daily Herald* reported demands coming from the original settlers, the soldier settlers, businesspeople, and the Prince Albert Board of Trade. The headlines for 13 March 1919 read "New Railways for Prince Albert. CNR Gives Promises of North Line. CPR Is Keen on the Northern Territory." The paper reported a "definite promise" of immediate construction of a line north to Paddockwood, and held out hope that it would go even farther, to "usher in a new era of prosperity for a country of unlimited possibilities in agriculture, lumbering, fishing and mining."[54] Boosters of the north Prince Albert edge landscape automatically melded the agricultural story with potential forest resources. No one knew exactly how far north the limits of agriculture might be, but resource industries were expected to provide equal, if not greater, opportunities. Marketing the local landscape meant defining opportunities for soldier settlement in two directions: pointing out the advantages of the ecotone as a mixed-farming paradise, and directing attention to off-farm economic potential.

MIXED-FARM ECONOMICS

Despite the lack of immediate rail transport to the lands set aside for soldier settlement, the Prince Albert SSB land branch was busy. There were several advantages to purchasing land in a recently homesteaded, forested ecotone region. Not only was such land considered the best bet for mixed farming, but also, in general, it was much cheaper than prairie land. In the Regina and Saskatoon districts, where free dominion land was scarce, the majority of soldier settlers took loans to purchase farmland or clear mortgages and liens on their own farms. The Soldier Settlement

Board had sweeping land power. It could negotiate and purchase land directly from farmers and hold the land under speculation for purchase by soldiers. Soldiers could also approach the SSB with agreements worked out with private owners on land that they wanted to buy. "Vendors of land to the board are always requested to reduce the original price of the land by sums ranging from $200 to $1000, and it is estimated that at least a saving of seven per cent has been effected on land purchased since the inception of the local office."[55] In Saskatoon, 1,364 soldiers purchased farms through the SSB; the average farm cost was about $3,000, requiring loans of $4 million. The Regina situation was similar: 1,322 soldiers purchased land averaging $3,500 at a cost of $4.5 million. At Prince Albert in 1919, the majority of soldiers, 590, settled on dominion land. The 559 soldiers who purchased land needed loans to the amount of $1,613,033, which worked out to less than $2,900 per farm.[56] This figure is an average and is somewhat misleading. An established farm in the settled districts around Melfort (south and east of Prince Albert) or Shellbrook sold for significantly higher prices than the just-proved-up farms in the north Prince Albert region. If a soldier bought a farm in that region, it cost about $1,200 per quarter. He faced smaller payments.

The Prince Albert district gave out significantly fewer loans overall, as settlers on Crown land were limited to loans for stock, equipment, and improvements, while their land was still in the proving-up stage. The soldier was expected to secure all of his loans through the SSB, which would also prepare bulk purchases of machinery, supplies, and stock, to pass savings on to the soldier. Soldier settlers who bought more expensive farms carried much higher and more risky loan portfolios, attempting to make payments on nearly everything: stock, buildings, and the land itself. Indeed, in the Prince Albert district up to 1921, the average loan per settler on purchased land was $5,663; on dominion land, it was $1,497. The majority of soldier settlers on dominion land across the country decided to go about "pioneering in the ordinary homestead use of the term without government financial assistance," choosing not to take any loans at all. Across Canada, the numbers were interesting. As of 1921, there were 25,443 soldier settlers. Of those, 5,672 settled on dominion land with no loans. A further 3,735 settlers on Crown land received loans, which were minuscule ($6,369,364) in comparison with the number of loans to settlers on purchased lands, with total loans of $69,259,608.[57]

In the Prince Albert district, more loans were given out for the purchase of stock and equipment than for land; in Regina and Saskatoon, land purchases were worth double the loans for stock and equipment. A soldier settler on free dominion land, able to secure both a soldier grant and a homestead grant, carried a lighter burden of debt spread across more land. The majority of soldier settlers in the north Prince Albert region took land at Paddockwood under the combined soldier grant/homestead option, with a significant minority purchasing cheaper, recently patented farms in the Alingly, White Star, Henribourg, and Albertville districts.[58]

As long as the soldier settler was still on his SSB farm, actively working and paying his loans (or at least the interest), the SSB continued to support him, offering further advice or loans to expand the farm or help in lean years. "Not only does it give him a start, but it sustains him, not through charity, but through a well-thought out system of credits by means of which everything needed by the settler may be purchased and paid for over a long term of years."[59] The ongoing, sustaining help, it was thought, would make the difference in successful soldier settlement. Although advertised as a new and welcome departure in land settlement policies, there was a considerable paternalistic overtone to the endeavour.

LAND CLASSIFICATION AND SURVEYS

F.J. O'Leary, district superintendent of the Soldier Settlement Board at Prince Albert, reported in 1921 that soldier settlers in the "timbered country" of the Paddockwood district, twenty-six miles north of Prince Albert, were showing evidence of "making good." Soil was listed as first-class "chocolate loam," a new railway into the district was "under construction," and the country was covered with black and white poplar.[60] With settlers taking both homesteads and soldier grants, about two townships of land were opened.[61] Although soldier settlers were given priority, civilian homesteading was once again allowed in the Paddockwood area, and settlement spread steadily north, filling Township 52, Ranges 23 to 26, and spilling over into Township 53. In fact, settlement was rapidly spreading to the end of surveyed land, forcing the dominion to face a land shortage or find new areas of expansion.

As land was being filled, the dominion government financed a land classification survey. It sent professional surveyors north of Prince Albert "to examine and report upon those lands suitable for immediate settlement ... [and] to classify the lands for general information, giving data that will afford prospective settlers and the general public a better knowledge of the country."[62] Surveyors classified the land by quarter section, specifically visiting abandoned homesteads or other land not yet settled. The survey provided information on the older settled districts around Alingly, White Star, Henribourg, and Albertville. It used these assessments to forecast the possibilities of the Paddockwood district, including the recent soldier settlement, and to classify the land that could yet be opened farther north.[63] In general, the report divided homestead land from unfarmable scrub and muskeg land, such as that found in the more northern townships. Good land, the survey noted, roughly ended in Township 53; few quarters were thought fit for homesteads in Township 54 and farther north. Settlement past this point was moving out of the relatively good land of the Shellbrook-Meath Park plain and onto podzolic-leached grey forest soil, with more white and black spruce, jack pine, and muskeg. Soldiers and other northern settlers were rapidly reaching the end of good land.

Figure 13. Department of the Interior surveyors, c. 1920.
Source: SAB, R-183 I.222 (6).

SOLDIER SETTLEMENT ON RESERVE LAND

The popularity of soldier settlement meant that the dominion was scrambling to find enough suitable farmland within fifteen miles of a railway to offer for soldier settlement. One of the most common places to find farmland was on First Nations reserves. During and immediately following the First World War, hundreds of thousands of acres of farmland were forcibly or coercively (and voluntarily) surrendered by reserves and sold to the Soldier Settlement Board. As the practice became more common, farmers in the Alingly district, stymied in their attempt to have Little Red River Reserve opened for homestead settlement, changed their tactics. The local Grain Growers Association petitioned for opening of the reserve, not for homesteading but for soldier settlement.[64] They believed that the added moral weight of servicing the returned soldiers would tip the balance in their favour.

The attempt to open the reserve for soldier settlement became a game of semantics. What one group (the Alingly Grain Growers Association and the Prince Albert Board of Trade) considered good mixed farmland, the other (the Department of Indian Affairs) dismissed as "questionable" and hardly fit for settlement. W.B. Crombie, the local Indian inspector, stated that "were this land put up for sale today it is very questionable if it could be sold readily, but on the other hand, were it thrown open for homesteading no doubt the most of it would be taken up for mixed farming purposes."[65] It was a telling statement. Crombie suggested that there was a different standard between land appropriate for purchase and land good enough to homestead. Purchased land had to be "improved," with fields ready to farm and buildings suitable for occupation to be worth its money. Homestead (and soldier grant Crown) land was essentially free. Clearing land and erecting buildings was a sweat equity process whereby a homesteader added marketable value through labour to change a homestead to a farm worth money. The reward of a patented farm to be sold for profit came at the risk of settling on possibly inferior land or land that could take a lot of time to clear and break.

Those demanding that Little Red be surrendered and opened for settlement continued to claim that few people lived there, even fewer year round. Others stated that as many as sixty people lived on the reserve and perhaps more. Still stinging from the underhanded tactics of the real estate agency and farm instructor who had duped residents into signing a land surrender,[66] the Department of Indian Affairs refused new soldier settlement surrender requests. It would have been a difficult surrender to obtain regardless, and the department knew it. What was the department to do with the families already in residence at Little Red? How would it deal with those who were farming, like Billy Bear, who had both a successful farm and a freighting business? Should he be offered homestead rights, which were not offered to First Nations men? What of those who were cutting hay and feeding cattle on reserve land? It was a reasonable use of the land, after all, given the growth of stock raising and the market at Prince Albert. Who was required to sign the surrender documents: the inhabitants of 106A or the reserve's legal owners, the Montreal Lake and Lac La Ronge bands? If the northern bands, then who would go up there and ask them? The journey was still a tremendous undertaking.[67] These were questions and concerns that no one at Indian Affairs wanted to answer. Considering the pressing need for farmland in the north Prince Albert region because of increased soldier settlement demand and the rather discouraging results of the land survey, the refusal to ask for the surrender of Little Red was remarkable.[68]

THE HOME BRANCH

Perhaps the most intriguing difference between soldier settlement and previous dominion homestead schemes was the development of the Home Branch in July 1919. The SSB literature decreed that "home conditions are a vital and often a deciding factor in the success of the settler. A branch, therefore, was formed to instruct and advise the wives and family dependents of settlers in home economics."[69] Creation of the Home Branch was in part a response to important social developments and public recognition of the role of women in society, particularly on the farm. Common complaints from women on homesteads in the western interior prior to the First World War included isolation and loneliness. In many cases, these feelings were exacerbated by complete bewilderment and lack of background knowledge in farming practices. The phenomenal growth of women's organizations, particularly the Women's Section of the Grain Growers Association and the Homemakers (Women's Institutes) prior to and during the war, began to alleviate these concerns. Combined with women's valuable contributions to the war effort and ongoing work by public women such as Nellie McClung in promoting women's issues and rights, the growing public stature of women in farm communities led to female enfranchisement, the right to vote, in 1917.[70] Perhaps the SSB, in keeping with its close alliance with mixed farming, understood what agricultural newspaper *Saskatchewan Farmer* had been saying all along: it was not possible to operate a successful mixed farm without a partner to shoulder part of the workload. And by 1919 those female partners had a much stronger voice for change.

Journalist Ethel Chapman wrote about the SSB Home Branch in *Maclean's* magazine in 1920. A woman, Chapman averred, was an "absolute necessity" on a farm. But her needs required due care and attention: "If the wife is not contented or if the home conditions are not liveable for the family, the farm business cannot prosper." Just as the SSB was there to look after the man and the farm business, the Home Branch was there to look after the needs of the wife and family.[71] A somewhat more derogatory view of a woman's role on a farm came from the SSB: "It is recognized that the wife's attitude towards the undertaking may be either a great help or a serious handicap to a settler. If she is cheerful, interested, capable, [all is well.] If she is discontented, not interested in farm life, or unthrifty and indolent, it is impossible to estimate the financial injury which she may do." The paragraph went on: "It is futile to loan money to a man for the purchase of land, stock and equipment if the mental attitude of his wife and her physical condition are such as to discourage and render him incapable of repaying that loan." In large part, the Home Branch was inaugurated to protect those loans by identifying, helping, and teaching the farm wife before her inabilities, attitudes, or accidents required money to fix or solve a physical, mental, or embarrassing financial situation.[72] The SSB looked at earlier homestead policies of the dominion government and decided that one obvious shortcoming was the lack of aftercare and support, particularly for women and families. Chapman suggested that the Home Branch operated as the women's branch of the SSB, just as there was a women's branch in many other social and political movements in Canada at the time.[73]

The Home Branch concentrated on providing information, bulletins, pamphlets, and courses designed to help women successfully support their family and farm. Assistance tended to fall into three general categories: educational and technical, medical, and information. Educational information and technical help (usually printed bulletins) were geared almost exclusively toward homemaking issues, teaching women the basics of farm life, including staples such as baking, milking cows, and making butter, looking after poultry, gardening, canning, sewing, and raising children. These skills were particularly useful to the wife of a mixed farmer raising beef and dairy cattle, sheep, goats, pigs, poultry, and a kitchen garden. Travelling libraries and homeschooling techniques and books, for those too far from established schools, were also important. The Home Branch established courses through university extension divisions across the country, including the University of Saskatchewan. They were often called "short courses" and operated from two days to several weeks. Board and tuition were covered at first by the Training Contingency Fund left over from the war effort. Courses and lectures reflected what the board thought were the duties of women, including "Poultry Raising," "Home Dairying," "The Kitchen Garden," "Personal Hygiene," "Bread-Making," "Beautifying the Home," "Canning," and "Remodelling of Clothing," to name just a few.[74]

Personal visits from qualified Home Branch staff helped to ease the loneliness and provide technical help and advice.[75] Chapman claimed that "it was made clear that their [Home Branch staff] purpose was not supervision, and not inspection—that they should go into the homes of the settlers and find out their greatest need."[76] Sometimes that "greatest need" was advice or even just a visit from another woman. Other issues came up. "Lost baggage has been traced, gratuities secured, employment found, information secured on selling houses, War Bonds, obtaining divorces, re-uniting parents and children, getting relatives out from England, and any of the hundred-and-one questions which may arise," the Home Branch report proudly declared.[77] The branch soon found itself with "a sheaf of letters on file from bachelors asking them to find them wives."[78] It effectively operated as a clearing-house for all other issues aside from the business of operating a commercially successful farm enterprise.

The Home Branch continued as an important component of settlement aftercare, and its many publications found their way into the hands of those who were not specifically under its scheme, including the popular book *Useful Hints on ... Home Management.* This book was published in 1930 by the Soldier Settlement Board as an amalgamation of household hints and tips collected by Jean Muldrew, in charge of the Home Branch throughout its existence. The book focussed on the practical aspects of being a farm wife, from cooking to raising poultry, doing laundry, raising children, and decorating the home on a budget.[79] All Home Branch publications were printed in English. It was thought that non-British immigrants were already well versed in mixed-farm life and had experience, while British war brides and those brought out under the 3,000 British Families scheme needed far more help, support, and advice. The Home Branch was eliminated when the SSB was reorganized in 1930–31.

While in operation, Home Branch representatives specialized in two areas in particular: first, an ability to liaise with other established organizations; second, a commitment to health. The Home Branch had a limited budget and could not meet specific requests or requirements itself. To compensate, it excelled at creating connections with groups such as the Imperial Order Daughters of the Empire (IODE), the Homemakers Clubs, the Patriotic Fund, the Women's Grain Growers Association, the Rotary Club, the Legion branches (once they were established), local churches, and various branches of the provincial or federal government, such as the Soldier's Civil Re-Establishment scheme. Chapman argued that "this is the long suit in the [Home Branch's] methods. ... Seldom, when they have fully carried out their campaign, do they fail to find sympathy and help."[80] The ability to link with other organizations allowed a fuller measure of help, support, and information to the soldier settler's wife.

The second, and perhaps even greater, strength of the Home Branch was "where sickness or unfortunate disaster occurs."[81] Health, hospital and nursing care, and health information were considered top priorities, and the Home Branch worked hard to initiate public health reform and promote local medical facilities. Working with each of the provincial Departments of Health, the Home Branch promoted health examinations of every dependant of the soldier settlement scheme. Its in-depth knowledge of local needs led to agitation for cottage hospitals, nurses, and other medical services. The branch found its greatest ally in the Red Cross.

RED CROSS OUTPOST HOSPITALS

During the war years, the Red Cross had operated a full-scale campaign to provide services and supplies to men at the front.[82] At the end of the war, flush with money, the Red Cross vowed to continue its campaign.[83] Activities following the war refocussed primarily on the health and welfare of returned soldiers and their families, though the Red Cross soon expanded into other areas. One of the first priorities, in part because of agitation from the Home Branch of the SSB, was establishment of Red Cross outpost hospitals. A pamphlet outlining postwar Red Cross initiatives noted that "the settlement of ex-service men on the land drew attention to the fact that many pioneer districts in Canada were woefully lacking in medical and

Figure 14. Paddockwood Red Cross Outpost Hospital, 1948. Ruth Shewchuk (standing in front) was the last nurse at the hospital before it was closed. Source: SAB, Ruth Shewchuk collection.

nursing care."[84] The first of what became several hundred small outpost hospitals strung across the entire British Empire was built at Paddockwood. It opened in the fall of 1920.[85]

The hospital was a unique combination of local and Red Cross resources but directed and initiated by the SSB. F.J. O'Leary, the Prince Albert SSB district superintendent, chaired a community meeting at the log hall at Paddockwood. The community was to build and maintain a suitable building, which the Red Cross would furnish and equip and for which it would provide trained staff.[86] The community got to work immediately. Situated on a hill just off the Montreal Lake Trail and near the burgeoning village of Paddockwood, the Red Cross Outpost Hospital, with its big red cross painted on the roof, could be seen for miles. It first accepted patients in September 1920. An opening ceremony attended by locals, members of the SSB, and the Red Cross was held on 8 October.[87]

A resident charge nurse took care of maternity cases, deliveries, cuts, wounds, and broken bones and dispensed medical advice. The hospital operated as a local clearing-house or triage service. Minor problems were attended immediately. Those with serious injuries or illnesses were sent to the larger hospital in Prince Albert. Doctors would visit from Prince Albert once a week, or on call as necessary, which reduced local expenses but maintained a high degree of care. A local Homemakers Club, also formed in 1920, was closely allied with the hospital and over the years donated time, money, linen, and other necessities.[88] The hospital operated continuously for almost thirty years, bringing a sense of self-sufficiency and pride to the burgeoning community.

It is hard to overestimate the implications of a local hospital for development of the Paddockwood area. At the time, though the railway had been promised, there was only a graded road between Prince Albert and Paddockwood. In dry weather, this trail was "suitable for motor traffic," an important consideration since cars were becoming more common in the Prince Albert area.[89] Most of the time, however, this trail was difficult to travel. Dominion land surveyor M.D. McCloskey pointed out in 1920 that "considerable work remains to be done on local road improvement before the needs of the vicinity will be supplied."[90] He went on to comment specifically on the settlement at Paddockwood: "Road grading gangs are working at present. ... This township is badly in need of roads and another big bridge over the Garden River."[91] Simply getting to the main road from a settler's homestead was trying. Cart tracks and trails slashed through the bush were all that could be expected of a pioneer community. If a person was sick or injured and immediate care was needed, bad roads were a complication. As settlement moved east, west, and north of the little village, transportation difficulties intensified. A hospital within the community helped to ease the fears of local settlers. In addition, the Red Cross was a universally recognized symbol of health and care. The cross-cultural appeal and recognition of the Red Cross no doubt helped Paddockwood to draw settlers to the area. Creation of the hospital in 1920 might have offset local settlement concerns caused by the delayed railway.[92]

DELAYED RAILWAY

District Superintendent O'Leary's assessment of soldier settlers "making good" in the north Prince Albert region was probably overenthusiastic. The soil might have been first class on some farms, but soil quality was not uniform. Some quarters were less arable, with more leached grey podzolic soil and less black chernozem. Muskeg and other problems of low-lying land limited cereal crop potential but provided important hay land. O'Leary's main description of the Paddockwood area—"timbered country"—told the tale. As the Buckland history book recorded, "those having places easily cleared, which had had light brush on them or had been well burned over, had a great advantage over the owners of land still covered with heavy bush or large stumps. These latter had a hard struggle to keep the pot boiling, let alone to pay off debts."[93] Large stumps, leftovers of extensive timber berths, had to be pulled out. Some stumps left holes deep enough to serve as root cellars.[94] Extensive fires had made excellent headway for clearing, but remaining deadfall, brush, and roots had to be cleared by hand, piled, and usually burned. Sometimes such burns resulted in runaway forest fires that killed more forest acres.[95] In other cases, fires went underground and consumed precious topsoil. Regardless, settlers on heavy bush homesteads had one commodity in demand on the open plains to the south: vigorous aspen regrowth could be converted into cordwood.

Local advocates understood that the CNR, as a business, was only interested in putting in *profitable* railways. The best commodity for short-term profit was cordwood. Local residents, the mayor of Prince Albert, and the Board of Trade united in their tactics. A railway would offer heavy transport capabilities so that homesteaders could turn their liabilities (trees) into assets (cordwood). To that end, these groups argued that "Paddockwood district alone can supply thirty carloads of cordwood a week for the next ten years if the railroad is built into this district. At $15 a car or $450 a week—freight charges show what revenue will be derived from this one commodity."[96] The implication was that other commodities, such as grain and cattle, would increase local revenue even further.

The communities waited in vain. By July 1919, the *Prince Albert Daily Herald* asked "what is wrong with the proposed railroad which was to be surveyed and graded this summer by the Dominion. A large amount of money has been invested and land has been taken up [at Paddockwood] with the expectation that these promises would be fulfilled."[97] The CNR replied that the line had not been started because the company had been unable to find an engineer to survey and grade the road but that work would commence soon. By early August, engineers and crews were busy.[98] For the next couple of years, expectations were high, but results on the ground were disappointing. Surveying and grading were one thing; laying steel and opening the track were quite another. The postwar recession ground progress to a halt. By 1923, there was still no railway. Local residents were indignant. In a meeting between Sir Henry Thornton, president of the CNR, and the Prince Albert Board of Trade and local representatives, Major J.H. Lindsay spoke for the Board of Trade:

We do not expect you are a wizard to just come along and lay the
steel, but so far as the Paddockwood line is concerned, in 1919, the
Government of Canada, as represented by the Soldier Settlement
Board considered that was a place which should be settled. That being
so, they placed in that district, two hundred, if I may say, returned
men. These men went into that district on a full understanding that
the line was to be constructed. These men have been waiting patiently
for its construction. They have seen the line graded but not finished.
If that line was finished then these people would be satisfied and
surely, if anyone is entitled to any consideration, then the returned
men who have settled in that district are entitled to the very best
consideration possible.[99]

The pressure of public guilt and loyalty to returned soldiers worked. The CNR succumbed and finished the line. The first train rolled into Paddockwood late in 1924.[100]

NORTHERN MIGRATION

Prince Albert celebrated when the Burns family of Calgary announced that it had chosen the city as the site of their new stockyards and meat-packing plant in 1919. Securing the stockyards was a tremendous achievement, and the *Prince Albert Daily Herald* reported it with jubilation.[101] The result of intense negotiation and heated rivalry among several cities, the stockyards heralded a significant rise in local fortunes and contributed to the popularity of the Prince Albert region as a soldier settlement and dryland resettlement destination. Cattle ranchers, long associated with southwestern Saskatchewan, looked north. Farmers and ranchers hard hit by the drought were supported by the dominion government in their efforts to secure feed or move their cattle north to graze. The temporary northern refuge became permanent for many. The *Daily Herald* exulted: "This whole north country is fine pasture land, and watered by innumerable lakes and streams. Grass grows in all the bush land ... and hay is cut around every little lake and slough. ... It will soon be a great cattle country."[102] Environment and local economics combined to recreate Prince Albert as the new ranching country.

The stockyards announcement renewed interest in the scrubland north of the soldier settlement land at Paddockwood, past Township 53. Some surveyors argued that the land was unfit for agricultural homesteading, with podzolic soil, rock, and muskeg throughout. Interest in stock raising and ranching changed the general consensus. It became common to suggest that the land, if not good enough to homestead, would make a good complement for established farmers who just needed a bit more pasture or hay land. The dominion land surveyor, M.D. McCloskey, reporting in 1920, disagreed. He cautioned that "cattle would [not] find sufficient grass until the summer is fairly well advanced."[103] He was ignored. By

1922, continued pressure pushed settlement onto marginal land, not as additional hay and pasture land, but for homesteading.[104]

Soldier settlers and drought migrants brought more and more cattle to the north Prince Albert region. The growing stock population led to both ecological and political distress, necessitating new farming techniques and intensifying local debates. In the first place, despite the praise of northern boosters, the supply of natural hay fell short of demand. One method commonly applied to stimulate extra hay involved manipulating the ecology of the Spruce and Garden Rivers. McCloskey reported that "numerous beaver dams existed along the streams, and smaller watercourses. To ensure a crop of hay in dry season [some of the settlers] close the beaver dam and keep the land flooded until June, or thereabouts, then open the dam and release the water."[105] Settlement thus generally followed the watersheds of the Spruce and Garden Rivers, or other well-watered quarters, before spreading out to other land.

Increased stock numbers placed pressure on hay resources and led to debate regarding herd laws and fencing versus free-range pasturage. Stock would benefit from accessing "waste places" not suitable for farming, but it was equally important to stop the cattle from grazing on newly sown oat, barley, and wheat fields and to keep them out of areas designated for the winter hay crop.[106] At times, a mixed farmer was torn: was his primary role to raise stock or to grow crops? Drought in the drylands, carloads of cattle shipped north to the forest reserves to graze, and requests for hay and feed permits from desperate southern farmers led to physical manipulation of the landscape through fences and flooding. The opening of commercial cattle facilities confirmed the connection between the edge landscape and more intensive diversification into stock raising, a hallmark of mixed farming as well as ranching.

The majority of settlers who initiated the considerable movement out of the Saskatchewan portion of the drybelt made this move under their own steam, with no provincial help and limited federal help. A few were given railcar relief to move their goods or pasture their cattle.[107] Settlers who managed to sell their farms in the south could move their stock and machinery north. If they had already homesteaded in the south and had proved up, then they could not homestead again, so they were forced to purchase or rent improved land.[108] In 1923, the Department of the Interior allowed "second homesteads" in the northern settlements for those who had to abandon the drybelt. Second homesteads were a targeted and strictly controlled measure by the federal government "to provide for the removal of homesteaders from the southern part of Saskatchewan, the drought area, to the northern part."[109] Too many, though, after years of trying to hold on in the south, arrived in the Prince Albert region with little or no capital left, their stock sold and their machinery repossessed by creditors.[110] It was a difficult prospect, at best, to start again under such conditions.

THE POSTWAR DEPRESSION

The settlement at Paddockwood—original homesteaders, soldier settlers, and in-coming dryland disaster refugees—faced the same agricultural pressures as did other farmers across the dominion. Despite the best intentions of the SSB to ease loans by negotiating farm prices and purchasing supplies in bulk, the soldiers took their loans and bought machinery and stock when prices were at their postwar peak. In the fall of 1920, agricultural commodities began a long financial slide that affected both stock and grain prices for several years. Historian Kent Fedorowich claimed that "the cost-price squeeze ushered in a period of failure, foreclosure, abandonment and indebtedness which haunted soldier settlers and politicians alike throughout the inter-war period."[111] The postwar recession hit those who had pur-chased their farms—the majority of SSB clients—particularly hard. As the difficult years went on and abysmal prices continued, soldiers with substantial loans either abandoned their farms or demanded that the government re-evaluate and renegoti-ate loans on land, stock, and machinery.[112]

Settlers in places such as Paddockwood on a combination of homestead and soldier grant land carried less debt than did their counterparts elsewhere and thus were somewhat better off than those who had purchased not only stock and equip-ment but entire farms at wartime high prices. The Toronto *Globe* reported on the successes and problems of soldier settlement in 1922. Major Barnett of the SSB was quoted as saying that "the men that are getting along best and the men that are paying best are quite clearly and unmistakably those who are working slowly, who have no large cash crops of any kind, but whose revenue is made up of dribbles from this and little dabs from that, a few dollars here and a few dollars there." Barnett continued: "These men are paying their way as they go. Their success from year to year is not large, but neither are their disappointments great, and there is never the bitter disillusionment that follows when the crop that was expected to realize thousands of dollars turns out an utter failure." Barnett was mouthing the mixed-farming rhetoric. The SSB continued to believe that mixed farming provided soldiers with resiliency and a sure path. The *Globe* went on to generalize from his observations, suggesting that "the settlement of the West will proceed on a more secure foundation if the 'one crop' idea is relegated to the background and the land is used primarily for the purpose of raising a sufficient variety of foodstuffs for man and beast to assure the tiller of the soil against the catastrophe that in re-cent years has too frequently overtaken the land miners of the prairies."[113]

Yet the mixed-farming rhetoric went only so far. When McCloskey toured the Paddockwood region in 1920, he found "all the settlers interviewed were satisfied with their holdings but stated that the land was difficult to clear and that without capital a settler would be obliged to spend a portion of that time working out in order to obtain funds to carry him along when improving his homestead."[114] The Paddockwood soldier settlers might have had fewer loans to pay back, but they, along with other soldier settlers across the forested regions of the dominion, also had the hardest uphill battle to clear and open their land to make it pay.[115] As local residents David Dunn and Frank Stoddart knew, farming required capital, mixed farming required more capital, and mixed farming at the ecotone required both time and money to create the land in the first place. As a result, "the enormous amounts of time, energy and money required to bring the land under cultivation proved too much for some."[116] The natural environment also took its toll: "Frequent and early frosts, hail, flooding and drought wiped out even the best and most determined soldier settlers."[117] Overcome by the dual prongs of agricultural price deflation and natural calamities, many soldier settlers across Canada (including those who took land along the forest fringe) were forced to give up, leaving historians with little choice but to call the overall program a failure.

In the Prince Albert region, however, the statistics tell a somewhat different tale. Although not justifying the booster-style exhortations of mixed-farming supporters, the local story adds an important layer of detail to the overall soldier settlement story. By 1927, the Prince Albert office of the SSB had almost twice as many soldier settlers on soldier grants established *without* loans as it did men *with* loans. It also had a higher number of overall settlers compared with Saskatoon and Regina combined: active entries in 1927 were 2,112 in Prince Albert, 1,294 in Regina, and only 494 in Saskatoon. Of course, there were also cancellations from the Prince Albert office: from an original 3,458 soldier grants in the district to 1927, 1,346 had been abandoned or cancelled.[118] The cancellation numbers (39 percent)—despite the aims of the SSB, the supposed advantages of mixed farming, and the policies of intensive ongoing support through loans, advice, and the Home Branch—were similar to the abandonment and cancellation averages from all of Saskatchewan (including what was considered good agricultural land) of the prewar years. On the surface, it appears that the intensive and ongoing support was not making a difference. Abandonment, cancellations, and desertions were not any worse, though, despite complications of forested land and a severe economic deflation.[119] These statistics (which, at over 60 percent, should be seen as successful) stand in contrast to those who tend to refer to soldier settlement as a failure—a failure that depended at least in part on *where* the farm was located and *which* kind of farming was done there.

ASSISTED LAND SETTLEMENT EXPANSION

Soldier land abandonment created a new set of problems for the Soldier Settlement Board. Farms reverted to the SSB, which found itself the owner of empty, unproductive farms. The SSB had a support structure suitable for facilitating extensive agricultural settlement, including its successful Home Branch, loan system, purchasing system, land base, and inspectors. As early as 1922, various groups were calling for the SSB to expand its services to look after the needs of civilian settlers. The *Globe* pointed out the wisdom of accessing SSB experience for general land settlement: "The placing of thousands of returned soldiers on the land involved the consideration of many difficulties that [also] confront the civilian settler. The solution in both cases must be the same." Since the methods of soldier settlement have "proven successful," the *Globe* went on, "there is every reason to suppose that they would be equally effective in continuing the work of settlement hereafter for the benefit of civilians." The paper urged the government to make the SSB service available in a broader mandate.[120] In conjunction, there was pressure to open dominion land previously held exclusively for soldiers to civilian settlement. In response, the SSB was transferred to the auspices of the Department of Immigration and Colonization. It was reformed to encourage civilian settlement, becoming the Land Settlement Branch.[121]

One program developed to take over forfeited SSB land was the 3,000 British Families scheme.[122] To alleviate continued shortages in Britain in the postwar era, British families were encouraged to emigrate to Canada to take up farming. The British government advanced loans of $1,500, and the Canadian government supplied land and support through the Land Settlement Branch using the old SSB infrastructure.[123] The railways also pushed for a return to prewar immigration. They petitioned the government to give the railways a more active role in recruiting immigrants. The federal Railways Agreement, signed in 1925, allowed the CNR to create its Department of Colonization and Agriculture. This move to promote agricultural immigration complemented the CPR's land settlement branch. The CNR, however, supported primarily northern development areas where its main and branch lines were located. The head of the CN Department of Colonization and Development, Dr. W.J. Black, was a Manitoba chairman of the Soldier Settlement Board. The CNR colonization platform declared that it would "encourage

Figure 15. M. Brodacki family, 1929. Settled at Paddockwood through the CNR land settlement scheme. Source: SAB, R-A32659.

in every way possible the development of mixed farming and better farming methods."[124] The CNR owned the railway north from Prince Albert to Paddockwood and brought in settlers along that line.[125]

The majority of CNR settlers took over homesteads that had been proved up and then put up for sale. Real estate agent E.T. Bagshaw of Prince Albert claimed that "often where a small shack had been built, and a few acres cleared and broke round about the buildings the abandonment of the farm meant the buildings were falling to pieces, and what small piece of land had been cultivated in the past reverted to seeds and sod, and desolation reigned."[126] Real estate agencies had many quarter sections for sale in the north Prince Albert region, proved up for title and hastily put up for sale. Once a quarter was proved up and patented, it was open to taxation. To pay taxes, a farmer *in situ* often traded work with the municipality or local improvement district, doing jobs such as building roads and bridges.[127] Landowners who left to pursue other opportunities had to pay taxes out of their own pockets, so often they were anxious to sell. Some land changed hands for little more than taxes owing.[128] To their credit, though, titled farms near developed communities usually offered better farmland and prospects than the new homesteads farther north that edged swamps, muskegs, and rocks into Township 54.

The two colonization schemes epitomized a major divide within Canadian postwar colonization. The first, the 3,000 British Families scheme, favoured British settlement and built on the infrastructure of the SSB (used by both Canadian and British soldiers). The railways, in contrast, pushed for immigration from wherever it would come, including continental and eastern Europe.[129] CNR colonization agents were particularly accepting of the ethnic "group settlement" strategy. As a result, the north Prince Albert region, with its existing network of Ruthenian (Polish and Ukrainian) settlement along the Garden River, was targeted for more settlers from these countries. Henribourg and the east Paddockwood district drew extensive eastern European immigration.[130]

Both colonization schemes also encouraged internal migration and recolonization within Canada, particularly within Saskatchewan. Settlers from southern regions could apply to either the dominion Land Settlement Board or the CNR and access land and loans, facilitating an easier transition to the ecologically mixed landscape of the northern regions.

The ongoing work of the SSB as the Land Settlement Board, the colonization work of the CNR along the Paddockwood branch line, and continuing south-to-north migration from the arid regions throughout the 1920s swelled settlement in the north Prince Albert region. Between 1925 and 1927, the Department of the Interior noted a steadily rising demand for new homesteads in Saskatchewan, rising from 2,363 in 1925 to 2,961 in 1927, the majority of them taken along the parkland and forest edge. New homesteads were fuelled by a combination of natural growth, northern drift of southern migrants, and immigration from outside Canada.

The steadily rising homestead numbers throughout the 1920s were swamped by a rapid increase in 1928, when a whopping 5,808 homesteads were taken, and a further 6,089 in 1929.[131] The increase came when the Department of the Interior opened Crown land to permit second homesteads to the general population. Farmers who had successfully completed all the requirements for their first homesteads by 1 January 1925 could apply for second homestead grants. The majority of these second homesteads were taken in northern regions.[132]

The northern movement in the latter half of the 1920s was not built on either economic crisis or environmental disaster. For a brief period, prosperity, rather than paucity, led the movement. Agricultural returns on the prairie had improved, as had prices and markets. Saskatchewan farms were diversifying at a fantastic rate, expanding the crop base beyond wheat to include more oats, barley, and other grains and increasing animal production. Although the diversification movement could be found across the province, it was a noticeable aspect of the northern surge. Owing in part to concurrent growth in urban areas, the number of milk cows in Saskatchewan rose dramatically from 225,000 in 1918 to almost 500,000 in 1925.[133] Oats and barley, crops that grew well in northern conditions, also increased. Wheat remained the major cash crop on *all* farms, prairie and northern. After 1925, when wheat prices recovered from their postwar slump, wheat contributed significantly to the overall wealth of the province's farmers.

One outlet for that wealth was mechanization, and historian Bill Waiser claimed that mechanization in the 1920s "began a revolution in Saskatchewan farming whose repercussions are still being experienced today."[134] Larger acreages could be planted and harvested far more quickly, adding to farm wealth and security. With adoption of the gasoline tractor and development of brush-breaking equipment, the prospect of clearing and breaking a northern bush homestead was less daunting.[135] Researchers at the University of Saskatchewan actively engaged in developing and testing brush-cutting machines, finding a mechanical solution to clearing acreage for agricultural purposes on northern land. Evan Hardy, a professor of agricultural engineering, wrote to Deputy Minister of Agriculture F.H. Auld in 1928, noting that "ten acres was all that one man could cut by hand in a year, and that [one farmer] was almost able to cut 10 acres a day with his John Deere tractor and brush cutter."[136] Brush cutting was necessary on land where the trees were too small to be valuable for timber or cordwood but too large to permit agricultural development. Land with recent burns, willows, and young poplars could be cleared efficiently with the technology. The move to northern farms in the latter half of the 1920s was facilitated by the opportunity to acquire a second homestead, contemporary agricultural affluence, and mechanization.

CONCLUSION

The sometimes tragic consequences of unsupported homestead settlement leading up to the Great War led the dominion government to radically change its settlement policies. Instead of a *laissez-faire*, sink or swim, attitude, the federal government initiated significant investment in the settlement process beyond simply enticing people onto the land. Soldier Settlement Board policies put both the land and the settler under closer scrutiny, emphasizing their fit. Loans, targeted purchasing power, sweeping land power, and investment in training became hallmarks. Women and their needs moved to centre stage along with health and welfare. Soldier settlement marked a significant new direction in dominion land settlement policies and should be viewed along this continuum. It laid the foundation for later settlement strategies, including the Land Settlement Branch, the 3,000 British Families scheme, the colonization departments of the railways, and the opening of second homesteads. All of these schemes were important in opening up new agricultural and potential resource lands along the forest edge and in changing the face of agricultural development and support in Canada.

Flipped on its back, the question becomes: did the forest edge have a significant impact on the direction and prosecution of soldier settlement and, by extension, later land settlement or resettlement schemes? The answer, clearly, is yes. Although dominion loan policies were agile enough to help soldiers across a range of personal situations and ecological opportunities across the country, the SSB directed its attention to a particular *kind* of farming. The push to promote mixed-farming practices directed soldier settlers, if and when possible, onto ecologically mixed land that contained forest, meadow, and water. Soldier settlement became the poster child of a distinct move away from wheat mining and toward ecologically and economically mixed farming.

Soldier settlement also had a significant impact on the agricultural growth and development of *this* edge place. The push for mixed farming meshed well with the promotional activity provided by the Prince Albert Board of Trade for the region north of the city. Moreover, the devastating fires of 1919 helped to purge the old timber berths. Renewed green growth enticed mixed farmers and ranchers to the northern regions, encouraged by both the landscape and the economic opportunities of the new stockyards and meat-packing plant at Prince Albert. The ongoing drought in the southwest corner of the province, the old Palliser Triangle, also redirected settlement efforts to the forested, mixed-farming region.

Beyond all of these changes, though, lies an important point: mixed farmers at the forest edge engaged in much more than farming. They moved north to engage in a mixed *lifestyle* that combined mixed farming and opportunities and products of the forest edge landscape.

CHAPTER SIX

POOR MAN'S PARADISE

In 1919, land settlement adviser A. McOwan, writing in the *Prince Albert Daily Herald,* claimed that the north was "a Poor Man's Paradise." "There may be no bonanza," he wrote, "but from the first day of entering it the adaptable man with initiative is assured of sustenance through all seasons and the reward of industry and thrift is the certainty of a margin and ultimate independence." It was determined advertising, repositioning the region as a mecca for those with little capital. The promise of small but incremental gains, providing self-sufficiency and leading to independence, was a hallmark of mixed-farming rhetoric. McOwan went on to claim grandly that "the north country is no country for the slacker or the faint-hearted. ... I often think that the man who has least to lose progresses most rapidly." The north region, he believed, would reward brave men who worked hard—a positive way of positioning the backbreaking work of making a living on a forest homestead. Economic success would be found by marketing the following list of products: "grain, potatoes, small fruit, vegetables, Seneca root, hay, cattle, hogs, sheep, poultry, fish, venison, eggs, butter, furs, lumber, cordwood, fence posts, and such a seasonable necessity as Christmas trees."[1] McOwan advocated a mixed-farming base that combined not only products typical of a mixed farm (eggs, butter, cattle, hogs, sheep, and poultry) but also products particular to the forest edge environment: venison, furs, lumber, cordwood, fence posts, Seneca root, and Christmas trees.

To the weary drylander wrung out by crop failures and drought, McOwan's list of northern products seemed a cornucopia of simple but basic delights. Promoters worked hard to connect the forest edge with cheap living, recreating the north Prince Albert region as a destination for poor but ambitious and hard-working immigrants. Unfortunately, the variety of products blithely listed did not tell the whole story. A settler needed at least some money to invest. A good milk cow cost $40 to $50, a yoke of oxen $100, and a team of horses $350. Stock diversification was expensive.[2] The natural products of the land were supposed to make the difference for incoming settlers as ways to generate, or save, capital. The fact that permits and licences, guns, ammunition, traps, knives, saws, axes, and grubhoes were needed—and cost money—was glossed over.

Prince Albert took pride in and actively created its "northern" identity, taking as its motto "Gateway to the North." A northern identity, though, had a few drawbacks. Local historian R. Mayson suggested that "twelve persons could be asked about Prince Albert and ten would answer that it is the door to the Arctic Circle and one step across the threshold of the frozen north would send its icy blasts to the marrow. Even so well-informed a person as Lady Macdonald said in one of her published letters that "'Prince Albert is the most northerly city in the world.'"[3] Nonetheless, the city thrived on its northern gateway identity. It became the pivot point of the two solitudes of resource boreal north and settled agricultural south in the western interior—an edge place where the two "personalities" of the province combined.

The dual role of agriculture and off-farm resources suggested the growing connection between mixed farming and the forest landscape. Mixed farming was a traditional agricultural practice and at the ecotone took the idea several steps further. It became a place-based idea that encouraged combining on-farm products and off-farm forest resources. It was a good place in which to live and from which to draw other products or sources of income—an excellent interpretation that reflected older, First Nations models. Considering the deep-time history of human use that deliberately drew from a mixed resource base, it was painfully ironic that the First Nations families at Little Red River and Sturgeon Lake Reserves, well versed in using local resources, were denigrated for doing so. Despite diversified landscape use, which would eloquently satisfy McOwan's list of forest and farm resources, these First Nations continued to fend off attacks from those who wanted their land. At the same time, non-Native homesteaders were encouraged and applauded for tenacity and inventiveness in pulling a living from off-farm opportunities in the local landscape.

Off-farm industrial opportunities in the north Prince Albert region were varied. Timber was an important industry until 1919, when devastating fires swept through the landscape. Nonetheless, trees remained, including a new rank growth of poplar. Timber was largely replaced by a full cordwood and railway tie industry, particularly after branch railway lines snaked through the region in the postwar era. The large lakes supported commercial fisheries. Prince Albert remained a major centre of the fur industry and kept its important north-south links to the communities of the Churchill River system. A growing interest in mines and minerals contributed to a northward surge. Underpinning the growth of industry, though, was transportation. The old east-west water-based "highways" of the Churchill and the Saskatchewan were replaced by a north-south overland link that crossed the ecotone. Moving away from the rivers meant flipping the region from river to landscape-based knowledge—good tree stands, potential mineral sites, large lakes—that signalled new knowledge, control, and use of Saskatchewan's northern reach. Land transportation links connected the communities in new ways and for different reasons. Soon overland freighters moved goods in both directions, serving the new industrial businesses. All of these off-farm opportunities were dominant "pull" factors that encouraged migration. The ability to draw a living from several possibilities—"occupational pluralism"[4]—and an extensive barter economy took the community beyond a basic mixed-farming practice to develop a cultural, social, and economic lifestyle rooted in the landscape.

OVERLAND FREIGHTING

Nothing changed the face of transportation across western Canada like the railway.[5] For northern regions, railways started the long decline of northern supply and shipping posts, including hardship for Aboriginal people who derived important income from the water transportation empire as York boat and canoe builders, paddlers, freight haulers, lumbermen, and suppliers. For many, canoe and York boat freighting provided a means of summer employment and wage labour, often used to supplement winter trapping and hunting returns.[6] Yet northern communities still required goods and services, and in truth the fur-trade empire "remained strong and vibrant and expanded in the north until after the Second World War."[7] Trading companies and the federal government were both anxious to find efficient transportation links.

Northern historians tend to refer to overland freighting in passing, as part of a general discussion on the problems of northern transportation and development or as one of several options for moving goods from one place to another.[8] For provincial north historians of Manitoba and Alberta, water transportation remained an important component, with much of both the north-south Athabasca and Peace Rivers in Alberta, and the extensive large lake system of Manitoba, navigable by steamers. Developers would link rail lines to the most southern navigable point, creating an effective rail-to-water system. Yet the implications of overland freighting deserve greater attention as an early critical transformation link to the modern northern highway system used today. Such attention would also explore questions of seasonality, encompass the shift from horse transport to industrial gasoline and diesel vehicles, and consider weight and the boreal environment as compounding factors. Saskatchewan serves as an exemplary case study, for the natural waterways move east-west rather than north-south. There were few natural (water) or human-made (rail) corridors into or out of its north country. Funnelling goods into and out of the far northern communities in Saskatchewan required road building and the services of overland freighters.

If the lumber industry exploded in the immediate Prince Albert area following completion of the Qu'Appelle, Long Lake, and Saskatchewan rail line in 1890, other industries were also quick to take advantage of this new transportation route. Completion of the railway to Prince Albert dovetailed with several regional interests, in particular those of the Indian Department and the Hudson's Bay Company. The treaty party that met First Nations bands at the north end of Montreal Lake in 1889 to sign the adhesion to Treaty 6 was lucky. It was winter, and the party sleighed up the rude cart trail past Red Deer Lake (Waskesiu) and then through the bush to Montreal Lake, carrying the traditional gifts that normally accompanied a treaty signing. These gifts included flour, tea, bacon, and tobacco in addition to treaty medals, flags, and money. Goods had been purchased at local trading posts.[9]

Sledding up in the frozen winter was one thing; delivering yearly treaty payments following the successful adhesion created a host of transportation problems. Treaty payments were much more extensive than treaty gifts and included agricultural implements such as plows, large quantities of food and seed, twine, ammunition, clothing, and miscellaneous goods. The sheer bulk of these items posed a serious logistical problem for the Indian Department. It asked Reverend J.A. Mackay of Prince Albert for advice on how to go about making the payments effectively and efficiently. He suggested that it would be better to ship the goods for the La Ronge band by canoe through Grand Rapids and Cumberland and from there north to the Churchill system following the old fur-trade routes.

For supplies destined for Montreal Lake, Mackay offered a radical idea: "It would be an immense advantage if the cart road were opened to Montreal Lake. This would do away with all difficulties in the way of transport. The road has been commenced and I believe about $200 judiciously spent would complete it."[10] Asking the Indian Department to build a road revealed the costs involved in not only purchasing treaty supplies but also freighting them to their destinations. Treaties changed the relationship between Euro-Canadian newcomers and First Nations: it was no longer primarily a business relationship between two relatively equal partners. Whereas fur-trade companies factored in freight transportation as part of their costs and included the people and infrastructure required, the dominion government had to look to outside contractors to support its new treaty-based relationship with First Nations.

Mackay directed the Indian Department to contact a local trading and supply firm, Stobart and Company, to see if it would freight in the treaty supplies. Hillyard Mitchell, the proprietor, replied with surprising bluntness: the route north from Prince Albert using the cart road to Red Deer Lake (Waskesiu), then by river to Montreal Lake, "would be both risky and expensive, and I would not care to undertake it except at your risk and expense." The cart trail connected Prince Albert to Red Deer Lake. From there, canoes could travel on the Red Deer River to the south end of Montreal Lake. Brigades went north across the lake to the Montreal River and up that river to Lac La Ronge. The weak link in this route was the water level of the Red Deer River. It was never reliable for navigation, and canoe brigades faced low water levels and several gruelling portages. Low water in the river and the heavy amount of supplies complicated matters, Mitchell said. Canoes could not carry those weights if the water was low. He concurred with Mackay's suggestion, stating that "the N.W. Government last year expended $150 on a road cutting from Deer Lake toward the South End of Montreal Lake about 15 miles was cut (being about half the distance) the balance could be cut for about the same amount, thereby opening a cart road direct from Prince Albert to Montreal Lake." From that point, it was a one-day sail or paddle up the lake to the north end, where the treaty had been signed during the winter. "Until this road is cut," Mitchell went on, "I may say there is no practicable road to Montreal Lake during summer (excepting heavy rain rising the water in Deer River) except via Cumberland and Stanley. This is a long distance round and it would pay your Dept. to at once open the road mentioned." Freight costs on the portion of the road that was usable were high: Mitchell cited $2.50 to $3.00 per 100 pounds overland; canoe freight was fifty cents per pound cheaper but only on the lakes.[11]

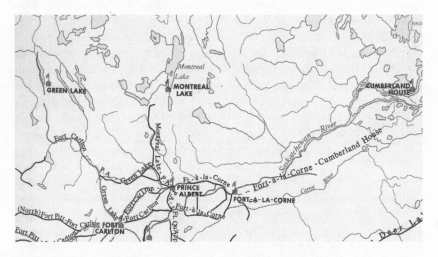

Map 10. Trails near Prince Albert, c. late 1800s. Note that the Montreal Lake Trail did not reach Montreal Lake.
Source: *Atlas of Saskatchewan*, 1969, 11. Used with permission.

Considering the lucrative government contract, Mitchell's letter underscored the precarious nature of industry and transportation through the boreal forest. Mitchell was reluctant at best to take on the logistics of transport and refused to take on the cost and risk except at the Indian Department's insistence and payment. Unless the department put forward the money to finish the road, he recommended that it freight the supplies to Cumberland House and then north to Stanley Mission on the Churchill River, using the old river transportation route.

Or perhaps the department could convince the bands to meet at his post at Red Deer Lake and have them take charge of moving the goods.

Mitchell's assessment of road conditions and freight rates scared the Indian Department. Hayter Reed, in an uncharacteristic spending spree, ordered the department to find money to finish the road. Costly in the short term, it would save money in the long term. Yearly treaty payments would be made more easily, and the road would help future freight, communication, and survey parties.[12] It was commissioned and cut, and most of the treaty supplies were sent in by wagon to the south end of Montreal Lake and then in canoes north in time for the treaty payment in mid-September 1889. The old canoe transportation route through Cumberland House to Stanley Mission, recommended by Mitchell for treaty payments for the La Ronge band, was soon superseded by the new overland route. The completed road to Montreal Lake initiated the overland freighting industry in the Prince Albert region, linking the railway to the northern communities.

The Hudson's Bay Company immediately grasped the implications of the new trail as a cheaper transportation route to Lac La Ronge and Stanley Mission. The company used the old cart trail to Red Deer Lake to service its post at The Narrows, listed in the *McPhillips' Saskatchewan Directory* in 1888. The new trail marked new opportunity. In previous years, the Hudson's Bay Company had shipped its goods via the Churchill system or the North Saskatchewan by canoe brigade or steamship to Carlton Post. From there, the long-established overland cart road to Green Lake was in constant use. The Green Lake route had its own problems, though. It was a long haul, parts of it impassable in wet weather. At its terminus, it accessed the Beaver River system north to Île-à-la-Crosse, which in dry weather was not navigable. This, of course, was a two-pronged dilemma: too wet and the goods could not be shipped; too dry and the goods could not be shipped. In 1885, Carlton Post was burned by accident during events surrounding the rebellion, ending its role as a shipping point on the supply chain. Prince Albert took over Carlton's role, from the HBC post known as Fort Albert.[13]

As soon as the new cart road all the way to Montreal Lake was finished, the HBC shipped a small portion of its northern supplies to Prince Albert by rail, then overland using this route. Historian Bill Waiser explained that the initial trial must have been a success, because "the following season the Company shipped all of the district's supplies north from Prince Albert and established a large depot on the southwest shore of Montreal Lake."[14] The HBC also moved its post to Montreal Lake and began operations there, effectively making the post at Red Deer Lake redundant. It was closed by 1893. Within one year of its establishment, the cart road from Prince Albert to the south end of Montreal Lake became a major north-south artery, frequented by freighters serving the HBC, the Indian Department, local traders, First Nations, and lumbermen. Teams of horses, ponies, or oxen could be regularly seen plying this new route.

In many ways, overland freighting north of Prince Albert extended transportation practices common in the western interior of North America. In what became western Canada, freighting was a distinctly Métis industry. Métis supplied inland fur-trade posts (mostly on the prairie) and hauled the meat, hides, and pemmican of the massive yearly buffalo hunt to supply posts on the canoe brigade routes.[15] The height of western cart freighting from the 1860s through the 1880s coincided with the development of railways south of the border and to Winnipeg. Goods and messages brought cheaply and quickly to Minnesota or Manitoba were freighted overland to the posts in the interior over the Carlton-Edmonton trail.[16] Similar trails were used by "bullwhackers" running large shipments of goods from Fort Benton in Montana north to Fort Macleod, and early settlers followed these trails, establishing farms. The difference in twentieth-century freighting lay in its relation to the ecotone and its new and developing knowledge of the boreal environment.

Overland transportation stitched the prairie south to the boreal north and offered economic opportunities for both First Nations and local homesteaders. Men could take contracts for individual freighting trips, work as contract teamsters for a company, or supply farm produce, hay, and oats either to the freighters or to the wholesalers. Such options appealed to those who were developing forest edge farms. Often these men had stock or families to look after and tended to prefer or require short-term employment or a service role rather than a full winter commitment in a bush logging camp. Freighting developed a co-dependent relationship with local farmers (both Aboriginal and non-Aboriginal): when farming was slack in the winter, freighting was a viable opportunity to make some much-needed cash money; in the summer, putting up hay and growing oats for the freighters injected cash into the local economy. A manpower- and horsepower-intense activity, successful freight hauls required freighters, strong teams of horses, sleighs, and large amounts of hay and feed oats. Records of the Department of Indian Affairs and annual reports of the Indian agents indicated that many First Nations men found employment. The Indian Department reported in 1900 that "freighting ... enables some to make a comfortable living without assistance from the agency."[17] In 1901, W.B. Goodfellow, the Indian agent at Carlton Agency, reported that in William Twatt's band (now Sturgeon Lake First Nation) "some are hired by lumbermen; others earn money by freighting or putting up hay."[18]

First Nations communities, both along the forest edge and deeper in the boreal forest, participated in overland freighting. In addition to work as teamsters in the winter, First Nations men were often engaged to cut and stack hay for stopping places and barns along the freight trails. In summer, many had employment improving trails, laying corduroy roads, stacking cordwood, and building or fixing barns and shacks. HBC magazine *The Beaver* noted in its "Stanley Notes" of December 1920 that "there was plenty of work all summer at Stanley Post and vicinity. The Brooks Construction Company was engaged in repairing and making stables, leveling portages, and putting up hay."[19] Men from Little Red River Reserve could commonly be found on the freight trail or helping to operate the stopping place on the reserve. Billy Bear, a noted Cree man from Little Red, engaged several of his neighbours in his freighting business in addition to his farm operations. Through to the First World War, forest fringe bands reported considerable income through freighting. As non-Aboriginal settlers penetrated the forest fringe, occupying cut-over timber berths and commencing farming operations, they began to crowd out the Aboriginal freighters. Details are sketchy and numbers are not available, but both oral and written documentation and photographs seem to show a decline—but never a complete absence—of Aboriginal men in freighting and lumbering after the First World War.

Figure 16. Freighting swing at Prince Albert.
Source: Prince Albert Historical Society (PAHS), T-133.

SEASONALITY

Overland freighting was never a successful summer activity, despite completion of the cart trail. Boreal forest trails were generally incapable of supporting heavy wagon loads of goods. Indeed, Montreal Lake HBC employee Sydney Keighley recalled a particularly brutal stretch of trail south of the lake on the cart trail where "a wagon entering it immediately sank to the axles. The stretch was corduroyed but the logs were constantly sinking out of sight." To shore up the road, wagon drivers were forced to improvise, adding road-building to their boreal repertoires. "Axes and hatchets were standard traveling equipment in that area, as there was no possibility of getting a load of any weight at all through the muskeg without building impromptu corduroy roads," Keeley explained. A corduroy road was made by chopping logs and placing them crossways on the road to form an instant roadbed. All northern roads contained corduroy over soft spots.[20] The muskegs, endless sinkholes of water, sedges, and black, tarry ooze, claimed wagon axles and snapped wheels. They were also terrible on animals, which became hopelessly stuck and had to be pulled out by the neck. Black flies and mosquitoes added to the misery of both horse and man.

Freighting on northern boreal trails found its niche as a winter activity and developed into a significant regional winter occupation. The proverbial Canadian winter froze water and muskeg, offering a more efficient roadbed, easing passage over muskeg and creek, and providing wide open highways on frozen lakes. The cart trail became a passable, even good, winter freight trail, and freighters chose slightly deviated routes to take advantage of natural low-lying (and treeless) features of the landscape. Bush trails were heavier going, with deep snow and soft patches as well as rocks and ridges that could overturn a sleigh. Breaking trail with a full load would exhaust the horses.[21] Winter trails designed for horses deliberately crossed flat natural landscapes, but even lakes had their drawbacks. Drifts had to be plowed. Freighters usually travelled in "swings" of several sleighs and horse teams, which gave tremendous force to the plow in front of the lead team, shearing through snowbanks and pressure ridges to create a road. Cracks in the ice or slush holes were other hazards, particularly after a storm, when fresh snow would cover open water. Experienced horses would stop at the first sign of water; others plowed ahead and sank. If a team did go through, it was a struggle to retrieve both the horses and the load.[22] Even if the horses were pulled out alive, severe hypothermia would claim them if the freighter was unable to get them warm and dry. Through the years, hundreds of horses were lost on the freight trails.[23]

When possible, freighters tried to have a paying load in both directions—from the railhead heading north, and from the north coming back south. In some cases, they were paid to bring back furs from the major fur-trading companies. Prince Albert remained the centre of the fur industry in Saskatchewan, and most furs funnelled through the Hudson's Bay Company, its rival Révillon Frères, or smaller merchants such as Stobart and Company, which traded furs for groceries and supplies. These companies usually moved their Saskatchewan fur caches south to the railhead and urban fur market using overland freighters.

FREIGHT ECONOMICS

Overland freighting became a major component of the Prince Albert commercial enterprise. Contracts to haul supplies north came from the HBC, Révillon Frères, the Canadian government, First Nations reserves, fish and mining camps, stopping places, and private trappers throughout the north. Freighting was a subsidiary enterprise that allowed companies such as lumber and fishing camps to concentrate on their businesses and leave the logistics of supply freighting to others. Overland freighting on northern winter roads provided employment to a wide range of people. Loads varied, and over the years the types of supplies typically hauled

Figure 17. Crossing a northern lake with a freight swing. Note the plow in front.
Source: http://www.jkcc.com.

Figure 18. Freight swing with fish boxes.
Source: http://www.jkcc.com.

by freighters changed. Before the First World War, freight loads tended to favour supplies typical to an HBC post: flour, sugar, tobacco, dry goods and linens, frozen food, blankets, kerosene and lamps, kitchenware, harness and repair items, and occasionally canoes or stoves. As small gasoline engines became more common, outboard motors and drums of gasoline and oil were added to the list, connecting winter freighting opportunities with summer requirements. Supplies specific to certain industries carried their own challenges. For example, lumber companies sometimes requested bulky and heavy sawmill equipment that often had to be taken apart for transport. Commercial fisheries needed nets and boxes as well as food and clothing for the fishermen. As prospectors discovered significant mineral deposits, large mining equipment, drilling rigs, and engines were common loads— and far too heavy and large for York boat, canoe, or barge. Items were sacked and crated in large amounts: bags of flour or sugar weighed 100 pounds each, a drum of gasoline 300 pounds. The freighter and his team carried their own supplies as well, from hay and oats to a grub box, bed roll, basic toolbox, and change of dry clothing. Freighters gauged their loads carefully, depending on the size of the team, the route, and the strength of the sleigh.

At railway points such as Big River or Prince Albert, the noise was deafening in the early winter. John Brooks, who homesteaded in the Meath Park area of the north Prince Albert region, recalled the scene: "Every train into Big River was now swelling the population of this distributing centre to the north. It was the third week in November, 1928 and the town was a hive of activity." Everyone from commercial fishermen to freighters to "tie hackers," who cut railway ties, "were everywhere getting lined up for a job, getting their winter gear or just waiting for enough ice to travel. Blacksmiths were a busy lot, their anvils' ringing could be heard at all the major Companies' barns where horses were being shod all round in readiness for the freight road."[24] This description underscored the economic impacts of northern freighting on forest edge communities. As an example of the scale of the industry, on 15 January 1919, sixteen teams left Prince Albert in one day.[25] The *Daily Herald* reported each winter on the departure and arrival of freight swings, conditions along the trails and across the lakes, and news from the northern communities. The freight trails became a critical point of connection and exchange between the prairie south and the boreal north.

Individual freighters had two choices: they could hire their services to a freighting company as a teamster (driver) for a base pay of twenty to forty dollars per month, or sometimes one dollar per day, or they could become private contractors and use their own team and sleigh, negotiating with a supplier for rates based on load weight and distance. Professional freighting companies negotiated contracts with large businesses, then hired teamsters to take to the trail. The R.D. Brooks Company of Prince Albert, for example, held contracts with the HBC.[26] Livery barns also took contracts, then hired freighters. A 1919 advertisement from Prince Albert read thus: "Wanted immediately: 20 or 25 teams for freighting to Montreal Lake, Lac La Ronge and Stanley. Apply W.C. McKay or Star Livery."[27] A private contractor with his own team and sleigh could expect to earn about $300 to $400 per trip. Most hoped to make two to three trips a season, each lasting from two to four weeks, depending on distance, ice pack, and weather.[28] Private freighters looked to haul payloads in both directions to earn the most pay. Boxes were constructed to be "knocked down" to conserve space so that freighters could include them in their loads going north. After dropping off supplies, teams would visit local fish camps to load these boxes. Frozen fish, usually whitefish or lake trout, were hauled back and shipped to both Canadian and American cities. Each sleigh could carry about seventy boxes of fish, each weighing 150 pounds.[29] Freighters sold the fish for between one and five cents per pound.

A high proportion of income for a private freighter went into horse feed, warm clothing, food, and other supplies for the trip. Farmers who already had feed, horses, and a good sleigh could earn more than those who had to purchase such goods. But the risks were higher too. The trail was a harsh way to make a living. Broken equipment, and dead or weakened horses, had to be replaced by the contract freighter out of his pocket. Men who took up freighting as a winter occupation took paying loads up the Montreal Lake Trail to La Ronge, Green Lake, or other points along northern routes. Soldier settler David Dunn was a typical example. He would take one to three loads north every winter as a way to earn cash to build his farm.[30] Despite its risks and drawbacks, freighting fit well with northern homestead operations since the men were away on a freight haul for a shorter period of time than a winter commitment to a cordwood, tie, or commercial fishing camp. Wives and children left on the farms could manage with the help of neighbours.

COMMERCIAL FISHING

Overland freighting tied in with burgeoning commercial fisheries. In fact, the growth of fishing as a commercial enterprise led to an intriguing shift in freighting contracts. Hauling fish back for the large commercial fisheries or as private enterprise came to be viewed as the primary freight, offering the best profit. Other supplies going north were of secondary consideration.[31] Commercial fishing began on lakes close to Prince Albert as early as the 1890s, when Candle Lake, Big Trout (Crean) Lake, and Montreal Lake were fished. As with the lumber industry, commercial fishing was a winter occupation. Before mechanized cold storage, fish were transported frozen. The *Prince Albert Advocate* reported in November 1894 that one William Spencer, "whose seventy-odd years of age seem to have made but slight impression in either his appearance, spirits, or powers of endurance," recently returned from inspecting fisheries in the northern part of the district *on foot*. "He reports the fish very plentiful and the catch a profitable one," the paper noted, with a combination of glee and awe. The paper also reported an interesting story that connected boreal water landscapes and the new inroads into farming:

A good fish story comes from the north. It seems fish are very plentiful in Montreal and surrounding lakes, and when the settlers there run short of hay, as they frequently do, the cattle are induced to eat fish by sprinkling salt over them, which the cattle lick, and in this way eat the fish for the sake of the salt. That is only to get the appetite for fish cultivated, however. After that the cattle become addicted to the "fish" habit and in this particular instance a sagacious old ox is said to have frequently gone down to the lake, broken open a hole through three feet of ice, and feasted to satisfaction on the fish which swam into the hole thus made.[32]

The growth of commercial fishing—for whitefish, trout, pickerel, and northern pike—led to the posting of a fisheries overseer at Prince Albert in 1893 to issue permits and ensure compliance with fishing regulations.[33] Commercial fishing ebbed and flowed according to profits and environmental constraints. As early as 1909 there were complaints of overexploitation. A 1909 commission investigated the industry and made recommendations regarding season dates, net dimensions, licences, and other technical concerns. Cleaning and packing procedures, the demand created by the First World War, and improvements in cold storage and transportation led to higher prices and general expansion of the industry.[34]

During the First World War, northern inland commercial fishing grew. Prices for fish rose, allowing better profits and improvements, such as fish boxes and cold storage, that ensured a better end product. Between 1920 and 1940, the annual commercial production of northern Saskatchewan almost doubled.[35] A newspaper article dated c. 1926 on the Prince Albert region trumpeted that "fishing in the northern lakes and streams is important and last year more than 5,673,650 pounds of northern pike, pickerel, trout and whitefish, valued at about $450,000, were shipped to the eastern markets. The output from this area comprises annually about ninety percent of the fishing activity of the province."[36] Fishing camps, strung out along large lakes such as Doré, La Plonge, Churchill, and Peter Pond, were operated by large commercial interests such as Big River Consolidated or Waite Fisheries. Local lakes, such as Candle, Montreal, Waskesiu, Crean, and Kingsmere, were also fished but less extensively. In 1919, there were 684 commercial licences and 842 domestic licences sold to fishermen. By 1929, those numbers had more than doubled.[37] Like work in lumber camps, jobs in commercial fishing camps lasted for the winter months and suited primarily single men without extensive stock on their homesteads. The value of commercial fishing to the northern Saskatchewan economy was enormous: landed value of the fish regularly exceeded $250,000 per year throughout the 1920s.[38] Commercial fishing was a major driver in the forest edge economy, providing employment both at fishing camps and through contract freighting work as well as economic wealth to Prince Albert.

Commercial fishing, however, was a "white" and southern industry, even as it exploited northern resources. After 1890, as nearby commercial fishing grew, through to the explosion of the industry between 1920 and 1940, commercial fishing undercut—even actively worked against—Aboriginal subsistence or small-scale commercial practices. Although commercial fishing could be measured against an economic standard of price per pound or as a percentage of the provincial gross domestic output, its measurement within northern Aboriginal communities was elusive at best. Fish was primarily a food source for both humans and, perhaps even more importantly, dog teams. As Lac La Ronge chief Lorne Roberts indicated during the Treaty 6 adhesion negotiations in 1889, dog teams were integral to northern transport—he requested new dog harness instead of horse harness. It was cheap, practical, and easy to feed fish to sled dogs, which thrived on the diet. Fisheries inspectors found this practice rather horrifying, a waste of potentially commercially valuable fish flesh. Cultural and economic practices differed, as did legal rights. Although subsistence practices were protected through treaty, government workers chose to code First Nations fishing practices as non-commercial and even detrimental to commercial industry. First Nations, for all intents and purposes, were excluded from commercial fishing, both as large-scale contractors and as hired labour, except in a supply role through freighting.[39]

THE FOREST-FARM NEXUS

Between 1890 and 1919, the lumber industry was a major player in the regional economy at the forest edge. Rooted in the nearby, accessible, boreal landscape within transportation distance to Prince Albert, the lumber industry contributed to the growth of a labour class in Prince Albert as well as regional farming. Wage labour was an important, but too often underestimated, part of the homestead process.[40] When a sawmill owner leased a timber berth, he required equipment and men to operate the berth and cut the logs. Depending on the size of the mill, the corresponding bush camps might be small or large. Men were hired in the late fall for the camps. Homesteaders from both the prairie and the local area would congregate in Prince Albert after harvest to sign on with lumber camps. There is no way to know the proportion of logging camp men who were from the prairie as opposed to those who took nearby homesteads once the land north of the river began to be opened up for settlement.[41]

Homesteading, or creating a viable farm, was a capital-intensive activity. Until a farm had enough land cleared and enough equipment available to farm the land intensively, it turned little profit. In the meantime, homesteaders required ready cash to make up the shortfalls from their operations, purchase groceries and supplies, or expand. Working in lumber camps throughout the winter was an acceptable option since wages were good and board was provided. A.R.M. Lower completed studies of the forest frontier of eastern Canada that provide a good overview of how the Canadian lumber industry operated.[42] Two of his works offered his analysis of the peculiar interrelation between lumbering and farming. There remain limitations. The first book dealt only with eastern Canada, the second added the Maritimes and

British Columbia, but neither offered an analysis of forestry in the western interior.

Land in Ontario was clearly defined as either forest or farmland, and the lumber barons of Ottawa, for example, were held by Lower to be of a higher sort. There the relationship between farming and lumbering mirrored what happened in the north Prince Albert region, where land was actively managed as either commercial forest or opened for homesteading. Small farms were eventually established in the cut-over areas of forest, supplying labour and goods to the camps. The farmer-lumberjack relationship in New Brunswick in the 1800s Lower described quite differently. There a farm contained a belt or copse of merchantable timber, and the ideal was for a farmer to farm in the summer and work his timber for profit in the winter, marrying the two on a small scale. This ideal was seldom reached, according to Lower, who scoffed at small-scale efforts and dismissed the whole enterprise as bringing "much harm to the province as a whole." In some ways, though, the farmer-lumberjack, working his own land, bears some relation to the homestead-cordwood connection that grew in the north Prince Albert region after 1920.[43]

A few men, technically "squatters" on Crown Land, lived in the north Prince Albert region prior to homestead settlement in 1906, making their living as suppliers for large lumber camps. Two men, Pat Anderson and Mr. Vangilder, lived in what became the Alingly district between Sturgeon Lake and Little Red River Reserves. Anderson ran a stopping place on the trail to the Prince Albert Lumber Company camps at Shoal Creek (now the south end of Prince Albert National Park), providing hot food, beds, and a stable for the teams freighting to and from the lumber camps. He became the first postmaster. Vangilder also kept a stopping place, for the ice road from the Sturgeon Lake Lumber Company ran through his yard. He made extra money cutting hay in the area and selling it to the lumber camps, but he had to give up this practice when the land was surveyed and opened up to homesteaders.[44]

In 1907, the short-lived Edmonton-based magazine the *Wheat Belt Review* published an in-depth story on the lumber interests operating in Prince Albert. It gave a moral overtone to the connection between farming and lumbering: "The farm hand or rancher that has nothing to do in the winter months may, if he will, shoulder his axe and find steady employment in the logging camps until spring. There is no reason why any laboring man should be idle in winter. If he is idle it is because he does not care to work. There is no other town that can be called to mind that has the logging and the farming industry so closely allied."[45] Working in a lumber camp, in part to earn cash to build up a homestead, provided an important connection between farming and labour in the north Prince Albert region.

Homesteaders in the newly formed Alingly district east of the Sturgeon Lake Reserve and south of the Little Red River Reserve became intimately tied to lumber camps, providing stopping places, hay, and produce, working in the camps and on the spring river drives, and purchasing finished lumber.[46] A high proportion of the food for the camps was supplied by local homesteaders, especially after 1906. Richard Dice, who recorded Alingly's early history in an unpublished manuscript kept by the Prince Albert Historical Society, noted that "the Sturgeon Lake Lumber Company at what is now Deer Ridge and the Prince Albert Lumber Company at Shoal Creek and the Soup Kitchen was a splendid market for baled hay, oats, dressed beef, and potatoes in the settlement's early days." Men with supplies were welcomed at the camps and treated like kings: "We would unload, put our horses or bulls into their huge barns, feed them the company's oats and hay, free of charge; eat at the company's well-filled table, put up with the men in the bunk house and leave the next morning with a good fat check in our pockets." The practice brought a measure of early investment: "Many thousands of dollars found their way into this settlement in the early days which was its real start financially." Hay and oats for horses, milk and cream, eggs, poultry, pork, and beef were traded directly to the camps, providing a local cash market.[47] The road to Alingly went east from the Sturgeon Lake lumber and freight road, instead of straight north from the city, further bolstering the connection between new farms and local lumber interests.

Other homesteaders travelled north and slightly east from Prince Albert up what became known as the "Sand Hill" road, ending at or near the large, shallow body of water known locally as Egg Lake. Homesteaders would break off these primitive roads to slash trails through the bush to their own homesteads. As more homesteaders arrived, the need for roads, bridges, and other municipal requirements (such as fence laws and herd laws as well as taxes and school boards) became more important. The district directly north of Prince Albert formed a Local Improvement District in 1910 but quickly became the Rural Municipality of Buckland No. 491 in 1911.[48] The post office at Alingly was soon joined by post offices at Spruce Home in 1908, Henribourg in 1911, and Albertville in 1914.[49] Farther north, the homesteaders in what became known as Paddockwood opened their post office in 1913. As homesteaders moved onto their quarter sections, post offices became the nucleus of small commercial centres, with livery barns, general stores, churches, schools, barber shops, and later mechanic shops and other commercial enterprises emerging. Not all of those who lived in the region farmed for a living.

THE CORDWOOD ECONOMY

Although the lumber camps and lumber businesses in Prince Albert provided excellent local employment, barter, or cash opportunities, extensive fires during the dry spring of 1919 effectively shut these businesses down, leaving settlers (along with their First Nations counterparts) searching for other options. Possibly the most popular option was to cut and haul cordwood (firewood).

Paddockwood, and other forest fringe towns, capitalized on a continuously growing prairie fuel demand. It was, in many ways, a double-win situation for forest edge farmers: the land had to be cleared of trees in order to farm and gain patent, and cash could be made from selling the logs and timber. Settlers pursued this industry either on their own, cutting from their own homesteads, or working for a cordwood contractor who leased and operated a cordwood berth, similar to the old timber berths. Such jobs were paid by the month or as piecework.[50] The cordwood industry was more profitable closer to the city. Heavy hauling over long distances—Prince Albert was at least twenty miles away—meant that profits were low. The private cordwood industry did not explode in the new settlements until the coming of the railway to Henribourg and Paddockwood in 1924.

In 1926, Prince Albert commercial photographer William James travelled to the "end of the steel" at Paddockwood. The little village, with its four false-front frame buildings and assortment of log shacks, was the last village on the new CNR line, but that was not its claim to fame.[51] What brought James to Paddockwood that cold winter day was cordwood, stacks of firewood for sale and barter, piled along the tracks and down the main street in every direction. To capture the sight, James climbed onto the railway car to snap a panoramic view of Main Street, cordwood, and a countryside fast becoming denuded of its trees.[52]

Figure 19. Paddockwood cordwood, 1926.
Source: William James, from copy in the author's collection.

Cordwood was the basis of the ecotone's local commercial success after 1924. It became the main local commodity, a bulky substitute for cash. Settlers brought the wood to town and piled it all along Main Street. Each pile was owned by a different resident. It could be traded to local stores for supplies, to each other in exchange for labour or services, and even to the local hospital, in payment of fees. Continued bartering eventually placed it with local merchants. A merchant's pile would be sold to a cordwood dealer in Prince Albert or elsewhere and transported by rail.

Cordwood exemplified the Paddockwood identity—and the north Prince Albert region more generally—as a hybrid place, at the juncture between prairie/farming and forest/resources. A barter item similar to the eggs, butter, and cream common to mixed farms, cordwood in some ways replaced the cash wheat crop of the prairie south. The difference was that cordwood was a local currency geared to subsistence needs and local barter situations, but could not be mortgaged. Banks and implement dealers were willing to offer loans based on future wheat production but not on cordwood production. Although cordwood drove the local subsistence economy and, in some cases, brought cash investment in farms, it was not conducive to long-term economic development.

PROSPECTING AND THE POTENTIAL OF MINING

Prospecting for potential minerals and mines was a profitable activity in Canada throughout the late nineteenth century. Major finds in British Columbia and the Yukon, northern Ontario, Quebec, the Maritimes, and Manitoba spurred further reconnaissance trips into northern boreal and Canadian Shield landscapes. Gold

fever in particular gripped the entire nation in the late 1890s. As the lure of the Yukon took hold and prospectors from all over the world were searching for the best route to Dawson City and the gold fields, Prince Albert merchants capitalized on the town's "northern" identity, situating the town as a logical jumping-off point to more northern destinations. An 1897 pamphlet from the local Board of Trade advertised "Yukon Via Prince Albert: How to Get to the Klondike. The Safest, Best, and Cheapest Route to the Yukon Gold Fields."[53] The route was "unanimously recommended" by the Legislative Assembly of the North-West Territories in 1897. The pamphlet charted a route through Prince Albert, Green Lake, and Fort McMurray using the old fur-trade water highways. Each week Prince Albert newspapers reported Klondikers passing through.[54]

Saskatchewan prospectors not aiming for elusive Klondike gold had much to keep them busy. Local reports of amber, silica, coal, and other commodities excited interest. Gold dredging in the North Saskatchewan River was pursued around the turn of the twentieth century, though it soon became clear that the placer gold recovered during the process barely covered expenses.[55] Prince Albert newspapers reported prospecting activity, claim staking, and rumours of big finds with breathless excitement, always hoping for the next lucky strike. Mineral claims had to be registered at Prince Albert, an added advantage to entice this clientele.[56] Local advertisers pursued the prospector dollar with zeal.

Figure 20. Mandy Mine, 1917.
Source: SAB, R-B3553-1.

Prospecting was clearly related to tourism and local businessmen geared advertisements to this clientele while expecting future development. The *Prince Albert Advocate* reported in 1897 that "Capt. Bell and Mr. White were in town a few days ago last week, on their way through on a prospecting tour for gold in the limitless and untrodden country to the north. They are proceeding on their journey overland and by canoe with Indian servants and guides, expecting ultimately to arrive at Norway House, from there proceeding by boat to Winnipeg. ... The tourists expect to make some valuable finds of mineral in the country they are to traverse."[57] This story raised several key points. First, it showcased the growing self-identity of Prince Albert as the Gateway to the North, a natural point of departure for anyone heading into the forested wilderness north of the prairie region. Second, it reiterated the old fur-trade narrative of First Nations as guides, as experts in wilderness and forest navigation by canoe or trail. This role remained a complex combination of guide and servant, navigator and employee, but though the article explained the backgrounds of the potential prospectors the Indian men were not named. Such narrow-minded reporting, focussed only on the Anglo participants, was a common product of colonial thinking. First Nations were the labouring class, worthy of work but unworthy of name and respect. In many ways, early prospectors such as Bell and White viewed First Nations labourers as part of the "wilderness" scenery, akin more to trees and animals than to Anglo humans. It is also interesting that the newspaper could call the north "untrodden" yet acknowledge that the First Nations employees were "guides"—presumably, they had been there before. Third, the story presented a specific link between prospecting for potentially precious finds of ore and tourism. A tourist was someone who travelled to wild places to appreciate their scenic beauty; a prospector looked for sites of future potential wealth. Putting the two needs together shows the combination of sublime beauty and future economic potential.

While northern development may have slowed while the prairies filled with homesteaders, prospecting activity continued, particularly around Amisk Lake and Flin Flon on the Saskatchewan-Manitoba border. Caught up by a renewed northern fever in the 1920s, both federal and provincial governments initiated extensive reconnaissance surveys. To help northern prospecting options, the government blasted several large boulders out of the Montreal River to open it for heavier traffic loads and shorten portages. A well-publicized canoe trip by provincial attorney

New Saskatchewan Water Route For Prospectors in North

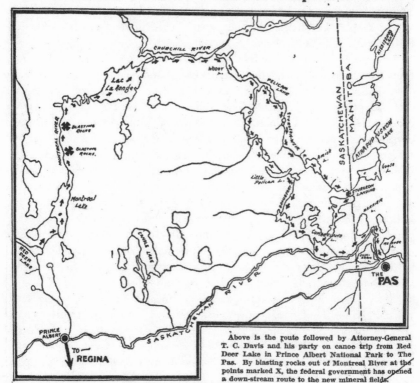

Above is the route followed by Attorney-General T. C. Davis and his party on canoe trip from Red Deer Lake in Prince Albert National Park to The Pas. By blasting rocks out of Montreal River at the points marked X, the federal government has opened a down-stream route to the new mineral fields.

Map 11. New Saskatchewan prospecting route, 1928.
Source: *Regina Daily Post*, 17 September 1928.

general T.C. Davis (originally a Prince Albert MLA) in 1928 showcased the new river route. Davis and several colleagues, along with their wives and four Indian guides, made the trip. Travelling overland from Prince Albert to Montreal Lake, the group canoed up the Montreal River to La Ronge, then down the Churchill River system to Amisk Lake, Cumberland House, and The Pas.[58] Their trip capitalized on the growing resource development of the provincial north, such as the Rottenstone mine near La Ronge and the mineral development at Flin Flon/Creighton on the Saskatchewan-Manitoba border.

CONCLUSION

The northern surge showed Saskatchewan people flexing their muscles, broadening their resource base, and settling into the *whole* province rather than just the southern half of it. The resource potential of the northern boreal and Canadian Shield regions drew extensive interest from across the country. Freighters and commercial fishermen visited far northern points such as Reindeer Lake and Lake Athabasca on a more regular basis, and prospectors, trappers, and government survey teams could be found. By August 1929, the north was touted as the province's—and the country's—place of future wealth and growth.[59] Fish, furs, and minerals in particular drew interest and investment.

If the potential of the north lay wrapped in the dreams of investors and stripped from the Aboriginal inhabitants, internal colonization along the forest edge, or "colonization within Canada," advanced the northern push. Space became place as people gained knowledge and flexed differential power. For those at the forest edge, such as the city of Prince Albert, the Gateway to the North led to increased development, community growth, and a close connection between on-farm and off-farm opportunities, all of which accelerated and energized the northern surge. The chance to draw on a mixed economic environment and its resulting combination of opportunities drew increased attention, not only from individuals, but also from government and business leaders.[60] Although neither government nor industry could have predicted the importance of internal recolonization and development schemes at the boreal edge and throughout the north, the northern surge of the early twentieth century helped both government and industry to be at least partially prepared for the onslaught of internal migration that arose during the Great Depression.

The northern push of settlement and development in the western interior fascinated the editorial staff of *Saturday Night* magazine. It consistently reported on the "trek northward" throughout the 1920s. Not only was the northern surge an agrarian movement, according to *Saturday Night,* it also reflected a growing interest in minerals, timber, furs, and fisheries.[61] For northern settlers, economic prospects included not only potential mixed-farm products but also other products drawn from the local forest edge landscape. Occupational pluralism combined farm income with wage, contract, or piecemeal work. There were extensive connections between the lumber industry (from winter work in the camps to spring lumber drives, work in the mills, food supply, or contract freighting) and local homesteaders. After the decline of the commercial lumber industry, completing the spur rail line through the north Prince Albert region in 1924 opened the cordwood economy, which allowed homesteaders to reap non-agricultural profits from their lands. Growth of the commercial fishing industry, as well as trapping and prospecting, led to a rise in overland freighting opportunities. Although many researchers have characterized the pursuit of off-farm income as an indication of the marginal nature of forest edge farms, those who recorded their stories in local history books viewed such income as a significant aspect, and part of the draw, of forest fringe life. Off-farm economic prospects melded with on-farm work to produce a local, occupationally pluralistic society. The concept of mixed farming at the forest edge adapted to include both on-farm and off-farm income—McOwan's list of farm and forest products suitable for "poor man's land." The opportunity to earn a cash wage or its equivalent through the barter economy gave forest edge residents an added measure of resilience. The ecotone landscape supported a "mixed" farm that was much more than just a farm.

By the late 1920s, provincial and national commentators boasted that the future of the province would be found in the north. In 1927, writer F.C. Pickwell quoted Member of Parliament (and former Saskatchewan premier) C.A. Dunning, whose new slogan was "Go North, Young Man," which *Saturday Night* claimed was "more truth than poetry."[62] Yet there was poetry too. Striking scenery, green trees, freshwater lakes, camping, and fishing awaited travellers to the north. The north stood ready to turn tired and dusty prairie residents into intrepid and healthy tourists. Building on the contrast between the agricultural prairie south and the boreal forested north, tourism enticed travellers to northern Saskatchewan. Even if farms were full of trees and difficult to develop, or potential northern resources such as mines a distant dream, the northern forest still had something to offer: it was culturally remade as Saskatchewan's own place of beauty.

CHAPTER SEVEN

ACCESSIBLE WILDERNESS

It was "the most interesting, the most unusual, and most beautiful holiday I ever had," declared Christina Henry. In 1919, Henry (later Bateman), a clerk at the University of Saskatchewan registrar's office in Saskatoon, went on a holiday. Not east to Ontario, nor west to Banff, nor south to the United States; instead, she went north, through the boreal forest and Canadian Shield to Lac La Ronge and Stanley Mission. Travelling with her friend, Nan McKay, whose father was the HBC factor at La Ronge, Henry gaily recorded a travel diary and took numerous photographs. They took a train from Saskatoon to Prince Albert, then bounced through a three-day trip via horse-drawn wagon up the freight trail from Prince Albert to the south end of Montreal Lake. Billy Bear, a Cree farmer, freighter, and businessman from the Little Red River Reserve, drove his wagon and provided the escort. From Montreal Lake, two more Cree men, Adolphus Ross and William Bird, canoed the women across the lake and up the Montreal River to La Ronge, a further four-day trip.[1] Henry's trip bridged modern and traditional transportation, from train to canoe to get to their destination. The core of the trip, though, flipped northern seasonality and use. McKay and Bateman saw the winter landscape of lumbering and freighting between Prince Albert and La Ronge through a new, summer tourist gaze.[2]

Although western Canada was well known as a tourism destination for British sportsmen throughout the nineteenth century, sustained tourism development in the north Prince Albert region began after the introduction of northern trails, improved roads, and eventually motor cars. Henry's 1919 trip offers a vivid snapshot of an exceptional transitional point in Canadian tourism history. At the time, local promoters were at a crossroads, in conflict with themselves, urging opposite uses *at the same time:* cut down the trees for lumber/cordwood and to make farms, or keep the trees as majestic examples of vigorous northern health and beauty, a landscape of relaxation and refuge. Balancing opposing development ideas meant judging each piece of land at the local level. Who owned the land, did it have good transportation, were the trees merchantable, was the soil good for farming, did the lake have fish? These questions became the guide. Setting aside swaths of territory for forestry reserves, parks, or farmland drew lines on a map that, in turn, had an effect on how the landscape looked and what it was used for.

The north Prince Albert region is known today as Lakeland, a tourism destination with resort communities at Round, Sturgeon, Christopher, Emma, Anglin, and Candle Lakes and Waskesiu in Prince Albert National Park. In 2013, Saskatchewan set aside a further 11,000 hectares as a provincial park in the area.[3] Modern tourism began in the north Prince Albert region at the turn of the twentieth century, when tourism literature across North America enticed urban residents to flee the concrete jungle to find a restful holiday in idyllic, green, rural surroundings. In a predominantly rural province such as Saskatchewan, this call had limited scope. North Prince Albert tourist promoters found their strongest voice exploiting Saskatchewan's forest/prairie divide: treeless, dry, open plains versus watered, lush, boreal forest. Part of the reason was practical. Promoters wanted to keep precious tourist dollars at home, urging prairie residents to be patriotic, to "See Saskatchewan First." The boreal forest became vacationland, "accessible wilderness" on the prairie doorstep. Recreational opportunities such as fishing, hiking, canoeing, and camping expressed domestic enjoyment, a nearby interlude from everyday life. Saskatchewan's north was the original "staycation." But the north/south contrast provided more than a mere marketing tool. It struck a chord of surprise and intrigue in tourists who did not know that Saskatchewan had anything to offer other than prairie. The opening of Prince Albert National Park in particular stamped Saskatchewan's national identity in the boreal forest. Tourism painted a vision of Saskatchewan beauty, accessible and wild at the same time, a story to contrast and counteract its practical image of hard-working prairie wheat farms.

PICTURESQUE PRINCE ALBERT

Future Canadian author Lucy Maud Montgomery came to visit her father in Prince Albert as a sixteen-year-old girl in the fall of 1890. Already a fledgling writer, Montgomery kept a diary to record her experiences. Prince Albert, she penned, was a "straggly" town, strung out along the south side of the North Saskatchewan riverbank for several miles. "Across the river," she wrote, "are great pine forests, and the views upstream are very beautiful."[4] Her description of Prince Albert's pine forest and river landscape as "beautiful" mirrored the thoughts of the Lorne Agricultural Society of Prince Albert. In the same year as Montgomery's sojourn, the society published its advertising pamphlet *Prince Albert and the North Saskatchewan*. It confidently boasted that one of the most significant selling features of the region was its beauty: "The country is beautiful in its general appearance," full of lakes, trees, and hills, notably different from the "plain country to the south."[5] Settlers in the north country were assured that their properties would enjoy added value in the "charm [of] the beautiful groves of aspen ... and in the abundance of small but refreshing ponds or lakelets, one of which is almost certain to be found in every settler's 'park.'"[6] The society pamphlet presented a vision of a landscape remodelled and controlled, identified as "park" rather than "wilderness." It also suggested that the beautiful and the picturesque held an unknown but tangible economic worth.

An Edenic garden or a park landscape built on British ideals has been well studied.[7] Concepts such as picturesque and beautiful, as specific aesthetic comments on landscape, carried multiple meanings. Within the British context, owning a park, or land kept for enjoyment rather than economic benefit, marked the upper classes of society. Only the rich could own land whose sole purpose was beauty. In the colonial context, picturesque idealism was often combined with a sense of economic end-use or potential exploitative possibilities, such as farming. The picturesque ideal identified riches in good soil, water, trees, and game—beautiful but also necessary for colonization.[8] Suggesting that the North Saskatchewan area was picturesque and park-like would have been immediately understood as representing its potential value for both beauty and future riches. The dual ideal of use and beauty would reverberate through both the mixed-farming literature and the development of tourism.

A SPORTING PARADISE

Although Montgomery and the Lorne Agricultural Society promoted Prince Albert's beauty, the region had much else to offer. Lumber industrialist Captain Moore, who opened the first steam-powered mill in the district in 1879, found his way to the fledgling settlement first as a sportsman. On a hunting expedition across the west, Moore and his group stopped at Prince Albert to purchase supplies.[9] He was just one of many British men of class, enticed by newspaper articles and brochures, visiting the Canadian west to hunt.[10] Sportsmen-tourists created an imperialistic image of the old North-West as idyllic and Edenic, overflowing with game.[11] Western Canada developed a reputation as a sportsman's paradise, a tourist destination for the idle rich.[12] In its 1890 brochure, the Lorne Agricultural Society promoted natural abundance, which meant both scenery and game: "The sportsman and the tourist will find within our borders all the keenest could desire. Game of all kind in abundance, and scenery which has already excited the admiration of the English and Canadian explorer."[13] Primed with such advertising, sportsmen and tourists arrived at Prince Albert with preconceived notions of a landscape both full of game and inherently beautiful.

Figure 21. Spoils of the hunt north of Prince Albert, 1917.
Source: SAB, R-B3507-1.

In a practical sense, and for the purposes of Prince Albert merchants, both tourists and sportsmen required lodging, food, transportation, and guiding.[14] Hotels, general merchants, and livery barns catered to this market, offering rooms, supplies, and rentals of horse teams and outfits. Advertisements lauded sparkling lakes, good fishing, and excellent game on both hoof and wing to entice the reader. To add to the general picture, Prince Albert's local newspapers participated in presenting the region as a sportsman's paradise, continually reporting good game hunting, trapping, and fishing. The *Prince Albert Advocate* reported, for example, that "prairie chicken and duck are very plentiful this year, and local sportsmen come home with large bags of game as a rule."[15] Tourists and sportsmen, eager to participate, brought wealth.

The close of the nineteenth century saw the opening of several northern lakes, such as Montreal, Candle, and Red Deer (Waskesiu) Lakes, to a burgeoning commercial fishery.[16] Although commercial fishing and sport fishing were entirely different endeavours, stories of immense fish wealth would reinforce the idea of Prince Albert and the North Saskatchewan region as a sport paradise. Those interested in northern development connected sportsmen and potential economic possibilities. Prince Albert newspapers cajoled upper-class sport tourists to visit in the hope that they would stay to develop economic industries. Major Ernest J. Chambers, in his 1914 report to the Senate on the resources of northwestern Canada, pointed out that the "tourist sportsman, the cultured business men, who find their greatest pleasure, relaxation, and physical benefits from trips into the wilds, are quick to discern the commercial value" of such "wild" lands in addition to their aesthetic qualities: "park-like groves of fine trees, its sylvan lakes teeming with fish, and every prospect a gem of nature's own perfect landscape."[17] While walking through the woods, scouting game, or portaging to the next lake, sportsmen would keep an eye firmly on the economic potential of the landscape, quick to spot exceptional timber resources, future mines, or water power. Tourism and sport combined could lead to intensive and extensive economic development.

PRINCE ALBERT'S BACK YARD

Not all of the people moving through the landscape of the north Prince Albert region were from far away. The majority of people were local. "Wild" areas across the North Saskatchewan River from Prince Albert were a favourite destination for day hikes, berry-picking excursions, picnics, and hazelnut hunts in addition to more prosaic uses such as tourism, hunting, fishing, prospecting, and firewood berths or commercial timber limits. One child was lost on such an expedition and not found for four days. Over 300 people participated in the search.[18] These uses show the local and domestic, rather than the commercial and sport, aspects of the landscape.

Figure 22. Picnic at Round Lake.
Source: Prince Albert Historical Society (PAHS) E-156

During her stay in Prince Albert, author L.M. Montgomery took a trip across the river in 1891. The ferry did not accept passengers other than farmers or freighters with loads of goods, so Montgomery and her party of female friends had to beg canoe rides across the river from passing canoeists (going over) and local First Nations women (coming back). Taking "enough cans and buckets for an army," Montgomery and her companions crossed the North Saskatchewan to a landing point near the mouth of the Little Red River, then hiked along the "road to the Indian camp" and on to the "berry barrens," a distance of over five miles. The blueberries, unfortunately, were "few and far between," probably already picked over and dried by the First Nations women.

Montgomery waxed rhapsodic in her journal regarding the scenery: "What a wilderness it was! Steep banks covered with mighty, heaven-sweeping pines, weird with age; below, a thick undergrowth of poplar through which we forced our way to a most romantic little spot ... that wild yet beautiful wilderness, where nature ran riot in untrained luxuriance." The ladies returned late that night to Prince Albert completely exhausted, with sore feet and limbs. "No more over the river excursions for me if you please!" Montgomery declared.[19] Clearly, the beauty that she had witnessed was not enough to entice her a second time on such a tiring excursion.

Montgomery filled her journal with comments on the scenic beauty of the Prince Albert area; in fact, the highest compliment that she could pay was that the scenery reminded her of Prince Edward Island. Other comments contrasted the northern greenery with the plains area of the south, through which she travelled on her train journey. She was "delighted to see that it was fair and green and fertile-looking—altogether unlike those dreary wastes around Regina." Montgomery pushed the same contrasts made by the Lorne Agricultural Society: the District of Saskatchewan centred on Prince Albert, while the District of Assiniboia centred on Regina. Within months of her arrival, Montgomery penned an article for the *Saskatchewan Times* newspaper on the Saskatchewan country, "a flowery peroration on the possibilities of the country as a whole," she admitted. Despite her comparatively brief visit, she duplicated the local habit of tying scenery to economics and noting the contrast between the barren open plains and the lush northern forests.[20]

EARLY COMMERCIAL TOURISM: ROUND LAKE

The boom period in western Canada after 1896 and into the first decade of the twentieth century saw rapid industrial growth in the Prince Albert region: lumbering, commercial fishing, prospecting and gold dredging, and freighting. Commercialization of the local lumber industry was particularly important. The modern lumber mills at Prince Albert employed hundreds of workers in wage labour and shift work. Industrialism on this scale disconnected urban life from an older, pre-industrial, and rural life.[21] With structured work hours came structured free time, and industrial workers—and their bosses—were quick to find ways to fill it. As the lumber industry expanded north of the city, trails into the north were continuously improved. Those drawn across the river to pick berries, hunt, or otherwise amuse themselves could safely and quickly expand their explorations.

The most important trail leading north was the original artery of the Montreal Lake Trail. First created to serve lumber interests and access the timber basket, the trail was a direct link between urban and wild. From the ferry at Prince Albert, the trail angled west through the jack pines and past a body of water known to the local First Nations as Moon Lake but to the freighters, lumbermen, and settlers as Round Lake. About eighteen miles north and west of the city, the small lake was filled with fish and populated by wild fowl. From Round Lake, the trail went north toward Sturgeon Lake, the Little Red River Reserve, and the heavy wood basket, eventually leading to Red Deer Lake and Montreal Lake over the winter freighting trail.

By 1905, probably at least partially in response to the industrial pollution of the North Saskatchewan by city effluence and lumber mills, Round Lake drew attention from Prince Albert residents as a picnic and recreational destination.[22] Local lumbermen James Sanderson and Mayor William Cowan, along with merchants, druggists, real estate agents, and lawyers from the city, created the Prince Albert Outing Club,[23] which purchased land around the lake.[24] The group built a club house in 1911 that housed a common recreational area, kitchen, dining area, and

Figure 23. Two ladies fishing on unidentified lake, c. 1900.
Source: SAB, R-A5628-2.

store. In 1918, a dance pavilion was erected. Lots were leased from the club and modest cabins built. Docks, swimming platforms, and slides were also added, as well as a tennis court in 1930.[25]

Despite proximity to the Dakota Sioux Reserve at Wahpehton, the Outing Club and Round Lake recreational activities remained tied to private, non-Native use. Primary shareholders in the Outing Club were the city's merchant class. The families of lumbermen (particularly foremen and clerks) came to use the facilities as well. Round Lake soon grew in fame, drawing tourists from southern Saskatchewan. The *Prince Albert Daily Herald* reported in 1916 that "Round Lake Is Wonderful to Prairie People. Many Campers Expected at the Local Resort This Summer." An unidentified mayor of one prairie city was quoted: "If the people living in the south of the province only saw this beautiful lake with these trees surrounding it, and within a distance of 15 miles from a city, with good trails leading to it, through all those pine trees, well I do not know what they would say." He went on: "You know I have been sending my family to a small lake on the prairie where the only shade trees we have are small willows and the heat and wind, well there really was no pleasure in it."[26] The words of this unknown mayor, contrasting prairie recreational opportunities with those found in the north Prince Albert region, were almost prophetic.

After homesteads were surveyed and opened in 1906 and 1907 north of the city, roads and trails were continuously created and improved. The majority of these trails, however, were cut on a north-south axis. There were few east-west trails, isolating the new communities from each other. The main lumber and freight trail that went past Round Lake bypassed Christopher, Emma, and Anglin Lakes to the west. In fact, so little was known about Christopher, Emma, and Anglin Lakes that they were often depicted on maps as a single lake.[27] Lack of access, and lack of knowledge, meant that these lakes could be visited only by determined trailbreakers. The Sand Hills Trail northeast of the city, toward the burgeoning communities of Henribourg and Paddockwood, led to the "new" Montreal Lake Trail cut during the First World War and the Mosher Trail to Candle Lake. Montreal and Candle Lakes were much farther away from the city over uncertain bush trails. They did not draw early tourists or corollary development to any appreciable level. Round Lake remained the primary developed tourism spot until after the First World War.[28]

During the 1920s, the recreational site at Round Lake boomed. Churches and schools met there for picnics, and the annual sports day with swimming, diving, sailing, canoeing, and motorboat races (and prizes) created lots of excitement.[29] Stuart Anderson, whose family owned a cabin at the lake, recalled that, "as a young boy coming from Prince Albert, I was amazed at the number of tin signs nailed to jackpine trees in promotion of businesses."[30] Outdoor camps for children were organized at the lake, and by the mid-1920s weekend trips to Round Lake were common not only for Prince Albert residents but also for those beyond. Round Lake continued to attract visitors and commercial development until the 1950s, when it began to decline. With developed roads blocking drainage patterns and increased agricultural clearing, water levels receded in Round Lake. Lower water levels led to a commercial decline for the Outing Club, and many cabins were abandoned from the 1950s on. However, the club remained viable, and there has always been a tourism and recreational presence at the lake, though not on the same scale as in its earliest years of activity. In the late 1990s, water levels rose, and recreationists once more began to frequent Round Lake in both summer and winter.

TRANSITION FROM FREIGHT TRAILS TO TOURISM ROADS

The freight trails became more familiar as reliable access points into and out of the north. Recreationists, following the trails, ventured further afield. Nan McKay and Christina Henry's 1919 trip is an excellent example. The women used personal connections with church leaders at Prince Albert and merchants of the Hudson's Bay Company to organize their trip. They travelled overland on the freight artery intended for lumber, furs, and fish coming south and goods going north to various settlements. On the trail, First Nations men who owned the necessary equipment— wagon and canoe—and were familiar with the route accompanied, guided, and transported the women. The men drove horse teams or paddled, set up tents, and conveyed belongings, but the women reciprocated by doing some of the cooking. Yet aspects of their journey were new. Henry clearly considered the trip a holiday. The women travelled without white male chaperones, showcasing an important gender shift. Whereas Montgomery was chaperoned on her rail trip across Canada to Prince Albert in 1890, Henry and McKay were not. Women's emancipation, clearly represented by Henry in her journal through comments on clothing, tenting, and cooking in the outdoors, reflects a postwar change in women's behaviour and realm of possibility. Henry and McKay dressed in overalls and pants as it suited them, which Henry noted in her diary aroused comment from both Bird and Ross. The women flipped the seasonal dynamic, using the bumpy wagon road in summer, whereas it saw most of its traffic in winter. Henry commented extensively on the environment, particularly that the landscape had been devastated by the firestorm that May: "Not very far from Prince Albert we came upon miles and miles of burnt over woods—only blackened trunks left—a very sad sight." "But," she noted with optimism, "the fireweed was springing up making a bright pink carpet for the black tree trunks. The road was terribly rough—nothing but tree roots and rocks, bump, bump, bump."[31] She also noted the danger of stormy water on the lakes as well as the beauty and bounty of the natural world around them. Henry's trip is an example of a broad redefinition of the trails leading north of Prince Albert as a bridge between traditional and modern uses of the north Prince Albert region: the old freight trail to La Ronge viewed with a new, tourist gaze.[32]

Figure 24. Montreal Lake trail, 1919 through fire-killed trees.
Source: SAB, Christina Bateman fonds, S-B491.

Figure 25. Possibly Adolphus Bird with Christina Henry (left) and Nan McKay, 1919.
Source: SAB,S-B510.

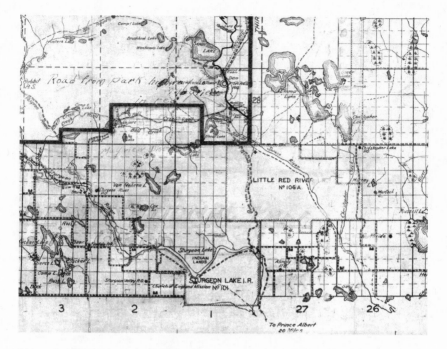

Map 12. Road from Prince Albert to Montreal Lake, c. 1925. Shown as the double-dotted line (centre), the road ran along Sturgeon Lake and through Little Red River, heading north.
Source: Sturgeon River Forest Reserve map, Friends of Prince Albert National Park.

TRAILS NORTH

From 1910 on, reports from the Rural Municipality of Buckland (the first RM in the north Prince Albert region) in the *Prince Albert Daily Herald* remarked on road conditions and pressed for improvements. Each year citizens (either on their own or with municipal funding) built bridges, filled in holes, and created drainage systems to improve road conditions. By 1920, in response to the exploding new soldier settlement and incoming settlers from the prairie, local roads and trails received more attention. Motor vehicle traffic was on the rise, and roads began to be judged by their ability to permit cars. The *Daily Herald* reported a fascinating story in 1920:

> To Montreal Lake. Jack Woods Drives to Within Twenty Miles of the Place. J. Woods of the City Auto Livery made a trip by car into the north country last week and succeeded in reaching a point within 20 miles of Montreal Lake, having passed the Bear Trap by 7 miles. This is considered to be the most northerly point in the province yet reached by an automobile and Mr. Woods intends next spring to try to reach the lake itself. The journey which covered 93 miles was made

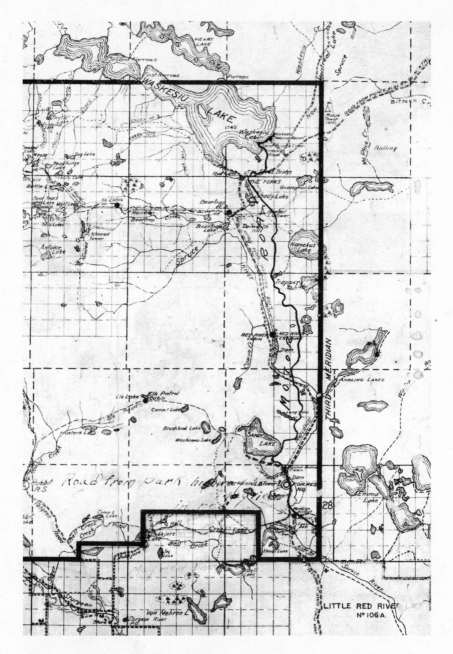

Map 13. Sturgeon River Forest Reserve roads, c. 1928–29. The motor road was hand-drawn on this map to contrast the freight trails that existed before it. Today cyclists and hikers use portions of the old freight trail west of the auto road.

Source: Friends of Prince Albert National Park, Waskesiu. Scan by the author.

in 7 hours, which is not considered a bad record, as Mr. Woods says that the last 15 miles of the trail was pretty bad. The trip is another evidence of the invasion of the northern territories by the advancement of progressive civilization, which is gradually bringing settlements, at one time considered remote, in easy contact with the city.[33]

Although the trail is not specified, it would have been the same trail taken by Henry in 1919, passing through the Little Red River Reserve and the Sturgeon River Forest Reserve, where Bear Trap Lake was a notable feature. The lake had been dammed by the Prince Albert Lumber Company, and a canal had been constructed south to the Spruce (Little Red) River to facilitate water flow and handle log volumes. If Woods reached a point seven miles beyond Bear Trap, he did not reach Waskesiu, though he would have been close to "The Forks," a stopping place where the trail branched one way to Montreal Lake and the other way to Green Lake.[34]

A map owned by Friends of Prince Albert National Park showed the forest reserve boundaries prior to creation of the park. The map, issued originally in 1923, showed roads in the region as of the mid-1920s. The road "from Prince Albert to Montreal Lake" bypassed Sturgeon Lake, snaked through the west side of the Little Red River Reserve, and went into the forest reserve. This main road branched at "The Forks" to go east and north to Montreal Lake. Although a trail is shown leading to "Waskesiu Summer Resort" and "Primeau Road," the original freight road did not deliberately access resorts or lakes.

Neither Woods nor Henry mentioned any of the smaller lakes near that road, with the exception of Montreal Lake as their destination. Yet both parties made their trips for no other purpose than leisure and travel tourism. It seems somewhat odd from our present perspective that the lakes now considered key points in the Lakeland landscape—Emma, Christopher, Anglin, and Red Deer (Waskesiu)—received no reference. The trail as it wound through in 1919–20 bypassed all of these lakes. Drawn in ink on the map shown above is the "Motor Road" built when the forest reserve became the nucleus of Prince Albert National Park. This road took a slightly different route, deliberately drawing near the shores of Sandy Lake and ending at Waskesiu Lake. The trip by Henry and McKay blended the practical freight road with tourism, and the trip by Woods (partly to advertise his business, City Auto Livery, which rented cars to motorists for short-term jaunts), introduced motor tourism to the north Prince Albert landscape. Their escapades marked a major turn in regional tourism development.

EMMA LAKE AND CHRISTOPHER LAKE

In an effort to find land suitable for soldier settlement, the dominion government sponsored an in-depth land classification survey of Canada in 1918. Dominion land surveyor M.C. McCloskey investigated the north Prince Albert region and reported in 1921. His report continually commented on the state of the roads, the north-south direction of trails, and the lack of cross-trails.[35] He and his surveyors were forced to change from wagons to pack horses to complete much of their work. Of particular interest for McCloskey, aside from finding decent soil and potential agricultural lands, were the smaller lakes in the area. He appraised these lakes for their fishing potential and scenic beauty. Emma Lake was singled out as "beautifully situated among rolling hills," with "all the features desirable for a summer resort. A broad sandy beach with gentle slope extends around the southern part, with excellent facilities for boating. The water is clear and fresh. Whitefish, pike and pickerel are reported plentiful."[36] At the time, the majority of the land around the south, east, and west portions of both lakes was either available homestead quarters (or partial quarters) or leased by trappers.[37]

Emma and Christopher Lakes were beginning to attract local tourist interest. In September 1920, the same year that Woods drove his car to Bear Trap, the Northside correspondent to the *Prince Albert Daily Herald* reported a couple and their baby spending a weekend at "Lake Emma."[38] Local popularity soon exploded. By the mid-1920s, numerous local residents from Henribourg, Northside, Alingly, and Paddockwood jaunted to both Emma and Christopher Lakes. A typical community report would state that "quite a number of parties from this district have been away camping this summer at Christopher Lake."[39] McCloskey's call for more cross-trails to connect the communities on an east-west access helped Paddockwood residents. A road was built in 1925 on the 14th baseline, connecting Paddockwood with Christopher Lake and bridging the Garden River. Although the road had been cut by surveyors in 1919, it needed grading and extensive improvements, including gravel, corduroy over muskeg, and a bridge over the Garden River, before it could be used by cars. The Paddockwood correspondent to the *Daily Herald* reported in 1925 that "Riley, Endicott and Gould motored to the lake on Sunday. Mr. Riley's being amongst the first car to traverse the road direct from Paddockwood to Christopher Lake."[40]

Increased mobility through cars and extensive road construction and improvement by local homesteaders and municipal governments enticed not only locals but also non-locals to Emma and Christopher Lakes. G.A. Crowley of Northside wrote to the Department of the Interior in 1925 urging it to improve the road to Christopher Lake. The lake, he wrote, "has the prospect of being one of the Greatest Summer Resorts in Saskatchewan. I've counted as many as 38 cars to this Lake on one Sunday and road not fit for a team on account of hummock and temporary corduroy for about four miles south of lake ... Cars run on low gear and are pulled or pushed through low places."[41] Defining the north Prince Albert region as a tourism destination required a spirit of adventure, putting cars through miles of mud to get to their destination. It also marked the dual places of origin of tourists: some were from close by, some were from far away. The trappers and homesteaders who owned lakeshore property soon converted some of their energy into building camping, boating, and bathing facilities, improving access, and providing services.

STURGEON RIVER FOREST RESERVE AND TOURISM

Prior to the First World War, the lumber industry dominated the landscape. The dominion government established the Sturgeon River Forest Reserve in 1914 on land east of the Sturgeon River to the third meridian, south including much of Township 53, and north to Township 57. The forest reserve allowed the dominion to increase surveillance on the lumber interests operating almost wantonly in the region, but it had other repercussions. It stopped agricultural settlement—land could not be taken for homesteading within its boundaries. Forestry reserves, the Department of the Interior insisted, were set aside to promote monitored forest production and reproduction, including a program of silviculture. The idea was to maintain healthy forests that could be continuously and economically exploited for human benefit—a "gospel of efficiency" and "wise use" of forest resources.[42] An emphasis on fire suppression and reforestation anchored the dominion's interests. Other uses included permit-controlled grazing and haying on open glades. After the devastating fires of 1919, which effectively halted large-scale lumbering in the area, the Sturgeon River Forest Reserve remained a legal entity.[43] Local residents continued to lease areas within the reserve to operate sawmills, cordwood berths, and railway tie camps, as well as haying and grazing permits, but the large-scale economic benefits for Prince Albert businesses from the lumber industry—supplies, food, clothing, transportation, and entertainment—melted away. These businesses were left with a frustratingly underused forest reserve landscape on their doorstep.

Enter the Department of the Interior, which operated the forestry reserve system. The forestry branch began to publicize forest reserves as recreational space across the dominion. The new marketing ploy emphasized camping as a domestic experience accessible to all: hiking, taking pictures, tenting, canoeing, cooking, eating ice cream, swimming, boating, and fishing. These experiences could be had just as easily on short weekend trips to forest reserves as on expensive month-long rail adventures to the mountains. The forestry branch encouraged such recreation, despite the increased risk of forest fires: tourism "enables many citizens to see the forests, and thus leads them to appreciate their importance," thereby heeding calls for fire prevention strategies, officials hoped.[44] To increase demand, the forest service began to provide camping and picnicking facilities "at favourable points."[45]

E.H. Finlayson, the director of forestry, wrote of the "eager manner in which the public have grasped the possibilities for holidaying and recreation." The department invested in road maintenance and signage to encourage this new traffic.[46] Northern Saskatchewan benefited. The forestry branch took on an "ambitious programme of improvement work." It dug canals on the Montreal River, cleared and widened portages, improved campsites, built log cabins for shelter and wood storage, and erected signs at portages and other important trail points along the way.[47] The branch knew that "our northern watercourses are extremely bewildering to a traveller not perfectly familiar with them," so it put up signs and widened trails so that "they could be followed by even a novice."[48]

Promoting tourism in forest reserves tapped a growing commercial market. During the 1920s, tourist recreation rocketed to public consciousness across North America in conjunction with the spread of motor vehicles and improved roads.[49] The post–First World War period saw a dynamic change in social expectations, leisure time, and increased affluence. Cars, along with tents and other camping supplies left over from the war effort, and an increasingly improved road network, encouraged the rise of auto tourism on a more modest budget. The 1922 annual report of National Park Commissioner J.B. Harkin noted with pleasure and expectation that "the prosperity that has followed the building of motor highways ha[s] convinced everyone that tourist travel pays, and that it can be developed like any other industry."[50]

TOURISM PROMOTION: URBAN, RURAL, NORTH, AND SOUTH

As Harkin rightly noted, despite being rooted in landscape, tourism is not a natural product. It is "developed, managed, and packaged by people and organizations," particularly on a large scale.[51] When a landscape is unique, it can be marketed and sold. The act of visiting drives the experience. In most cases, Canadian landscape tourism during the twentieth century appealed most strongly to urban residents. By 1921, Canada found half of its population residing in urban centres, working wage or salary positions with set hours and set leisure times.[52] Excursions to nearby lakes or resorts—for day trips, weekends, or a few weeks—became affordable holidays that could be taken with little preparation and modest investment. The rise of camping and picnicking in forest reserves was "becoming a regular habit of the people even from long distances, and this traffic is particularly heavy on Sundays and holidays."[53] Historian J.M. Bumsted noted that, during the early twentieth century, "urban Canada revelled in its neighbouring wilderness," flocking to accessible lakeshores and forested camping areas.[54] Brochures, maps, and films promoting tourist destinations were distributed in cities to receptive audiences.[55] The Department of the Interior expressed the opinion that tourism was becoming popular because of "alarm at the changes in the face of the country due to the rapid extension of our present industrial civilization, [which] has emphasized the necessity of conserving a few untouched areas."[56] National and provincial parks, forestry reserves, and other "natural" areas would provide charm, peace, and solace, as well as a healthy vacation in the outdoors, away from the urban jungle.

Saskatchewan, however, bucked the national trend toward urbanization. The rural/urban divide was still evident in 1921, with 70 percent of the Saskatchewan population living in rural areas.[57] While other provinces could assume that urban residents were more numerous and create marketing campaigns directed at busy urban lives, appealing to city residents had limited mileage in Saskatchewan. Recreating the north Prince Albert landscape as a tourist destination—a place that was "different," "beautiful," and "worth seeing"— largely depended on a different model. This model exploited Saskatchewan's north/south divide: open plains versus northern forests became the central marketing tool.

MLA T.C. Davis, the newly elected representative of the Prince Albert region, rose during one of his first sessions in the legislature in Regina in 1925 to expound on the north/south divide in Saskatchewan. It was as "crippling" as the east/west divide in Canada, he argued, where all the development, investment, and knowledge went to one part and not to the other. The divide within Saskatchewan, Davis claimed, was both physical and economic. The Saskatchewan north presented a non-agricultural landscape that did not fit the prairie development model. The result was "a lop-sided province. For those who don't wish to farm, there is little to do." Davis believed that the best way forward was through interaction: "The cleavage between the North and South in this province can be avoided by the people of the South getting acquainted with the people and the conditions of the North and the people of the North getting acquainted with the South." To support and develop this new acquaintance, Davis proposed tourism: "We are becoming ... a nation on wheels. During the summer time we are away seeking beautiful spots to visit. We go to Banff and Jasper Park and Yellowstone National Park and to the Lake of the Woods and Muskoka, and leave right here in our own province, a country which rivals them all to great advantage in point of natural beauty. We want first of all to get you to know that great country and we best do this by inducing you to go there on a pleasure bent."[58] His speech outlined a program of northern Saskatchewan tourism, appealing to a growing sense of provincial patriotism. It was not necessary to travel far away, Davis argued, when a beauty spot "which rivals them all" could be found closer to home. Prince Albert became the gateway to a northern vacation land, targeting prairie dwellers to discover the boreal forest and spend their money up north.

Improved roads and recreational facilities, as well as increased promotion, drew people from farther and farther away. "Whereas in former times visitors were mostly persons residing in the neighbourhood," the forestry branch wrote in 1926, "the records now show use by people living at considerable distances," including tourists from the United States.[59] A 1925 article in the *Prince Albert Daily Herald* reported that tourism had become Canada's third most important industry and claimed that in Saskatchewan this industry was worth about $10 million.[60] Whether tourism was worth that much or was that important to the national or provincial economy is irrelevant. The message was clear: tourism meant money. Merchants provided food, equipment, and services, from boat rentals to boarding houses to full-scale camps. For Prince Albert businessmen, supplying the new tourist trade offset the losses experienced by the close of the lumber industry. The merchants believed that the north Prince Albert region offered as good a recreational landscape as any. If people were willing to travel and spend money to visit a lake, do some fishing, and hike among the trees, then Prince Albert businessmen were ready to promote the north as the logical recreation destination of choice for prairie residents—and

Prince Albert as the point of departure. It was an *accessible* wilderness. Instead of spending a lot of time driving far away, a car full of tourists could arrive faster and spend more time having fun.

A "SASKATCHEWAN BANFF": PRINCE ALBERT NATIONAL PARK

The forestry branch created a cottage lot subdivision at the beach at Primeau Landing at Red Deer (Waskesiu) Lake in 1925.[61] The new development capitalized on increased tourist interest and looked to model success on similar developments at Clear Lake in the Riding Mountain Forest Reserve in Manitoba.[62] Cottage leases, camping fees, permits, and other revenues offset fire control and other operational costs. O.M. Lundlie, a Prince Albert resident who owned a large machinery dealership with a branch in Henribourg, visited Red Deer Lake in early July 1925. He reported with enthusiasm that in Red Deer Lake, Prince Albert had an asset that would more than repay development. The article in the *Prince Albert Daily Herald* declared that the lake would be an "Ideal Site for a Saskatchewan Banff."[63]

Rebranding the forest reserve as a "Saskatchewan Banff" had nothing to do with mountains and everything to do with economics. Tourist traffic, Lundlie exclaimed, would involve not just recreational tourists but also hunters, trappers, and prospectors. He imagined a cottage community in the forestry reserve that would combine landscape recreation with the supply trade. He believed that the resort community would become a new "jumping off point" for northern exploration and exploitation. Lundlie called on the Prince Albert Board of Trade to take up the cause of resort creation. Calling Red Deer Lake a "Saskatchewan Banff" foreshadowed the move to change the Sturgeon River Forest Reserve into a national park. His enthusiasm put a public face on an idea that was already in the making.

The national parks branch had already expressed some interest in Saskatchewan. In 1922, in keeping with the recreational aspect of the new car tourism, its annual report announced the creation of "recreational areas." These were areas "adapted for public use and enjoyment for summer resort and recreational purposes but which do not possess scenery of sufficient importance to justify their creation as national parks." Land suitable for recreation but not large enough to create a national park usually fronted a lake. As such, it was not good for agriculture and was unalienated Crown land. The first such reservation in Saskatchewan under this scheme was Vidal's Point, now known as Katepwa Point, on Katepwa Lake, within the Qu'Appelle Valley chain of lakes known as the Calling Lakes. Although not called a national park, the area came under the protection and administration of the national parks branch. The point had been in use for recreation for years. National designation gave Vidal's Point increased status and publicity.[64]

The Sturgeon River Forest Reserve north of Prince Albert was a large, publicly owned, and federally managed landscape, large enough to convert into a national park. Public ownership gave clarity and ease to the transition from one kind of federal ownership to another. The growing economic boom in regional tourism development at Round, Christopher, and Emma Lakes, combined with the enthusiasm of Lundlie and others who wished to turn the forestry reserve into a "Saskatchewan Banff," provided the idea and the willpower. Prince Albert politicians and businessmen knew that a national park commanded greater dominion involvement than a forest reserve, particularly financially, to build infrastructure and create an advertising campaign. Local merchants and entrepreneurs would ride the tourism wave with less effort on their own part. Political circumstances and manipulation added first possibility and then reality.[65]

The critical bargaining factor in creating the new national park was its situation. The Sturgeon River Forest Reserve straddled the ecotone, offering a transitional landscape of burnt-over areas and old logging berths, alongside open meadows and bursting poplar groves. National park officials were unconvinced that such a mixed landscape was sufficiently beautiful. In a letter to parks commissioner J.B. Harkin in April 1926, the deputy minister of the interior spelled out what a national park should be: "it is desired to have scenic wonders and beauties in sufficient abundance." The forest reserve had trees but few picturesque rocky outcrops and no waterfalls. It was not "north" enough because it was not the Canadian Shield. An internal memorandum suggested instead that the Lac La Ronge region, in the Canadian Shield, would be better suited: "Before a successful national park can be created, you must have a natural park. The territory lying north of and within easy reach of Prince Albert is not naturally a park country, so it requires a critical selection to choose any area which might form a satisfactory national park. ... The territory in the Lac La Ronge district and north is much more attractive as a natural park area."[66]

Prince Albert advocates were appalled. Such a park would be beyond Prince Albert's reach. In fact, it would be beyond anyone's reach, for there were no roads farther than the south end of Montreal Lake—and that was only the winter freight trail bumped over by McKay and Henry in 1919. The road past Waskesiu was unfit for summer motor vehicle traffic. The only tourists able to access a park at La Ronge would be occasional canoe adventurers such as Henry or those able to pay for an airplane flight, not the far more lucrative weekend car excursionists or cottage leaseholders. This fact gave the Prince Albert group leverage in their fight to create a park closer to the city. Not only did a national park need to have "scenic wonders and beauties in sufficient abundance," as the national park official stated, but local promoters pushed the official's own argument. In that same 1926 letter, the deputy minister admitted that scenic wonders were not enough. A national park also had to be "sufficiently accessible to attract that type of tourist who... travel(s) in the open."[67] By 1926, accessibility referred to roads for cars.

Department of the Interior annual reports between 1925 and 1930 reiterated the need for accessibility for motor traffic and the new trend to motor tourism. "While the national parks movement has its root in the instinct for beauty and love of wild places ... the economic importance which outstanding scenery has come to possess as a result of the remarkable development of tourist travel is very great and constitutes a potential source of wealth which has as yet been barely touched."[68] With the logic of accessibility, the forest reserve and the larger Lakeland area became the "playground of the prairie." The subdivision at Waskesiu, reported C. MacFadyen, district forest inspector for Saskatchewan, suited "residents of the prairie districts ... more than ever casting about for summering places within the province," places different from the already established resorts on prairie lakes such as Vidal's Point (Katepwa).[69] Building on the rising popularity of car tourism, local success at Round Lake, and emerging possibilities of Emma and Christopher Lakes, Prince Albert boosters had strong bargaining power.

It might have been more convenient to deny the national park and continue with the burgeoning recreational use of the forest reserve or merely to convey national "recreational status" rather than national park status to Waskesiu. In the end, however, Prince Albert interests prevailed. National park status allowed both lakeshore activities and protection for regional flora, fish, and game.[70] Conservation of natural areas was of growing international and national political importance. The general suggestion was that each province should have a national park set aside within its borders. Prince Albert advocates fought hard to have the province's first full national park not within the prairie area but within the invisible boreal forest. It was, in many ways, a political statement: Saskatchewan is beautiful.

The Department of the Interior and the national parks commissioner relented. Prince Albert National Park was created by Order-in-Council 524 on 24 March 1927. Justification for the park was formally stated: the park was desirable "to provide recreational areas for the prairies."[71] If the north Prince Albert landscape was not "sufficiently beautiful" in and of itself, it certainly was when viewed in contrast to the open plains. Prince Albert National Park was created to provide a "playground" for prairie residents, exploiting the physical and cultural contrasts between the north and the south of the province. It was accessible enough, and wild enough, to draw tourists.

EXPANSION, ARRESTED DEVELOPMENT, AND FIRST NATIONS

The new national park included the original Sturgeon River Forest Reserve as well as adjoining areas east and north, for a total of 1,377 square miles. The dominion actually set aside even more land for investigation. Potential homestead land north of Paddockwood in the Forest Gate district was removed from settlement for more than a year, pending investigation of the region as an addition to the park. This reserved area stretched past Candle Lake to the Whiteswan Lakes region. The land was assessed and released back to the Crown for homestead purposes in 1928. Even so, the park borders continued to expand north. A major addition in 1929 of several townships north of Waskesiu added another 400 square miles.[72]

One part of the new park, east of the third meridian toward the First Nations community at Montreal Lake, was never part of the original Sturgeon River Forest Reserve. The area, which encompassed Bittern, McPhee, and Clearsand Lakes, was the nearby hunting domain of the Montreal Lake Cree community. Montreal Lake itself, and the Montreal Lake Reserve land, were excluded, but the larger territory became park. It was a strange decision. These small lakes were only indirectly connected to the "chain of lakes" at Waskesiu, not easily accessible by canoe, and hazardous in a dry season. The lack of connected water routes, as well as poor trail conditions, reduced the tourism potential of this eastward extension of the park. The primary purpose of this section appeared to be as a large game preserve, though fishing was good at Bittern Lake.

Despite its limited tourism potential, the eastern extension might have been added in the hope of a proposed railway extension from Paddockwood. The track had indeed been surveyed, and partly graded, to several miles north of the village. The projected line probably would have gone up the east side of Bittern and Montreal Lakes to La Ronge. Local promoters had high hopes that the rail line would be extended. Prince Albert was the first national park not to have railway access. The rise of auto tourism for the most part offset the lack of a railway, but it seems probable that park designers might have had rail links in mind. The eastern extension, though it was recovering from damage from the 1919 fire, might have been made in part on the hope of facilitating a future link by rail. History enthusiast James Harris argued that both the CPR and the CNR were battling to control northern Saskatchewan. The CNR, planning to build a railway to Lac La Ronge and a luxury hotel at Waskesiu, built a golf course at Waskesiu in an effort to compete with the luxury courses in Jasper and Banff.[73]

During the First World War, freighters and surveyors cut a second "new" Montreal Lake Trail straight north from the burgeoning farm district around Paddockwood. By the end of the 1920s, following formal creation of the national park, there was a drive to transform this trail into a highway, both to increase homestead traffic and to provide a second road into the national park. Ultimately, the road would connect to Waskesiu via Montreal Lake, providing a "loop" drive through the park. "There is a possibility that the much talked of road from Waskesiu to Montreal Lake and then south to Bittern Lake and Paddockwood and Prince Albert, will be started this year as a relief measure," the *Prince Albert Daily Herald* declared in 1931. "The provincial government is ready to go ahead with the provincial portion from the park boundary to Paddockwood, and link up with the existing park highway. Both governments would undertake the project as a relief measure, and it is felt this would create considerable employment," the staff writer enthused. "The deputy minister ... visualizes the proposed road as serving a double purpose. The first would create a loop highway making it possible for park visitors to have the choice of two routes into the park, both of them being scenic. The other viewpoint is from the utility angle. The present land settlement movement is verging into the north via Paddockwood to a considerable extent and future settlement as well as the present would justify a road as proposed." Despite the enthusiasm, the road was never completed.[74]

Prince Albert National Park might have been meant as the playground of prairie residents, but a signed Order-in-Council could not change thousands of years of First Nations history. Nearby First Nations had already struggled with legislative restrictions on land and its use. Game and bird laws, open and closed seasons, and other ordinances imposed by both the territorial assembly and the provincial administration after 1905 created previously unknown restrictions on First Nations communities. Little Red River Reserve was particularly hampered by the creation of the Sturgeon River Forest Reserve in 1914, which restricted hunting, trapping, and gathering activities. By 1920, hunting and trapping licences had been imposed. Lydia Cook of Little Red, interviewed in 1997, claimed that

> The hunting and trapping went on for many years, people were free to hunt and trap where they always had, until one day, resources put a restriction on hunting and trapping and gathering. The people couldn't trap or hunt just anywhere anymore, they were told to move away from their usual trapping areas, but they refused to move. The resources then went around snapping the traps, so that trappers wouldn't catch anything. Eventually, the poor trappers were forced to leave their trapping areas. As a result of this invasion many of our people suffered from hunger, some were near starvation, and some became very sick, and died. ... This was no doubt a conspiracy to weaken the Indians, but it only brought the people closer together and made us a stronger nation.[75]

Cook's words provide a chilling and poignant reminder of the power of government regulations to disconnect humans from landscapes, with tragic results. For the inhabitants of Little Red, creating the Sturgeon River Forest Reserve and regulating trapping, hunting, fishing, and gathering (including birds' eggs, outlawed in 1914) led to hardship. Such hardship was particularly noticeable, and growing, after the great fire of 1919 and the loss of the lumber industry in the north Prince Albert region. Jobs in nearby lumber camps disappeared. Throughout the 1920s, some inhabitants of Little Red turned to freighting and farming on an increased scale, but forest resources of fur and game remained important to the family economy.

The formation of Prince Albert National Park in 1928 was devastating for those who relied on the products of the land. What was restricted by the forest reserve became outlawed. No hunting or trapping, even within season, was allowed within park boundaries. With increased agricultural use of the landscape around the reserve to the east, west, and south, and a national park to the north, Little Red River Reserve was surrounded and cut off from its traditional forest edge resource base. Those who continued to hunt and trap on their traditional lands, as Cook noted, could be caught and fined or even jailed for poaching.[76] The new park, in effect, placed hundreds of square miles of traditional territory beyond the reach of its original inhabitants. Many were forced to move out, abandoning holdings that they had spent years building up, with gardens and farm plots, homes and cemeteries.

The Department of Indian Affairs, along with George Exton Lloyd, the Anglican bishop of Saskatchewan, immediately tried to leverage special consideration for the First Nations people affected by park borders.[77] Hunting of any kind was prohibited within national parks, which operated as national game preserves. Fishing was limited to recreational permits and limits, which were of no use to the First Nations communities that had derived considerable dietary subsistence from netting and

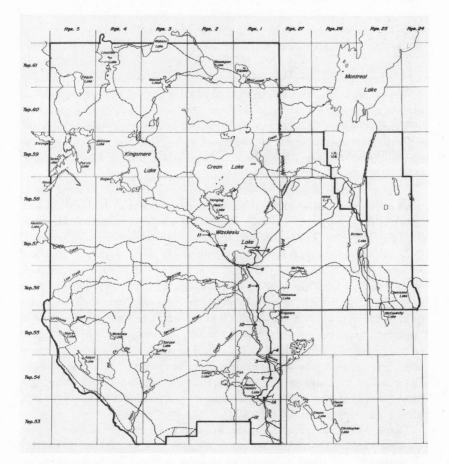

Map 14. Prince Albert National Park, 1935. Montreal Lake Indian Reserve 106 is on the southwest side of Montreal Lake, encompassed by the eastern portion of the park. Little Red Reserve is south of the southern boundary.
Source: Waiser, *Saskatchewan's Playground*, 53. Used with permission.

smoking or freezing fish in large quantities. In a letter to Deputy Superintendent of Indian Affairs Duncan Campbell Scott, Bishop Lloyd asked, "what about the Indians who were there before the National Park and surely are entitled to the right to live"? It was one thing to make a recreational site at Waskesiu, Lloyd maintained, but quite another to create a national park of nearly 1,400 square miles. At the least, Lloyd suggested, the band at Montreal Lake should be allowed to fish on alternative years on Bittern Lake and Trout Lake but would leave Red Deer Lake "entirely free for the summer tourists, which is the object of the National Park."[78]

National Park Commissioner J.B. Harkin flatly refused to consider Lloyd's reasonable request. After all, he noted, the Indians could still fish, within regulations, "as this is a privilege extended to all." As for game hunting, creation of the park would, in effect, strengthen game stocks in the region. The animals protected within the game preserve would provide a "constant overflow" to the surrounding area, he argued.[79] Harkin's haughty and condescending opinion did not fit reality on the ground: the majority of the band's sustenance was derived from whitefish, taken in large quantities by net, and not game fish such as jack (northern pike) or pickerel (walleye). The national park granted a short-term reprieve to the bands to continue their normal practice of fishing as long as they did not take game fish. Regardless of restrictions, however, isolation and lack of roads meant that Montreal Lake inhabitants operated much as usual for both hunting and fishing. Game wardens found themselves on constant watch for poaching, and band members devised strategies of stealth and misdirection.

Creation of the park reignited treaty land entitlement issues in the north Prince Albert region. It was believed that the future of these northern First Nations bands lay not in their traditional hunting and fishing grounds but in the already established farming reserve at Little Red. In many ways, creation of the park re-created the "north" in the mind of the southern white public as a place of recreation and relaxation, not a place to live permanently. It added strength to the continued push to move the northern bands to Little Red to engage in farming. Indian Affairs began to push for additional lands to be attached to Little Red for the La Ronge band, in lieu of lands in the north that had still not been surveyed. The band at Little Red wanted the new land added in a bloc to the west side of the original reserve. Even though soil quality was marginal, it was "as satisfactory for farming purposes as any other that could be obtained in the vicinity."[80] Settlers were reaching the end of good homestead land in the Paddockwood region, and interest was shifting west, so Indian Affairs believed that there was urgency to secure the land before it was designated as homestead land.

Adding more farmland to Little Red was easier said than done. The new park boundaries encroached on the reserve to the west and north. Negotiations between Indian Affairs and National Parks ensued, which Commissioner Harkin misunderstood. He thought that the Montreal Lake band was willing to give up its Montreal Lake Reserve in return for an addition to Little Red and possibly a reserve at Candle Lake. Such an exchange of land would facilitate both a southern exodus of reserve residents to the farming reserve and an extension of national park boundaries to include all of Montreal Lake and eliminate the main boreal reserve. Indian Affairs was quick to present the terms more clearly, pointing out that the extension of Little Red was not in fact a negotiated exchange with Montreal Lake but a simple proposal to finally bring the La Ronge band up to its treaty land entitlement. Harkin was upset. Montreal Lake Reserve residents, living and using the landscape as they always had, quickly became framed as a problem for park staff. Band members rightly unwilling and unable to change their subsistence and hunting activities within their traditional territory put excessive pressure on game wardens, forced to arrest reserve residents for "poaching." A proposal to extend the park to include all of Montreal Lake would engulf the reserve there, exacerbating the poaching problem. Harkin considered such a move, without elimination of the reserve, "entirely objectionable."[81]

Montreal Lake never became part of the national park. No exchange was negotiated, nor did the idea of a new First Nations reserve at Candle Lake come to fruition. The borders of Little Red were revised and extended over time, but the reserve at Montreal Lake remained. By 1947, in response to years of debate and lobbying by wardens and the park commissioner, Prince Albert National Park was downsized. The area east of the third meridian—the trapping and hunting area most used by Montreal Lake residents—was declassified as a national park.[82] After twenty years of "poaching," Montreal Lake residents no doubt drew a quiet breath of relief.

Although the creation of Prince Albert National Park and the growth of tourism developments at the new Lakeland region had adverse impacts on traditional resource use of the local landscape, they also offered new opportunities. First Nations residents along the forest edge and at the Montreal Lake Reserve participated in the tourist economy, as provisioners, employees, and tourists themselves, culturally shaping the boreal forest as a First Nations inheritance. First Nations cultural stories of the region, particularly the legend of the Hanging Heart Lakes and stories of forest denizen Wisk-ee-chack featured prominently in the *Prince Albert Daily Herald* park commemorative edition and found their way into Department of the Interior promotional brochures. Montreal Lake residents made publicized annual visits to Waskesiu, usually in conjunction with the annual regatta, where band members handily won canoe races. They often participated in ceremonies, speeches, and pow-wow dances throughout the 1930s.[83]

In 1931, the national parks branch of the Department of the Interior created *Modern Voyageurs*, a short silent film to advertise the new Prince Albert National Park. The main characters in the film were white tourists, but colour and life came from the First Nations men hired by the tourists to take them on a canoe journey through the park. Film viewers were encouraged to come and "circumnavigate the park under the protection of the Indian guides skilled in the use of rod, paddle and frying pan." It seemed idyllic for non-Native audiences—the Indian guides were shown carrying and loading all the gear and doing all the paddling while the tourists put their feet up and read books in the middle of the lake. Other duties included putting up tents, cooking (and fish cleaning), and serving tea. Even the most laborious tasks were trivialized: "The Indians carry the big canoes as if they were steamer trunks on the shady portage to Crean Lake."[84] Although it is unknown how many First Nations people capitalized on tourist opportunities, it was a way to use traditional outdoor skills for a new audience and become part of the new tourist economy, extending to a new clientele the local knowledge and services that Christina Henry used in 1919. Some of the members of Little Red and Montreal Lake spent their summers working at Waskesiu, either for businesses as cooks or general workers or for the park as guides.[85]

The connection between First Nations and the outdoors was exploited by the owners of the "Teepee Tea Room" (built in the shape of a traditional teepee) near Emma Lake and Little Red River Reserve on the highway leading to Waskesiu. It offered meals and confectionery items, an auto camp, supervised guides, cottages and boats for rent, camping and fishing, and souvenirs made from antlers and wood.[86] Women from Little Red, Fish Lake (a nearby Métis community), and Montreal Lake participated in the tourist economy by making moccasins and other handicrafts such as purses and shopping bags. Some were sold at the Teepee Tea Room, more at Waskesiu and a specially built store on the roadside between Waskesiu and Montreal Lake. Despite the economic depression during the 1930s, there was strong demand for the products. One Waskesiu business owner claimed that he could have sold over $1,000 worth of Indian crafts one summer but lacked a sure supply.

Supplying handicrafts was a delicate issue. In the Depression, under pressure from trapping and hunting restrictions, crafters found it difficult to afford supplies. To help out, the Indian agent from the Carlton Agency in charge of the area requested and received a fund to offset and underwrite these costs. This provided a non-refundable loan in the amount of $300. The proceeds of craft sales were to be put back into the fund to purchase more supplies. The agency also purchased a stamp that read "Guaranteed Indian Handicraft, Carlton Agency, Leask, SK," which promoted the agency and its involvement in the crafts rather than the First Nations women who did the work. Nonetheless, traditional crafts sold well.[87] In addition to crafts, First Nations and Métis women took babysitting, cleaning, and cooking jobs around the lakes during the summer tourist season.[88] In some ways, summer work within the burgeoning summer tourist economy offset winter losses caused by the end of the large-scale lumber industry and reduced hunting and trapping returns.

UP NORTH ON VACATION

Despite deep concerns registered by local First Nations communities, the new national park initiated a bold new tourism campaign. It developed from two sources: the businessmen of Prince Albert anxious to cash in on their nearby accessible wilderness, and the Department of the Interior, national parks branch, desperate to find a way to promote the best features of the new park. Promotion centred on enticing Saskatchewan residents first, marketing the prairie south as a workplace and the boreal north as a playground. Provincial Secretary S.J. Latta, at the park's opening in 1928, suggested that the new slogan should be "See Saskatchewan First!" He declared that "nothing will serve more to create that love of country upon which national patriotism is founded, or have greater influence upon the ultimate solidarity of our people, than an intimate knowledge of the Province which is our home."[89] Although stirring, such rhetoric tried to hide the fact that Saskatchewan politicians and merchants were eager to see potential tourist dollars spent at home. The new vacationland sold its landscape of trees and lakes to promote a happily domestic holiday of camping, fishing, boating, and swimming.

The tourism campaign also focussed on the astonishing idea that Saskatchewan had its own beauty spots. Advertisements targeting national and international audiences zeroed in on the romance of the fur-trade voyageurs and placed the park firmly as the gateway to a northern canoeing wilderness. In the annual report following creation of the park, Commissioner Harkin blended the prairie/boreal divide with the northern wilderness ethos:

> North of the great fertile belt devoted to agriculture there lies in this province a region of rocks, woods and water which seems almost to have been formed by nature as a special playground for man. Here are found thousands of crystal lakes, from tiny rock basins ... to great bodies of fresh water. Between, tying one to another into an intricate network of waterways, run innumerable little rivers and streams offering to canoeists and lovers of the wilderness water routes extending for hundreds of miles ... Irresistible to the adventurous, [these] lakes and streams form a natural gateway to the ... hinterland of Canada.[90]

The message of northern beauty and vacations was familiar in Canadian public life. In Ontario, for example, the northern wilderness ideal powered much of the northern cottage movement and the development of Algonquin and other rugged northern parks.[91] The Canadian public consciousness, however, did not have a vision of northern wilderness in Saskatchewan. The province bore a "mental map" of flat, treeless prairie.[92] As the comments of T.C. Davis in the Saskatchewan legislature in 1925 revealed, even few Saskatchewan residents had ever been north of the treeline. Acknowledging the prairie mentality, the Department of the Interior wrote in a natural resources publication in 1925 that, "though it may seem like a paradox to refer to the forests of the Prairie Provinces, the wooded sections ... are nevertheless very extensive."[93] During the opening of Prince Albert National Park, one visitor wrote that "to many people the word 'Saskatchewan' calls up a mind picture of great stretches of open prairie, unrelieved by lake or forest. To them a description of the beauties of the new Prince Albert National Park will come as a surprise."[94]

The Department of the Interior recognized the importance of image. Its tourist campaign consistently worked to overcome regional stereotypes.[95] The national parks branch invested in a wide variety of promotional materials, from pamphlets and maps to enlarged and framed photographs, lectures, articles, sheet music, magic lantern slides, and moving pictures. The silent film *Modern Voyageurs* was distributed in 1931; other films, such as *Prairie Land to Fairy Land* (1933) and *Summer Days at Waskesiu* (1936) also advertised the accessible wilderness of Saskatchewan's north.[96] Shown to audiences across Canada and the United States, as well as around the world, the movies were a bold move to overcome assumptions and stereotypes regarding Saskatchewan.

In addition, several moving pictures were filmed at Ajawaan Lake, showcasing the celebrated public speaker and author Grey Owl and his beaver friends.[97] Grey Owl, or Archibald Stansfeld Belaney, was an intriguing figure in the early promotion of Prince Albert National Park. Despite the now-common attitude that he was an imposter who stole First Nations ancestry, Grey Owl was the rock star of environmentalism in his time. He spoke to sold-out audiences in eastern Canada, the United States, and Great Britain. His books were bestsellers. And he lived at Beaver Lodge, the cabin that he built during the Great Depression at Ajawaan Lake, a full day of travel for an experienced canoeist, north of Waskesiu. Grey Owl *was* accessible wilderness. He was a popular and prolific author and speaker whose message was about the protection of wilderness. His cabin at Ajawaan Lake remains a pilgrimage site, hosting thousands of visitors every summer who recreate his wilderness travels and agree with him that "this is a different place."[98]

Despite Grey Owl's national and international appeal, most visitors to the park were provincial residents. J.A. Wood, newly appointed park superintendent, "embarked on a one-man campaign" through Saskatchewan to promote the new park.[99] Using slides and moving pictures, he gave fourteen lectures across the province.[100] There is no record of Wood going to any northern communities such as La Ronge or Stanley Mission to advertise the new park. Clientele would be drawn first and foremost from prairie residents with cars.

Car tourism forced both national and provincial authorities to give immediate attention to the state of roads to and through Prince Albert National Park. In fact, historian Bill Waiser suggested that Prince Albert merchants pushed for national park status in large part because the dominion, not the municipality or the province, would be responsible for major road improvements.[101] The park's first order of business was to build a road from its south entrance to the budding resort at Waskesiu. The freight road existed, but it was never built with scenery in mind. Its main use as a winter freight road required it to follow flat land as much as possible, and in summer portions of it were all but impassable through muskeg and swamp. Harkin noted in the annual report for 1928–29 that over 5,000 people visited the park the first year, "a large number, considering the fact that its reputation was as yet largely local and that parties traveling had to bring with them tents and camping equipment." Moreover, "road conditions were not good" that first year.[102] A better road, more scenic and crossing higher ground, built for car traffic, was necessary. Soon a graded road was in the works.

While the park built its road, engineered with "as many curves as possible,"[103] the provincial government agreed to improve the road leading to the park entrance. Disregarding the oldest route past Sturgeon Lake and through Little Red River Reserve, the government chose to improve the road straight north from Prince Albert, giving better access to the agricultural communities at Buckland, Alingly, Spruce Home, Henribourg, and Northside. It swung west at the 14th baseline, passing just south of Christopher and Emma Lakes. Resort owners at Christopher and Emma lobbied strongly for this route since it would bring national park tourist traffic right past their doorsteps. The original park road is now Highway 263, advertised as the "scenic route" to Prince Albert National Park.[104] The road hooks up with the park highway at its southern terminus. A provincial-grade road led to an explosion in tourism traffic and economic expansion for both the burgeoning Lakeland region and Prince Albert National Park.

Following the official opening of the park in 1928, the number of visitors to the north Prince Albert region skyrocketed. Over 5,000 people visited the park in 1928; in 1929, that number doubled. In 1930, it almost doubled again, with over 17,000 people visiting it, but that number was dwarfed in 1931, when a staggering 29,537 tourists registered at the park.[105] "That the people of Saskatchewan, and tourists generally, appreciate Prince Albert National Park is clearly indicated by statistics," exclaimed the park report for 1931.[106] Prince Albert businessmen eagerly championed the new tourist industry. They outfitted tourists, selling everything from bathing suits and tents to fishing supplies and canoes. Business boomed for the R.D. Brooks Company, which specialized in freight hauling into the north and began hauling camping outfits and gear from Prince Albert to Waskesiu, with stops in the Lakeland area.[107] The Saskatchewan Motor Club turned its attention to providing information and signage along the way to direct tourists both through Prince Albert and up to the Lakeland and park region.

The Lakeland region, on the road to the national park, grew as tourist traffic expanded. A road was built from the provincial highway heading north past Oscar Lake to the excellent fishing to be found at Anglin Lake, linking the three resort areas (Oscar Lake was never developed—it is essentially a big slough with few fish). Thus, Anglin Lake's development kept pace with that of Christopher and Emma Lakes. A small portion of Anglin Lake falls within national park boundaries, so its history has always been intimately tied with park issues.

Developments outside park boundaries were unfettered by strict national park protocols. Resort and cottage development outside the park, as well as fishing regulations, were monitored by provincial and municipal authorities. A group of citizens formed the Emma Lake Outing Club sometime in the late 1920s and purchased land around the south end of Emma Lake.[108] Development at Sunnyside beach, Macintosh Point, Neis Beach, and Sunset Bay at Emma Lake was mirrored by resort work at Christopher Lake, particularly at Johnson's (now known as Bell's) Beach. Daily correspondence throughout July and August from both Emma Lake and Waskesiu, reported in the Prince Albert *Daily Herald* under the heading "Vacationland," gave information on fishing, weather, cabin building, dances, news, and events throughout the 1930s. That decade, researchers and local residents reported, was a boom period of recreational development. "Lake water levels were considerably higher" (in the 1930s), offering easy access from one lake to another. Close to 100 cottages and seven-day-use resort areas had been built. In addition, several institutional camps had been built, such as several church-owned summer camps. "In less than ten years the land had totally changed its character from wilderness trapping to recreation."[109]

The phenomenal growth of tourism in vacationland carried on despite the severe economic effects of the Great Depression. It was "striking evidence of the fact that the people realize the necessity for recreation in a period of economic stress even more, perhaps, than at other times," Commissioner Harkin believed.[110] And, compared with lengthy car trips or railway excursions west, east, or south into the United States, a visit to Lakeland and Prince Albert National Park was an inexpensive holiday for both local and prairie residents. The majority of visitors recorded at the park gates registered from Prince Albert and surrounding towns; the next largest group came from cities, towns, and farms on the prairie. The *Daily Herald*, eager to promote the park to a broader audience, consistently sought out travellers from other provinces or the United States, soliciting their comments on the park. Invariably, the paper recorded enthusiastic reviews that declared the park among the best recreational facilities and beauty spots anywhere.[111] Reviews catered to local and provincial audiences, offering a message of reassurance: Prince Albert National Park and Lakeland are as nice as any vacation spot anywhere.

TOURISM AND PERMANENT SETTLEMENT

As early as 1922, the national parks branch proclaimed that tourist travel should be valued not only for tourism development but also for its role "as a forerunner of permanent settlement and financial investment. ... Tourist travel, in fact, is one of the best immigration agencies, one of the best methods of attracting ... capital."[112] People travelling to or through a region for tourism purposes would be more inclined to return and settle permanently or invest in development schemes. Certainly, the Department of the Interior (of which national parks was a branch) promoted permanent settlement.

The relationship between permanent settlement and scenic park areas was highlighted by the Paddockwood Board of Trade in 1933.[113] This group, made up of local businessmen, created a booster-style immigration pamphlet to advertise Paddockwood as a destination of choice for dried-out prairie farmers heading north.[114] During the 1930s, an estimated 45,000 people moved from the open plains north to the forest fringe, fleeing the dual prongs of agricultural depression and drought. Paddockwood merchants saw this movement as an opportunity to grow their businesses, and they set out to draw settlement.

To entice prairie refugees, the pamphlet promoted Paddockwood's situation ad-

Saskatchewan Unrolls Northward

PROVINCE BECOMES NORTH-MINDED AS SETTLEMENT AREA EXTENDS

Provincial Control of Natural Resources has made possible this year, the largest bona fide Settlement Activity North of the North Saskatchewan, in the History of the Country.

564 ENTRIES HAVE BEEN GRANTED IN THE PRINCE ALBERT DISTRICT, ALONE, SINCE NOVEMBER 1, 1930.

SOUTH LOOKS TO NORTH FOR NEW RECREATIONAL PLAYGROUNDS

With the National Park already firmly established as one of Canada's Premier Tourist Resorts, the North has additional recreational attraction to offer at Emma Lake Provincial Forest—

EMMA LAKE PROVINCIAL FOREST IS 150 SQUARE MILES IN EXTENT, AND HAS MANY DISTINCTIVE FEATURES.

Lands Posted For Settlement And Pasture Purposes

Nipawin District	200
Witchekan Lake and Big River District	700
North Prince Albert District	200
Total Quarter Sections	1,100

In addition, there are 100 quarter-sections to be posted in T.54,R.12, West of 3rd Meridian.

MINING ACTIVITY

As at June 30, 1931, the following are the number of Mining Leases and Claims in good standing:

Alkali leases	45
Coal leases	158
Petroleum and natural gas leases	544
Quarrying leases	62
Quartz leases	318
Quartz surface leases	22
Quartz claims	1007
Miners' licenses issued	155

Emma Lake Is Accessible From Highway To Park

The Provincial Forest is 30 miles north of Prince Albert; has heavy stands of White Spruce, Poplar and Jack Pine; and many varieties of Wild Fruit.

Moose, deer, bear, partridge and ducks abound; its lakes teem with pike and pickerel, while bathing beaches enhance the lure of the many lakes within the forest bounds.

FINGERS OF SETTLEMENT PUSHING NORTHWARD WILL HASTEN DEVELOPMENT OF NORTHLAND'S MINERAL WEALTH

THE DEPARTMENT OF NATURAL RESOURCES

Hon. J. T. M. Anderson, D.Paed.,
Minister.

Broder Building, Regina, Sask.

Major John Barnett,
Deputy Minister

Figure 26. Saskatchewan unrolls northward.
Source: *Prince Albert Daily Herald*, 5 July 1931.

jacent to the Lakeland region, just off the "National Park all weather highway."[115] The burgeoning resort at Candle Lake featured centrally in the pamphlet, emphasizing that the new road to Candle Lake passed through Paddockwood and "miles of virgin forest, untouched by the ravages of fire and unblemished by the axe of man, ... without equal for scenery." The road, built to allow car traffic, "will attract tourists to Candle Lake, one of the finest lakes in the Province for size, beaches, and fishing."[116] Clearly, Paddockwood merchants believed that people would be more likely to immigrate to places that were not only economically viable but also beautiful. Situating Paddockwood close to Lakeland and the national park pushed an aesthetic agenda intimately tied to economic development. The resorts offered nearby beauty and recreation and markets for farm products from local homesteaders.

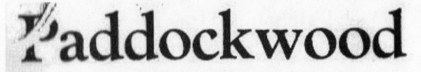

Paddockwood

The Mixed Farming Paradise of Saskatchewan

— ISSUED BY —

The Paddockwood
Board of Trade
1933

Figure 27. Paddockwood, mixed-farming paradise.
Source: Paddockwood Museum.

Of course, Paddockwood promoted, first and foremost, agricultural settlement. Farmers would hew the trees to "make land" for cereal crops. The pamphlet therefore mixed extractive and essentially destructive development with beauty unblemished by human intervention. Yet the Paddockwood Board of Trade had no qualm about the obvious conflict. The dominion government quarter section surveys of 1920 identified the best use for land in the local setting. When the federal government transferred the natural resources of Saskatchewan to provincial control in 1930, the province initiated the Royal Commission on Immigration and Settlement to determine the best use of the land. The commission believed in scientific settlement. Studying the general malaise in agriculture and the deficiencies of the homestead system (in which farmers sometimes took poor land without knowing its crop-growing potential), the commission determined that part of the solution was to examine the land more closely. Advocates promoted increased land surveys and investigations, such as those completed for soldier settlement. Questioning the reeve of the RM of Buckland during proceedings in Prince Albert, the commission representative asked, "don't you think [settlement] should be directed a little more scientifically to stop this waste of effort? ... That the character of the land should be determined by experts, so that people would know what kind of land they are going on to?"[117] The reeve agreed. Soil testing and extensive land studies were needed to determine land capability and best-use practices across the province.

The commissioner's question revealed not only a heightened interest in securing successful settlement using scientific assessments of land but also an underlying belief that land could and probably should be used for purposes other than agriculture. Some land was not suited for farming but might support recreation, grazing, timber, cordwood, hunting, or berry picking, the commissioner suggested.[118] Site-specific understanding of best practices allowed for a nuanced and sometimes conflicting representation of the landscape as both recreational and agricultural. Sometimes both types of use could occur on the same quarter of land. For instance, farmers whose land straddled the Garden River or contained large bodies of water could provide diving platforms, docks, and even boats for neighbours and children to use for recreation. The same river could provide water for stock diversification. In winter, the Paddockwood hockey team, the Muskeg Elks, practised on that frozen river. How land could and should be used varied not only by place but also by season.[119]

Localized landscape use promoting recreation might not necessarily affect the economic capital of the individual farmer, but it did have an impact on community development.[120] During the Depression, recreation, fun, and a thriving social community drew people to the forest fringe. The overall message, as presented by the Paddockwood Board of Trade, was that farmland in the north Prince Albert region offered settlers beauty, water, greenery, and trees—an enticing contrast to the open plains. The board attempted to draw people north using a combination of agriculture and recreation, mixing agricultural hope with relaxation and leisure, both ultimately contrasts to the stress and pain of prairie life during the Depression.

MURRAY POINT ART SCHOOL

Although the boreal north/prairie south divide fuelled much of the tourist boom, the contrast also launched a new oasis of culture in 1936—the Murray Point Art School at Emma Lake, headed by artist Augustus Kenderdine. Professionally trained and mentored in Europe, Kenderdine immigrated to Saskatchewan in 1908. He started working as an art instructor at the University of Saskatchewan in the mid-1920s and soon after built a cabin at Emma Lake. His northern excursions fundamentally shaped the future of art in Saskatchewan. He convinced the University of Saskatchewan to build an art camp on a secluded peninsula jutting into Emma Lake, renamed Murray Point after Walter Murray, the first president of the university. Murray promoted development of the art department at the university and hired Kenderdine. Reporters followed creation of the art school with great enthusiasm. Kenderdine, one Saskatchewan reporter asserted, showed prairie residents "the way to the resorts, and he leads them into beauty." His canvases, depicting the northern landscape, offered "beautiful glimpses into the lovely lakelands."[121]

Art historian Keith Bell argued that the prairie landscape, with its agrarian settlement grid, was less and less "natural."[122] The north, with its trees and lakes, in contrast, was perceived as more natural and wild. Throughout the 1930s, prairie regions were increasingly disfigured by drought that was not only economic and ecological but also cultural. University of Saskatchewan president J.S. Thompson summed it up in 1947: "Life was becoming grim and weary [in Saskatchewan during the Depression]. It was then, of all times, that [Kenderdine] thought of beginning a summer school of art to let the young folk of Saskatchewan see beauty in a land that men were coming to hate as a place of darkness and defeat."[123]

Kenderdine's art school in a forested landscape provided a contrast familiar to both Canadian and British eyes. For Ontarians in particular, northern "cottage country" was well established by growing tourism and the work of the Group of Seven. For British audiences, Scottish landscapes were wild and northern, "visited and experienced as a tourist in the summertime, and then left for the south when the season was over."[124] Planting an art school in what was becoming cottage country was a Saskatchewan version of similar activities elsewhere. Reflecting in large part a nineteenth-century Romantic notion of the wilderness landscape as a primeval cathedral within which to commune directly with God, students would come north and find spiritual rebirth, sanctuary, and peace. Kenderdine believed that Murray Point offered a cultural renaissance for drought-stricken southerners: clear lake in contrast to dry earth; boreal forest in contrast to treeless landscape; hope in contrast to despair.

The main participants in the summer art school were high school art teachers from prairie agricultural communities hit hard by the Depression. Kenderdine's vision of northern beauty would reinvigorate the Saskatchewan identity beyond its current dry dustiness and develop a broader cultural inclusion of the provincial north. "Having absorbed this transcendental experience, artists and art teachers from drought affected farming areas would be able to return home after their

Figure 8. Emma Lake Art Camp, c. 1936. Augustus Kenderdine (in white hat) is standing at the back right. Source: Glenbow na,-63-23.

classes at Murray Point with both a strong personal experience and a new optimism about life in the province," Bell suggested.[125] The optimism would ideally reach students, who in future would incorporate both halves of the provincial landscape into their cultural paradigm. Kenderdine used art to do what T.C. Davis had called for in 1925—make the south acquainted with the north.

Kenderdine's effort to establish an art school in Saskatchewan in the middle of the Great Depression has been met with bewilderment by most commentators. A deeper analysis of the north Prince Albert region, in particular the rise of resort culture and tourism, balances this picture. The Great Depression and the classic images of dust and despair represented, in part, what Kenderdine and the art students were running *from*, while Emma Lake and the northern forested landscape showed what they were running *to*.

CONCLUSION

Tourism in the north Prince Albert region was promoted using a unique cultural paradigm. Traditional tourism promotion generally rested on an urban/rural divide. Tourism in the Lakeland/Prince Albert National Park region drew its force primarily from Saskatchewan's ecological divide, the boreal north and the prairie south. Tourism promoters understood that the majority of tourists would be Saskatchewan prairie residents with access to cars. "Northward Ho!" was the slogan that some used, eager to exchange "the bleak and dusty regions" for "the luring vista of vast expanses of forest land with silvery glimpses here and there of the small lakes." After a tremendous holiday spent fishing, boating, camping, swimming, dancing, and enjoying the landscape, the prairie holidayer would head "back to the dusty south with fond memories of the short holiday trip and with many resolutions to be back again next year determined to see the holiday paradise of the north to its fullest extent."[126] To entice prairie tourists, promoters consistently marketed contrast, as did Davis, Kenderdine, and Grey Owl.

Contrast was also used by those who promoted agricultural settlement along the edge of the forest, connecting the ecotone with mixed farming and off-farm economic opportunities. Although on the surface agriculture, forest resources, and trees/beauty might appear conflicting, those conflicts broke down in the local setting. The science of settlement and highly governed state intervention in the north Prince Albert region included evaluating and setting aside large areas for a forest reserve, national park, or resort. Only land considered fit for agriculture was left open to homestead regulations. Mixed-farming promoters such as the Paddockwood Board of Trade advocated a landscape-based lifestyle that promoted both use and beauty. Such marketing echoes author L.M. Montgomery's "flowery peroration on the possibilities of the country" and HBC servant Anthony Henday's description of the future Prince Albert region as "pleasant and plentyful." Intensive local knowledge and use of space accommodated all concepts—farming, resource extraction, and recreation—in the same general region and sometimes on the same quarter. Resort owner George Neis at Emma Lake provided a classic example. Although he worked to develop Neis beach, he also operated a farm on the same quarter, cutting cordwood in the winter and selling eggs, chickens, milk, cream, and butter to tourists in the summer.[127]

Artist Augustus Kenderdine's vision of a northern landscape of idyllic beauty resonated as a bold and hopeful contrast to the devastation of the dirty thirties on the prairie, using art to construct a new concept that incorporated both solitudes of the provincial identity. Contrast and connection provided a point of leverage not only for local tourist development but ultimately for all non-agricultural development in the north. Responding to Davis's claim that Saskatchewan had experienced "lop-sided" development, the agricultural, resource development, and tourism push into the north Prince Albert region provided a strong multifaceted foundation for both social and economic development. That strength underscored the pull of the north for refugee migrants of the Great Depression.[128]

CHAPTER EIGHT

EVEN THE TURNIPS WERE EDIBLE

April 1934. In the midst of a violent early spring dust storm, tenant farmer Sargent McGowan of the east Weyburn district of southern Saskatchewan loaded a boxcar at the local siding. Stripping his farmhouse, machine shed, and barn, McGowan put everything he had into the boxcar: cows, chickens, plow, other implements, seed grain, household furniture, kitchen supplies, bedding, and provisions. He loaded his horses and wagon last, driving them up the ramp and into the boxcar. Unhitch, stow, organize, tie up, and tie down. At last, all was ready. He stepped down to hug his wife, Muriel, and two young daughters, who would take the passenger train to join him after one last visit with parents and grandparents.

McGowan climbed in to keep the animals settled, fed, and watered. As the train prepared to leave the siding, McGowan turned for one last look at the drought-stricken land that he was abandoning, wondering once again if he was making the right decision. But the landscape answered him. A brutal wind sent clouds of once-productive black soil billowing straight across the field toward the track. Dust blocked his vision. He could not see the caboose, though his settler car was just in front of it. With a face full of dirt, he withdrew, shut the door, wiped his eyes with a handkerchief and settled in for the three-day journey.

The train headed north to the village of Paddockwood. When the train pulled into the station, McGowan slid open the boxcar door and gasped. There were still two feet of snow on the ground, and the little town was ringing with the sights, sounds, and smells of hundreds of teams and sleighs. It was more activity than he had seen for years in the broken communities around Weyburn. The contrast between the violent prairie dust storm and the snow and busy humanity was "enough to put the memory of Weyburn back behind a huge cloud of dust, and there it stayed."[1]

In Saskatchewan, an estimated 45,000 people moved north during the Great Depression.[2] The massive internal migration, known as the Great Trek, changed the face of the province: prairie farms were abandoned or sold to neighbours, parkland regions filled to capacity, and agriculture pushed back the eaves of the forest. Great Trek refugees moved, not just away from the dried-up prairie, but also toward a place of hope, a place with water, trees, garden produce, and hay. Trekkers defined the new landscape in terms of the old, comparing what they had left behind with what they found in the north. The forest edge landscape was desirable because it was *not* the prairie.

The ecology and the economy were different along the forest edge. In the midst of the worst depression in living memory, forest fringe towns across Saskatchewan, including those in the north Prince Albert region, became oases in a desert landscape. "The 1930s were boom times for Paddockwood," local residents remembered.[3] Mixed farming, lumber and cordwood, freighting, commercial fishing, wild game, berries, and tourism combined to offer Depression migrants an economic as well as an ecological refuge.

For some, moving north was a temporary retreat; others found long-term resilience, drawing back full circle to traditional First Nations use of the north Prince Albert region. The ecological edge had provided a seasonal place of refuge for prairie First Nations in times of stress, such as a harsh winter or when bison were scarce. Small forest-adapted bands found long-term resilience at the ecological edge. During the Great Depression, wheat farmers—like their bison-dependent First Nations counterparts sixty years before—faced starvation and were forced to rely on government assistance. Many chose to move north to the forest edge simply to obtain the basic essentials of life: food, shelter, and warmth. There they encountered a small but temporally deep culture embraced by both First Nations and newcomers. It was a northern paradigm of resilience that drew heavily on mixed farming, occupational pluralism, and forest resources to provide a practical, self-sufficient way of life in which subsistence was the first priority.

As analysts have indicated, some migrants experienced worse conditions and moved away, overwhelmed by the attempt to bring agriculture to the forest landscape. Overall, though, northern migration—while difficult—was successful. Families at the forest edge required less relief than did their southern counterparts. In many places, migration continued to climb until the Second World War, after which both the southern prairie and the northern parkland/forest fringe experienced extensive out-migration. Increased farm mechanization and consolidation, urban industrialization, and the postwar population shift to urban centres were important factors underlying the movement away from both prairie and forest fringe farms. Those who stayed expanded their acreage, and in time some farms at the forest edge became indistinguishable from those in the adjoining parkland and prairie. The experiences of the Great Depression resonated strongly, though, and the forest edge culture continued to embrace self-sufficiency as a primary hallmark of success.

Much has been written about the Great Depression in Canada, in particular its effects in Saskatchewan, where environmental and economic disaster spelled ruin for many.[4] The Great Depression has been categorized as "ten lost years," a time when "our world stopped and we got off."[5] Certainly, the defining image of those years came from the prairie, the immense dust storms that simply blew the land—and the people—away. That image, however, has obscured the story of forest edge migration, northern boom, adaptation, and hope within the province in the face of the Depression.

Figure 29. Tractor buried in drifting soil.
Source: Glenbow Archives, NA 2291-2.

Tempted by stories of desperation and despair, Great Trek analysts have focussed on hungry and frantic families, devastated by drought and poor agricultural prices, forced north to a "place of last resort." Geographer J. David Wood in particular advocated the theory that hapless migrants occupied northern farms "in desperation after the more accessible land further south had been colonized."[6] Historians and geographers have presented the migration through government relief and resettlement policy analysis, agricultural hazards, and the shocking stories of loss, brutal conditions, and bewilderment of urban and prairie people trying to eke out a living in the bush.[7] Although there is ample evidence to support these characterizations, the story is incomplete. To assume that northern lands were taken only when the better agricultural land of the prairie had all been settled negates the experience of northern migrants who had already tried prairie farming and found it wanting. For those who abandoned the prairie, which was the more "marginal" landscape? The "place of last resort" storyline also dismisses the extensive "pull" factors that drew people north. Depression migration was not, in fact, a radical reaction to particular environmental and economic circumstances. The Great Trek was a proactive response, an injection of hope and energy to improve living conditions and open new possibilities for earning a living. Drought migration continued, and increased, internal migration practices that had been in place for a long time.

PRELUDE TO THE GREAT TREK

The first reference to a trek of southern refugees was in 1919—ten years before the start of the Great Depression. Northern migration gained strength throughout the 1920s, as trekkers from the Palliser Triangle or other drought regions found their way to the parkland and forest edge. Northern settlement throughout the 1920s was augmented by soldier settlement, the 3000 British Families scheme, and the work of the CNR Department of Colonization. The changing policies of the dominion government that began to invest in creating farms, not just enticing people to become farmers, supported the exodus north. Mechanization, agricultural prosperity in the latter half of the 1920s, and the new provision for second homesteads led to an explosion of interest in northern regions. The branch line from Prince Albert to Paddockwood, owned by the CNR, was a favourite northern route.

The surge in second homestead applications in 1928 and 1929 has often been blurred by memory and faulty analysis and presented as part of the Depression migration. The two, however, should not be intertwined. A large number of families filed on second homesteads prior to the Depression, when the agricultural situation in Saskatchewan was buoyant. The Prince Albert land agency recorded a respectable 2,162 homestead applications in 1927. In 1928, that number more than doubled, to 5,615, and increased again in 1929, with almost 6,500 new homestead entries.[8]

The opening of second homesteads caused a virtual land rush in northern districts across Saskatchewan, which contained the vast majority of remaining homestead quarters. Second homesteads were popular for several plausible reasons. A homestead, through hard work and good luck, could become a patented farm, to be kept and farmed or sold for profit. Much prairie land changed hands in this way, as a business endeavour rather than a lifestyle choice. Some prairie farmers, with enough capital to expand and diversify, took northern homesteads or purchased farms in an active bid to change their physical environment from prairie to parkland/forest edge. The northern environment was promoted as better suited to mixed-farming practices. A few of these farmers might have been interested in owning two farms, one on the prairie devoted primarily to wheat farming, one near or at the forest edge to access resources of timber, fuel, hay, and wild game. The north Prince Albert region was a popular hunting area, and some Depression migrants claimed their first experiences of the region from hunting trips. Others came to visit the new national park and the northern vacationland and liked what they found. A few families commuted between prairie and northern farms (depending on the season) throughout the Depression as finances and situations permitted. Finally, some might have experienced a pull toward the trees as a place of beauty and recreation. All of these factors contributed to the popularity of second homesteads. Families moved to those northern homesteads on a permanent basis when economic and environmental conditions in the south imploded.[9]

The classic story of contrast between prairie and forest drove interest in northern farms. In some cases, the move was a rejection of the prairie environment; in others, taking a northern homestead allowed diversification and access to a broader range of locally available resources to supplement and balance farm opportunities. In either case, second homesteads could only be taken by those who had already fulfilled the requirements of their original homesteads. Those interested in second homesteads were coming from the prairie, not elsewhere.[10]

RESOURCE DEVELOPMENT

The creation of Prince Albert National Park led many to speculate on the imminent rise of tourism and the possible "opening" of the provincial north to resource development. During the park's opening ceremonies in 1928, Prince Albert MLA T.C. Davis and several other prominent men commented on this theme. "The park will not only serve as a place of recreation for all time," Davis declared, "but as a step nearer to the greatest period of development that northern Saskatchewan has yet experienced." Rosthern MLA J.M. Uhrich added, "standing virtually at the gateway to the great northern hinterland with its wealth of mine, of forest, lake, and river, the new Park stretches out a beckoning and inviting hand." Uhrich went on: "The proposed utilization of Churchill River power sites in this province for the mining operations in the Pre-Cambrian zone, coupled with the timely opening of the new National Park, augurs, in my mind, a development of mining, timber, fish, fur and power resources of the province likely to be as inspiring and expansive as that which marked agricultural development of Saskatchewan's fertile prairie belt."[11] His comments foreshadowed what historian Liza Piper documented as an expansive boom period in northern Canada. In contrast to the dust and devastation in southern agricultural and manufacturing regions, the north experienced "a period of economic growth and expansion" during the 1930s. This story, she argued, "inverts classic accounts of the impact of the Great Depression in the Canadian west." The north, she declared, followed its own "economic trajectory."[12] Increased commercial fishing and extensive mining development (including the boomtown of Goldfields at Lake Athabasca in Saskatchewan's far north), brought a measure of prosperity through extractive industrial development. Communities at the forest fringe, tied to northern resource development through employment, freighting opportunities, and provision of foodstuffs, experienced a significant boom.

An important aspect of the Great Trek migration and northern boom was the 1930 transfer of Crown land resources from the dominion to the three western

provinces of Manitoba, Saskatchewan, and Alberta.[13] The transfer, long negotiated by the provinces, led to extensive changes in homestead regulations and land
settlement practices. New homestead entries were suspended in the fall of 1929 to
allow each province to create its own legislation. Saskatchewan initiated a Royal
Commission on Immigration and Settlement to look into the issue of how to set
up land, homestead, and immigration policies for the province. Instead of continuing the ten-dollar filing fee and dominion regulations, the province decided that all
remaining Crown agricultural land should be sold for no less than one dollar per
acre, with a down payment of 10 percent, or sixteen dollars. The balance was to be
paid in yearly instalments. As a legal agreement between buyer (homesteader) and
seller (Crown), the new regulations seemed innocuous at first, but they soon forced
potentially cash-strapped northern settlers to make land payments each year with
money that could otherwise have been put into land-clearing or operating costs.
Payments, in some cases, were soon in arrears.

Policy makers understood that Saskatchewan land was prized most of all by
Saskatchewan residents, reflecting an in-depth understanding of a long-practised
provincial south-to-north migration and the popularity of second homesteads during the 1920s. Land was offered on an inverted pyramid to Saskatchewan residents
first, then to Canadian residents, and then to British and other immigrants. The
commission also recommended a detailed investigation of lands to determine suitability for farming or industrial development—a land classification system such as
the dominion used to determine soldier settlement land in 1919. Historian Dawn
Bowen argued that, "unfortunately, the Commission's findings were released during a period of unprecedented economic turmoil, so in spite of the practical advice
offered to ensure orderly and efficient settlement, most of its recommendations
were ignored." The economic devastation caused by the Depression, which mani-
fested quickly in Saskatchewan, halted land investigation. Good or bad, northern
land was soon filled with drought refugees.[14]

Another casualty of the natural resources transfer was the effective demise of the
dominion-sponsored Land Settlement Branch. This branch had been shepherding
the dominion's assisted land settlement schemes to soldiers and others, whereby
families were offered transportation reductions, loans, and other supports to promote successful settlement. The provincial government under J.T.M. Anderson
moved with surprising alacrity to continue a provincial version of this scheme. The
Land Settlement Act, proposed in 1930 after the formal transfer of Crown land
from the dominion, gained formal assent in the spring of 1931. An assisted land
settlement policy, this act targeted farmers intending to move north to the diversified mixed-farming areas. In place with modifications for several years, the Land
Settlement Act has consistently—and incorrectly—been interpreted as a Saskatchewan response to the Depression.[15]

In light of the tradition of dominion land settlement schemes during the 1920s,
it is more appropriate to think of the new Land Settlement Act, at least initially,
as a continuation of dominion schemes within a Saskatchewan framework. Trac-

ing changes in government-assisted settlement from the homestead policies through soldier settlement to land settlement shifts the focus and gives a clearer picture. The Great Depression, however, radically changed execution and even purpose of land settlement policies. The difference between the land colonization schemes of the 1920s (sponsored by either the Department of the Interior or the railway companies) and the relief land resettlement schemes of the Depression was that the Depression land policies were interpreted, administered, and used as essentially short-term relief measures to ease southern prairie resident problems rather than a promotion of permanent northern settlement.[16] But land settlement as short-term relief could not remain the driving force. As northern migration continued and trekkers stalled in their attempts to convert the forest into farmland, the provincial government refocussed its attention to solving northern problems. The mandate of the Northern Settlers Re-Establishment Branch, created in 1935, was to promote and support permanent settlement and resilience in the communities across the forest edge.

THE GREAT TREK

Geographer Denis Patrick Fitzgerald used the term "the Great Trek" to describe the south-to-north migration of prairie settlers into the northern forested environment during the Great Depression, but he drew the words from Depression migrants and contemporary commentators.[17] As southern farmers felt the dual prongs of dust and economic disaster, northern migration escalated.[18] From 1931 to 1937, the worst year of the drought, northern migration was part of the fabric of life in Saskatchewan.[19]

Environmental devastation and economic depression slammed prairie farmers in a double whammy. Wheat prices slumped and then plummeted after the stock market crash in the fall of 1929. In addition, extreme drought conditions devastated cereal cash crops. Farmers reaped poor returns. Those who had taken mortgages, purchased equipment, or had other loans in the boom years of the mid- to late 1920s were faced with payments that they could not meet. Nor did they have enough crop to keep any for seed for the following year. Those who relied on wheat returns to meet payments or purchase basic supplies were soon in trouble.

Perhaps even more devastating, the drought burned fodder crops such as oats and hay to a crisp. Farmers faced the dilemma of owning animals that they could not feed. Relief feed and fodder—the majority from northern regions that had not been hit by the drought—eased the burden, but hundreds of animals died from malnutrition and starvation. Others were taken north or into Manitoba to graze, reinforcing the image of parkland and forest as a place of natural abundance. Animals were also shot to save feed and fodder costs.[20] "I thought of our stock trying to get feed off the sand-filled pasture," Mrs. A.W. Bailey said.[21] Moving north, where feed and water were more accessible, seemed the only humane option.

Drought conditions and sand storms shredded prairie gardens and crops, leaving sand and dust piled and covering what remained. Historian Peter Russell suggested that drought-prone farms "had a limited capacity for either subsistence or diversification," preferring to use their cash crop (wheat) to purchase all household staples, including food. Some wheat farmers neither kept animals nor grew gardens prior to the Depression, he noted.[22] The economic slump pushed many to attempt those traditional farming practices, but environmental devastation stymied those attempts. The same drought that shattered the wheat economy would not allow diversification or even simple subsistence strategies such as growing a garden, keeping some hens, or feeding a milk cow. Grass, water, and feed were scarce, and farmers began to rely on government handouts. Those who wanted to keep body and soul together moved north.

Moving was indeed a trek for many families. Although the McGowan family chose to move their possessions north in a boxcar, thousands of migrants made the move overland, using their own cars, trucks, wagons—"makeshift vehicles constructed from old implement wheels and boards torn from an empty granary"—or ubiquitous Bennett Buggies. To make a Bennett Buggy, you would remove the engine of the family car (since there was no cash for gas, oil, or repairs) and lash a wagon tongue on the front. After harnessing and hitching a team of horses to the wagon tongue, the driver carefully removed the front window and slid the reins through. Most drivers would disengage the steering mechanism, but leave the brakes intact. Cars had springs and nicer interiors, and many had a roof to keep off the rain and snow. The resulting crossover vehicle was named after R.B. Bennett, the prime minister of Canada from 1930 to 1935—a folk tribute and public commentary on his leadership during the Depression.[23]

During the Great Trek, motley vehicles, from trucks to wagons to Bennett Buggies, were loaded precariously with furniture, goods, children and grandparents, food for the journey, as well as any agricultural implements, crates of chickens, or the family cat. Larger stock, such as horses, milk cows, and the family dog, walked alongside. Migrants likened their outfits to those of gypsies or the great wagon trains that snaked across the Great Plains in an earlier time. Families, often several from one community making the move together, or several adult siblings moving as an extended unit, camped out each night, their fires dancing along the roadsides for miles. Soldier settlers commented that the exodus reminded them of war refugees in Europe.[24]

Many people in Saskatchewan still remember those years, both those who participated in the Great Trek and those who watched the caravans go by. Drought and economic devastation had brought the Weyburn region virtually to its knees. Bill Grohn of Weyburn, a hale ninety-nine-year-old in 2013, told me that "our community was broken."[25] Lila Sully of Biggar, on Highway 4 from southwestern Saskatchewan to the Meadow Lake region, remembered roads choked with migrants on their way north, stopping to water their animals, eat a picnic lunch, or camp for the night.[26] Depending on place of origin and destination, the trek would take anywhere from two to six weeks, barring unforeseen circumstances.

Edna Dobie (née Brook) of Prince Albert was a twelve-year-old girl when her extended family made the move from a farm near Moosomin to the north Prince

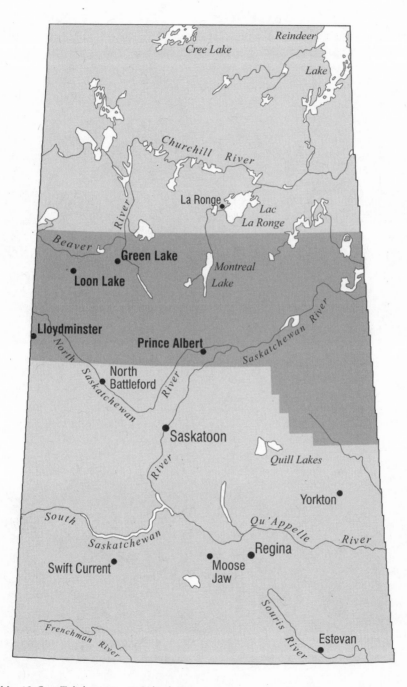

Map 15. Great Trek destinations in Saskatchewan.
Source: Adapted from Fitzgerald, "Pioneer Settlement."

Figures 30 and 31. Trekking north.
Sources: Glenbow Archives, NA-1609-1; SAB, NAC-A044575.

Albert region in late 1931. A flat tire on the first day caused the overloaded Model T to roll, smashing the windshield and top and tumbling all those inside. Edna recalled her mother screaming when she saw her children splattered in bright red in the back seat. A quart of precious strawberry jam had smashed. Her parents and uncles breathed a sigh of relief, righted the car, used barbed wire to hold things together, poured oil into the engine, and were then ready to continue. The family eventually arrived at their homestead about fifteen miles north of Paddockwood, in an area bypassed by fire. Tall spruce and deep moss greeted the prairie children, who thought that they had moved to fairyland—it was green, damp, and filled with Christmas trees.[27]

The contrast between the environmental devastation of the prairies and the green northern forests resonated in family histories published in *Cordwood and Courage* and other local history books from forest fringe communities. Trekkers— even those who eventually moved away—reminisced about the transition from dust to mud (or snow) and from brown to green. "How green everything looked!" said Elsa Blumer, who moved to the Paddockwood district in 1931. "I really did not care where we moved to as long as we could get away from that windy dust-bowl prairie," she declared. Esther Craig remembered that, when she arrived at their Paddockwood farm in 1930, "the clear air and the green trees were lovely after the dusty prairie."[28] The striking contrast formed a large part of Mrs. Bailey's published account of her family's move north: "We talked of moving to a place where there were green grass and shade. It would be a veritable heaven after so much dust and wind," Bailey recalled.[29] When the family arrived, Mrs. Bailey, born a prairie girl, was overcome with homesickness, but her children delighted in climbing trees, making forts in the brush, and swimming in lakes and ponds. For the parents, though, a rough bush homestead meant an enormous amount of work. Historian Jim Wright commented that "once more the log cabin with earthen floor swept by a broom made of willows became a reality in Saskatchewan. Dad ploughed the grey bush soil for a garden plot. The lads tracked and snared bush-rabbits, and rabbit pie appeared with monotonous regularity on the family table."[30]

The number of acres farmed in Saskatchewan went up during the 1930s across most of the census divisions. The rising acreage reflected a threefold expansion: the surge north to develop new farms, the opening of more acres in parkland regions, and the expansion of prairie acreage to try to grow more crop. When wheat prices declined dramatically, farmers increased their acreage to grow more bushels on newly broken, fresh land—a move that signalled their recognition that the land was not able to hold its fertility.

Each family's situation or inclination dictated the decision to make the move, but economics and drought were two primary motivations. "For the past six or seven years crop failures have occurred..., and once prosperous farmers who had fairly large bank accounts were reduced to near poverty. Seeing their savings dwindle every year, with no returns from the land or their livestock, they decided to leave," reported the *Regina Leader* in 1934.[31] G.J. Matte, minister of the Northern Settlers Re-Establishment Branch (created in 1935), explained that trekkers included farmers from every class:

> All manner of people were to be found in this movement. There was the rich farmer, owner of vast acres of wheat fields turned overnight into a drifting sea of sand. There was the small landowner who made a fine living from a small farm which cost little in effort and gave large returns. There was the man who had been expanding, farming many acres in which he had a large equity. We might call this man the greatest loser because he not only lost all he owned, but was left with enormous debt which he despaired of ever paying. There were the renters, and those who had always been on the edge of poverty but found themselves now in equal circumstances. They were all completely destitute.[32]

The decision to move north was a strategy of adaptation that addressed the immediate needs of the farmer and his family: the choice was either to accept relief and stay on the prairie or move to a place where at least part of the family's needs could be met with garden produce, natural hay to feed stock, and local forest resources of fish, game, and berries. Those who moved north in the early years, 1930 or 1931, generally had more savings and established a firm hold. Others hung on in the south, breaking more prairie land and hoping each year for a crop until their savings were exhausted. By the time they trekked north, some were virtually destitute.

ANALYSIS OF THE GREAT TREK

W.J. Mather, writing for *Maclean's* magazine in 1932, called the Great Trek "the greatest internal migration Canada has seen." Compared with such a migration, he noted, "the movement of the historic Barr colony of 1,200 persons to the country around Lloydminster is small." Mather estimated that 10,000 people made this move in 1931 alone; if so, then the estimate of 45,000 people over the whole of the migration period is probably too small.[33] Surprisingly, despite his description, there has never been a detailed, scholarly examination of the Great Trek.[34] Articles, theses, and government reports abound, along with novels and stories in local history books, but for the most part the story of the Depression migration in Saskatchewan (as well as somewhat smaller movements in Alberta and Manitoba) has almost disappeared from Canadian public memory. Saskatchewan provincial historians Jim Wright, John Archer, and Bill Waiser each devoted some attention to the movement, but it deserves broader investigation.[35] Even public historian James Gray, known for his swashbuckling storytelling style, denied the trek its depth and impact: "There was no massive migration or general exodus; there was only a steady trickle."[36] Clearly, he was wrong. Gray went on to note, in a spectacular case of analytical mediocrity, that "the prairies lost 247,000 people between 1931 and 1941; ... the short grass country of Saskatchewan alone lost 73,000."[37]

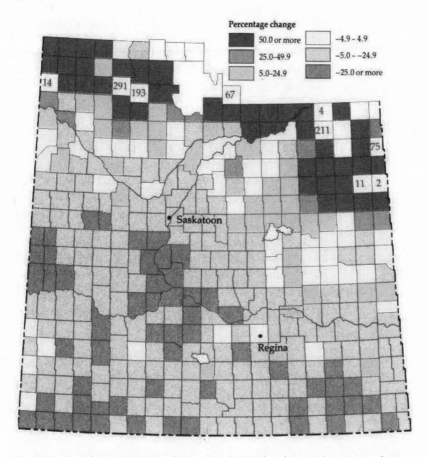

Map 16. Rural population change, Saskatchewan, 1931–41. Numbers show population increase from zero. Source: Adapted from Holdsworth and Kerr, eds., *The Historical Atlas of Canada*, 152. Used with permission.

Not only were Gray's numbers shockingly incorrect, but also their presentation glossed over the nuances of what really happened. Saskatchewan's population continued to *climb* throughout the Depression, peaking in 1936, contrary to Gray's popular depiction.[38] The provincial population stood at 921,785 in 1931. By 1936, despite the brutal effects of the Great Depression—which hit Saskatchewan the hardest—the provincial population had grown by 10,000 people, to 931,547. There was a population decline in the southern census regions but a corresponding increase in communities and municipalities across the forest edge.[39] As well, there was a drop in the urban population of Saskatchewan from 1931 to 1936 of over 10,000 people. Overall, these numbers show a preference for rural life in the forest fringe over either prairie or urban options during a time of social and economic upheaval.[40] By the end of the 1930s, largely as a result of northern migration be-

225

tween 1919 and 1937, it was estimated that one-third of the province's population lived in "northern" areas.[41] Saskatchewan's population fell to 895,992 in 1941, due in large measure to the war effort and the opening of manufacturing, service, and military positions elsewhere. The net out-migration of 35,555 people, though significant, was far less than Gray's gross overestimate of 73,000 plus.

BACK TO THE LAND

The social safety net that Canadians enjoy today did not exist prior to or during the Depression, when the inability to feed or clothe yourself or your family was generally a source of shame.[42] For many, the move north allowed a measure of pride and self-sufficiency in providing (at the least) food, shelter, and fuel for their families. For the first few years of the Depression, relief measures were municipal matters, handled at the local level, with considerable assistance from churches and other volunteer groups that ran soup kitchens, shelters, or organized clothing drives. As the Depression wore on, the provincial government took over and coordinated direct relief efforts with substantial loans from the federal government. Government aid in the form of agricultural loans such as seed grain or fodder relief, direct relief for families, or assistance in moving north was recorded as a loan or lien and as such was expected to be repaid by the recipient as soon as possible.[43]

One of the key drivers of northern migration was a back-to-the-land idealism, a "mixture of romanticism and practicality" that emphasized self-sufficiency for families. There was a social call of back-to-the-land movements, with country life seen as a panacea to the ills of modernity. A return to a more rigorous, healthful, and wholesome life would alleviate crime and other despicable aspects of city life.[44] Hallmarks of self-sufficiency included growing a large garden, keeping livestock (particularly milk cows, pigs, chickens, and sometimes sheep, goats, or turkeys), and generally "living off the land" or using the natural produce of the local environment, including fish, game, and berries.

Historian Dawn Bowen studied the municipally supported urban back-to-the-land movement in Saskatchewan during the Depression, particularly schemes from Saskatoon, Regina, and Moose Jaw, which accounted for approximately 1,000 families who went into the northern bush.[45] These families were urban residents already on relief. Urban newspapers avidly followed their stories of success and dismal failure, especially those who settled around Loon Lake, sometimes called Little Saskatoon. In the final analysis, Bowen claimed, the programs were successful. They cost less than direct relief, and neither the government nor the participants expected land settlement to be permanent. Despite hardships and continued relief payments, Bowen argued, bush homesteads offered a chance for land ownership, self-respect, a measure of self-sufficiency for families and their animals, and places of refuge to ride out the Depression until times were once again good. Bowen noted that 23 percent of the participants abandoned their land within two years, but only 27 percent abandoned it after four years, significantly less than either the

40 percent homestead abandonment or the whopping 80 percent plus abandonment of the dryland disaster. At Loon Lake, two-thirds eventually gained title to their homesteads, though the settlement at Tamarack (Moose Jaw relief recipients) was more disappointing, with fewer than half gaining patent.[46]

Urbanites were exchanging city sidewalks for country landscapes, but not just any landscape. Saskatchewan newspapers consistently described the devastation of the open plains by dust storms and recurrent droughts, grasshoppers, and cutworms. Who wanted to move there? Urban families, both those who accepted municipal back-to-the land relief and those who made the move on their own, hoped for short-term self-sufficiency as they headed north. Stories of back-to-the-landers who left their farms after only a few years, however, have contributed to the overall assessment of the northern migration as a failure, as if the sole purpose of northern migration was to build a new farm that a family would occupy for several generations. This assessment is flawed. A proportion of northern migrants, urban relief recipients or prairie farm migrants, viewed their northern homesteads as temporary refuges—a few months to, at most, a few years, until a job came up or the prairie again had rain. As such, bush homesteads, for the most part, fulfilled their role.

THE NORTHERN BOOM

The village of Paddockwood, at the end of the CNR railway line running north of Prince Albert, experienced a significant boom during the Depression in part because of the influx of southern and urban refugees. In a risky move, the local Board of Trade issued a pamphlet in 1933 that crowed *Paddockwood: The Mixed Farming Paradise of Saskatchewan.*[47] Relief at the time was a municipal burden. Actively recruiting migrants during a major economic depression was acutely ironic. Southern municipalities were overburdened by relief requests and discouraged destitute individuals and families from relocating to nearby towns or empty farms.[48] In contrast, Paddockwood not only encouraged migrants but even enjoyed a boom:

At this time Paddockwood had five general stores, a butcher shop, a drugstore, two harness repair shops, a lumber yard, hardware store, two blacksmith shops, one pool room, two hotels, three restaurants, a bakery, a second hand store, a barber shop, and twice weekly the ladies of the community could visit a beauty parlor operated in the hotel. The implement companies were represented by agents for International Harvester, Case, Massey Harris, Oliver and Cockshutt. A resident MD set bones and performed minor surgery (without anesthetic) for the people, at most reasonable rates. Talent abounded in other fields too. There were men who filed saws, repaired radios, practiced veterinary medicine, tanned robes, made illegal spirits and told fortunes. One individual was known as the "Pea Man." He made a living of sorts by growing and selling seed peas.[49]

Paddockwood was full of bustle and hustle, with piles of cordwood for trade and barter, garden produce and berries in abundance, easy access to resorts and water recreation, the Red Cross Outpost Hospital, and plenty of stores and services. The nearby communities of Henribourg and Albertville, and the growing resort communities at Christopher and Emma Lakes, shared the north Prince Albert boom. They were islands in an ocean of Depression despair. The boom created an economic and cultural flow, a movement of goods and services at odds with the "broken" communities of the open plains.

Just like the urban back-to-the-landers, prairie families looked to the northern ecological edge to provide a landscape of diversity and resilience through the mixed-farm ideal. The McGowan family's experience was an excellent example. On their newly purchased quarter section near Paddockwood, Sargent and his wife, Muriel, concentrated on self-sufficiency, using a combination of ingenuity and exchange:

> We exchanged "clucking" hens for an orphan ewe lamb from our
> neighbour. This was the nucleus of a small flock kept for a few years
> until coyotes became a nuisance. Dairy cattle provided us with milk,
> meat, cream and butter for home use, as well as some cash from
> butter sold, or whole milk sold to a cheese factory at Henribourg, or
> cream sold to dairies in Prince Albert. Pigs thrived on surplus skim
> milk and provided meat, especially the cured pork so necessary for
> summer protein before refrigeration. Chickens provided meat and
> eggs. Turkeys, although more difficult to raise, provided meat as well
> as some cash when sold in the fall. Sheep gave us meat and wool. We
> learned how to clip the sheep, wash and card wool for quilt batts. The
> garden soil produced a bountiful supply of vegetables. Wild fruit and
> some hardy tame ones were usually available. Blueberry, Saskatoon,
> and raspberry picking expeditions were not only necessary but a
> pleasant break from our daily routine. Everyone canned food of every
> kind—fruit, meat, vegetables, and pickles.[50]

Muriel McGowan's description (though idyllic) of the techniques of barter and exchange, and the combination of cash and subsistence strategies, were essential components of back-to-the-land practicality. The ideal subsistence farm was a mixed farm.

The majority of those who heeded the call to move to the forest edge found their land in one of three ways. Some found a farm to rent. Others, such as the McGowans, purchased a farm through a private deal with the landowner, with a down payment and yearly payments until the debt was cleared. Farms that had been patented with only the minimum acreage cleared were cheaper than developed farms with a larger acreage. Deals between buyer and seller were often private since banks were reluctant to issue mortgages. Finally, a migrant could enter a homestead claim and build the place of residence. The primary method of farm acquisition varied from one region to another along the forest fringe: in older settlements, such as Paddockwood or the Carrot River country, 36 percent of the farms were homesteaded, while almost half were purchased. In areas developed as new settlements, such as Pierceland in the northwest, almost 90 percent of the farms were new homesteads.[51]

Years of mixed-farming boosterism and advertising proclaimed a difference between wheat monoculture and a more diversified, stable, and resilient mixed farm at the forest edge.[52] Yet creating a mixed farm took time, energy, luck, and investment. Each family of southern refugees experienced better or worse conditions depending on several key factors: their previous residence and vocation (particularly farming experience); their method of acquisition of land (purchased or homesteaded); their age and composition when they went north; their net worth when they started (including implements, tools, stock, and furniture); their progress in clearing and breaking the land; and the productivity of the soil. A family with some cash, stock, and equipment who purchased a partly cleared farm with moderate to good soil generally did better than a virtually destitute family with few resources or stock who ended up on a new homestead with 160 acres of heavy bush covering grey podzolic soil.[53]

Figure 32. When wheat prices crash.
Source: *Prince Albert Daily Herald,* 28 July 1931.

Great Trek migrants spread out across the forest fringe. In some cases, as in the north Prince Albert region, migrants both filled out the existing land base by purchasing patented farms from previous residents and entered new homestead land. In other areas, new communities and service centres sprang up virtually overnight. In the northwest, for example, communities such as Goodsoil and Pierceland, along with the urban back-to-the-land communities of Little Saskatoon and Tamarack near Loon Lake, grew exponentially as a result of the Great Trek. In the northeast, the communities east of Albertville along the new railway to Nipawin in the White Fox Valley (Shipman, Snowden, and Choiceland, for example) exploded with Depression refugees. In general, older communities such as those in the north Prince Albert region absorbed newcomers with more ease and less social and economic distress. An established service base, a transportation system, schools, and hospitals provided infrastructure. In new communities, everything from roads to homesteads, schools, and service centres had to be built, straining limited local resources.[54] In every case, the northern boom created economic opportunities similar to those experienced on the prairie during the immigration boom between 1896 and 1910.

ENVIRONMENTAL DIFFICULTY

On each farm or homestead, agricultural progress varied. Those facing heavy scrub and trees took longer to clear less acreage. Those who rented or purchased partly developed farms, or found new homestead land with light scrub or open glades, could clear more land in less time. In five years, a homesteader on light scrub might clear sixty acres; those who faced heavy clearing and breaking would accomplish less than half that amount. As well, clearing rates quickly went down over time. A homesteader would clear the easiest areas of the farm first. Clearing and breaking became more difficult once the farmer encountered larger trees and more scrub.[55] Although mechanized methods of land clearing were available, few prairie refugees had the capital to invest in, operate, or hire tractors to do the work. Clearing trees, pulling stumps, picking stones and roots, and other duties were done by hand or with horses. It was as if "the clock of history had been turned back" to a more primitive type of agriculture.[56]

The amount of land that each family managed to clear, break, and turn to productive agriculture meant the difference between the continued need for relief help and the ability to eke out a living. Land clearing in northern areas to 1928 was completed primarily by the farmer, but just over 20 percent of the land was cleared by hired labour. During the Depression, farmers cleared more of their land on their own, as much as 87 percent. Hired labour rose again between 1938 and 1940, to pre-Depression levels. Stone and root picking, however, was overwhelmingly completed by the farm family, with a tiny proportion—between 1 and 3 percent—picked by hired help, often local First Nations casual day labourers.

During the Depression, later analysts noted, a family on black or transitional soil needed at least fifty acres cleared and worked to manage a bare living; on grey podzolic soil, eighty-eight acres would support a family without any off-farm income. Unfortunately, it took as many as ten years—or even fifteen—to clear that many acres on the heavy bush land common to grey podzolic soil.[57] Even if a family moved north to a new homestead early in the trek—1930 or 1931—they might not have found economic sufficiency strictly from agricultural pursuits until the end of the decade, when farmers once more could afford mechanized land-clearing techniques. A family who moved later in the trek, with no cash reserves or resources left, faced an even more difficult battle.[58]

The amount of time and back-breaking work that it took to clear and break enough land to make a farm profitable was the single most important factor in encouraging or discouraging those who tried northern settlement. In the bush, as few as ten acres cultivated and seeded were sometimes enough to convince the homestead inspector to approve a farm patent. Patent, however, did not make a farm profitable. Settlers had to choose between continuing clearing, breaking, and seeding activities and accessing off-farm cash labour opportunities or selling the land and moving. As with the initial choice to migrate away from the prairie, the choice to stay on or leave a northern farm varied from family to family as circumstances and inclination—and opportunity—dictated.

Although optimism and hope infused most of those who went north, the reality of trying to establish a viable mixed farm in the bush produced much adversity. Historian John McDonald suggested that "many half-truths about conditions in the north continued to be circulated, engendering an optimism ... based on a distorted image of true environmental conditions in the forest fringe."[59] Another historian, T.J.D. Powell, suggested that people who moved north "received assurance through the media, government officials and word-of-mouth that the northern lands would certainly provide the necessities of life if not improve their standard of living. Some families, in fact, did improve their economic status, but others experienced poverty or even worse conditions."[60] The difference, later analysts declared, lay in the combination of experience, rate of land clearing, soil profile, and sheer good luck.[61]

Indeed, northern refugees "had much to learn before becoming adapted to living in bush country," wrote "Prairie Immigrant" for the Paddockwood local history book. To clear the land to create a farm, they "first had to learn to use swede saw, axe and grub-hoe without endangering life or limbs." Fire, though a useful tool for clearing scrub brush, had a dark side: "An innocent-looking fire, started in a brush pile, can smoulder all winter under feet of snow, consuming much of the good topsoil." Not just people but also prairie animals had a tough transition from prairie to bush. Prairie immigrants "watched and wondered as animals began chewing on sticks, bones, harness and sweat-pads, until realization dawned that the poor beasts were in need of salt, an ingredient that was seldom lacking in their diet on the prairie." Although the mixed-farming movement and other promoters lauded the lush northern hay crop, trekkers learned that it "proved to be more filling than nutritious and compared unfavourably with the prickly prairie wool. Brome grass and alfalfa had to be seeded to keep the animals satisfied." Stock farmers and their animals valued the northern water sources, but farmers soon learned to fence their animals "away from dangerous muskegs, after some had become mired more than once and dragged out by the neck to dry land." Unlike the open prairie, where a farmer could see for miles, stock hid in the northern bush. Farmers learned to "hang a bell around the neck of the 'boss' cow, if ever they hoped to find the herd."

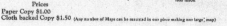

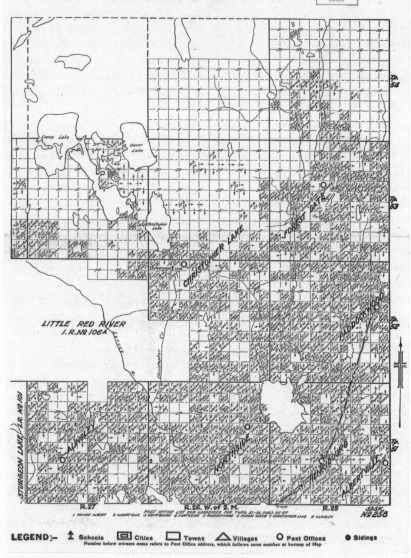

Map 17. Cummins Map 258, Moose Lake and Hell's Gate. Moose Lake was in TWP 54 R25 W2. Hell's Gate was in TWP 54 R 26 W2.

Source: SAB, Cummins files.

Other nasty surprises included "swamp fever," an infectious anemia thought to reside in wet marsh grass. Many horses died, and this placed incredible pressure on farm families. With agricultural commodity prices still at an all-time low, where would a family find the money to replace valuable horses, the main mode of transportation and motive power for the farm? Such a calamity could wipe out a sense of hope or optimism and place a family in even more desperate straits than they had been in on their prairie farm.[62]

In the north Prince Albert region, homestead land with grey podzolic soil had been avoided or abandoned, for the most part, by soldier settlers and other northern recruits during the 1920s. The demand for land created by refugees flung north during the Great Trek, however, overwhelmed the available land base. In the Paddockwood region, a tongue of settlement north following the Montreal Lake Trail passed beyond the last vestiges of transitional soil and found itself on grey podzolic land. The area became known as Moose Lake and, west of Moose Lake, Hell's Gate (west of the Montreal Lake Trail, across the Garden River). Its isolation, muskeg, mosquitoes, and tree cover became legendary in Paddockwood, and it carries the name Hell's Gate to this day. Families in Hell's Gate eked out a harsh and meagre existence, their land covered in knee-deep moss and muskeg, surviving on wild game and continued relief until a better farm or job came up somewhere else. As early as 1920, dominion land surveyor M.D. McCloskey characterized the entire township (which encompassed the Hell's Gate settlement) as not "well adapted to farming." He elaborated by noting that "while there are some areas of fair soil ... these areas are comparatively small and are isolated. The land is badly broken by spruce and tamarack swamps. Sandy ridges and banksian pine are prominent, with a mixed forest of aspen, spruce and pine. Boulders are plentiful in places." Not even grazing, McCloskey noted, would be a good idea in this area. Cattle would not find sufficient grass "until the summer is fairly well advanced." Thick forest growth, much of it untouched by the 1919 fires, shaded the ground. It stayed colder and wetter longer into spring and summer than the areas farther south.[63]

Cold and wet conditions plagued many northern homesteads. As settlement pushed north, the growing season, or average number of frost-free days necessary for cereal grain ripening, shrank. Late spring or early fall frosts hit farmers hard. Cereal crops, particularly wheat, suffered. Just as on the prairie, expected income from wheat disappeared when environmental disaster struck. As Muriel McGowan noted, the grain grown on their northern farm was more often than not converted to animal feed. Wheat prices were abysmal throughout the Great Depression, so meagre wheat crops were rarely worth the cost of harvesting. Freight deductions were also higher for northern farms. In addition, northern grain typically graded lower. In some years, after deductions and fees, grain cost more to ship than to keep. Farmers found themselves facing a bill rather than a cheque.[64]

Flooding was a problem in some areas or on some quarters. The homestead inspector for the north Paddockwood area, James Barnett, commented on a homestead at Moose Lake in 1931: "The wetness of this country probably appeals to those from the dried out areas. This may prove the other extreme and not turn out so pleasant as it first seems."[65] In a wet season, the settler had to wait longer to get seed in the ground, further courting the risk of frost. Over time, settlers noticed that, as more land was cleared, roads built, and ditches dug, drainage and frost issues improved. As tree cover and roots were removed, the land warmed up and dried out. Soldier settlers and other older residents assured newcomers that they had also faced bush, frost, and water. Their larger acreages, somewhat more prosperous despite the ravages of the Depression, offered hope.

As Depression refugees pushed north along the Montreal Lake Trail, it would have been difficult to tell at a glance the difference between the relatively prosperous farms near Henribourg and Paddockwood and the land farther north. Few to none of those refugees would have had access to the information provided by the original surveyors. For the Hell's Gate region, the dominion land inspector report unfortunately turned out to be accurate. Settlers abandoned their holdings within a few months or, at most, a couple of years. Many, however, did not go far. After the Great Trek, few were willing to move on such a massive scale again. The majority of Hell's Gate settlers relocated just a few miles south to better farmland at Forest Gate or Paddockwood.[66] In their study of northern land settlement, analysts R.A. Stutt and H. Van Vliet noted that, across the forest fringe, an average of 30 percent of the settlers originated from southern Saskatchewan. Astoundingly, though, over two-fifths of the settlers, or 44 percent, came from other places in northern Saskatchewan. If their first choice of land did not work out, then many settlers merely relocated to another part of the forest edge, continuing to reject the open plains.[67]

Like the urban back-to-the-landers at Loon Lake, though, it is difficult to tell if land abandonment and out-migration represented failure or merely short-term success as a refuge for a few months, a few seasons, or a few years. Initial enthusiasm and in-migration at Hell's Gate led to a short-lived attempt to create a new school, the Deerness School District No. 5056, in 1934. Logs had been cut and piled, but by 1936 the idea had to be abandoned. Mr. Crispin, the secretary, wrote to the Department of Natural Resources claiming that "most of the settlers have moved out and more are going ... At the present time there is not enough to form a school board."[68] Other Hell's Gate residents were denied loans or other support from the Northern Settlers Re-Establishment Branch because their farms were too remote—they still did not have a decent wagon road or proper bridge connecting them to the Montreal Lake Trail. The Hell's Gate community crumbled, to live on primarily in the memories of Forest Gate and Paddockwood residents as the epitome of the worst that could happen, even to those homesteaders who had come north full of hope, looking for a better life.

RELIEF

Unlike modern welfare, relief was registered as a loan by municipal or provincial authorities. Families and individuals tried to keep their relief requirements to an absolute minimum, loath to accumulate debt that would be difficult to pay back.

Settlers might have hoped that the ecological edge environment would allow a measure of self-sufficiency, but the forest did not yield its living easily. The economic impact of the Great Depression was too severe. For those on poor land who faced difficult clearing with few resources, hope soon turned to resignation and almost despair. Although garden produce was usually more than sufficient, families required clothing and other supplies. Most northern families—at one time or another in their sojourn—required help, whether in the form of food, clothing, or medical relief.[69] Analysts have pointed to relief records, newspaper accounts, and letters from northern settlers desperate for help as further indication of the north's marginality and inability to adequately support newcomers.[70] Within the context of the Depression, however, that analysis is unfair. No place was free of the Depression's heavy hand. Prices for all agricultural products, not just wheat, were depressed. Although a northern farmer usually found a greater degree of self-sufficiency consuming rather than selling farm products, agricultural returns were necessary for certain expenditures or services that could not be negotiated without cash. Relief vouchers filled that gap.

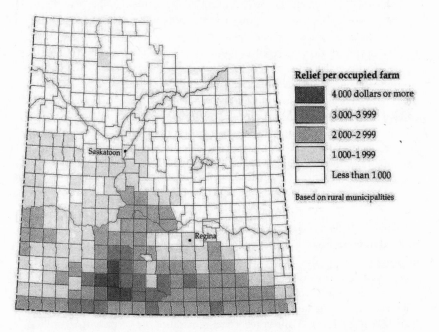

Map 18. Farm relief, Saskatchewan, 1929–38
Source: Adapted from *Historical Atlas of Canada Vol. III,* 152. Used with permission.

Relief was actually a malleable tool. One family might have lost its garden crop to frost, requiring interim food relief to get through the winter. Another might have had a bountiful garden but needed warm clothing. A third might have been doing well, but an unexpected illness or hospitalization gave them a bill that they were unable to meet. One family might require relief for several months or years; their neighbour might need only occasional or specific help. Although it has been common to speak of Depression families "going on relief" for prolonged periods of time, relief payments were generally more sporadic. Relief was tailored to each family's situation and operated on a month-to-month basis. Officials (and personal pride) encouraged families to provide as much as possible for themselves. Through operating a mixed farm where subsistence, fuel, barter, and exchange were common, relief could be kept to a minimum.[71]

A reporter for the *Regina Leader* investigated the northward trek to the Meadow Lake region in late 1931. The article claimed that the majority of trekkers had hopes of "making their living, arduous as it may be, with less government assistance than would have been required to maintain them on their original holdings."[72] *Less* government assistance, but assistance if and when necessary, the reporter emphasized. Researcher Robert McLeman noted that on average, larger families were more inclined to make the Great Trek north, while smaller families stayed on their southern farms. The chance to grow a garden, operate a mixed subsistence farm or access forest resources appeared to be a stronger pull factor for larger families.[73] Yet, the optimism that the reporter found in 1931 dimmed as the years went by. Agricultural conditions stemming from poor soil, heavy bush, frost, water, and continued economic depression cast a pall over early enthusiasm. As the Great Trek continued, later migrants had fewer resources. Relief vouchers and relief work entered the northern picture in ever-increasing amounts.

But the flame of northern hope never died out completely. Northern relief, in fact, was minimal in comparison with the seemingly endless relief rolls of prairie and urban centres. Geographer Denis Patrick Fitzgerald calculated a "startling difference between the amount of relief required in the prairies and the parklands compared with the pioneer region."[74] The amount of per capita aid per year between 1930 and 1937 averaged $385.64 on the prairie and only $2.85 along the forest fringe.[75] Fitzgerald's calculations might be high. The Saskatchewan report to the dominion Royal Commission on Dominion-Provincial Relations, however, calculated that northern relief (both direct relief and agricultural aid and re-establishment) was less than one-tenth the cost of aid to the drought regions. In 1934–35, direct relief in the drought area cost $6.5 million, while in the northern relief areas costs were $690,083. Agricultural aid that year cost $14 million for the whole province. In 1935, direct relief and agricultural aid cost about $8 million, in the drought region, while northern areas required $793,028. In 1936, costs escalated. To the end of the relief year in August 1937, costs were an astronomical $8 million for direct relief and $10 million for agricultural aid in the drought regions. Government assistance in northern relief areas amounted to $1,030,976. Government aid for the north increased over the years, reflecting the growing population base, but clearly northern settlers required far less relief than did their counterparts in the drought regions.[76] The difference, Fitzgerald noted, lay in the northern environment. Food and heating fuel, in particular, were easily procured in the forest edge landscape. He contended that the relief records provided "a very clear illustration, and abundant proof, of the north's attractiveness during this period, repudiating some common beliefs."[77]

Analysts have typically pointed to government resettlement schemes as evidence that both the provincial and the federal governments actively encouraged northern migration. Certainly, in the case of urban back-to-the-land schemes, forest edge agricultural settlement was an important part of municipal relief management. In terms of prairie agricultural resettlement to northern farms, government aid cannot be categorized as overtly encouraging. Although loan and other aid schemes were in place, the provincial government made it more difficult for settlers to obtain land in the north through their new purchased-homestead policies. It screened applicants for the available northern resettlement schemes prior to 1935 and rejected more people than it accepted.[78] Historian and economist G.E. Britnell claimed in 1939 that "government assistance in the form of loan schemes can scarcely be said to have been an important factor in northern settlement from 1930 to 1935 ... even after allowance has been made for government aid in meeting the costs of transferring settlers' effects and livestock."[79]

Despite substantially reduced relief requirements in northern settlements, both the provincial and the federal governments were reluctant to abandon the once-profitable prairie wheat economy. In 1931, the Soldier Settlement Board of Canada sent a circular letter to its field superintendents, and copied the letter to the Saskatchewan Department of Agriculture, which endorsed it. The letter stated that "we do not wish to encourage a general or even an individual exodus from the south country. In fact, every effort should be made by our Supervisors in the south country to discourage settlers from moving north unless under the most exceptional circumstances." The "exceptional circumstances" included tenant farmers or those on "extremely poor farms." Northern farms, "whilst presently better so far as moisture is concerned, may not be all as he believes them to be."[80]

The Prairie Farm Rehabilitation Administration (PFRA) was created in 1935 to investigate the drought problem and initiate erosion control and water solutions. Its creation proved the importance of the prairie wheat economy. As late as 1939, despite the economic, social, and environmental havoc wreaked by the Depression and drought, the provincial minister of agriculture defended the importance of the grain-growing open plains. Astonishingly high expenditures on southern relief efforts in the drought regions were acceptable, the minister contended, since those expenditures were "small in relation to the wealth produced in this drought area" in the years prior to 1930. Although it was a good idea to promote "thinning out the settlement of submarginal areas," the minister steadfastly argued that "complete depopulation is not the solution to the problem."[81] Northern settlement during the 1930s found its impulse less in government support than in past northern migration, word of mouth, and the pull of mixed farming and off-farm opportunities available at the forest edge.

ORIGINS

· One settler family
◉ Concentrations of settler families

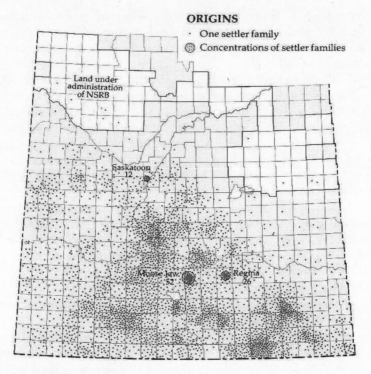

Map 19. Origin of relocation settlers.
Source: *Historical Atlas of Canada Vol. III*, 152. Used with permission.

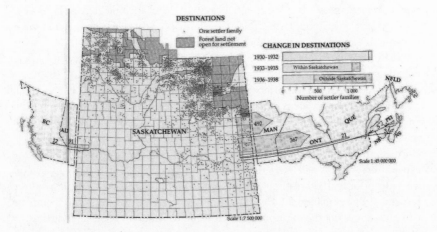

Map 20. Destination of relocation settlers. As the Depression worsened, more and more people moved by the government went outside the province.
Source: *Historical Atlas of Canada Vol. III*, 152. Used with permission.

THE NORTHERN SETTLERS
RE-ESTABLISHMENT BRANCH (NSRB)

The movement of thousands of drought refugees on their own, to sometimes precarious or dismal northern situations, forced the provincial government—reluctantly—to act. Some who went north "in despair had merely stopped in their tracks. They were found squatting on road allowances, on forest reserves, or in any other spot where they hoped to remain undisturbed for the time being." Squatting meant setting up a camp, digging and planting a modest garden, and living, as much as possible, off the land. "Trappers' cabins, old sawmill camps, and shacks of all descriptions were occupied by this latest army of pioneers," declared Northern Settlers Re-Establishment Branch (NSRB) commissioner G.J. Matte.[82]

With settlers squatting on unsuitable (even illegal) places, northern settlement was described as "chaotic," even "intolerable."[83] Administrators were besieged with requests for assistance. Settlers refused to pay taxes, interest, or land payments. Reports declared that some northern settlers burned government offices or threatened officials. Officers sent to evict squatters were met with force.[84] For those facing years of clearing marginal land, prospects were daunting, even overwhelming, and their anger and frustration boiled over. In response, the new Gardiner Liberal government made three critical policy changes in 1935 that affected northern settlers. First, the government changed its Crown lands policy. Homestead fees rolled back to the traditional ten-dollar filing fee, and the government refunded to the settler all land payments that had been made between 1930 and 1935.[85] For some, the refund gave a much-needed cash infusion. For others, the land on which they had been "squatting" could be converted into a legal homestead. In the first year of the revised scheme, 10,000 inquiries regarding northern land were received.[86] Between 1935 and 1939, almost 2,000 homestead entries were filed across the forest edge, indicating continued public pressure for northern land, despite its by then well-known drawbacks and hardships.[87]

Second, the Land Utilization Act of 1935 gave the government sweeping power to convert land already under homestead or purchase agreement back to public land.[88] Across the forest edge, land considered too marginal for grain farming—because of poor soil, excessive tree cover, or too much water—was evaluated by municipalities, often with one eye on their relief rolls. The government then required municipalities to halt financial assistance to occupants of inferior lands, essentially forcing those who had not already moved to do so. The Hell's Gate region was an example. Refused help, the people left. Such land reverted to public control.

Third, the government consolidated the various programs and policies administered by several departments under the NSRB. Relief aid for northern settlers was coordinated through this branch. Settlers whose land had reverted to public control received resettlement assistance to move to better land. Drainage projects, initiated to create both employment and more arable land, were established in places such as Shand Creek and the Carrot River Valley.[89] Most importantly, settlers gained access to "re-establishment" funds. These funds bought everything from horses and other stock, to equipment and tools, to land clearing and breaking. The government realized that settlement schemes from the 1920s—soldier settlement or land settlement—succeeded in large part because of loans and ongoing support to farmers. Much of the northern land (after the backbreaking work to clear it) was, in fact, capable of growing crops—including the best of the grey podzolic soil.[90] The NSRB purchased mechanized land-clearing equipment to break land or authorized payments to private contractors to clear and break larger acreages. From 1935 to 1940, over 6,000 families received re-establishment funds; of those families, well over 5,000 had become entirely self-supporting by 1941. Any northern resident, not just drought trekkers, could apply for re-establishment funds, extending the loan initiative to those who might have made the move north years earlier.[91]

Creation of the NSRB signalled a major change in policy for the provincial government. Whereas relief and resettlement schemes administered in the early part of the Great Depression were regarded as little more than "stop-gap" measures to alleviate conditions in the short term, the NSRB represented a return to land settlement policies constructed to provide long-term resilience for Saskatchewan farm families. Relief records often separated direct relief from agricultural aid, and much of the aid required during the Depression was for seed grain, feed and fodder relief for stock, tractor fuel and oil, and repairs to farm machinery. Agricultural aid was calculated to help a farmer in the short term. Re-establishment aid looked to the future, providing loans for a farmer to build up stock and make machinery purchases. The NSRB initiated educational campaigns that promoted mixed farming as the most secure base for northern settlers and provided the support and funds to allow land clearing and diversification. A policy shift from relief to re-establishment indicated the provincial government's commitment to overall northern development and expressed a measure of hope for future success.

FOREST RESOURCES

Although northern settlement initiatives sponsored by the various levels of government focussed primarily on agriculture and its successes and failures, trekkers and established settlers relied on—and expected—non-farm income to supplement mixed farming, relief, and re-establishment measures. Although drought and depression on the open plains sent many trekkers looking for water, green grass, and trees, they were also drawn to the economic and cultural prospects offered at the forest edge.

Of all the non-agricultural resources and opportunities found at the forest edge, the most important was the forest itself. The 1933 Paddockwood Board of Trade pamphlet declared that "all through the brief history of Paddockwood there can be little doubt that the great beckoning force has been the trees—the timber." The primary farm product, more important than grain or stock, came from the trees: "Thousands of cords of wood and millions of feet of lumber, ties and fence posts are sold annually to nearby points."[92] Clearly, in the north Prince Albert region, wood was a crop to be harvested and sold for profit. The concept of mixed farming at the forest edge took on a new meaning: not only was the mixed forest suited to stock raising and cereal grain growing, but also the forest itself could be turned into cash.

Local men Pat O'Hea and Herb Endicott wrote a history of Paddockwood for the Royal Commission on Agriculture and Rural Life in 1953. Cordwood was the bedrock of the Paddockwood economy during the Depression, they insisted:

> Came the lean and hungry 30s: Up to this time the forest growth, made up principally of white poplar, was a barrier to a settler being granted title deed to his homestead. There being no mechanized method of clearing the land, it was a monotonous, ding-dong battle of chopping, clearing, and grubbing. One did well to have five acres ready for breaking in a year. Then our enemy, the poplar, became our ally when turned into cord wood, and was a big factor in our weathering or surviving the thirties. ... We beat the 30s, also the bush, thereby winning two battles, but "'twas a tough fight."[93]

As the Depression deepened, the cordwood industry symbolized both the ecological and the economic struggle. Trees were the enemies of progress for homestead development but became the allies when converted into fuel for sale. Cordwood became the Paddockwood equivalent of the "made beaver" currency of the old fur trade; all else was measured against it.

During the Depression, the cash economy virtually disappeared, particularly in southern Saskatchewan. Communities were paralyzed. Without some form of flowing economy outside relief payments, families were unable to go to dances or the lake, pay a teacher's salary, or buy a new teapot. Bill Grohn pointed to this paralyzing effect when he claimed that the east Weyburn district was broken by the Depression. Community life, in almost all of its forms, stopped, and the community died. In contrast, the cordwood economy and healthy system of cash and barter that existed along the forest edge meant that communities could thrive, even boom. Cutting and hauling cordwood were hard and dangerous work, with sometimes pitiful cash returns, but most residents agreed that it was better than nothing, and it kept some of them off, or at least reduced, relief. If a farmer did not have adequate trees on his own farm, he could work in a cordwood or railway tie camp, leased from the provincial government. Several operated along the Montreal Lake Trail and the Mosher Trail to Candle Lake, just south and east of the original boundary of Prince Albert National Park.

The cordwood economy allowed community members to organize and build schools, invest in social and recreational clubs, take short holidays to lakes or even build cabins, support sports days and hockey clubs, and allow musicians to play for pocket change at dances held in homes, schools, and halls. The importance of the cordwood economy resonated through the years, leading the Paddockwood History Book Committee to call their local history *Cordwood and Courage* when it was published in 1982. Geographer Denis Patrick Fitzgerald commented that "the psychological role of forest resources might well have been of more significance than the material. Many pioneers ... felt that the forest lands themselves were a type of insurance policy; they acted as a safe refuge or shelter." The trees, as well as other forest resources, acted to sustain the morale of northern homesteaders, even when life was particularly grim.[94]

The forest edge environment provided household resources, particularly food through berry picking, wild game, and fish. Indeed, the Paddockwood pamphlet expressly advertised products of the landscape as a way to supplement household diet cheaply. Local history books proudly displayed photographs of these resources, including several canners full of blueberries from 1931, wild game piled on the railway station platform, and strings of fish from successful expeditions to local lakes. Numerous family histories recount excursions to hunt, fish, and pick berries as a way of adding to and varying diet. Some, however, admitted defeat in this regard. Muriel McGowan noted that "although living in this area where fish and game are plentiful neither Sargent nor I became enthusiastic hunters or fishermen." When Sargent accompanied a neighbour on a highly successful fishing expedition, Muriel was perplexed by the sheer amount of fish. Some were eaten fresh, some canned, and the rest salted "and later buried in the bush." A hunting expedition also went awry when Sargent became hopelessly lost. He "vowed never to go again, that he would pick his own meat, on the hoof, in his own farmyard, which he did."[95] Although hunting regulations were in place throughout the Depression, game wardens were encouraged to look the other way when it came to families clearly harvesting elk, moose, and deer as food resources—unless, of course, those animals were shot within the boundaries of the national park.

In addition to mixed farming, forest-based food resources, and the cordwood economy, the forest edge landscape supported labour opportunities from freighting, fishing, lumber and railway tie camps, mining camps, tourism, and trapping. These opportunities allowed occupational pluralism that combined on-farm with off-farm income. Such pluralism was characteristic of the northern boom, particularly for those who homesteaded within the wooded grey soil zone. These farms, the majority of which were homesteaded during the 1930s, rarely exceeded a quarter section, and most had only a few acres cleared, grubbed, and broken for cultivation.[96] Off-farm cash income supplemented mixed-farming returns and relief vouchers and contributed to the general northern boom.

Ernest Wiberg took his homestead at Paddockwood in 1931. He was a prairie boy from the east Weyburn district whose brothers either farmed with their parents or rode the rails across the country. Not yet married, Wiberg worked for fifteen years in the commercial fishing industry on the large lakes in northeastern Saskatchewan.[97] Typically, fish camps operated from freeze-up in late fall to spring thaw. Wiberg recalled walking into the camps in early winter over frozen rivers or poling scows loaded with HBC freight up the rivers in late fall.[98]

Other forest edge farmers made cash during the winter by freighting. Throughout the 1930s, freighting went through a transitional phase. Some freighters used sleighs pulled by teams of horses, but increasingly companies began diversifying into mechanized caterpillar tractors. Cat tractors were efficient—they could run day and night and did not require rest, as did horses. They could also pull far more freight. A small cat tractor could pull thirty tons of frozen fish or goods and push a plow to open a road. Another cat immediately behind on a clear road could haul even more.[99] The extra power provided by caterpillar tractors meant that northern posts, fishing camps, towns, schools, and the new mining camps could order heavier items. Indeed, much of the equipment in the Rottenstone mineral region near La Ronge, the Anglo-Rouyn mine, and Goldfields on Lake Athabasca was freighted in with cat swings. Northern commercial fishing and mining resource industries boomed during the 1930s and propelled the move to caterpillar tractors. Cats could haul equipment and supplies too heavy for water barges or horses. In the absence of rail lines in northern Saskatchewan, cat swings filled a specific need for power, speed, and heavy transport.

As technology advanced and caterpillar tractors became the motive force of the freight swings, there was a shift in the social and economic dynamics of freighting. Although some farmers continued to work as freighters in the winter to supplement their income, freighting as an industry decoupled from farming—horses, hay, and oats were no longer needed, and the skills required were not horse skills but machinery skills. The change to cat tractor technology escalated northern development. Cats used to haul freight in winter were hired to make extensive road improvements or agricultural brush cutting in summer. These changes transformed both the freighting industry and forest edge communities. Agriculture expanded rapidly in the late 1930s and throughout the 1940s as farms expanded and consolidated. Better roads opened the way for intensive development in the once-remote far north following the Second World War.

Figure 33. Cat train near Prince Albert, c. 1929.
Source: Glenbow Archives, PD-356-1132.

Homestead families in the Alingly, Spruce Home, Albertville, Paddockwood, Forest Gate, and Christopher Lake districts also engaged in the burgeoning tourism industry. Men with extensive bush experience became park wardens; others worked on park roads, cooked for the hotels (or relief camps), or opened tourist facilities such as cabin or boat rentals, bus services, or grocery and supply stores. Others loaded up their wagons with meat, eggs, milk, butter, and fresh garden produce and sold them to the camps and hotels or door to door at the cabins and on the beaches at the lakes. Earl Daley, for example, sold his milk for ten cents a quart and had enough cows to offer fifty to sixty quarts a day to picnickers and beachgoers.[100] Mrs. Oscar Anderson of the Elk Range School District (between Northside and Paddockwood) took butter and eggs to Neis beach on Emma Lake in 1931. But George Neis, who homesteaded the land and owned the resort, had his own butter and eggs to supply the campers. When he physically removed her from his property so that she could not sell her wares, Anderson charged him with assault. Neis hired John Diefenbaker as his lawyer and succeeded in having the case dismissed since Anderson had clearly been trespassing.[101]

The Jacobsen family, who initiated much of the tourist development at Anglin Lake, moved from Frontier, Saskatchewan, in 1930. "As soon as the car stopped [after the three-day trek north] one little brother grabbed a hatchet and claimed territory by cutting down a small tree. As I look back I realize that no one minded leaving the prairie, we loved the forest and lakes."[102] For the Jacobsens and many others, the move away from the open plains reflected what geographer Robert Rees called "the Cult of the Tree." For many immigrants to western Canada, the strangeness of the prairie landscape—treeless, flat, dry, hot, and immense—caused an intensely negative reaction.[103] For prairie-born children, that landscape was home but became disfigured and alien by drought. The love of trees and a connection between forest and beauty pervaded Anglo-Canadian culture.[104] The trek north was a move, in part, from poverty to subsistence, brown to green, despair to hope, ugly to beautiful.

Trapping fur-bearing animals was another important activity along the forest edge. A number of north Prince Albert region residents earned extra cash in the winter and spring by operating traplines on their homesteads or on nearby Crown land. They sought primarily squirrel, weasel, skunk, rabbit, muskrat, wolf, coyote, fox, and lynx. Pelts could be bartered at local merchants or turned to ready cash. With squirrels worth ten cents a pelt and muskrats sixty-five cents a pelt, a kid with a trapline could easily earn considerable cash. Bryce Dunn of Paddockwood, whose father, David Dunn, claimed both homestead and soldier settlement land, remembered taking his spring pelts to Prince Albert in 1933 and receiving a tremendous $21.45. Dunn splurged on new leather boots, went to the movies, and loaded up a gunnysack with groceries and treats at the store. Jam, for example, could be bought for twenty-five cents for a four-pound pail. He took home six pails.[105] Paul Hayes of Candle Lake claimed unconditionally that "trapping was the key to survival in the hungry thirties." He claimed that a winter's take of the more lucrative fox, lynx, otter, marten, and wolf pelts "could gross $3500.00," an immense amount of money during the Depression.[106]

The Depression placed significant stress on the fur industry. The sheer number of homesteaders moving into the forest fringe placed increasing pressure on fur resources. As well, prices dropped. Muskrat pelts worth a dollar and a half in 1928 dropped to sixty-five cents, mink from thirteen to less than four dollars. In addition, beaver were scarce, and trapping them was officially prohibited in 1938.[107] Despite the drastic slip in prices, the number of trappers overall increased. The files of the Saskatchewan Department of Natural Resources show that the money earned by trapping in northern Saskatchewan grew from half a million dollars in 1930 to over a million dollars by 1933–34, then declined slightly to 1937, when there was a severe drop. A spike in overall returns in 1939, just prior to the onset of war, reflected the return of good prices.[108] The number of trappers was highest in 1934 and 1936, but overall returns were not higher.[109] Even so, despite low returns, trapping offered an opportunity to increase cash flow or barter power for some northern homesteaders. And, though fur prices dropped, the prices of goods also dropped, narrowing the difference.

Figure 34. Trapping White Gull Creek, Walter Haydukewich, 1933.
Source: *Fur, Fish, and Game: A Candle Lake Legacy*, 27.

Since the publication of A.L. Karras's beautiful *North to Cree Lake* and *Face the North Wind*, there has been considerable interest in the history of white (non-Native) trapping in northern Saskatchewan. Karras was perhaps the most well known of men who, as a result of the Depression, went into the northern boreal forest to operate traplines.[110] Depictions of these men have spanned a narrative range. Archibald Belaney, or Grey Owl, wrote during the 1930s that "we ... are seeing the last of the free trappers; a race of men who ... will turn the last page in the story of true adventure on this continent, closing forever the book of romance in Canadian History. The forest cannot much longer stand before the conquering march of modernity, and soon we shall witness the vanishing of a mighty wilderness."[111] Despite his opposition to trapping, Grey Owl believed that trappers (of all races) and other northern sojourners understood the "Last Frontier" best and thus would be in a position to defend it and act as champions of the wild.

Those "Last Frontiersmen," or at least the non-Native trappers who inspired the fulsome praise of Grey Owl, have been harshly condemned in recent historical work. Historian David Quiring criticized white trappers for lacking a "long-term commitment" to the north, harvesting furs in winter and drifting south after spring breakup. Their lack of foresight and commitment led to overtrapping and a severe depletion of fur stocks in northern Saskatchewan prior to 1945, he suggested.[112] Overtrapping had a deeper impact on the First Nations population than on the itinerant trappers because it affected the whole region over a longer period of time. White trappers could take other jobs in other industries; First Nations people often could not. In this sense, the Depression story of trapping as a northern opportunity has evolved to emphasize First Nations hardship.[113] Increased trapping pressure from white southern trappers spread the resources thinly for everyone, particularly First Nations on whose traditional trapping areas the newcomers encroached.

The prolonged drought of the 1930s had a severe environmental impact on northern trapping. Drought, contrary to popular perceptions driven by images of dust storms, was not confined to the south. The northern boreal forest was also touched. Although the north was comparatively wetter than the devastated plains, the northern forests, streams, and lakes did experience an overall drier era, particularly after 1935 and during 1937, when even the parkland and much of the forest fringe agricultural region experienced drought. Dry conditions set off massive forest fires, which affected the game and fur-bearing populations drastically.[114] Heavy smoke from the forest fires, it was claimed, cut off the sunshine, which led to low oxygen levels in the lakes. Thousands of dead fish were found floating on the lakes, and beaver and muskrat populations plummeted. Beaver dams and ponds, an important part of a northern forest ecosystem, were burnt out and not rebuilt. Experiments were carried out to dam small lakes and streams to encourage muskrat and beaver populations.[115] Streams normally used for transportation purposes either completely dried up or were too low to allow the passage of freight canoes or barges. As a result, northern communities demanded road work as relief projects to try to establish land links to the south.[116] These land links sometimes affected local ecosystems, changing water courses. The environmental impacts of the drought and forest fires should be considered along with the surge in non-Native trapping to explain the devastating drop in fur resources prior to 1945.[117]

FIRST NATIONS AND MÉTIS

As homesteaders pressed north past the Forest Gate region into the grey soil zone at Moose Lake, Hell's Gate, and east to Candle Lake, new homesteaders competed with trappers, cordwood and railway tie camps, hunters, and berry pickers for available resources. All were constrained by the boundaries of Prince Albert National Park, which disallowed homesteading, trapping, or hunting within its borders. First Nations families from Little Red River Reserve who traditionally used northern boreal territory had to share the trails and restricted resource base with an ever-increasing number of drought refugees. The results were devastating to the First Nations population. Moving farther and farther away from the reserve to access forest resources placed excessive strain on reserve families. Throughout the 1930s, increased hardship could be found.

Several Métis families, such as the Lavallées, were forcibly displaced by the creation of Prince Albert National Park. Louis Lavallée had a cabin on the shores of what is now known as Lavallée Lake, at the north end of the park.[118] He at first found a measure of fame at his home when journalists visiting the park arrived to take his picture. He was also featured in the Department of the Interior film *Modern Voyageurs* in 1931 as one of the more colourful personages living in the park. Sometime in the 1930s, though, Lavallée was pressured to leave. Other families, such as the Clares, also lived within what became the park boundaries, where they made their living fishing, trapping, and hunting. When trapping and hunting were prohibited, the Métis families found their livelihoods severely diminished. Banished from their homes, they were eventually offered land at the Green Lake Métis settlement north and west of Big River under the direction of the Northern Settlers Re-Establishment Branch.[119] Several families eventually settled at Fish Lake, a Métis settlement that grew between Little Red River Reserve and Prince Albert National Park within the Emma Lake Provincial Forest.[120]

The "road allowance" people, as many Métis were known, found themselves a people "in between." They were not allowed to reside on Little Red since they were not status Indians of either the Montreal Lake or the La Ronge band, even though many had relations on the reserve. They were entitled to land consideration through their Métis heritage. The provincial government set aside otherwise unused Crown land for these small, family-oriented communities, such as Fish Lake or the Crescent Lake settlement south of Yorkton.[121]

The nature of First Nations and Métis life at the forest edge reveals opposing and ironic twists in how the story of the forest fringe has been told. Agricultural analysts considered wheat monoculture the apex and norm of farming. As a result, occupational pluralism and off-farm income commonly found along the forest fringe—freighting, fishing, hunting, picking berries, harvesting lumber, and trapping—became indicators of a marginal environment. Within the agricultural paradigm, families were "forced" to use off-farm resources to supplement meagre farm returns. At the same time, First Nations and Métis inhabitants of the forest fringe routinely combined landscape resources with occupational pluralism. The culture embraced seasonal movement and flow. Through cultural racism, their lifestyle was often denigrated. Yet during the Depression, off-farm occupations and forest products provided the key to the northern boom and were an important drawing card for many southern refugees. Racist explanations separated Aboriginal pursuits from homesteader practices by emphasizing the role of time: white homesteaders would use the resources of the landscape only until their farms were large and profitable enough to sustain their families; First Nations bands had no intention of changing their pluralistic pursuits, in which farming provided only a portion of income or food.[122] Although each family's daily activities might be the same, racial profiling and slurs created difference.

The struggle to turn bushland into farmland, hard enough for white settlers, was almost impossible for First Nations families without access to government loans for tools, supplies, horses, or machines. Land was owned by the band, and without some form of land collateral, loans to underwrite agricultural expansion were limited. Some reserve inhabitants, such as Billy Bear, succeeded in developing a prosperous mixed farm, but Bear combined farming with a successful freighting business and lumber interests, thereby accessing much-needed cash to allow for farm improvements.[123] For the Little Red band, one way to capitalize on their land and realize income was to lease their farmland to neighbouring settlers. Non-Native neighbours cleared and broke reserve land for agricultural purposes, and the band used the rent to fund much-needed services.[124]

SOCIAL CAPITAL

A key aspect of the Great Trek, and an important part of a trekker's success or failure in the north, was derived from social capital. Social capital is the spirit of connection and exchange among humans or social groups that creates networks of neighbours and friends and can provide extensive benefits. Although social capital is difficult to track or evaluate, it can be seen in knowledge exchange, cooperation, trust, sharing, security, acts of charity, chain migration, friendship, and kinship.

The experiences of the Wiberg and McGowan families of Paddockwood and the exchange of services and help offered by friends, neighbours, and relatives are excellent examples of the importance of social capital to northern resettlement success. Ernest Wiberg rode with a neighbour from Griffin, Saskatchewan (east of Weyburn), on his trek north in 1931. At Paddockwood, he worked with another Griffin emigrant, Axel Goplen, for the first year on the new northern homestead. As the Depression deepened, Ernest convinced his sister Muriel and her husband Sargent McGowan to try the north country. The Goplen family was there to offer a hot supper to Sargent in the spring of 1934, when he arrived by sleigh from Paddockwood with his settlers' effects. The McGowans lived with Ernest on his homestead for the first six years, looking after his farm in the winter while he was away working at the fish camps. Ernest looked after chores when Sargent was away doing road work with his big teams in the summer, which he often did for the municipality instead of paying taxes.

Sargent's brother, Norman McGowan, and his wife, Mabel, came north soon after Sargent and Muriel settled. They stayed up north for three years, where Norman (a hulk of a man at six foot four inches and broad shouldered) worked in tie camps and at other jobs. Mabel never adjusted to northern life, even though she bore a son at the Red Cross Outpost Hospital. When an opportunity arose for Norman to run a Pool elevator, they moved back to the Weyburn district. For them, their northern sojourn provided a short refuge until an opportunity came along to ease their return south.

Clarence Wiberg, brother to Ernest and Muriel, went north in 1934. He stayed with his siblings while taking local jobs. The three Wibergs were joined by their parents and other family members in 1940. Clarence and another brother, Allan, did some fire fighting in the Candle Lake area before joining the war effort. Muriel's sister Dagmar went north in 1940 and soon started teaching at Elk Range School, where Sargent was a trustee and the McGowan children went to school. Dagmar's husband, John Bentz, joined the army, and when the war was over John, Allan, and Clarence all took land in the Paddockwood area through the Veterans' Land Act, an updated version of the original Soldier Settlement Act land scheme. Clarence later claimed that, "upon returning to this warm and friendly atmosphere amongst loving relatives and congenial neighbours, I decided this was a good place to make my home."[125]

His sentiments played out for hundreds of other families across the forest fringe. For the McGowans and Wibergs, the social capital offered by friends and neighbours, and especially relations, provided shelter and food, hospitality, exchange of services, and local influence to help each other adjust to northern life and build new homes in the north. Their story is just one of many that can be traced through the local history books of neighbours and friends, siblings, cousins, and hired help whose social capital wove the fabric of existence. Historian Dawn Bowen tracked urban Depression refugees in the communities of Little Saskatoon and Tamarack, both near Loon Lake. Her findings suggested that one of the reasons Tamarack was a far less successful community than Little Saskatoon (more abandonment, fewer homesteads achieving title, little sense of community over the long term, for example) was that "social ties among the settlers were poorly developed." Migrants did not know each other prior to their arrival at Tamarack, nor did they develop strong bonds after taking homesteads. This lack of social capital, combined with poorer land, inadequate farming experience, lack of economic capital, and lack of support and infrastructure, "severely hampered their farming efforts."[126] Bowen found comparatively more social capital in Little Saskatoon, which developed a more prosperous community built in large part on cooperative effort, sharing, exchange, and cohesion. Her work suggested that social capital brought by Depression migrants—such as the social capital among the Goplens, Wibergs, and McGowans—helped to create an atmosphere that promoted success.

THE "GREAT RETREAT"?

Northern communities drew migrants because the forest edge, at least compared with the prairie, had moisture. In 1937, that distinction disappeared. The prairie, parkland, and southern edge of the forest fringe had "the most complete crop failure ever experienced." It was, for Saskatchewan, "the worst year yet." Provincial net farm income plummeted to minus $36,336,000, and wheat yields averaged an abysmal 2.7 bushels per acre.[127] Although the Great Trek had been reduced in the latter half of the 1930s, some southern farmers still felt the call of the north.[128] Others, however, saw the drought attacking even their northern refuge. For those who had fled dry conditions to go north in search of moisture, the 1937 drought signalled the end of hope. Starting in 1937, geographer Denis Patrick Fitzgerald noted, a "thin trickle" of people began to leave.[129]

That population loss was minor to the end of the Great Depression. In census division 15, which covered the Prince Albert region, 2,000 people (just over 2 percent of the population) left between 1936 and 1941. In the Paddockwood region, however, the population continued to climb. Over 500 more people lived in the region in 1941 than in 1936, a gain of almost 13 percent.[130] Fitzgerald commented that "the Great Retreat did not become apparent until after World War II."[131] The Prince Albert census district population sank by 8 percent between 1941 and 1951, dropping to just over 80,000 people.[132] The North Battleford district shrank by 15 percent of its population between 1941 and 1951; the Nipawin region, however, dropped by a mere 5 percent in the same period.[133]

These numbers cannot stand alone. Analysts have consistently—and incorrectly—attributed the "Great Retreat" to the abysmal farming conditions of the forest fringe. The Great Trek migrations, historian John McDonald asserted, overpopulated the northern forest fringe "relative to its true agricultural potential."[134] "Benighted settlers" left in droves, the narratives have consistently suggested, because they could not make a living.[135] Pushing agriculture beyond the forest edge had led to starvation and want, leaving analysts to declare that giving up was the only option. Poverty and harsh agricultural conditions, combined with sharply declining cordwood and lumber income, were contributing factors, of course, to northern out-migration. Compared with other areas of the province, however, net out-migration during and after the Second World War was substantially *less* along the northern parkland and forest fringe than on the prairie. The Swift Current region lost 18 percent of its population between 1941 and 1951, the Rosetown-Biggar district 20 percent—figures significantly higher than those along the fringe. Of course, these numbers do not include depopulation statistics in those regions from the 1930s. Rosetown had lost 15 percent of its population during the Depression, while the north was burgeoning. Swift Current had lost 13 percent.[136] In total, the Swift Current census district lost 29 percent of its population between 1931 and 1951, the Rosetown-Biggar district 31 percent.

What, then, accounted for the population drop across all rural regions of the province after 1941? The war, of course, drew many thousands of people to serve in the Armed Forces and in war service industries. The general economy improved, and business was healthy and full of opportunity. As well, farming changed drastically. Farm consolidation, real estate values, the resurgence of prairie land after the dust, price controls during the war years, and other factors affected agriculture as a whole. Although mechanized methods of land clearing and farming were available, their use was limited until after the war effort. The postwar period saw intensive farm mechanization and a switch from horses to motorized machines. Farming changed both on the prairie and at the forest edge. It turned from a way of life or a way to support the family to a business. Farmers were encouraged, and expected, to track their farm incomes and net returns, identify areas of loss and gain, and view their farms as economic—rather than social or cultural—endeavours.[137]

During the 1940s, agricultural progress in western Canada overcame its homestead origins. Although there remained a distinct difference between northern farms and prairie farms,[138] many forest edge farms on black or transitional soil enjoyed a large measure of success.[139] Fields continued to expand, year over year, as the forest acreage of each farm decreased. Paddockwood residents and local historians O'Hea and Endicott suggested that homesteaders of the 1930s, "having beaten the wilderness and being granted patent to their holdings, numbers of settlers, not farmers, sold their homesteads. Their places were taken over by ... farmers [who] got off to a good start." Homesteading, in this explanation, was a business venture different from building a farm: it was a way to create capital relatively quickly. Those who wanted to farm, not homestead, bought their land. The new farmers cleared "all land suitable for the purpose [of] cultivation." O'Hea and Endicott explained that the majority of these new farmers in their region were Ukrainian and Polish. The Kirychuk family of Paddockwood was one example. They came to Canada in 1939 on the wings of the European war and bought a farm northeast of Paddockwood.[140]

Although out-migration was indeed a noticeable part of Paddockwood life after the Second World War, farms that had been settled and cleared between 1920 and 1940 remained in production.[141] Population density maps of the province produced for the Saskatchewan Royal Commission on Agriculture and Rural Life in the 1950s showed a decided preference for parkland and forest fringe farms. Around Prince Albert and Nipawin, and north of Yorkton, the population density exceeded eight persons per square mile, while prairie regions rarely exceeded four.[142]

By the 1960s, the *Prince Albert Daily Herald* noted with a measure of surprise, the landscape at Paddockwood was "like the prairies."[143] It had passed the early homestead and development stages, and the physical landscape of mixed, livestock, and cereal grain farms bore little resemblance to the original mixed boreal forest. Some farms, of course, were less "successful" than others. In the Moose Lake region east of Hell's Gate and north of Forest Gate, the national Agricultural Rehabilitation and Development Administration (along with shareholders from the north Paddockwood region) initiated a community pasture project.[144] Farms in the region were sold to the government and transformed into pasture. Buildings were moved or burned, trees cleared, land seeded to grass, and farmsteads erased. Although productive, Moose Lake farms produced a smaller living with more work than the provincial average. Measured against prairie wheat farms, agricultural receipts were low at Moose Lake. The land was classed as sub-marginal, even though the farms were occupied and the majority were viable. Engaged primarily in a mixed-farm, occupationally pluralistic lifestyle geared to self-sufficiency, such farms were targeted for "improvement." Farmers were bought out.[145] As in the 1930s re-establishment movement, however, most of those who moved but continued farming stayed within the forest fringe, purchasing farms close by.[146] The majority of Moose Lake residents were Depression refugees or the children of refugees. For them, the cultural force of the forest edge as a place of refuge and resilience—where self-sufficiency and social capital were proven—remained strong.

CONCLUSION

The Great Trek from the prairie to the forest at a time of economic and ecological disaster signified the last time that there was a broad cultural definition in Saskatchewan of landscape as the point of connection between humans and sustenance. Back-to-the-land ideals and subsistence trumped market-oriented agriculture, and both urban residents and farmers embraced the northern, forested landscape. Since the mid-1940s, the growth of agribusiness, large-scale farming, and mechanization, and increased urbanization, have moved Saskatchewan increasingly away from its farm roots and coloured the way in which the past has been viewed. The concept of subsistence farming has too often been denigrated—by historians, agricultural analysts, and governments—as less successful and less desirable than large economic farm units tied to an export market. Too often the Great Trek migration and forest edge agriculture have been measured against an agricultural ideal built on market orientation and business rather than family self-sufficiency. Yet the Great Depression severed the connection between agriculture and the external market. Aspirations narrowed, and both farmers and urban residents saw farming through a practical lens that focussed on the products of the farm and the landscape: shelter, fuel, and food. The majority of northern farms—owned by Depression trekkers, earlier prairie migrants, or soldier settlers—were built within a culture drawn from self-sufficient mixed farming, the ecological edge, and occupational pluralism. They were not prairie farms.

The Great Trek migration, in many ways, was the end-game of the battle between wheat farms of the prairie and mixed farms of the parkland and forest fringe. Northern migrants, a *Regina Leader-Post* journalist noted in 1931, knew that the northern country "cannot afford a rapid career to a prospective wheat grower, but it will at least afford a living to a family with pioneer instincts better than that promised at present in the districts they have been forced to abandon."[147] The northern forest fringe did not offer single-cash-crop agriculture, and the vast majority of southern refugees knew it. What they searched for, and what many found, was a way of life that offered some balance: wood and water, garden produce, game and fish, and hay to feed stock. At the forest edge, migrants learned that mixed farming was more than just a mix of crops and livestock; it was culturally and economically embedded in the forest edge landscape, engaged in resource harvesting and the cordwood and barter economy. Like their First Nations neighbours, there were two kinds of people who used the forest edge: those who accessed its resources as a refuge for a short period to relieve economic or environmental stress, and those who developed a broadly mixed lifestyle that combined forest and prairie pursuits to find a measure of resilience.

Analysts who have used the government records of the Land Settlement Branch or the Northern Settlers Re-Establishment Branch found the stories of those who most needed and accessed government help. Those sources do not record the experiences of those who went north without government assistance. Local history books, and the reminiscences of drought trekkers, offer a new perspective on life at the forest edge.[148] Their stories of barter and exchange, a booming local economy, social capital and hope, short-term refuge, and long-term resilience in a mixed-farming and resource base tell a story at odds with traditional interpretations. Those who moved north considered a myriad of pull factors, primarily the contrast between the drought-ravaged open plains and the northern forested and wet landscape. They also wanted to access non-agricultural resources of fish, game, fur, and timber from the forest. The rise of tourism throughout the 1920s and 1930s culturally reinforced a divided Saskatchewan identity in which the south was flat and treeless while the north was lush, green, and forested. Weary drought refugees remembered, and celebrated, this contrast.

Today, in the north Prince Albert region, the line between farmland and Northern Provincial Forest is stark and entirely human made. Fields and pastures cut a straight edge along the quarter line. One step divides farmland from forest. Within that forest, past the agricultural edge, there remains Crown land that has either never been surveyed or was surveyed but not homesteaded. Hidden in the forest, though, are remnants of the northern push. Old sawmill sites, trappers' cabins, and Hell's Gate–type abandoned homesteads, with rotting shacks sinking into the bush, can be found. Acreages once cleared by axe or fire and cultivated have grown lush with poplar and willow in the ensuing years, to be succeeded once again by spruce, tamarack, and fir. The boreal forest stands, as always, at the ready to take over any farmland temporarily or permanently abandoned along the forest edge. But the overgrown caragana hedges, lilac bushes, and patches of rhubarb, remnants of long-forgotten garden plots, recall the Great Trek migrants who "watched in amazement as late-seeded crops and gardens grew inches, it seemed, overnight. They were thankful for the flavourful, bountiful harvest from the small garden plot, enough to last until the next harvest, and even the turnips were edible."[149]

CONCLUSION

SOUTH OF THE NORTH,
NORTH OF THE SOUTH

The north Prince Albert region is a transition zone between field and forest, an eco-tone binding the two solitudes of Saskatchewan. That place, both edge and centre, point of convergence and point of contrast, has shifted over time. In a cultural bat-tle between forest and prairie, forestry and agriculture, wilderness and civilization, north and south, the ecological and cultural edge moved. Trails and corridors of connection, exchange, resource extraction, and settlement crossed the ecotone on a north-south pattern, breaking the false east-west perception of Canada's develop-ment. Government intervention, in the form of forest reserves, recreational areas, and homesteads, dictated land use, change, and development. The physical land-scape now corresponds to human decisions, lines and boundaries drawn on maps: roads and road allowances, quarter section divisions between farms, recreational land, First Nations reserve land, and the edge between agriculture and forest.

With human intervention, the local landscape shifted from boreal forest to the mixed fields of parkland/prairie or, in contemporary terms, from north to south. Yet the local identity fits neither the prairie nor the northern paradigm. How can it be prairie when there are trees, lakes, and a local economy built in part on resource exploitation? How can it be north when there are farms? Residents of the north Prince Albert region are keenly aware of their in-between position, embracing at-tributes of both cultures and ecologies. While interviewing forest fringe residents for this book, I ended interviews by asking "is this community part of the north or part of the south?" Participants looked me in the eye, then looked away, out the window or across the room, tilting their heads and pursing their lips before answering. Then they hedged their answers. Technically, it is south, I was told again and again, simply because it lies south of the mid-point of the province. The geographical (and therefore "legal") centre of Saskatchewan is the middle of Montreal Lake—many miles toward the pole. Pointing through windows at fields, combines, and barns, they noted that is is a farming region. But without exception, all of the interviewees identified this place as north. They offered a local identity with distinctive characteristics and a history that proclaimed and upheld its defining attributes as a place that was decidedly not the prairie. The default iconography, since they could not accept the Saskatchewan prairie agricultural paradigm, was north.

Canada, it is almost axiomatic to say, is a northern country. Its nordicity is a defining characteristic. Geographer Peter Usher wrote that "our national mythology suggests that our identity and purpose lie in the North, that a truly distinctive Canadian nationality will only be achieved through the development and settlement of our northern lands. ... To the North lie not only our economic destiny, but also our moral and spiritual renewal."[1] From Group of Seven artistry to the 2010 Olympic Games in Vancouver, Canada is proud to "own the podium" of its northern distinctiveness.

The national northern character, closely identified with specific places such as the Arctic or the Canadian Shield, is absent from Canadian public identification of Saskatchewan. The province is the anchor and epitome of the "Prairie" Provinces. The Canadian penchant for dividing this vast country into easily understood places called regions has reduced Saskatchewan identity to its southern denominator: prairie. Home of Tommy Douglas, medicare, the Roughriders, and endless fields of grain, Saskatchewan has become "the Land of Living Skies," where open space is the defining characteristic. The reflexive nature of prairie identification belies the truth of the Saskatchewan landscape and has distorted cultural and historical interpretation to favour the prairie south. The north, as historians Ken Coates and William Morrison pointed out, has indeed been—all too often—forgotten.[2]

The northern identity, in defiance of the national prairie iconography of Saskatchewan, resonated through two distinctive local history projects from the Paddockwood region. The first was the local history book *Cordwood and Courage,* published in 1982. Many of the people who worked on the book, such as Muriel McGowan, were Depression migrants who remembered and identified a northern and wooded landscape that was emphatically not the prairie. The new landscape was quickly transformed through axe and fire to amalgamate agricultural characteristics and create a hybrid local identity that pulled from both farm and forest. In essence, they created an edge identity that found resonance with its northern roots. It was not an easy life. Few writers who contributed to the community history book romanticized the work that it took to build a farm and a life out of the forest. After the Second World War, non-agricultural opportunities drew many people north, south, east, and west. Yet their memories and stories, returned to the community and stored in the community's history book, reflected gratitude for the refuge found at the forest edge at a time of intense need.

The edge identity surfaced again in 2005 when a group of local volunteers erected a stone commemorating the Montreal Lake Trail that ran through the region. The bronze marker, fixed to a huge glacial erratic, pinpointed the origin of the trail as a First Nations pathway, a route that led past the lobstick tree and took forest bands onto the plains and plains bands into the forest. Over time, it became a freight trail and a route into the north for natural resources, recreation, law enforcement, and fire control. The stone also commemorated the homesteaders who had pushed their way into rather unforgiving bush country to establish farms and homes and introduce mixed farming into the area. In its inspiration, it drew heavily on stories from Hell's Gate settlers and their battle to create viable farms. The defeat at Hell's Gate, and the erasure of much of the Moose Lake School District by the community pasture, revealed the harsh conditions and precarious lifestyle at the forest edge that too often skirted abject poverty. The commemorative stone focussed on the trail itself, placing Paddockwood securely as a conduit between north and south, a place of transition and connection. The stone recognized the complexity of memory, and acknowledged success and failure, forest and farming, and adventure and despair, at a place of hybrid influence, fluidity, transference, and cultural interchange. It celebrated the connections, acknowledging First Nations, mixed farming, natural resources, and recreation, underscoring a hybrid understanding of the forest edge as an important and dynamic transitional zone that bound one way of life to another.

Figure 35. Remnant of Montreal Lake Trail.
Source: Merle Massie, 2009.

Figure 36. Charlie Elliott of Paddockwood at Montreal Lake Trail cairn unveiling ceremony, 2005. Source: John Dinius, Paddockwood.

This book has explored the story of Saskatchewan's transitional zone, where the two halves of the province meet. Through deep-time place history, layering and comparing successive cultures in the same place, this book cuts through traditional interpretations of Saskatchewan's prairie or northern past. Edge theory, where the forest fringe is viewed as both an ecological and a cultural edge where two distinct regions and peoples meet and exchange knowledge, offers a critical approach that bridges the constructed gap between Saskatchewan northern history and southern history. Regionally defined prairie and northern narratives, when combined and focused through a local viewpoint, give a fresh view of the provincial story.

This fresh take on Saskatchewan history has unveiled nuances that alter the Canadian story and, perhaps, suggest some paths forward for future historical research. The story of First Nations history in the western interior shows a cultural use of the landscape that deliberately combined prairie and forest ecosystems—whether through meeting and trade/exchange or through short-term or extended stays in the "other" landscape. The forest edge was a place of refuge for plains bands, and it contributed significantly to the resilience of the smaller boreal bands throughout the western interior. In the summer, the forest edge was marked by a feminine, domestic lifestyle that drew on the aquatic landscape. First Nations history, both pre– and post–fur trade, would benefit from a critical gendered examination. This book has touched only the outer edge of the wealth of information that can be drawn from archaeological and historical sources.

As non-Native settlement escalated in the western interior, traditional First Nations practices that combined boreal and plains landscapes were replaced by an exploitative model that developed the resources of one ecosystem to serve the needs of the other. The dominion government divided agriculture and forest. The absence of wood on the open plains meant that forest resources in the western interior were too valuable for private/farm enterprise, so they were kept within the public domain. The lumber industry codified the north Prince Albert region as a place of resource wealth. Commercial fishing, along with mining, trapping, and other economic pursuits, flourished at the edge. Freighters stitched the two halves of the province together, taking commercial goods north and bringing resources south. Ironically, older First Nations models that combined prairie and forest set the stage for future development. As investors looked to exploit northern resources, the dominion was forced to make treaty with the region's boreal First Nations inhabitants. Boreal bands sought an adhesion to Treaty 6, thereby trading supplemental bison-hunting traditions for agricultural practices, entrenching farming in the forest. They folded farm produce into diversified forest edge resource extraction, reinforcing traditional subsistence and resilience strategies. To support the long-held practice of the forest edge as an important "home" territory for boreal bands, and to ensure the development of agriculture, the Montreal Lake and Lac La Ronge bands succeeded in winning a second, agricultural reserve in addition to their boreal territories. The Little Red River Reserve planted a firm foothold for the bands at the forest edge, not far from the lobstick tree that marked their world.

The agricultural history of the Canadian western interior has been dominated by the wheat story. The prairie, it has been told repeatedly, was the domain of King Wheat. The agricultural history of the north Prince Albert region, however, followed a different path. The mixed-farming movement dominated the region. Dominion surveyors, Prince Albert promoters, and local farmers endorsed the forest edge landscape as an ideal place to create a mixed farm. Presented as morally and ecologically superior to a wheat farm, a mixed farm spread a farmer's asset base over a range of crops, livestock, and farm products. Mixed farms required a diversified landscape with a good water source, scrub land for hay and shelter for stock, and good land for cereal grain production. Farming practices became tied to landscape, and debate raged over the advantages of mixed versus wheat farms. Those debates were central to the development of agriculture in the western interior. The opening of the New Northwest as the site of mixed farming contrasted with the development of half-section pre-emption wheat farms in the Palliser Triangle. What has been analyzed as essentially a wheat story becomes, through the lens of place history, a complicated ideological and cultural battle that played against the backdrop of landscape.

When fire raged through the north Prince Albert region in 1919, its identification as a lumber basket collapsed. Remnants of the forest remained, along with a vigorous growth of aspen that helped to underwrite the future of the region as a cordwood capital. Soldier settlement, supplemented by internal migration from the open plains, recreated the north Prince Albert region as a haven for farmers eager to trade the open plains for the forest edge. Dominion focus shifted away from simply moving people into the western provinces and toward helping them to stay there and create viable farms. Tied to the mixed-farming movement, soldier settlement and other assisted land settlement schemes changed the relationship between government and agriculture, tying Crown land and agricultural development to dominion responsibility.

Like their First Nations antecedents, soldier and prairie settlers developed an economically diversified society that drew on both farm and forest. Although the lumber industry was diminished, cordwood production combined with postwar growth in other northern resource industries to create an occupationally pluralistic society, combining mixed farming with regional wage opportunities. Soldier settlement in forested regions, in contrast to the usual examples, could experience exceptional success. As the decade drew to a close, the north was recast as a place of opportunity. Economic buoyancy, increased mechanization, and second homesteads brought a wave of new settlers to the forest fringe. Prospecting and potential mineral exploitation joined forest products and commercial fishing and contributed to the call to "go north."

With the rise of the car culture and increased municipal and provincial expenditures on roads and infrastructure, the north Prince Albert region developed a new identity. Tourism marketing reinforced the contrast between the prairie south and the forested north. Promotion based on the rural/urban divide found little traction in Saskatchewan. Instead, the leverage to create Prince Albert National Park and the Lakeland region marketed and exploited the cultural and ecological divide. The north was recast as a place of beauty and relaxation, lakes and rivers, health and fun, in contrast to a dry, treeless prairie south. It was wilderness, but it was accessible—you could get there in a car, and the trip was short. As the "Playground of the Prairies," the northern vacationland drew widespread public interest, primarily within the province, that increased as the Depression deepened. As the prairie landscape became disfigured by drought, writer Grey Owl and painter Augustus Kenderdine worked to present the northern landscape as an oasis of beauty and the last frontier of wilderness and natural splendour.

Given the cultural presence of Saskatchewan's north at the end of the 1920s as a place of opportunity and natural beauty, it should come as no surprise that refugees flocked to the north in droves during the Great Depression. Instead, historians have consistently expressed a large measure of shock and confusion at the sheer number of prairie migrants who made the Great Trek north to develop farms at the forest edge, the so-called place of last resort. Through a deep-time history of the north Prince Albert region, it became clear that northern resettlement during the 1930s was an escalation of practices that had, in fact, been in place for a long time. Aboriginal landscape harvest practices, boreal resource extraction, mixed farming, and northern tourism were important cultural and economic precedents that drew migrants north by the thousands when the wheat economy failed. The story of dust and devastation, the archetypal prairie dust bowl narrative, broke open at the forest edge. While communities on the open plains hemorrhaged, the forest fringe—and the far north—boomed. I had a student from Flin Flon in one of my university classes studying western Canadian history. His perception of the 1930s, like that of Paddockwood, recalled a time of wealth and prosperity, not want. Families moved north toward a place of hope and opportunity. For some, it was a landscape of short-term refuge, for others of long-term resilience.

After the dust had settled, prairie farms returned to pre-drought productive capacity. Nonetheless, the rural populations of both the open prairie and the forest edge fell after the Second World War. As mechanization and farm consolidation gained hold, farming began the long march toward the agribusiness and indus-trialization that we see today. Technological advances in crop varieties, fertilizers, herbicides, and insecticides combined with crop insurance and large-scale water damming for power and irrigation schemes to give prairie grain farms more re-silience. Farming as a way of life, to nurture a family and build a subsistence liv-ing over the long term, gave way. Logging, cutting cordwood, freighting, fishing, and other forest edge resource economies also surrendered to industrialization and mechanization, making a large-scale transition from independently owned small businesses to commercial enterprises.

The northern push of settlement left a lasting mark on the Saskatchewan land-scape. As of the 2006 census, settlement in the north Prince Albert region—despite the inclusion of a large amount of uninhabited forest reserve within the census region—averaged over 2.4 people per square kilometre. Corollary rural munici-palities in the prairie south, such as Swift Current, supported half that population base, while municipalities that have seen significant depopulation since the 1920s, such as Happyland, support one-tenth the number of people.

For Aboriginal inhabitants of the forest edge, general agricultural retreat and rural depopulation after the Second World War eased pressure on traditional for-est resources. In 1947, the borders of Prince Albert National Park were changed. The section east of the third meridian, which effectively enclosed the Montreal Lake Reserve, was eliminated and reverted to Crown land. Aboriginal inhabitants at Montreal Lake and Little Red River could once again access the large area for fishing, hunting, and trapping purposes. In 1948, Little Red once more fought off a petition to have the agricultural reserve released and its inhabitants sent back north. The land was officially divided between the Lac La Ronge and Montreal Lake bands, facilitating band governance.[3] Through treaty land entitlement settle-ments, Little Red has continued to grow.

Along the forest fringe, vestiges of the mixed, ecologically pluralistic lifestyle remained. Some subsistence mixed farms were targeted as "marginal" and pur-chased for conversion to provincial pasture during the 1960s. During the 1970s and 1980s, a renewed back-to-the-land movement brought a new wave of migrants to the region, looking to develop a "dream of people living in harmony with na-ture."[4] Forest edge farms, with timber for building and fuel, were once again popu-lar. In the 1990s and after the turn of the twenty-first century, the cycle turned again. "Marginal" forest fringe farms were targeted by government researchers as expendable, their "best use" once again as forests to preserve and strengthen Canada's carbon-trading footprint. Climate change scientists forecast, however, that the open plains will undergo increasingly severe swings between droughts and floods as the earth warms. Decreased agricultural potential on the prairie might mean another Great Trek into the forest to develop the podzolic soil and take advantage of the comparatively wetter and potentially warmer climate of northern Saskatchewan. Cultural explanations of the forest edge economy will continue to swing on a pendulum between marginal and poor to flourishing and attractive.

Interpretations of Saskatchewan's northern history—and northern future— have reinforced a deep cultural contrast and divide between the boreal north and the prairie south. The north has been a place of resource exploitation, colonialism, and southern metropolitan control. Northern Saskatchewan is known for its "otherness," as "another country altogether." Although these interpretations bear validity and need to be folded into the Saskatchewan identity, they leave the provincial past deeply divided, as if there has been no point of contact or exchange. The north as the colonial fiefdom of the south has also consistently been a story of the recent past, a post–Second World War storyline that emphasizes overt public control, transportation innovation, and resource exploitation. Prior to that time, historians have asserted, the north was ignored.[5]

This book has shown that the north has consistently been an integral aspect of successful human adaptation in the region that became Saskatchewan. In fact, the biomes of prairie south and boreal north worked in concert to provide resources (whether natural or manipulated) for human adaptation, refuge, and resilience. Economic and cultural development has often used the tension and interplay of Saskatchewan's two solitudes, where the attributes and resources of one offset and complement the deficiencies of the other. When historical interpretation rests solely on one region or the other, however, the connections and sense of interchange between the two are lost.

The cultural ramifications of forest edge settlement, particularly drought migrations from the 1920s to the end of the Great Depression, created and reinforced a Saskatchewan identity that was neither wholly prairie nor wholly northern. Communities along the forest edge became places that were defiantly *not* the prairie, though large-scale agricultural practices would transform the landscape. Resonances of the non-prairie identity can be found in Meadow Lake, Big River, Paddockwood, Choiceland, White Fox, Nipawin, and Hudson Bay, all places that share similar economies and histories built on a mix of farm and forest resources. A deep-time place history of the north Prince Albert region replaces the split narrative of Saskatchewan with an inclusive perspective. From traditional First Nations use of the forest edge landscape through to that of the Depression migrants, resilience and longevity could best be found when northern and southern landscapes, economies, and cultures were folded together.

What does this mean for Canadian historians? Is this book anything more than a mere peek at the pre–Second World War history of one particular place? I say yes. Edge theory asks where are the artificial, internal boundaries that Canadian historians have created? What implications have those regional boundaries created? Which assumptions do we Canadians hold on to most dearly when it comes to telling the Canadian story? Which traditional plots, characteristics, regional stereotypes, and storylines do we cleave to when we think about our nation? Is the divide between east and west, for example, a construction or a constant? Is a road really heading nowhere, or is it—from the lens of those at the end of that road—a gateway to the world? What would a history of Canada look like, let's imagine, if it was told from the perspective of Churchill, Manitoba, or Thunder Bay, Ontario? Which Canadian places, events, or timelines considered foundational to the Canadian story would be tossed and lost in the stormy waters of Hudson Bay or Lake Superior? I could name hundreds of other points on the map, from Newfoundland to Nunavut to the Salish Sea, and ask what would Canada's past look, sound, and taste like from those perspectives? It's about viewpoint rather than weight in a mystical balance scale of importance. In the end, what matters is not that I have told some new stories about a place that you might never see. What matters is that I have now (I sincerely hope) upended some of your perspectives on Saskatchewan. Let this new view of Saskatchewan's past provide a roadmap or blueprint for those of us looking to shake up the way in which we tell Canada's story.

NOTES

INTRODUCTION: EDGE, PLACE, AND HISTORY

1   See http://atlas.nrcan.gc.ca/site/english/learningresources/theme_modules/borealforest/index.html (accessed 20 March 2008).

2   McGowan, "Under the Raven's Nest." McGowan wrote another manuscript, entitled "The Key is in the Horse," c. 2001–2002. Both manuscripts are in possession of author.

3   Friesen, "Defining the Prairies."

4   For an overview of the inherent problems of creating a national narrative, see Granatstein, *Who Killed Canadian History?*; Owram, "Narrow Circles." Recent essay collections that are regionally based and present some criticism on the concept include Wrobel and Steiner, eds., *Many Wests*; and Friesen, *River Road*.

5   Wishart, "Preliminary Thoughts on Region and Period."

6   Stanley, "The Western Canadian Mystique," 6–27.

7   Coates and Morrison, *Forgotten North*, 1. An important companion book is Abel and Coates, eds., *Northern Visions*. An excellent overview of recent writing on the Canadian north, including intriguing suggestions for further study which include a call for more investigation of the provincial norths and their "ties of corporations, governments, families, political parties and others between northern areas and southern regions," is from Coates and Morrison, "The New North in Canadian History and Historiography." Kerry Abel followed up her co-editing with the prize-winning *Changing Places*. See also Abel, "History and the Provincial Norths." The best example from northern Manitoba is Frank Tough's *'As Their Natural Resources Fail'*. For northern Alberta, see Wetherell and Kmet, *Alberta's North*.

8   Work on the Peace River region of Alberta and British Columbia made the physical connection between the west and the Far North (north of the sixtieth parallel) through the Peace and Athabasca River systems and the opening of highways to Alaska, the North West Territories and the Yukon. See Bowes, ed., *Peace River Chronicles*; Leonard and Lemieux, *Fostered Dream*. Others have pushed the western Canadian boundary south with comparative work on the American Great Plains and Canadian Prairies. See Higham and Thacker, eds., *One West, Two Myths* and Higham and Thacker,

eds., *One West, Two Myths II.* These were complemented by another important reader, Felske and Rasporich, eds., *Challenging Frontiers.*

9 Quiring, *CCF Colonialism*, x.

10 Ibid., xi; Bone, "Saskatchewan's Forgotten North," 13.

11 The classic interpretations of northern development remain Zaslow, *Opening of the Canadian North; Northward Expansion of Canada.*

12 Piper, *Industrial Transformation of Subarctic Canada.*

13 See Sandwell, "Rural Reconstruction"; see also Sandwell, *Contesting Rural Space;* Sandwell, "Notes toward a history of rural Canada."

14 Ommer and Turner, "Informal Rural Economies in History," footnote 9.

15 "Forest Fringe" is a term that is well-recognized within the Saskatchewan context.

16 Odum, *Fundamentals of Ecology.*

17 The use of the terms ecotone and edge effect within archaeology was criticized by Rhoades, "Archaeological Use and Abuse of Ecological Concepts and Studies." His point was that the current landscape may not reflect past landscapes; also, borrowing from another discipline without also understanding the nuances and controversies within that discipline provides shaky ground. Rhoades's criticisms convinced few.

18 Turner, Davidson-Hunt, and O'Flaherty, "Living on the Edge," 439.

19 Ibid., 452. Two pivotal works are relevant here: White, *The Middle Ground* and Pratt, *Imperial Eyes.* Both introduce similar concepts of a "middle ground" or a "contact zone" where two distinct cultures meet, interact, exchange ideas, engage, and generally grapple with one another.

20 Ray, *Indians in the Fur Trade*, 46–48.

21 Ibid., 36.

22 Ray's work is specifically cited in Turner, et al., "Living on the Edge."

23 Turner et al., "Living on the Edge," 441. It is important to define the concept of resilience, as it has a different, and almost completely opposite meaning within ecology. Resilience is a somewhat negative concept, used often in reference to plant or animal species that take over an area and come back again and again, despite natural or human attempts to control or reduce. Weeds would be an excellent example.

24 Turner, "The Significance of the Frontier in American History." This paper was first presented in 1893 and continues to draw both admiration and criticism. See also Cross, "Introduction," *The Frontier Thesis and the Canadas*, 1.

25 For examples, see the work of Vanderhill, "Observations on the Pioneer Fringe in Western Canada"; Vanderhill, "The Passing of the Pioneer Fringe in Western Canada." Vanderhill directly attributes Bowman with popularizing the term.

26 For a short, but detailed analysis of Bowman, his work, and his large sphere of influence, see Smith, "Political Geographers of the Past."

27 Bowman, *The Pioneer Fringe; Bowman*, et al., *Pioneer Settlement.* Bowman wrote and published several smaller essays that explained aspects of the project. See Bowman, "Planning in Pioneer Settlement"; "The Scientific Study of Settlement"; and "The Pioneering Process."

28 Fitzgerald, "Pioneer Settlement in Northern Saskatchewan," 3–4.

29 Ibid., 3.

30 Ibid., 561.

31 Wood, *Places of Last Resort*, 15. Astonishingly, Wood's book makes no reference to Fitzgerald's seminal thesis.

32 Environment Canada, Lands Directorate, working paper No. 38. "The Agriculture-Forest Interface: An Overview of Land Use Change" by Michael Fox and Sandra Macenko, 1985. For an excellent overview of Clay Belt settlement that contrasts Ontario with Quebec, see McDermott, "Frontiers of Settlement in the Great Clay Belt."

33 Atwood, *Survival*; Atwood, *Strange Things*.

34 Examples of this technique include Cronon, *Changes in the Land*; White, *Land Use, Environment, and Social Change*; Binnema, *Common and Contested Ground*; and Abel, *Changing Places*. A spectacular addition to this list is William Turkel's study of the Chilcotin region of British Columbia, *The Archive of Place*.

35 Dan Flores, "Place: An Argument for Bioregional History."

36 Stunden Bower, *Wet Prairie*.

37 Flores, "Place."

38 Massie, "Scribes of Stories, Tellers of Tales."

39 Voisey, "Rural Local History and the Prairie West," rpt. in Francis and Palmer, *Prairie West*, 497–510. For an example of a local history written along Voisey's dictates, see his own *Vulcan: The Making of a Prairie Community*.

40 Parr, *Gender of Breadwinners*.

41 For a discussion of the views for and against local history as an acceptable venture for academics and others, see Kammen, ed., *Pursuit of Local History*; Kammen and Prendergast, eds., *Encyclopaedia of Local History*. For a passionate call for writing innovative local history, see Amato, *Rethinking Home*.

42 Baker, "So What's the Importance of the Lethbridge Strike of 1906?"

43 Abel, *Changing Places*. Published by the same press and in the same year as Wood's *Places of Last Resort*, Abel's study region (the Iroquois-Porcupine Falls area) is part of the Ontario Clay Belt zone but Abel's work takes a much broader perspective, folding the agricultural story with that of Aboriginal, mining, and lumber settlement.

44 Abel, *Changing Places*, preface, xxii–xxiii.

45 Flores, "Place," 5.

46 See Cronon, "A Place for Stories."

CHAPTER ONE: ECOTONES AND ECOLOGY

1 McNeill and Winiwarter, eds., *Soils and Societies*, iv.

2 Canada Land Inventory, http://www.geostrategis.com/c_cli-prince-albert.htm. For example, Gerald Friesen characterized the parkland as the transition zone between prairie and boreal environments in his introduction to *The Canadian Prairies*, 3.

3 Coupland and Brayshaw, "The Fescue Grassland in Saskatchewan."

4 Bird, *Ecology of the Aspen Parkland*, 3–4.

5 Meyer and Epp, "North-South Interaction."

6 Ibid., 338. For a further investigation of the problems of using the term "ecotone," see Rhoades, "Archaeological Use and Abuse of Ecological Concepts and Studies," 608–14. The Boreal Shield and Taiga Shield ecozones are effectively incorporated as boreal.

7 Meyer, Beaudoin, and Amundsen, "Human ecology of the Canadian prairie ecozone."

8 Strong and Hills, "Late-glacial and Holocene."

9 For a map of Saskatchewan's ecoregions, see Fung, ed., *Atlas of Saskatchewan*, 174–5.

10 Canada Land Inventory classification, http://www.geostrategis.com/c_cli-prince-albert.htm (accessed 15 January 2009).

11 The *Atlas of Saskatchewan* classifies the research region as "Boreal Transition" and is described as "characterized by a mix of forest and farmland, marking both the southern advance of the boreal forest and the northern limit of arable agriculture." See *Atlas of Saskatchewan*, 162–3.

12 Hind, *Narrative*, 392.

13 Pyne, *Awful Splendour*, 37.

14 For an overview of the dynamics and historical context of prairie fires and the prairie/forest edge, see ibid., 38–40.

15 Campbell, et al., "Bison Extirpation," 360–2. The existence and extent of the "parkland" region in prehistoric and early historic times is under research by archaeologist Alwynne Beaudoin in Edmonton using proxy pollen records. Early results indicate that the parkland did not exist in prehistoric times.

16 Campbell, "Bison Extirpation," 361.

17 See Bird, *Ecology of the Aspen Parkland*, 3–4.

18 Pyne, *Awful Splendour*, 20.

19 Johnson and Miyanishi, eds., *Forest Fires*, v–x.

20 Ibid., 3.

21 An excellent report, created by Jeffery Thorpe of the Plant Ecology Section of the Saskatchewan Research Council for the Prince Albert Model Forest Association, outlined the transitions that lead from one forest canopy type to another (the predominance of one kind of tree over another), the ages at which such transitions can occur, and alternatives and factors that encourage one transition path or another. Thorpe, "Models of Succession."

22 Forest succession is drawn primarily from Thorpe, "Models of Succession." See also Kirby, *Growth and Yield of White Spruce-Aspen*.

23 Thorpe, "Models of Succession."

24 See Lewis and Ferguson, "Yards, Corridors, and Mosaics."

25 Ibid., 68–9.

26 Ibid., 69–70.

27 Ibid., 70–72.

28 Meyer, Beaudoin, and Amundsen, "Human ecology of the Canadian prairie ecozone."

29 For a well-written explanation of these and other typical Saskatchewan soils, see http://www.soilsof-sask.ca, which is provided by the Soil Science department of the University of Saskatchewan.

30 For an overview of land and soil types relevant to this area, and a map, see Kabzems, Kosowan, and Harris, *Mixedwood Section in an Ecological Perspective*, 9–12.

31 Waters to the north of this research area flow north into the Churchill River system.

32 Richards, *Saskatchewan*.

33 See, for example, the various discussions on "north" as defined by NiCHE—The Network in Canadian History of the Environment, http://www.niche.ca.

34 *Atlas of Saskatchewan*, 118.

35 Meyer and Epp, "North South Interaction."

36 See http://www.geostrategis.com/c_cli-prince-albert.htm (accessed 15 January 2009).

37 Ibid., 4.

38 See, for example, reports from the *Prince Albert Daily Herald* in late August 2008. http://www.paher-ald.sk.ca/index.cfm?sid=166907&sc=4.

39 Interview, Merle Massie with Miriam Swenson, 13 November 2008.

40 See, for example, the work of the Land Use and Land Cover Change program of the United States Global Change Research Program, http://www.usgcrp.gov/usgcrp/ProgramElements/land.htm.

CHAPTER TWO: THE GOOD WINTERING PLACE

1. Silversides, *Gateway to the North*.

2 Palliser, *Journals*, 92, 202.

3 Burpee, ed., *Adventurer from Hudson Bay*, 103.

4 "John N. Smith," in *Voice of the People*, 117. This book is an edited collection of biographies and reminiscences collected by the Historical Society. Most of the original manuscripts are kept in the Bill Smiley Archives, Prince Albert Historical Museum, Prince Albert.

5 Daschuk, "A Dry Oasis," 3.

6   Ray, *Indians in the Fur Trade*, 31–3. This model has been accepted by, for example, George Colpitts, as expressed in his essay, "'Victuals to Put Into Our Mouths.'"

7   See Chapter 1.

8   Those who have studied bison movement and migration have included: Arthur, "The North American Plains Bison"; Bamforth, "Historical Documents and Bison Ecology on the Great Plains"; Clow, "Bison Ecology"; Epp, "Way of the Migrant Herds"; Flores, "Bison Ecology and Bison Diplomacy"; Moodie and Ray, "Buffalo Migrations in the Canadian Plains"; Morgan, "Bison Movement Patterns"; Roe, *North American Buffalo*; Vickers, "Seasonal Round Problems on the Alberta Plains."

9   Another researcher who strongly refuted Ray's parkland co-occupation thesis was Dale Russell, whose important work, *Eighteenth-Century Western Cree and Their Neighbours* cited Ray extensively, while pointing out gaps in Ray's research and/or large errors in interpretation.

10 Malainey and Sherriff, "Adjusting Our Perspectives."

11 Ibid., 336–9.

12 Bird, *Ecology of the Aspen Parkland*, 3–5.

13 Vickers and Peck, "Islands in a Sea of Grass."

14 Ibid., 95.

15 See Haig, ed., *Peter Fidler's Journal*. Quoted in Pyne, *Awful Splendour*, 60. For a book-length discussion on energy (fire, wood, coal, oil, nuclear, etc.), see Schobert, *Energy and Society*, particularly Chapters 4 and 5.

16 Vickers and Peck, "Islands in a Sea of Grass," 98–9.

17 It is unclear whether they were Woods or Swampy Cree.

18 Ray, *Indians in the Fur Trade*, 41.

19 Ibid., 45–6. Russell disputed many of Ray's assumptions regarding the extent of these trips. He argued that Ray assumed this trip was "normal" and that it indicated a forest/parkland cycle that would only utilize the parkland/bison biome for a brief period in mid-winter. Russell argued that other influences, including a late start, illness, and a desire to wait for the French traders to arrive, accounted for their shortened route. See Russell, *Eighteenth-Century Western Cree*, 111.

20 Ray, *Indians in the Fur Trade*, 41.

21 For years it was kept in the basement of the old Presbyterian church, before being put on display in the renovated Fire Hall, the present home of the Prince Albert Historical Society. Further details have been added in conversation with Jamie Benson, curator of the museum.

22 A fantastic essay by Edward S. Rogers on "The Dugout Canoe in Ontario," was published in *American Antiquity* 30, 4 (April 1965): 454–9. Rogers argues that dugout canoes were an idea brought by Europeans to the interior. Using a combination of fire and European tools, both Aboriginals and Europeans could carve a canoe from a large tree. As forest fires and logging decimated valuable birch bark trees, Rogers argued that dugout canoes gained favour, but that they were always used in a local situation, never for portaging. This is an intriguing environmental and cultural explanation. The Christopher Creek dugout canoe has never been dated; it is possible that it was created as recently as the nineteenth century. It is unlikely, however, to have been of European make.

23 On the open plains of the South or the tundra to the north, where birch could not be found, hides were used to construct serviceable crafts of coracles or kayaks.

24 Meyer and Epp, "North-South Interaction."

25 Ibid., "North-South Interaction," 334.

26 Malainey, et al., "One Person's Food," 143, 154; Meyer and Epp, "North-South Interaction," 336.

27 Malainey et al., "One Person's Food." For a fuller investigation of Malainey's work, see Malainey, "Reconstruction and Testing of Subsistence and Settlement Strategies."

28 For an overview of the importance of isinglass and sturgeon to the fur trade, see Holzkam, Lytwyn, and Waisberg, "Rainy River Sturgeon," 194–205. Historical geographer A.J. Ray talked about the gender connection of isinglass at Prairie Summit Conference, Regina, 2010, where Ray was the keynote speaker.

29 Lewis, "Recognition and Delimitation." For more of Malcolm Lewis's work on the connection between First Nations and maps, see Lewis, *Cartographic Encounters.*

30 There has been considerable discussion in ethnographic literature regarding the origin and dispersal of the Cree into the western interior. For an overview, see Russell, *Eighteenth-Century Western Cree and their Neighbours.* The Assiniboin (for which group I like the historical term, Assine Poet), are sometimes referred to as Nakota in modern scholarship, and it was from this group that the Cree may have learned the art of bison pounding. See Meyer and Russell, "'So Fine and Pleasant, Beyond Description.'"

31 Russell, *Eighteenth-Century Western Cree,* 146–55.

32 Meyer and Russell, "The Pegogamaw Cree and Their Ancestors," 307.

33 These archaeological sites are sometimes known as Late Woodland. One site has been identified not far from the Garden River, as the Hulowski site, FiNi-3. See Meyer and Russell, "Pegogamaw Cree and Their Ancestors," map, 311.

34 The journals of the masters of both Cumberland House and its inland supply post, Hudson House, offer extensive references to this post, most of them quite negative in nature. See *The Publications of the Hudson's Bay Record Society: Cumberland and Hudson House Journals, 1775–82,* First and Second Series, 1952. The site of this fur trade fort has been professionally excavated on several occasions, but the North Saskatchewan River has now eroded all traces of the old fort. For an intriguing article on the Sturgeon River fort and its role in place, commemoration, and the work of the Historic Site Board of Canada, see Thompson, "Life on the Edge: The Cultural Value of Disappearing Sites," http://crm.cr.nps.gov/archive/20-4/20-4-18.pdf (accessed 8 September 2009). The most famous inhabitant of this fort was Peter Pond. A cairn was erected at the old site of the Sturgeon River fort to commemorate Pond.

35 The Pink journals are as yet unpublished. See Russell, *Eighteenth-Century Western Cree,* 98–105; see also Morton, *History of the Canadian West,* 277–81.

36 Russell, *Eighteenth-Century Western Cree,* 144. See also the letters of William Walker of Hudson House to Cumberland House, December through May, 1781–1782, in *Cumberland and Hudson House Journals, 1775–82 Second Series, 1779–82* and Meyer and Russell, "Pegogamaw Cree."

37 William Walker letters and journals, Hudson House, 1781–1782, *Cumberland and Hudson House Journals.*

38 Meyer, "Lands and Lives of the Pegogamaw Crees," 217.

39 Smith, *Voice of the People,* 117.

40 The best explanation of the impact of horse and gun technology on First Nations groups in the western interior is found in Binnema, *Common and Contested Ground.*

41 Erasmus, *Buffalo Days and Nights,* 231–2.

42 Ray, "Northern Great Plains."

43 Ibid., 278.

44 Turner, Davidson-Hunt, and O'Flaherty, "Living on the Edge," 456.

45 Ibid.

46 Morton, ed., *Journal of Duncan McGillivray,* 62.

47 Allan Bird identified this battle as being from the early 1700s. It is therefore not possible to correlate the Cree/Dene hostility to the local resource richness of the early 1800s. For an overview of the story, see Shortt, *Survey of the Human History* and Waiser, *Saskatchewan's Playground,* 4 and endnotes.

48 Elliott and McGowan, "Links with the Past," *Cordwood and Courage,* 2. See also Hayball, "Historic Lobsticks and Others," 62–6.

49 Podruchny, *Making the Voyageur World.*

50 As quoted in Hayball, "Historic Lobsticks," 64.

51 Ibid., 64.

52 Meyer and Thistle, "Saskatchewan River Rendezvous." Meyer later rejected the term "rendezvous centre" for the term "ingathering centres." See Meyer and Russell, "So Fine and Pleasant, beyond Description," 234.

53 See Lewis and Ferguson, "Yards, Corridors, and Mosaics." The farmer who owned the land throughout the 1970s and 1980s would often find bison skulls when cultivating. Walter Mindiuk, personal communication to Merle McGowan (later Massie), 1985. Burned grass regenerates into new growth up to three weeks faster than natural grass.

54 See in particular Meyer, *Red Earth Crees* and "Waterfowl in Cree Ritual."

55 A modern comparison would be the Catholic Church steeple at Albertville, on the same open plain not far from where the lobstick tree would have been. This steeple can easily be seen on a clear day from the crest of the Waskesiu Upland near Christopher Lake. The lobstick would have been similarly easy to find.

56 If the exact location of the tree could be identified, an archaeological investigation of the site might produce more information on cultural use.

57 Net-Setting or Sturgeon River, and Carp River are excellent toponymic examples of local exploitation practices.

58 See Russell, *Eighteenth-Century Western Cree and Their Neighbours.*

59 Goode, "A Historical/Cultural/Natural Resource Study," 3.5. Note that these lakes did not carry their current names at this time. Maps of the region from 1885 show references to lakes called Little Swan Lake and Little Bittern Lake. Little Bittern was most likely Christopher Lake. When the Little Red River reserve was surveyed, what we now know as "Christopher Creek" was listed as "Little Bittern Creek." See http://cartweb.geography.ua.edu/lizartech/iserv/getimage to view the 1885 map.

60 Waiser, *Saskatchewan's Playground*, 1; Goode, "A Historical/Cultural/Natural Resource Study," 3.1–3.5.

61 Waiser, *Saskatchewan's Playground*, 9.

62 Goode, "A Historical/Cultural/Natural Resource Study," 3.5.

63 See Ibid., "The Journal of the Reverend J.A. Mackay."

64 The Hudson's Bay Company Archives has HBC post records from 1851 to 1930 for this post. The general account book for Candle Lake for the years 1887–1889 is also extant in the archive.

65 See Waiser, *Saskatchewan's Playground*, 4–9.

66 For an overview of this transition, see Binnema, *Common and Contested Ground.*

67 Colpitts, "Pemmican Empire: Environment, Food and Trade in the Northern Great Plains," History and Classics Colloquium, University of Alberta, 13 November 2009. See also Colpitts, "'Victuals to Put into our Mouths'"; Ray, "Northern Great Plains."

68 Green, "'The House in Buffalo Country.'"

69 Colpitts, "'Victuals to Put into our Mouths.'"

70 Mandelbaum, *The Plains Cree*, 68. This book was based on Mandelbaum's extensive fieldwork among the Cree, and his doctoral thesis, both of which were completed in the 1930s. See "Preface to the New Edition," xiii.

71 Mandelbaum, *The Plains Cree*, 68.

72 Ibid.

73 See James Nisbet letters and papers, published by the Presbyterian Church of Canada as Nisbet, *Home and Foreign Record of the Canada Presbyterian Church.* Some of the letters were reprinted in *Voice of the People*, Letter from N. Saskatchewan, 30 July 1866, from Rev. J. Nisbet to Rev. R. F. Burns, 25.

74 The decline of the bison has been well-documented and extensively explored by historians, ethnographers, and biologists across the entire Great Plains. Excellent works on this subject include Isenberg, *Destruction of the Bison*; Flores, "Bison Ecology and Bison Diplomacy"; Foster, Harrison, and MacLaren, eds., *Buffalo*; Dobak, "Killing the Canadian Buffalo."

75 Erasmus, *Buffalo Days and Nights*, 248, 249.

76 The signing and implications of the numbered treaties have been well-served by others and will not be repeated here. See, for example, Ray, Miller, and Tough, *Bounty and Benevolence* for the most recent, and comprehensive, Saskatchewan overview.

77   Ray, Miller, and Tough claim "Treaty Six was negotiated primarily with the buffalo-hunting First Nations of the parkland/grassland region." *Bounty and Benevolence*, 143.

78   See the copy of Treaty 6 on the Indian Claims Commission website, http://www.indianclaims.ca (accessed 14 September 2009).

79   Ray, Miller, and Tough, *Bounty and Benevolence*, 132.

80   Treaty 6, p. 4, http://www.indianclaims.ca.

81   Nisbet, "Three and a Half Years," rpt. in *Voice of the People*, 32.

82   The Order-in-Council that outlined the reserve stated: "Sturgeon Lake is a long narrow expansion of Sturgeon or Net-Setting River, and runs easterly, across the reserve. This stretch of water has high bold shores, and abounds with fish and fowl. It is used by lumbermen to get out timber." This description would have been taken from the surveyor's notes. See Order-in-Council PC 1151, 17 May 1889, 50–51.

83   Library and Archives Canada [LAC], RG10 Vol. 2656, file 9092. James Walker, Acting Indian Agent, Battleford, NWT, to Lt. Governor, NWT, Battleford, 20 August 1877.

84   For wording from Treaty 6, see http://www.indianclaims.ca/pdf/authorities/6%20eng.pdf. Bob Beal, "Treaty Six," *Encyclopedia of Saskatchewan*, 951–2.

85   Ray, *Canadian Fur Trade*, 34, 35, 38.

86   LAC, RG 10 Vol. 3601, file 1754, John Sinclair, Prince Albert, to D.H. Macdowall, M.P., Ottawa, 26 May 1891.

87   As noted in Goode, "Historical/Cultural/Natural Resource Study," 3.8. See also LAC, RG 10 Vol. 3601, file 1754, John Sinclair to D.H. Macdowall, 26 May 1891.

88   Goode, "Historical/Cultural/Natural Resource Study," 3.8. For an overview of Treaty 6 and the Treaty 6 external adhesion at Montreal Lake, see Miller, *Compact, Contract, Covenant*, 175–200; see also Ray, Miller, and Tough, *Bounty and Benevolence*.

89   Lac La Ronge band is sometimes referred to as "Rocky Cree." See Roberts, *Historical Events of the Woodland Cree*, 4. The signing of the adhesion and its ramifications have been given a brief overview by Waiser in *Saskatchewan's Playground*; by Ray, Miller, and Tough in *Bounty and Benevolence*; Champ in her essay "Difficult to Make Hay"; and Goode, Champ, and Amundson, "Montreal Lake Region."

90   LAC, RG 10, Vol. 3601, File 1754, Ottawa, 6 December 1888.

91   Ray, Miller, and Tough, *Bounty and Benevolence*, 144.

92   LAC, RG 10 Vol. 3601, File 1754, Superintendent General of Indian Affairs, Edgar Dewdney to Indian Commissioner Hayter Reed, 6 December 1888.

93   Champ, "Difficult to Make Hay," 27.

94   Waiser, "John Alexander Mackay," *Dictionary of Canadian Biography online* (accessed 8 May 2013).

95   For an overview of the yearly trapping cycle, see Massie, "Trapping and Trapline Life."

96   Interview, John Charles with Joe L. Roberts, 14 April 1997; Vicky Roberts with Walter M. Charles, 18 August 1996. *Historical Events of the Woodland Cree*, 15 and 21. See Roberts, "Biography of Chief James Roberts," *Historical Events of the Woodland Cree*, 8; Waiser, "John Alexander Mackay."

97   LAC, RG 10, Vol. 3601, File 1754, Notes taken by Mr. McNeil, of the Indian Department, at the treaty made at the north end of Montreal Lake, on 11 February 1889.

98   Ibid.

99   Ibid.

100 Three ploughs and twenty scythes were ordered for his band, possibly under the assumption that he would want them in the same quantities and for the same reasons that James Roberts did.

101 See LAC, RG 10, Vol. 3601, File 1754, "Montreal Lake band articles to be delivered next spring," late fall 1889 (after fall annuity payment had been given and requests received).

102 Ibid.

103 Piper and Sandlos, "Broken Frontier."

104 Moodie and Kaye, "Indian Agriculture," 83.

105 The best overview of the idealized role of agriculture and its intended effect on First Nations was put forward by Sarah Carter in *Lost Harvests*. Carter's work reflected a Plains Indian and government dynamic. See also Buckley, *Wooden Ploughs to Welfare*; Bateman, "Talking with the Plow." For a historiographic overview, see Dawson, "Roots of Agriculture."

106 See Roberts, "Biography of Chief James Roberts," in *Historical Events of the Woodland Cree*, 6–7.

107 For a brief overview of these discussions, which included the divided opinion that the band should settle at Red Deer (Waskesiu) Lake, see Waiser, *Saskatchewan's Playground*, Chapter 1.

108 LAC, RG 10, Vol. 7766, File 1754, Hayter Reed to the Department of the Interior, 25 January 1890.

109 LAC, RG 10, Vol. 7766, File 27107-4 Pt. 2, Annuity Payment report, October 1890.

110 Merasty, "History of Little Red River."

111 For an excellent overview of residential schools that strives to present a balanced picture, see Miller, *Shingwauk's Vision*.

112 Merasty, "History of Little Red River." See also *Historical Events of the Woodland Cree*.

113 LAC, RG 10, Vol. 7766, File 27107-4 Pt. 2, Hayter Reed to the Superintendent General of Indian Affairs, 5 November 1890.

114 Ibid., quoted in letter, Hayter Reed to the Deputy of the Superintendent General of Indian Affairs in Ottawa, 4 June 1891.

115 Hilliard Merasty, interview with Vicky Roberts, 14 March 1997. *Historical Events of the Woodland Cree*, 11.

116 LAC, RG 10, Vol. 7766, File 27107-4 Pt. 2. Quoted in letter, Hayter Reed to the Deputy of the Superintendant General of Indian Affairs in Ottawa, 4 June 1891.

117 The Montreal Lake band also remembered agitating for a farming reserve near Sturgeon Lake in this period. Goode, "Historical/Cultural/Natural Resource Study," 3.22.

118 LAC, RG 10, Vol. 7766, File 27107-4 Pt. 2. Department of the Interior to L. Vankoughnet, Deputy Superintendent General of Indian Affairs, 13 July 1891.

119 There is some indication in the departmental correspondence that the Indian Department considered other land, but none as acceptable as the land recommended by Surveyor Ponton.

120 LAC, RG 10, Vol. 3815, File 56622, W. Sibbald, Duck Lake Agency, to the Indian Commissioner, 29 September 1894.

121 LAC, RG 10, Vol. 7766, File 27107-4 Pt. 2. Memorandum for the Information of the Minister re Farming Lands in the Saskatchewan District wanted for Indians of the Montreal Lake and Lac La Ronge bands. Hayter Reed, 23 February 1895.

122 Ibid., Hayter Reed to A.R. Burgess, Deputy Minister of the Interior, Ottawa, 5 March 1895.

123 Ibid., Department of the Interior to Hayter Reed, 11 March 1895.

124 Ibid., T. Clarke to Indian Department, 23 February 1897.

125 Department of the Interior requested a survey to conform with township lines. The survey avoided the railway lands, addressed the school lands, and challenged the one remaining timber berth licensee to give up the berth, arguing that there was no merchantable timber on that land anyway.

126 The reserve was created by order-in-council on 6 January 1900 as "reserved for the 'Montreal Lake' and 'Lac La Ronge' Indians," without specific reference to the proportion of the land owned by each band.

127 LAC, RG 10, Vol. 7766, File 27107-4, Pt.2, J. Lestock Reid to T.O. Davis, MP, no date. For a biography of Reid, see Parker, ed., *Who's Who and Why*, Volume 2. See also Ray, Miller, and Tough, *Bounty and Benevolence*, 127.

128 The Almighty Voice story resonates in the Prince Albert region. The bare facts are recorded by Rob Nestor in *Encyclopedia of Saskatchewan*, but other details, such as where he hid during the manhunt, are drawn from local lore.

129 Carter, *Lost Harvests*, 193–258.

CHAPTER THREE: WOOD IS SCARCE

1 Macoun, *Manitoba and the Great North-West,* 294–323.

2 Howlett, "The Forest Industry on the Prairies."

3 Ibid., 240.

4 Kennedy, "Reminiscences of a Lumberjack."

5 The story of Captain Moore and his mill can be pieced together through the reminiscences of John Smith and Thomas Miller in *Voice of the People,* 57–9 and 117–24. For the north Prince Albert forest industry, see Smiley, "The Forest Industry in Prince Albert to 1918"; and Silversides, *Gateway to the North,* 12.

6 For a recent overview of these settlers, see Code, "Les Autres Métis."

7 Abrams, *Prince Albert,* 1–2. Reverend James Nisbet established a Presbyterian mission at Isbister's Settlement in 1866. Nisbet is popularly referred to as the "father" of Prince Albert. Although he gave the settlement its name, he was not the first to settle there.

8 For an overview of the uprising of 1869–1870 that led to extensive Métis migration westward, particularly into the Saskatchewan River region, see Friesen, *Canadian Prairies,* Chapter 6, "The Métis and the Red River Settlement 1844–70," 92–128. For comprehensive studies of the Métis communities in Red River, see Ens, *Homeland to Hinterland* and Pannekoek, *Snug Little Flock;* see also Code, "Les Autres Métis," 33–8.

9 Abrams, *Prince Albert,* 16. See also Saskatchewan Archives Board [SAB], Department of the Interior, Dominion Lands Branch, file 753, Rev. James Nisbet to Lt.-Gov. Alexander Morris, 25 Janurary 1874.

10 Mochoruk, *Formidable Heritage,* 20.

11 Ibid.

12 Bob Ivanochko wrote a short overview of steamboats in Saskatchewan for *The Encyclopedia of Saskatchewan.* See also Barris, *Fire Canoe;* Peel *Steamboats on the Saskatchewan;* Ballantine, "Recollections and Reminiscences."

13 Abrams, *Prince Albert,* 18.

14 As noted in Stanley, *Birth of Western Canada,* Chapter 9, "Growth of Settlement in the North West," n. 17, quoting *Saskatchewan Herald,* 16 December 1878.

15 Stanley, *Birth of Western Canada,* 184.

16 For an overview of the decision to reroute the CPR, and its effects on the development of the western interior, see ibid.; Waiser, "A Willing Scapegoat."

17 Abrams claimed that it "caused no apprehension when the CPR built steadily westward towards Moose Jaw in 1881, or when the southern route was definitely fixed upon in May, 1882." His sources for this assertion were the local newspapers, notably the *Prince Albert Times* and *Saskatchewan Review.* Abrams, *Prince Albert,* 45.

18 See Black, *History of Saskatchewan,* 227. Black claimed the provisional district divisions were for the benefit of the Post Office Department, but clearly the Saskatchewan district was based largely on the major basin of the North and South Saskatchewan including the Forks and the Lower Saskatchewan. See http://www.canadiangeographic.ca/mapping/historical_maps.

19 For the evolution of the boundaries, see http://www.rootsweb.ancestry.com/evolution.boundaries. By 1887, the Saskatchewan district boasted its own Member of Parliament at Ottawa.

20 Abrams, *Prince Albert,* 48–9.

21 The 1885 Rebellion has been examined in depth by many historians. In particular, see Stanley, *Birth of Western Canada;* Beal and Macleod, *Prairie Fire;* Flanagan, *1885 Reconsidered;* Stonechild and Waiser, *Loyal Till Death.* For Prince Albert's contribution and reaction, see Abrams, *Prince Albert,* Chapter 6, and Code, "Les Autres Métis."

22 An example of the Saskatchewan territorial identity is found in an editorial from Prince Albert when a Toronto newspaper, recounting an exhibition of grains from the west, mentions only three of the four major western districts: Manitoba, Assiniboia, and Alberta. Saskatchewan, the indignant editorial

contended, was worthy of pride and filled with righteous anger at being left out. See *Prince Albert Advocate*, 10 September 1900, "Saskatchewan again gets the go-by."

23 SAB, R-A4535, photograph by William James of the first train to Prince Albert, piled high with cordwood to feed the steam engine. See Silversides, *Gateway to the North*, 42.

24 For an interesting overview of the context of "home" for First Nations versus non-First Nations in the western interior, see Bradford, "'Home Away From Home.'"

25 For a discussion of the prairie market, and how it spawned its own "hinterland" around Prince George with prairie capital, labour, and a market, see Hak, "Prairie Capital."

26 Anderson, "Population Trends," *Encyclopedia of Saskatchewan*, 706.

27 See "The Advantages of the Prince Albert District, Saskatchewan, are unsurpassed for rich lands," CIHM 30434, 63. Smiley, "The Forest Industry," 8.

28 For a full investigation of the Dominion Lands Act, see Martin, *"Dominion Lands."*

29 Martin, *"Dominion Lands,"* 182–3. To view the act and its amendments, see Early Canadiana Online http://eco.canadiana.ca/search?q=dominion+lands (accessed 26 November 2013).

30 Ibid., 182–5. See also Dominion Lands Act.

31 Black spruce and Jack pine were smaller than white spruce. They were sometimes cut by special permit for railway ties or fenceposts. See Saskatchewan, Department of Agriculture pamphlet, "Saskatchewan," 1909, 59–62.

32 For an extensive investigation of timber policy in the western provinces, see Martin, *"Dominion Lands,"* Chapter 11, "Swamp Lands, Grazing, Timber, Mining and Water Rights."

33 Some of the earliest maps of the north Prince Albert region were made by timber cruisers, defining and describing timber berths. See the collection of the Prince Albert Historical Society and the Department of the Interior files at the Saskatchewan Archives Board.

34 It is difficult to follow the many variations and changes in the Dominion Lands Act as it related to timber, and my figures may not correspond with others if the sources were from different years. Chester Martin's detailed study focussed primarily on homestead land.

35 Martin, *"Dominion Lands,"* Chapter 11.

36 See SAB, MS W586, W.W. Whelan, "Echoes of Yesterday," unpublished manuscript. There is a copy of this manuscript in the Prince Albert Historical Society archives. See also Lumby Production Company, *Giants of their Time: The Lumberjack*, movie, c. 1970s; Smiley, "The Forest Industry"; SAB, Skuli Bachman manuscript; and Kennedy, "Reminiscences of a Lumberjack."

37 See *Saskatchewan Times*, "Saw-Mill Destroyed by Fire," 20 April 1905.

38 Silversides, *Gateway to the North*, 12.

39 *The Wheat Belt Review*, November 1907.

40 See Silversides, *Gateway to the North*, 12; Kennedy, "Reminiscences of a Lumberjack."

41 *Prince Albert Times*, 15 January 1903.

42 Beames, *Gateway*.

43 The Lumby Production Company movie, *Giants of Their Time*, contains live footage of lumber drives, several photographs taken by Prince Albert photographer W.J. James, and an interview with Odias Cartier of White Star, north of Prince Albert, who had worked in the lumber camps and on the drives. A copy of the film was provided to me by the Prince Albert National Park archive, Waskesiu, Saskatchewan.

44 Kennedy, "Reminiscences," 30.

45 *The Wheat Belt Review*, November 1907.

46 The community is now known as Deer Ridge.

47 Dice, "Alingly and Surrounding Districts," 1.

48 See *Prince Albert Times*, "Big Engine is Working. Sturgeon Lake Lumber Company are Hauling Lumber from their Mill to the City—Many are Witnessing the Novel Method of Moving Lumber," 14 February 1907.

49 *The Wheat Belt Review*, November 1907. For an example, see *Footprints of Our Pioneers*, 814.

50 These reserves were just south of the area that was set aside as the Sturgeon Forest Reserve in 1914.

51 The logdrivers on the Little Red River system, in particular, were drawn from these reserves. See *Wheat Belt Review*, November 1907.

52 Saskatchewan Archives Office, "Index to Material Relating to Saskatchewan Indian Reserves in Annual Reports of Department of Indian Affairs 1900–1973."

53 See Thompson, "Sturgeon Lake First Nation," *Encyclopedia of Saskatchewan*, 914.

54 LAC, RG 10, C12112, Vol. 7839, File 30107-4, Frank Pedley, Deputy Superintendent General of Indian Affairs, Ottawa to James Macarthur, Indian Agent at Mistawasis, 3 July 1903.

55 Ibid., Indian Agent's Office, Carlton Agency, 249831. Each person signed with either an X or in Cree syllabic.

56 Ibid. The surrender was signed by Isaac Itawawepsim, Edward Charles, John Hunt, Alfred Charles, Elias Hunt. In the presence of W.E. Jones, Agent. Rupert Pratt, Interpreter and A.I. Wilkinson (possibly a witness or JP). These were not the same people who signed the original surrender document. These men were living on the New Reserve and other documents indicate that at least three of these men were originally from the Lac La Ronge band.

57 The manager of the Canada Territories Corporation was A.J. Bell, who also managed the Sturgeon Lake Lumber Company and ran the sawmill at Bell's Lake, just to the west of the Little Red Reserve.

58 LAC, RG 10, C12112, Vol. 7839, File 30107-4. James Hines to Indian Commissioner, 8 August 1904. In reply, it was pointed out that only the white spruce saw timber had been sold; the pine for fenceposts and aspen/poplar for building and cordwood had not been sold.

59 Ibid., Indian Agent's Office, Carlton Agency, Mistawasis, to Hon. D. Laird, Indian Commissioner, Winnipeg, 19 January 1905.

60 Ibid., J.D. Maclean, Secretary of Indian Affairs, to David Laird, 7 April 1905.

61 Ibid.

62 LAC, RG 10, Vol. 7766, File 27107-4. Letter to the Accountant from the Indian Department, 14 October 1910.

63 Ibid., Letter to the Accountant.

64 See LAC, RG 10, C12112, Vol. 7839, File 30107-4.

65 LAC, RG 10, C12112, Vol., 7839, File 30107-4. J.D. McLean to Silas Milligan, Indian Agent at Mistawasis, 17 January 1916. 1 February 1916, Reply from S. Milligan.

66 See in particular the documentary, *Jim Settee: The Way Home* by Jeanne Corrigal (Inner Nature Productions, 2009).

67 LAC, RG 10, Vol. 7766, File 27107-4. Letter to the Accountant from the Indian Department, 14 October 1910.

68 Waiser, *Saskatchewan's Playground*, 18–9. Waiser documented much of the early freighting, fishing, and general transportation history of the region. See Chapter 2, "Prince Albert and the New Northwest."

69 See *Prince Albert Daily Herald*, 6 May 1916.

70 The state of the roads was an ongoing problem throughout the first three decades of the twentieth century in the north Prince Albert region. Once municipalities were formed, local governments sought provincial assistance to improve or create even the most rudimentary roads and bridges. These calls filled the meetings of the local municipal boards and the pages of the *Prince Albert Daily Herald*.

71 Shortt, "Survey of the Human History of Prince Albert National Park," 15.

72 Burtman, *Sustainable Management*, 485. There continue to be extensive jack pine forests in the north Prince Albert region. These were selectively logged but never as intensively as white spruce. Jack pine regenerates far more efficiently than white spruce. See Thorpe, "Models of Succession," 9.

73 *Cordwood and Courage*, 9.

74   Shortt, "Survey of the Human History of Prince Albert National Park," 13–4; Waiser, *Saskatchewan's Playground*, 14.

75   The Reserve was formally created by an act of Parliament in 1914. Waiser, *Saskatchewan's Playground*, 16.

76   Waiser, *Saskatchewan's Playground*, 16.

77   Shortt, "Survey," 16–7.

78   *Prince Albert Daily Herald*, 24 March 1916.

79   Shortt, "Survey," 16. Shortt references a letter from C. Putlick to R.M. Treen, 28 April 1919, SAB, Crown Timber Agency Files, NR5, B.12.9, and noted that this number is significant, as it represented almost 25 percent of the total area within the Sturgeon Forest Reserve.

80   *Prince Albert Daily Herald*, 7 October 1918; Shortt, "Survey," 14.

81   *Prince Albert Daily Herald*, 28 April 1919.

82   *Prince Albert Daily Herald*, 4 June 1919.

83   Tobi McIntyre, "Canada's Incendiary Past." McIntyre states that the fires were natural.

84   *Prince Albert Daily Herald*, 12 June 1919.

85   Ibid.

86   See, for example, Weir and Johnson, "Effects of escaped settlement fires." This essay is based in part on Weir's MSc thesis, "The fire frequency and age mosaic of a mixed wood boreal forest" (University of Calgary, 1996). This research focussed on Prince Albert National Park. It does not explore or understand the wider implications of the logging industry in the north Prince Albert region on a broad scale. Instead, it argued that incursion into the mixedwood boreal forest north of Prince Albert was for agricultural purposes only outside the Sturgeon Forest Reserve. This is inaccurate.

87   *Prince Albert Daily Herald*, 3 June 1919. The forest reserves were beginning to see increased use by tourists and campers. It is possible that the fires were started by fishermen or campers, instead of homesteaders.

88   Northern road improvements in the post–Second World War era took foresters deeper into the boreal North: commercial timber operations resumed, and the pulp and paper industry was created in the 1960s. For an overview of the origins of the pulp and paper industry in Saskatchewan, see Novosel, "Pulp Fictions."

89   Saskatchewan Department of Agriculture pamphlet, "Saskatchewan," issued 1909.

CHAPTER FOUR: A PLEASANT AND PLENTYFUL COUNTRY

1   Belyea, ed., *A Year Inland*, 64.

2   The dairy and beef industries in Saskatchewan have been explored by Church, "Dominion Government Aid"; Williams, "Always the Bridesmaid." Church claimed that by 1889, cheese was a major Canadian national export and it was thought that butter could be, too. Mixed farmers were the centre of the dairy industry.

3   For overviews of the wheat-growing culture as it developed in the western interior, see Britnell, *Wheat Economy*; Fowke, *National Policy*; Thompson, *Harvests of War*. See also Spector, *Agriculture on the Prairies* and MacEwan's popular history, *Between the Red and the Rockies*.

4   Lorne Agricultural Society, "Prince Albert and the North Saskatchewan: A Guide to the 'Fertile Belt' now being opened up by Railway from Regina to Prince Albert, The Central City and Capital of Saskatchewan," printed by the *Prince Albert Times*; CIHM 30434. The difference between sub-humid or humid "prairie" versus semi-arid or arid "plain" in the United States is more clearly defined and understood.

5   Murchie, *Agricultural Progress*, 46.

6   Saskatchewan, Department of Agriculture booklet, "Saskatchewan," 1909, 10, 6.

7   Ibid., 48.

8   See, for example, Johnson, "Relative Decline of Wheat."

9   Maps of potential wheat-growing land can be found in many books, and formed the overly optimistic estimates of the future potential of the western interior. See, for example, Bowman, ed., *Pioneer Settlement*, 5.

10 "Prince Albert Investments."

11 *The Northwestern Miner*, Minneapolis, Minnesota, 1 July 1908. "Wheat is Wheat—Prince Albert— The Gateway to Hudson Bay" by Mae Harris Anson. For more on Seager Wheeler, see Shilliday, *Canada's Wheat King*.

12 Clark, "Settlement in Saskatchewan."

13 Thompson and MacPherson, "How You Gonna Get 'em Back to the Farm?"

14 Russell, "Subsistence," 16. Russell pointed specifically to Britnell, Fowke, and Thompson.

15 This quote, taken from Britnell, was the central point of Russell's paper. The statement, Russell argues, is not so much wrong as radically incomplete. See Russell, "Subsistence," 26, 15.

16 One of the best reports regarding the cash nexus on grain farms was Britnell's *Wheat Economy*, particularly Chapter 5, "Income and Expenditure," and Chapter 7, "Standards of Living." See table, 167.

17 See Clark, "Settlement in Saskatchewan."

18 Russell, "Subsistence," 19.

19 Mavor, "Economic Results," 670–1.

20 One of the most accessible overviews of the battle between mixed farming and wheat monoculture was presented by Voisey, "A Mix-up over Mixed Farming." A similar version is found in Voisey, *Vulcan*, Chapter 4, "Crop Selection."

21 McInnis, "Changing Structure of Canadian Agriculture."

22 Ibid., 191.

23 For short biographies of prominent men who promoted mixed farming, see Spector, *Agriculture on the Prairies*, 7–11; 217–49. See also Dyck, *Farmers 'Making Good'*.

24 See Voisey, "A Mix-up over Mixed Farming," 179.

25 Although some particularly fervent advocates touted mixed farming as the easier path to riches. See Voisey, "A Mix-up over Mixed Farming," 180.

26 See Spector, *Agriculture on the Prairies*, 48–58; Ankli and Millar, "Ontario Agriculture in Transition."

27 For an examination of the moral and intellectual ideals of farming, see Nesmith, "Philosophy of Agriculture."

28 Ingalls Wilder, *Farmer Boy*, 370.

29 For the most severe indictment on such practices, see Thompson, "'Permanently Wasteful,'" 193–206.

30 For a correlation between social consequence, investments, and the rise of the ranching industry, see Breen, *Canadian Prairie West*; Elofson, *Cowboys, Gentlemen, and Cattle Thieves*; Morgan, "The Bell Farm."

31 Clark, "Settlement in Saskatchewan," 36–7.

32 An investigation of the "wheat boom" of 1880–1910 through the perspective of economics can be found in Ward, "The Origins of the Canadian Wheat Boom."

33 Clark, "Settlement in Saskatchewan," 36–7.

34 As an example, see the extensive publications of John Lehr on the Ukrainian communities of western Canada. In particular, see Lehr, "Rural Settlement Behavior of Ukrainian Pioneers in Western Canada"; "Government Coercion in the Settlement of Ukrainian Immigrants in Western Canada."

35 Hawkes, *Story of Saskatchewan*, 732.

36 "Mixed Farming is Need of West," *Saskatchewan Farmer* 2, 3 (December 1911): 30.

37 See some of the recent work by Sandra Rollings-Magnusson on the role of women and children on prairie farms: Rollings-Magnusson, "Necessary for Survival"; "Canada's Most Wanted."

38 Spector, *Agriculture on the Prairies*. For a detailed look at the homestead and general land settlement policies, see Martin, *'Dominion Lands' Policy*.

39 "Efficiency" became a byword of the modernist movement during the twentieth century. For a forestry analysis of wise-use and efficiency in the United States, see Hays, *Conservation and the Gospel of Efficiency*.

40 An excellent analysis of trees on the prairie can be found in Rees, *New and Naked Land*, particularly Chapters 8, "The Cult of the Tree," and 10, "Gardens, Parks, and Shelterbelts." For a view from the United States, see Drake, "Waving 'A Bough of Challenge,'" 156–8. For a narrative look at the challenge of growing trees on the open plains, see Ingalls Wilder, *First Four Years*.

41 For an overview of this period, see Abrams, *Prince Albert*, Chapters 1–7.

42 See ibid., 101–3.

43 See *Prince Albert Times*, 14 September 1872. For stories of the Earl of Southesk, see *Saskatchewan and the Rocky Mountains*.

44 Lorne Agricultural Society, "Prince Albert and the North Saskatchewan."

45 Clark, "Settlement in Saskatchewan," 90.

46 See, for example, "Overland Route to the Klondike," *London Times*, 23 October 1897. See also "Yukon via Prince Albert," pamphlet c. 1898, CIHM 15253.

47 An anonymous pamphlet, "Prince Albert district Saskatchewan" was published c. 1891. It reiterated much of the same claims made by "Prince Albert and the North Saskatchewan" in 1890, particularly the connection to mixed farming. CIHM 30434.

48 *Prince Albert Times*, 7 February 1907.

49 West of Prince Albert, the north branch of the Saskatchewan bends toward the south. As a result, Shellbrook is west of Prince Albert but on the north side of the river.

50 For an overview of the creation of Wahpeton for the Dakota Sioux who came to Prince Albert in the aftermath of their victory over Custer, see Elias, *Dakota of the Canadian Northwest*. For a description of the Dakota Sioux at Prince Albert from a missionary perspective, see Byers, *Lucy Margaret Baker*; SAB, Lucy Margaret Baker fonds, F375 S2005-15, Speech by Lucy Baker.

51 LAC, RG 10, Vol. 7766, file 27107-4, Prince Albert Board of Trade to T.O. Davis, 30 April 1904: *Melfort Moon*, rpt. in *The Saskatchewan Times*, 20 April 1905.

52 LAC, RG 10, Vol. 7766, file 27107-4, Prince Albert Board of Trade to T.O. Davis, 30 April 1904.

53 LAC, RG 10, Vol. 7766, file 27107-4, pt. 2. J.B. Harkin to Mr. Pedley, 15 March 1906.

54 Ibid., Wells Land and Cattle Company Limited of Davidson, SK, to the Minister of the Interior, 4 July 1906; W.J. Perry, Napinka, Manitoba to the Department of the Interior, Lands Branch, 1 October 1906. Such letters were important as the dominion homestead and timber permit applications were based on a first-come, first-served basis.

55 This entire story is found in LAC, RG 10, Vol. 7766, file 27107-4, pt. 2, T. Eastwood Jackson, Acting Indian Agent, Carlton Agency, to the Secretary, Department of Indian Affairs, 20 August 1907.

56 Ibid., J.A. Mackay to Frank Pedley, 31 August 1907.

57 Ibid., Borthwick to Frank Pedley, 27 September 1907; no. 314903, John Macdougall to Frank Oliver, 30 September 1907; no. 315293 handwritten surrender agreement for 106A signed by Borthwick and members of Lac La Ronge and Montreal Lake bands; Borthwick to Secretary, Department of Indian Affairs, 7 October 1907, regarding homestead promises to settlers on 106A.

58 See LAC, RG 10, Volume 7766, file 27107-4, pt. 2, no. 324178, Montreal Lake and Lac La Ronge bands to Frank Pedley, 9 April 1908.

59 Ibid., no. 335082, W.J. Chisholm to Secretary, Department of Indian Affairs, 16 December 1908.

60 For an investigation of surveys and settlement in the western interior (particularly Manitoba), see Tyman, *By Section, Township and Range*.

61 At the time, the Surveyor General had already commissioned nine townships to be subdivided, including those lands recently opened by the Galician settlement. The Board of Ttrade was asking

for even more land, a total of fifteen townships. SAB, R-183, I.352. Telegram, Prince Albert, 16 July 1906, Prince Albert Board of Trade to Hon. J.H. Lamont, Ottawa.

62 Quoted in Abrams, *Prince Albert,* 124.

63 SAB, R-183, I.352. Memorandum, Surveyor General to Deputy Minister of the Interior, Ottawa, 21 July 1906.

64 SAB, B11.10, Richmond Mayson fonds, Histories of Prince Albert. "Prince Albert Board of Trade," transcript of broadcast over CKBI by R. Mayson, 7 May 1954.

65 Historian Joe Cherwinski has made a special study of that brutal winter. Some of his findings were presented at the annual meeting of the Canadian Historical Association in Toronto in May 2002 as "Cold Comfort: the Brutal Winter of 1906–07 and the Defining of the Prairie Regional Identity"; another essay, "The Rise and Incomplete Fall of a Contemporary Legend: Frozen Englishmen in the Canadian Prairies During the Winter of 1906–07," was published in *Canadian Ethnic Studies/Études ethniques au Canada* 30, 3 (1999): 20–43. Many thanks to Dr. Cherwinski for sharing these papers with me.

66 Cherwinski, "Rise and Incomplete Fall."

67 For a detailed analysis of the strike, see Baker, "Miners and the Mounties"; Baker, "Miners and the Mediator." See also den Otter, *Civilizing the West,* 282–304; McMan, "Trade Unionism in District 18," 49–57; and Seager, "A Proletariat in Wild Rose Country," 208–17.

68 Writer Joseph Kinsey Howard, in *Montana: High, Wide and Handsome,* reported that it was so cold, railway tracks snapped.

69 See Cherwinski, "Rise and Incomplete Fall," and "Cold Comfort." The *Killarney Guide* called it the earliest, most violent and longest storm in living memory, 23 November 1906, quoted in Cherwinski, "Cold Comfort" and Waiser, *Saskatchewan,* 56.

70 *Prince Albert Times,* "Sugar and Spice are Scarce," 17 January 1907.

71 *Prince Albert Times,* "The Fuel Situation," 7 February 1907.

72 *Prince Albert Times,* "Telegraphic Notes," 7 February 1907.

73 Historian Jim Wright concluded, in discussing that awful winter: "people who lived in the Parklands and Forest regions were thankful for the native trees which meant shelter from windchill and firewood for their stoves." Wright, *Saskatchewan,* 129–30.

74 Taché, *Sketch of the North-West of North America.*

75 See announcements in the *Prince Albert Times,* 7 February 1907.

76 Abrams, *Prince Albert,* 130. For an overview of the drawn-out process of bringing in the second railway and the frustrations of the city, see pp. 125–30.

77 *Prince Albert Times,* 16 May 1907.

78 *Prince Albert Times,* 28 February 1907.

79 *Prince Albert Times,* 7 March 1907.

80 The notes of Archie Ballantine, the timber inspector who made an inspection of the proposed route of the railway from Prince Albert to Beaver Lake in 1914, contain a superb map. See SAB, 102, Ra.220, Department of Railways, "Petition General Prince Albert." The rail line was completed to Shellbrook in 1909, north to Big River by 1910, and west to North Battleford by 1914.For a history of the Hudson Bay Railway scheme, see Fleming, *Canada's Arctic Outlet;* Bickle, *Turmoil and Triumph;* Pratt and Archer, *Hudson's Bay Route.* The popular version remains MacEwen, *Battle for the Bay.*

81 Canada, Senate *Debates,* 24 January 1907, 138.

82 *Prince Albert Times,* 31 January 1907. See Waiser, *New Northwest.*

83 See Waiser, *New Northwest,* 9–11.

84 Ibid., 23. The name "The New Northwest" had variations in Manitoba and Ontario. In Manitoba, whose borders were pushed north in 1912, the non-prairie North became known as New Manitoba. In Ontario, New Ontario was the name given to the Clay Belt region that was being opened for settlement.

85 See *Prince Albert Times,* 7 March 1907.

86 A typical example can be found in Canada, *Sessional Papers*, Vol. 25, 8–9, Edward VII, A, 1909. A.L. McClennan, Dominion Land Surveyor, reporting on Township 51, Range 25, west of the Second Meridian.

87 Canada, *Sessional Papers*, Vol. XLII, No. 12, 4 April 1907. Report of R.S. Cook Agent of Dominion Lands, Prince Albert.

88 *Prince Albert Times*, 9 May 1907.

89 Canada, *Sessional Papers*, Vol. 25, 8-9, Edward VII, A, 1909. Report of the Agent at Prince Albert, R.S. Cook, 11 April 1908.

90 More townships were opened to the west of these reserves, in the same township range of 49 through 52, but west of the third meridian, opening the land around what became the communities of Holbien, Briarlea, Crutwell, Wild Rose, and Deer Ridge. Their development is similar to that of the region directly north of Prince Albert, but cross-country interaction was limited and continues to be so. There were few and only poor roads through the Indian reserves running east-west. Before 1912, another township, 53, on the north side of the baseline, was opened for settlement in ranges 24 through 26, to the north of the new settlement at Paddockwood. These surveys completed the northern advance until 1919, when townships 54 and 55 were surveyed in 1919 in anticipation of the press of soldier settlement.

91 SAB, Department of Agriculture files, R-266.IV.40, "Homestead Entries 1905 to 1943 by Land Agencies and Census Divisions."

92 Stegner, *Wolf Willow*, Chapter 3, "Carrion Spring." See also Cherwinski, "Cold Comfort." For an overview of the winter as it related to the cattle industry, see Kelly, *Range Men*; Breen, *Canadian Prairie West*; McGowan, *Grassland Settlers*; Elofson, *Cowboys, Gentlemen and Cattle Thieves*; Waiser, *Saskatchewan*, 57–8.

93 "Saskatchewan Homestead Entries."

94 McManus, *Happyland*. The Moose Jaw land office was the only one in operation in southwestern Saskatchewan in 1907–1908, and had to handle the new claims of all the homesteaders pouring into that newly opened region. In 1908 alone, over 8,000 homesteads were filed at the Moose Jaw office, compared to less than 2,000 at Prince Albert. A land office at Swift Current opened soon after to alleviate the demand, and one in Maple Creek in 1912–1913. See "Saskatchewan Homestead Entries."

95 For an excellent overview of dry farming and the scientists who studied and promoted it, see Russell, "Far-From-Dry Debates." See also Hargreaves, *Dry Farming in the Northern Great Plains*.

96 Several pamphlets were published in 1910–1911. See SAB, Morton Manuscript collection, Mss C555/2/10a, "Prince Albert: Europe's Easiest Way," Prince Albert Board of Trade, 1910; 10b, "Prince Albert, Saskatchewan: The Ideal Spot for the British Settler," Prince Albert Board of Trade, 1910; 10c, "Prince Albert, Saskatchewan: The Easiest Way," c. 1911, and 10d, "Prince Albert Investments: Issued Monthly in the Interests of Prince Albert and Vicinity," November 1911. Quote from "Prince Albert Investments."

97 "Prince Albert: Europe's Easiest Way."

98 Ibid.

99 Ibid.

100 "Prince Albert, Saskatchewan: The Ideal Spot for the British Settler."

101 "Saskatchewan Homestead entries."

102 *Prince Albert Daily Herald*, 15 January 1916.

103 SAB, Saskatchewan School District Jubilee Histories, Micro S-8.15. "Alingly School District Jubilee History," 1955.

104 For an example of the physical and economic problems of swamp fever, see Roe, "Alberta Wet Cycle of 1899–1903," 112–20. McGowan, "Gee and Haw," *Cordwood and Courage*, 634.

105 This rule of thumb became particularly entrenched during the 1930s, in the post-1930 homestead records. See SAB, S43, R2004-220, post-1930 homestead records. See also Prince Albert Historical Society, Bill Smiley Archives, Local history fonds, Buckland, "From Ox-Team to Combine," 4.

106 *Prince Albert Daily Herald*, 4 March 1916.

107 See Dice, "Alingly and District." See also *Prince Albert Daily Herald,* 15 April 1916.

108 The continued delays were most likely bound up in the ongoing financial problems of the Canadian Northern Railway. By 1917, in large part due to the disruption of the war, the Canadian Northern failed. It was bought by the federal government who amalgamated the Canadian Northern and Grand Trunk Pacific lines to create the Canadian National Railway. For a history of the Canadian Northern railway, see Regehr, *Canadian Northern Railway.*

109 SAB, Department of Railways files, Ra 400. CNR plans and construction (b) (20). William Knox to The Honorable Frank Cochrane, 6 May 1916.

110 SAB Ra 220. Department of Railways, General File (2) (a). Petition to James Calder, Minister of Railways.

111 *Prince Albert Daily Herald,* 15 January 1919; *Buckland's Heritage,* 469.

112 "From Ox-Team to Combine," 5.

113 *Prince Albert Daily Herald,* 8 April 1919.

114 For a somewhat problematic but still important overview of agriculture during the First World War, see Thompson, *Harvests of War.*

115 LAC, RG 10, Vol. 7766, File 27107-4 Pt. 1. Letter from Alingly Rate Payers Association.

116 Ibid., "Petition to open up "Hunts" Indian Reserve in Township 52, Range 26, 27, and 28, West of the 2nd Meridian for homesteading."

117 Ibid., Lands and Timber Branch, file 72,438, 5 June 1914. Duncan Campbell Scott, Deputy Superintendent General of Indian Affairs, wrote to Alingly to repeat the same point.

118 Ibid., Office of the Inspector of Indian Agencies, North Saskatchewan Inspectorate to Mr. Scott, 23 July 1917.

119 Bear was referred to as "that fine young Cree" in both Indian Affairs documents and letters from the local Anglican Diocese in Prince Albert. Since Little Red was owned by the Montreal Lake and Lac La Ronge bands, it did not have its own chief, although most people both on and off the reserve considered Billy Bear to be the leading public figure.

120 See Saskatchewan Archives Office, *Index to Material Relating to Saskatchewan Indian Reserves.*

121 Dominion Field Naturalist John Macoun is generally skewered by historians as the leading proponent of the wheat boom, and at least indirectly responsible for the disastrous march into the Palliser Triangle. Tyman, *Section, Township and Range* was particularly critical of Macoun.

CHAPTER FIVE: QUALITY OF PERMANENCY

1 *Prince Albert Daily Herald,* 6 January 1916, "Fuel Boom Follows Close on Cold Spell. Local Wood and Coal Dealers are Having Their Harvest Season."

2 Dunn and Stoddart, *Cordwood and Courage,* 186–7; see also O'Hea and Endicott, "Early History of Paddockwood," *Cordwood and Courage,* 9–10.

3 The Dominion Lands Act set out rules by which women could apply for homesteads or patents. For a discussion of women who farmed by purchasing South African scrip, see Carter, "Daughters of British Blood."

4 See Chapter 6, "Land I Can Own," in Waiser, *Saskatchewan.*

5 Land abandonment or cancelling a homestead was not necessarily a "failure," although many historians and government inspectors have branded it as such.

6 Waiser, *Saskatchewan,* 105.

7 See Martin, *"Dominion Lands" Policy,* 172, 174.

8 Jones, *Empire of Dust,* 80. See also Jones, *"We'll all be buried down here."*

9 See, for example, the story of the McGimpsey family who moved from Hearn, Saskatchewan (near Moose Jaw) to Paddockwood in 1915. *Prince Albert Daily Herald,* 6 May 1916. Mrs. McGimpsey took patent on her land in 1920, after her husband and daughter died in 1916. See SAB, homestead file 3448546, SW 20-52-25 W2.

10 *Prince Albert Daily Herald*, 2 June 1919. The story was a reprint from the *Toronto Times*.

11 Military historian Kent Fedorowich has made a detailed international study of soldier settlement, including the Canadian context, in Fedorowich, *Unfit for Heroes*.

12 According to the *Prince Albert Daily Herald*, many of the soldier settlers looking for land in the area were from "the southern part of the province." 16 January 1919, "Settlers are coming into North Country."

13 *Prince Albert Daily Herald*, 1 August 1919.

14 McManus, *Happyland*, 34.

15 These numbers are estimates at best, derived from census statistics and other sources. See Jones, *Empire of Dust* and McManus, *Happyland*.

16 See Jones, *Empire of Dust*, 212–3.

17 Permits to ship hay to the south, or stock to the north, were common as early as 1914. See *Saskatchewan Farmer* 8, 12 (1918): 1. In 1918, using the provisions of the War Measures Act, the dominion outlawed the burning of straw stacks. The feed situation was so important for the war effort that it became a criminal code offence to burn straw stacks left over from harvest. See *Saskatchewan Farmer* 9, 1 (1918): 17.

18 *Prince Albert Daily Herald*, 1 August 1919.

19 *Prince Albert Daily Herald*, 21 August 1919. The term "Rush to North" was also used, alluding to the Great Land Rushes of the southern prairie.

20 Ibid.

21 Ibid.

22 See *Report of the Royal Commission of Inquiry Into Farming Conditions*, Province of Saskatchewan, 1921; "Federal Government Gives But Little Hope of Relinquishing Control of Natural Resources," Regina *Morning Leader* 16 December 1920.

23 As noted in Marchildon, "History of the Special Areas of Alberta."

24 *Regina Leader*, 2 October 1919, "140 soldiers settled at Swift Current."

25 "Soldier Settlement on the Land," 1926, 5.

26 *Prince Albert Daily Herald*, 28 January 1919.

27 Greening, "Arne Jacobsen and Family," *Tweedsmuir*, 86.

28 *Prince Albert Daily Herald*, 22 February1919. "Paddockwood Area Shows Great Activity in Attraction of New Settlers from Prairie Districts."

29 See Morton and Wright, *Winning the Second Battle*; see also Morgan, "Soldier Settlement in the Prairie Provinces"; McDonald, "Soldier Settlement and Depression Settlement." The head of the Soldier Settlement Board, E.J. Ashton, wrote a contemporary account, Ashton, "Soldier Land Settlement in Canada."

30 Morton and Wright, *Winning the Second Battle*, 146. Reserve land, on the other hand, had to be purchased by the dominion on behalf of the Soldier Settlement Board, once it was surrendered by the First Nation band.

31 Fedorowich, *Unfit for Heroes*, p. 106.

32 Murton, *Creating a Modern Countryside*. For an explanation of the liberal order framework and its usefulness as a lens through which to view Canadian history, see McKay, "Liberal Order Framework," 620–3.

33 Murton, *Creating a Modern Countryside*, 43.

34 See, for example, the full-page advertisement from the Soldier Settlement Board, 6 April 1919, *Prince Albert Daily Herald*. See also stories in *Saskatchewan Farmer*, particularly "Farm Training for Soldiers," 7, 1 (1916): 17; "Land for Soldiers," 7, 9 (1917): 13; "Land Settlement Plans Announced for the Soldiers; For Experienced Men," 9, 3 (1918): 9.

35 The Canadian Pacific Railway had also developed an extensive land settlement scheme to sell their immense land holdings. In some cases, they partially developed farms, with irrigation, houses, or

other improvements, and sold the land to incoming settlers. Typical mortgages were twenty years. See *Saskatchewan Farmer* 7, 6 (1917): 15; Hedges, *Building the Canadian West*. The Soldier Settlement Board scheme no doubt drew from these ideas.

36 The Soldier Settlement Act may be found online at http://laws.justice.gc.ca/S-12.8/text.html. It is the consolidated version which includes all the additions and changes made to the act up to 1946.

37 Three examples of block settlement schemes on forested Crown land are: the Kapuskasing Colony in Ontario, the Merville settlement on Vancouver Island, and the Porcupine Soldier Settlement in Saskatchewan north of Yorkton on the old Porcupine Forest Reserve. See Wood, *Places of Last Resort*; Murton, *Creating a Modern Countryside*; Harris, *Book of Memories*; Morgan, "Soldier Settlement in the Prairie Provinces," and MacDonald, "Soldier Settlement and Depression Settlement."

38 Fedorowich, *Unfit for Heroes*, 70. Geographer J. David Wood, in Wood, *Places of Last Resort*, provided the best example of the argument that northern settlers were duped.

39 Murton admitted in his Appendix that "Perhaps the LSB did have some success in helping people to establish themselves as farmers." Murton, *Creating a Modern Countryside*, 198.

40 See Morton and Wright, *Winning the Second Battle*, 146.

41 "Soldier Settlement on the Land," Report of the *Soldier Settlement Board of Canada*, 31 March 1921, 90. In Saskatoon, 76 had been recommended for training, 114 in Regina, for a total of 230 for Saskatchewan; 244 in Edmonton and 167 for Calgary, a total of 411; 378 in Manitoba, 508 in Ontario.

42 "Soldier Settlement on the Land," 10.

43 SAB, Micro S.183 Records of Premier William Martin, Soldier Settlement files.

44 "Soldier Settlement on the Land," 10.

45 See "Land for Soldiers," *Saskatchewan Farmer* 7, 9 (1917): 13.

46 Dunn and Stoddart, *Cordwood and Courage*, 186–7.

47 "Soldier Settlement on the Land," 10.

48 For these quotes, see "Soldier Settlement on the Land," 11–12.

49 "Soldier Settlement on the Land," 11–12.

50 There were individual instances of soldiers being granted land or loans to develop specialized farms (such as poultry, fruit, or market garden ["truck"] farms), but these were in cases where the soldier had extensive previous experience.

51 *Prince Albert Daily Herald*, 13 February 1919.

52 "Land Problem," *Prince Albert Daily Herald*, 17 January 1919.

53 See "Soldier Settlement on the Land," 28–30.

54 *Prince Albert Daily Herald*, 13 March 1919. It was understood that a settlement railway would be built following the north bank of the Saskatchewan, through Meath Park and the White Fox plain, following the White Fox River, where other soldiers were settling the land. The spur to Paddockwood was finished in 1924; the eastward line, from Henribourg to Nipawin, was finished in 1929, just in time to carry Depression refugees and their effects.

55 "Soldier Settlement on the Land," Prince Albert board report, 89.

56 SAB, Micro S.183 Records of Premier William Martin, Soldier Settlement files.

57 "Soldier Settlement on the Land," 1921, 13.

58 See statistics for Prince Albert, Saskatoon, and Regina, "Soldier Settlement on the Land," 88–9, 95, and 105.

59 *Prince Albert Daily Herald*, 2 June 1919. The story was a reprint from the *Toronto Times*.

60 "Soldier Settlement on the Land," 93.

61 A map prepared by the Information Services Corporation (ISC) on Dominion Land Grants in what later became the RM of Paddockwood No. 520 listed 130 quarters of land positively identified as Soldier Settlement land. Many other quarters may have passed through the Board after being homesteaded, and their records may be hidden in Dominion Land files, destroyed, or otherwise unavailable at the time the map was made (c. 2005).

62   SAB, Department of the Interior files, R-183, I. 290. Report on surveys completed in 1920. M.D. McCloskey, Dominion Land Survey to E. Deville, Esq., LL.D., Surveyor General, 30 March 1921.

63   Such reports, on a quarter-section level, were not published for the general public as they would be out of date almost immediately, as quarter sections were taken up faster than printing could be accomplished. However, it is possible that the report may have been kept on hand at the Dominion Lands Office for reference.

64   LAC, RG 10, Vol. 7766, File 27107-4, Pt.1. Alingly Grain Growers Association to Indian Affairs, 3 April 1918. The idea to open the reserve was reported in the *Prince Albert Daily Herald,* 1 March 1919.

65   LAC, RG 10, Vol. 7766, File 27107-4, Pt.1. W.B. Crombie, Inspector to the Secretary, Department of Indian Affairs, 27 June 1918.

66   See Chapter 4.

67   By this time, the Lac La Ronge band had split into two bands, making the legal ramifications even more complicated.

68   For an overview of Soldier Settlement and reserve land, see Carter, "Infamous Proposal." See also Dawson, "Better than a Few Squirrels."

69   "Soldier Settlement on the Land," 17.

70   A favourite book on women and the western frontier remains Rasmussen, Rasmussen, Savage, and Wheeler, *Harvest Yet to Reap;* others include Silverman, *Last Best West;* Strong-Boag, "Pulling in Double Harness or Hauling a Double Load"; Sundberg, "Farm Women on the Canadian Prairie Frontier"; Strong-Boag and Fellman, eds., *Rethinking Canada,* 95–106. Recent work includes Rollings-Magnusson, "Hidden Homesteaders"; Cavanaugh, "'No Place for a Woman.'"

71   Chapman, "For the Soldier Settler's Family," in the section "Women and Their Work," edited by Ethel Chapman, *MacLean's Magazine,* c. 1920.

72   "Soldier Settlement on the Land," 38.

73   Ibid., 39.

74   See ibid., 39–41.

75   Ibid., 91–2.

76   Chapman, "For the Soldier Settler's Family."

77   "Soldier Settlement on the Land," 92.

78   Chapman, "For the Soldier Settler's Family."

79   Muldrew, "Home Management."

80   Ibid. See also "Soldier Settlement on the Land," 92.

81   Chapman, "For the Soldier Settler's Family"; "Land Settlement: Sixth Report of the Soldier Settlement Board of Canada, December 31, 1927," 12.

82   For a delightful narrative version of the work of these clubs, including the Junior Red Cross, see Montgomery, *Rilla of Ingleside.*

83   Glenbow Archives, Canadian Red Cross Society, Alberta-North West Territories Division fonds, M8228 Series 6a pamphlet collection 224, "Nation Builders: Are You One? Red Cross Campaign, November 5th to 11th, 1922."

84   Glenbow Archives, Canadian Red Cross Society, Alberta-North West Territories Division fonds, M8228 Series 6b-226, "A Brief Summary of the Work of the Canadian Red Cross Society Since the War."

85   For an overview of the Red Cross Outpost network, including a list of all Saskatchewan Red Cross Outpost hospitals, see Massie, "Red Cross Outpost Hospitals," *Encyclopedia of Saskatchewan,* 680. See also http://esask.uregina.ca/entry/red_cross_outpost_hospitals.htmlin. For an overview of the Paddockwood hospital, see Massie, "Ruth Shewchuk: A Red Cross Outpost Nurse." See also Elliott, "(Re) constructing the Identity of a Red Cross Outpost Nurse"; Elliott, "Blurring the Boundaries of Space"; and Elliott, Dodd and Rousseau, "Outpost Nursing in Canada." For other stories from Red Cross nurses and outpost hospitals, see Miller, *Mustard Plasters and Handcars;* Martin, *Red Cross Nurse on the Bay Line.*

86 Crawford-Petruk, "Memoirs of the Paddockwood Red Cross Outpost Hospital," *Cordwood and Courage,* 12–17.

87 The first overnight patient at the hospital was Nellie Hambleton, who was admitted 29 September 1919. Her baby son was born the next day, and they greeted visitors at the official opening ceremonies. See University of Saskatchewan Archives, miscellaneous fonds, "Paddockwood Red Cross Outpost Hospital record of patients 1920–1947." See also *Prince Albert Daily Herald,* 2 October 1919.

88 University of Saskatchewan Archives, Paddockwood Homemakers fonds, "A History of the Paddockwood Homemakers Club," c. 1980.

89 SAB, R-183 I.290. Reports of M.D. McCloskey, Dominion Land Survey, 1920.

90 McCloskey report, Township 51, Range 25, West of the 2nd Meridian.

91 Ibid. The village of Paddockwood was (is) in this township.

92 A young Swedish mother was quoted in a Red Cross campaign: "I am engaged to my husband five years. He is out here, my people won't let me come—no good place, no doctor, no nurse. Then one day he write, 'The Red Cross has come, they have hospital.' We know Red Cross. I come by next boat." Glenbow Archives, Canadian Red Cross Society fonds, M-8228-226, "The Story of the Red Cross."

93 "From Ox-Team to Combine," 5.

94 Ibid.

95 See *Saskatchewan Farmer* 8, 8 (1918): 9, "Bad Year Ahead in Forest Fires"—"Settlers' fires continue to be the very worst source of forest conflagration, although campers and careless smokers are close competitors."

96 *Prince Albert Daily Herald,* 15 March 1919, "Paddockwood."

97 Ibid.

98 *Prince Albert Daily Herald,* 25 July 1919. "Start Survey North Line in About Two Weeks. Canadian National Railway Wires Board of Trade."

99 SAB, Department of Agriculture files, B11 13. PA Board of Trade. "Report of Meeting Held at Empress Hotel."

100 The coming of the railway led to the erection of elevators and a huge spike in the local cordwood industry. See *Cordwood and Courage,* 10, 26–7.

101 *Prince Albert Daily Herald,* 25 January 1919.

102 *Prince Albert Daily Herald,* 1 February 1919.

103 SAB, R-183 I.290. Report of M.D. McCloskey, Dominion Land Surveyor, on Townships 54, 55, and 56, Ranges 23 through 27, west of the second meridian, August 1920.

104 At least fifteen men from Mozart, Saskatchewan, of Icelandic descent, filed on land in this township. It would have been a large colony, but only a few of the men who filed actually went to their northern homesteads, and none of them stayed. Any outstanding homestead entries not actively worked were cancelled in 1927 in preparation for the new National Park borders. See SAB post-1930 settlement files, R 2004-220, S43, File S10140.

105 SAB, Department of the Interior files, R-183, I. 290. Report on surveys completed in 1920. M.D. McCloskey, Dominion Land Survey to E. Deville, Esq., LL.D., Surveyor General, 30 March 1921.

106 See *Prince Albert Daily Herald,* 1 April 1916; 8 March 1919.

107 SAB, Department of Agriculture files, AG 2-7, General File. Application for Free Shipment of Settler's Stock and Effects from points in Dry Area, 1923.

108 Prince Albert Historical Society, Bill Smiley Archives, "From Ox-Team to Combine," unpublished history of the Buckland district, 5.

109 Quoted in Martin, *"Dominion Lands" Policy,* 167. The original legislation can be found in the Statutes of Canada, 13-14, George V, c. 44.

110 "From Ox-Team to Combine," 5.

111 Fedorowich, *Unfit for Heroes,* 81.

112 Determined demands for re-evaluation were heeded. The first loan writeoffs occurred in 1922, and a massive re-evaluation was completed in 1927–1928. See McDonald, "Soldier Settlement and Depression Settlement," 41.

113 *Globe*, 28 September 1922, "Land Settlement Plans."

114 SAB, R-183, I.290, M.D. McCloskey, Report on Twp. 52, R. 25, W. Of 2nd Meridian.

115 An advertisement in the *Prince Albert Daily Herald* June 1919 read: "Be Sure and See the LAND CLEARING DEMONSTRATION at the same time and place as the P.A. Agricultural Society Annual Plowing Match. THE MACHINE USED WILL BE A KIRSTIN, CLUTCH TYPE, ONE-MAN STUMP PULLER."

116 Fedorowich, *Unfit for Heroes*, 83.

117 Ibid. Fedorowich references the work of McDonald, "Soldier Settlement and Depression Settlement." See also Wood, *Places of Last Resort* for many anecdotes of the problems of northern settlement.

118 See "Land Settlement," 22, 23. By 1929, the soldier settlement statistics for the Prince Albert region were, from a total of 3,876 soldier grant entries, 1,657 had been abandoned or cancelled, leaving 2,219 active entrants and just under 43 percent cancellations.

119 I calculated the homestead entries between 1904 and 1914 to be 288,782; cancellations in that same period, 108,678, almost 38 percent. These statistics were from the document "Saskatchewan Homestead Entries 1905 to 1943 by Land Agencies." Soldier settlement abandonments, at 40 percent, were far less than overall Saskatchewan abandonments between 1911 and 1931, which economist Chester Martin calculated at a horrifying 57 percent. See Martin, *"Dominion Lands" Policy*, 174. In comparison, the soldier settlement scheme in Prince Albert was a resounding success.

120 *Globe*, 28 September 1922, "Land Settlement Plans."

121 Morton and Wright, *Winning the Second Battle*, 153. See also Fedorowich, *Unfit for Heroes*, 102.

122 The 3000 British Family Scheme was seen as a way to bring British people to Canada, to combat the floodtide of immigration from non–English speaking eastern European countries. See Kitzan, "The Fighting Bishop," and "Preaching Purity in the Promised Land." Although the Prince Albert area was not as popular as other places, it nonetheless had over 200 families come to the region through this scheme.

123 There has been scarce academic work on the 3000 British Family Scheme. See, for example, Schultz, "Canadian Attitudes Toward Empire Settlement." More information can be found in the annual reports of the Soldier Settlement Board throughout the 1920s.

124 For an excellent overview of the work of the Canadian National Railway and its Department of Colonization and Agriculture, see Osborne and Wurtele, "The Other Railway."

125 Julius Androchowiez was a colonization agent for the CNR, working to establish families along the Prince Albert-Paddockwood line. He was interviewed by the Saskatchewan Royal Commission on Immigration and Settlement, 25 April 1930, in Prince Albert. See SAB, R249, Vol. 35, 87–103. See also the interview with A.J. Hanson, also a CNR colonization agent, same evening and venue, 65–83. Mr. Arthur William Hilton arrived under the British Family scheme in 1928; he testified to the Commission on the same evening.

126 SAB, R249, Vol. 35, 113–5. Testimony of E.T. Bagshaw, managing director of Bagshaw-Holroyde Agencies Limited, General Financial Agents, Prince Albert to the Royal Commssion on Immigration and Settlement, Prince Albert hearings, 25 April 1930.

127 Such work-for-taxes prevailed in the north Prince Albert region well into the 1940s. See "McGowan, Sargent Hugh and Muriel," *Cordwood and Courage*, 355.

128 The homestead files for the north Prince Albert region list many quarter sections sold for little more than the taxes owing, and sometimes less.

129 See Osborne and Wurtele, "The Other Railway." See also Kitzan, "Preaching Purity in the Promised Land"; Macarthur, "Immigration and Colonization in Canada."

130 See LAC, Canadian National Railways fonds, Graphic material (RG 30) for photographs of families who came via these CNR colonization schemes.

131 Canada, Department of the Interior, Lands Branch, *Annual Reports* 1923–1930. Reports were presented to the end of the fiscal year, March 31, so the calendar year did not exactly correspond to the fiscal year.

132 For example, the Department of the Interior records indicated that in Saskatchewan in 1928, 5,808 homesteads were filed. Of those, 4,197 were filed at the Prince Albert district land office, and of those, 1,262 were second homesteads. In 1929, Saskatchewan had 6,089 homesteads, 4,873 at the Prince Albert office. Of those, 1,435 were second homesteads. These reports differ from the homestead entries recorded by census division found in SAB, R-266 IV.40. This document lists 8,007 homesteads taken in Saskatchewan in 1928, of which 5,615 were filed at the Prince Albert land office. In 1929, 8,374 homesteads were filed, 6,480 at the Prince Albert office. The balance were recorded at Moose Jaw, the only other active land agency in those years.

133 See table V, "Number of Milch Cows in Prairie Provinces," Murchie, *Agricultural Progress on the Prairie Frontier*, 26. The number of milk cows moderated between 1926 and 1929, but averaged a respectable 434,500 animals, or one milk cow for every two people.

134 Waiser, *Saskatchewan*, 273.

135 See Ankli, Helsberg, and Thompson, "Adoption of the Gasoline Tractor." See also SAB, Department of Agriculture fonds, R.266.1. Evan Hardy, Professor of Agricultural Engineering, University of Saskatchewan, to F.H. Auld, Minister of Agriculture, 28 September 1928.

136 SAB, R-266.1, Department of Agriculture fonds. Evan Hardy to F.H. Auld, 26 September 1928.

CHAPTER SIX: POOR MAN'S PARADISE

1 McOwan, "The Great Northland," *Prince Albert Daily Herald*, 14 January 1919.

2 These numbers were supplied by Dominion Land Surveyor Ernest Hubbell, based on his knowledge of prices in northern Saskatchewan in 1908. By 1919, just before the postwar slump, these prices would have been much higher. See *Sessional Papers*, Vol. 25, 8–9, Edward VII, A, 1909.

3 SAB, R-73 Richmond A. Mayson fonds, File I, Pioneer Trails, CKBI Broadcasts, transcripts, "Prince Albert Board of Trade" broadcast 7 May 1954.

4 Sandwell, "Rural Reconstruction"; Ommer and Turner, "Informal Rural Economies in History."

5 Zaslow, *Opening of the Canadian North* and *Northward Expansion of Canada* are the best starting points to discover the north and its social and industrial development. See also Mochoruk, *Formidable Heritage*; Piper, *Industrial Transformation of Subarctic Canada*.

6 See Tough, *'As Their Natural Resources Fail'*.

7 Ray, *Canadian Fur Trade*, xv.

8 Ray, *Canadian Fur Trade*.

9 See LAC, RG 10, Vol. 3601, File 1754, Dewdney's office to Hayter Reed, 6 December 1888.

10 LAC, RG 10, Vol. 3601, File 1754, J.A. Mackay to Hayter Reed, 20 May 1889.

11 Ibid., Hillyard Mitchell to Hayter Reed, 24 June 1889. Hillyard Mitchell, in addition to part ownership in Stobart and Co., was an MLA.

12 Ibid., Hayter Reed to Deputy Superintendent General of Indian Affairs in Ottawa, July 1889.

13 See McPhillips, *McPhillips' Saskatchewan Directory*, 127. Cited in Shortt, "Survey of the Human History of Prince Albert National Park," 4 and footnote 7. Shortt suggested that this post was operational as early as 1886.

14 Waiser, *Saskatchewan's Playground*, 7. See also Prince Albert National Park historical files, "HBC Post at Red Deer Lake, Saskatchewan," 24 March 1969 (historical material on Red Deer post compiled by Hudson's Bay Company Archives, Winnipeg); *Prince Albert National Park Archives*, Waskesiu, cited by Waiser. See Shortt, "Survey of the Human History of Prince Albert National Park," 7–8.

15 For an overview of this period of Métis history, see Ens, *Homeland to Hinterland* and Sprague, *Canada and the Metis*.

16 Klaus, "Early Trails to Carlton House," 32–9.

17 "Index to Material Relating to Saskatchewan Indian Reserves," 2.

18 Ibid., 10.

19 "Stanley Notes," *Beaver*, 1921. H.M.S. Kemp described freighter R.D. Brooks's attempt to take a horse freight swing from Stanley to Lac du Brochet, on the north end of Reindeer Lake in 1919. The trip was disastrous, and many horses died on the route for lack of feed. See Kemp, *Northern Trader*, 210–3. This trip was also reported in the *Prince Albert Daily Herald*, 15 January 1919.

20 Keighley, *Trader, Tripper, Trapper*, 64.

21 "Horses," "Freight Swing Era," http://www.jkcc.com/horses.html (accessed 28 January 2008).

22 *A Look at the Past*, "Freighting," at http://www.jkcc.com/dlfreight.html (accessed 21 April 2008).

23 Ibid. See also "Hale—Stanley and Millie," *Cordwood and Courage*, 242.

24 Brooks, *Strange Hunters*, 9. Brooks's book recounted hair-raising and interesting tales of northern life and spoke of the integration of commercial fishing and overland freighting.

25 *Prince Albert Daily Herald*, 15 January 1919.

26 The *Prince Albert Daily Herald* reported that Brooks started out working for Colin and Stanley McKay, who had the contract in 1919, but it was clear that in later years, the Brooks Transportation Company took over. See Prince Albert *Daily Herald*, 15 January 1919. Brooks' winter freighting outfit was captured on film in 1928 by the Canadian Film Board. See LAC, V1 2008-12-0004, "Freighting in Northern Canada." See also numerous photographs in the Prince Albert Historical Society collection.

27 *Prince Albert Daily Herald*, 7 January 1919.

28 It is difficult to discuss wages, since they varied widely depending on the length of the trip, the year, and the local economy. These figures were suggested in local history books: DiLella, *Look at the Past*; *Buckland's Heritage*; *Cordwood and Courage*.

29 These are the numbers provided by the essay "Freight Swing Era," http://www.jkcc.com/brfreight.html (28 January 2008).

30 See "David Dunn and James Stoddart," *Cordwood and Courage*, 186–7.

31 An example is the Sigfusson family in northern Manitoba. They developed an overland freighting industry built on commercial fishing. Any supplies going up were for their own use in the fish camps, but often loads would go north empty and return full. They expanded their enterprise to include road building and became experts in ice roads over the vast inland lakes, particularly Reindeer Lake in northern Saskatchewan, which was linked to the Manitoba rail system at Lynn Lake. See Sigfusson, *Sigfusson's Roads*.

32 *Prince Albert Advocate*, 28 November 1894. *Prince Albert Advocate*, 6 October 1895.

33 Waiser, *Saskatchewan's Playground*, 11. See also Canada, House of Commons *Sessional Papers*, 1894, Vol. 27, No. 11, App. 10, "Annual Report of the Department of Marine and Fisheries," 299.

34 Seymour, "Geographical Study of the Commercial Fishing Industry," 15–9.

35 Ibid., 25.

36 "City Gateway of Wealthy and Fertile North Country."

37 Seymour, "Geographical Study of the Commercial Fishing Industry," 32.

38 Ibid., 22.

39 Gulig, "Sizing up the Catch," 3–12.

40 Historian Donald Avery rightly acknowledged the relationship between farming and wage labour. See Avery, *Dangerous Foreigners*.

41 See SAB, A 241, manuscript division, Reminiscences of Skuli Bachman. Bachman worked in the Saskatchewan logging industry throughout the early part of the twentieth century.

42 Lower and Innes, *Settlement and the Forest Frontier in Eastern Canada* and Lower, *North American Assault on the Canadian Forest*. See Howlett, "Forest Industry on the Prairies."

43 Lower, *Settlement and the Forest Frontier in Eastern Canada*, 33.

44 Information on Vangilder and Anderson was provided by Richard Dice, "Write up Alingly and surrounding Districts," Manuscript 705b, Prince Albert Historical Society.

45 University of Saskatchewan Archives, Davis Family fonds, f373. *The Wheat Belt Review, Canada's Most Popular Magazine, Milford B. Martin Owner and Publisher*, November 1907.

46 Prince Albert Historical Society, Bill Smiley Archives, Manuscript 705b, Richard Dice, "Write-up of Alingly and District."

47 Richard Dice, in his unpublished memoir of the Alingly district, Prince Albert Historical Society manuscript 705b, "Alingly and Surrounding Districts."

48 See "Local Improvement District, No. 491," *Buckland's Heritage*, 14–20. The Paddockwood/Christopher Lake area operated as Local Improvement District no. 959 for over sixty years more, incorporating as the Rural Municipality of Paddockwood, No. 520 only in 1978. *Cordwood and Courage*, 36.

49 Chapter 8, The Royal Mail. *Buckland's Heritage*; *Cordwood and Courage*.

50 *Prince Albert Daily Herald*, 6 January 1919.

51 For years, both Prince Albert and Paddockwood residents believed that the rail line would eventually be extended further north, through the boreal forest to tap into the mineral resources of the Shield near La Ronge, or swing east through the rich Flin Flon region and become the long-sought railway to Hudson Bay. Various newspaper articles in the *Prince Albert Daily Herald* from the opening of the bridge in 1909 and throughout the next twenty years, as well as notes from the Prince Albert Board of Trade, suggested this. See, for example, University of Saskatchewan Archives, Davis family fonds, "City Gateway of Wealthy and Fertile North Country," newspaper article, no date, circa 1926.

52 The photograph became so well-known, and so iconic for the town, that many regional residents · purchased a copy. To take a similar picture today would be difficult; the rail line has been taken out, and the landscape has once again filled in with poplar trees.

53 "Yukon Via Prince Albert," CIHM 15253.

54 See, for example, the *Prince Albert Advocate*, 9 March 1897. Gold was also found at Rat Portage (presumably in Saskatchewan) as well as in the Birch Hills near Prince Albert, which led to a short-lived local gold rush.

55 References to the gold dredge are found in local newspapers, and are reported in Abrams, *Prince Albert*.

56 The claims office was moved to The Pas in 1920, a move that was vigorously protested in Prince Albert.

57 *Prince Albert Advocate*, 15 June 1897. The *Advocate* reported each week another one or two men off to the gold fields of BC and the Yukon. For an oral history of prospecting and mining in Saskatchewan, see Kupsch and Hanson, eds., *Gold and other stories*.

58 *Regina Daily Post* 17 September 1928, "New Route in North Success;" 20 September 1928, "More Details of New Route to the North." See also *Regina Leader* 12 August 1929, "North's Growth Greatly Aided by Government." The *Regina Daily Star* 1 November 1928 predicted a "sensational race" between the CNR and CPR to develop northern rail lines. See "Rail Lines to Develop Rich Field."

59 *Regina Post* 10 January 1929, "Sees Future in Far North;" *Regina Leader*, 12 August 1929, "North's Growth Greatly Aided by Government."

60 "Ninth Report of the Soldier Settlement of Canada," Ottawa, 1931, 9.

61 F.C. Pickwell, *Saturday Night's* western correspondent, "Saskatoon and the North," *Saturday Night*, 16 April 1927.

62 Ibid.

CHAPTER SEVEN: ACCESSIBLE WILDERNESS

1 SAB, A-281 Christina Bateman fonds, "Northern Saskatchewan Holiday." Bateman's typewritten document and its accompanying pictures can be found on the Our Legacy website, http://scaa.sk.ca/ourlegacy, database ID 27383. See also Spafford et al., "Amazing adventures of Christina and Nan."

2 Bateman, "Northern Saskatchewan Holiday."

3 Weather reports, real estate listings, provincial advisories and community events designate the area as "Lakeland." The new provincial park will be called Great Blue Heron and runs from the north side of

Christopher and Emma lakes north surrounding Anglin Lake. It abuts the east side of Prince Albert National Park. See http://www.gov.sk.ca/news?newsId=b02112db-3d0d-4ea9-948c-dafbc44a79d2 (accessed 28 May 2013).

4   Montgomery, *Selected Journals of L.M. Montgomery Volume I*, 30.

5   "Prince Albert and the North Saskatchewan." Lorne Agricultural Society. Printed by the *Prince Albert Times*, 1890. CIHM 29478.

6   "Prince Albert and the North Saskatchewan."

7   See, for example, Gillespie, "The Imperial Embrace"; MacLaren, "The Influence of Eighteenth-Century British Landscape Aesthetics" and "Limits of the Picturesque"; Coates, "Like 'The Thames Towards Putney'"; Jasen, *Wild Things*; Owram, *Promise of Eden*; and Francis, *Images of the West*. For an Australian interpretation, see Ryan, *Cartographic Eye*.

8   See Gillespie, "The Imperial Embrace," Chapter 3.

9   Moore's group was unsuccessful in getting flour, although Prince Albert harvests had been good and grain was available. The mill, however, operated only on wind power and as there had been no adequate natural breezes, there was no milled flour available in the whole settlement. Moore saw the opportunity to develop a business, and took it. See Chapter 3.

10   Another British sports-tourist was James Carnegie, the Earl of Southesk, whose travels and exploits in 1859–1860 through what was then still Rupert's Land were published as Carnegie, *Saskatchewan and the Rocky Mountains: A Diary and Narrative of Travel, Sport and Adventure in 1859 and 1860*.

11   For an exceptional overview of the concept of sport and game in western Canada, see Colpitts, *Game in the Garden*. See also Loo, *States of Nature*.

12   Canadian politician Peter Mitchell visited the North-West in the late 1870s. He wrote "The West and North-West: Notes on a Holiday Trip: Reliable Information for Immigrants, with maps, etc.," published in 1880. A sixty-three-page pamphlet, it combined tourism promotion with immigration. CIHM 11139.

13   "Prince Albert and the North Saskatchewan."

14   The Lorne Agricultural Society, despite its name, was essentially a forerunner of the later Prince Albert Board of Trade. The Society consisted primarily of Prince Albert businessmen.

15   *Prince Albert Advocate*, 25 September 1899.

16   See *Prince Albert Advocate*, 28 November 1894; Waiser, *Saskatchewan's Playground*, Chapter 1.

17   Chambers, "Preface," *Unexploited West*. Chambers seemed unable to distinguish between north and west.

18   See *Prince Albert Advocate*, 3 September 1900.

19   For this particular excursion, see Montgomery, *Selected Journals*, 60–1, 13 August 1891.

20   Montgomery, *Selected Journals*, 29, 52. The Prince Albert Historical Society (Bill Smiley Archives) has an original copy of this newspaper, which was handwritten rather than set with type.

21   See Ommer and Turner, "Informal Rural Economies in History." The work of E.P. Thompson is also important here, particularly his *Customs in Common* and *The Making of the English Working Class*. For the connection between urbanites and rural tourism in a specific context, see Shapiro, "Up North on Vacation," 2–13.

22   The local newspapers reported on the state and quality of the water in the North Saskatchewan for drinking. See, for example, the *Prince Albert Advocate*, 20 January 1909 which reported a typhoid epidemic in the city's east end, downstream from where the city released its untreated sewer effluent.

23   The club was originally called the Round Lake Outing Club but was incorporated as the Prince Albert Outing Club, reflecting its urban origins and customers. See *Prince Albert Outing Club, Round Lake, Saskatchewan 1905 to 1990* .

24   This land would have had a township survey completed because of the lumber interests, but it is unclear whether the land was subdivided by the quarter section survey. Certainly it would have been subdivided by 1907 at the latest. For an overview of township surveys for settlement purposes, see Chapter 4. The club in fact purchased Métis scrip to buy the land. Scrip was an important commodity

in the Prince Albert region. Scrip hearings were regularly announced and debated in Prince Albert, which had a strong mixed-blood community. See Augustus, "Scrip Solution"; Code, "Les Autres Métis." See also *Prince Albert Advocate*, 1897–1900, numerous articles.

25   See *Prince Albert Outing Club*, 22.

26   *Prince Albert Daily Herald* 11 April 1916.

27   Christopher Lake was originally called "Little Bittern Lake." Christopher Creek was known as "Little Bittern" Creek and the community that developed on the creek was known as "Little Bittern" throughout the 1920s. *Prince Albert Daily Herald*, 1920s.

28   For an overview of roads and trails in the north Prince Albert region, see Waiser, *Saskatchewan's Playground*, Chapters 1 and 2. See also *Cordwood and Courage*, 6.

29   *Prince Albert Daily Herald*, 7 July 1923.

30   *Prince Albert Outing Club*, Stuart Anderson memories, 92–4. Round Lake remained essentially a private destination, its advertisements and notices confined primarily to the 'Society' pages of the *Prince Albert Daily Herald*.

31   Bateman, "Northern Saskatchewan Holiday."

32   For an overview of the women's movement and its relation to tourism, see Jasen, *Wild Things*.

33   *Prince Albert Daily Herald*, 12 October 1920.

34   See Waiser, *Saskatchewan's Playground*, 16–9.

35   SAB, R-183, I.290, Department of the Interior fonds. M.D. McCloskey to E.E. Deville, 30 March 1921.

36   Ibid.

37   See SAB, Cummins Map Company, map no. Sask. 258, 1922 and 1930.

38   *Prince Albert Daily Herald*, 11 September 1920.

39   *Prince Albert Daily Herald* 8 August 1925.

40   Ibid. See also SAB, R-183, I.222, J. Hardouin General Report 15 April 1921.

41   LAC, RG 10, Vol. 7766, File 27107-4 Pt. 1. G.A. Crowley to Department of the Interior 20 April 1925. As the letter was primarily another call to open all or part of the Little Red River Reserve to homesteading, the letter was forwarded to the Department of Indian Affairs.

42   Hayes, *Conservation and the Gospel of Efficiency*.

43   For an overview of the creation of the Sturgeon River Forest Reserve, see Chapter 3.

44   Canada, Department of the Interior *Annual Report* 1922. Report of the Director of Forestry, R.H. Campbell, p. 139.

45   The Forestry Department laid out resort areas at Clear Lake in Manitoba and at points in British Columbia in the early 1920s; similar work was carried out in Saskatchewan between 1922 and 1925.

46   Canada, Department of the Interior *Annual Report* 1926. C. MacFadyen, District Forest Inspector, Dominion Forests in Saskatchewan, 75–8; E.H. Finlayson, Director of Forestry, *Report* for 1926, 69.

47   Canada, Department of the Interior *Annual Report*, Forestry Report, 1922, 156.

48   Forestry Report, 1922, 156.

49   To understand the rise of motor tourism in North America, see Hyde, "From Stagecoach to Packard Twin Six"; Dawson, "Taking the 'D' Out of Depression"; Apostle, "Canada, Vacations Unlimited"; Rothman, *Devil's Bargains*; Urry, *Tourist Gaze*; Louter, *Windshield Wilderness*; Sutter, *Driven Wild*. An excellent article that is a good comparison to the north Prince Albert region is Shapiro, "Up North on Vacation."

50   Canada, Department of the Interior *Annual Report*, 1922. Report of the Commissioner J.B. Harkin, Canadian National Parks.

51   Shapiro, "Up North on Vacation," 8.

52   See Sandwell, "Notes toward a history of rural Canada," in Parkins and Reed, eds., *Social Transformation in Rural Canada*.

53 Canada, Department of the Interior *Annual Report* 1924, Forestry Division. See report of H.I. Stevenson, District Forest Inspector for Manitoba report, 97.

54 Bumsted, *Peoples of Canada*, 142.

55 The Department of the Interior was largely responsible for tourism literature on a national level. The National Resources Intelligence Service compiled and created tourist information for both the National Parks and Forestry Branch. See Canada, Department of the Interior, *Annual Report* 1926, 23–5. The Department of the Interior annual reports are valuable resources for tourism historians, as they chart the change from railroad to car tourism, and report visitors by country of origin. By the end of the 1920s, the Department of the Interior reported that Canadians were more inclined to use cars, but foreign visitors often saw the country via train travel, even though visitors could cheaply bring their own cars to Canada by boat.

56 Canada, Department of the Interior *Annual Report* 1928. Report of the Commissioner, J.B. Harkin, Canadian National Parks.

57 See table, "Urban and Rural Population of Saskatchewan," in Waiser, *Saskatchewan*, 498.

58 See Saskatchewan, *Sessional Papers*, 1925. Speech delivered by Mr. T.C. Davis, MLA Prince Albert in the Debate on the Address in Reply to the Speech from the Throne in the Legislative Assembly of Saskatchewan, 7 December 1925.

59 Canada, Department of the Interior *Annual Report* 1926. Report of Charles Stewart, Minister of the Interior, Ottawa 1925–1926.

60 *Prince Albert Daily Herald*, 23 July 1925.

61 The Forestry Department had five resorts within three forest reserves in Manitoba. The department also had a new resort subdivision at Fish Lakes in the Moose Mountain forest reserve in Saskatchewan, opened in 1923. This new subdivision was an expansion to an already existing resort, now known as Kenosee.

62 Canada, Department of the Interior *Annual Report,* 1926. H.I. Stevenson, District Forest Inspector for Manitoba, Dominion Forests of Manitoba report, 1925–1926, 75.

63 *Prince Albert Daily Herald,* 4 July 1925.

64 It was popular: by 1929, 17,000 visitors registered annually, far more than the 10,000 or so who journeyed north to the new national park. The area was turned over to the Saskatchewan provincial government in 1930 with the transfer of all remaining Crown land. Canada, Department of the Interior *Annual Report* 1922, Report of the Commissioner J.B. Harkin, Canadian National Parks, 100. For yearly reports, see the *Annual Reports* of the Canadian Parks Branch, 1922–1930. See also LAC, "Vidal's Point Park, History and Establishment", micro reel T-11266. For a personal view and history of the park, see Archer, *Lake Katepwa*.

65 See Waiser, *Saskatchewan's Playground*, Chapter 3: The Political Art of Park Making, 25–35.

66 LAC, Parks Canada fonds, Vol. 1726. Memorandum to file, F.H. Peters to J.B. Harkin, 27 October 1926. Referenced in Waiser, *Saskatchewan's Playground*, 29. Quoted at length in SAB, S-Q80, S2000-51, John Webb, unpublished document, "Forward: Legal Surveys of Prince Albert National Park, Waskesiu, Saskatchewan."

67 Deputy Minister to J.B. Harkin, 26 April 1926. Quoted in Webb, "Legal Surveys."

68 Canada, Department of the Interior *Annual Report* 1925–26. Report of the Hon. Charles Stewart, Deputy Minister of the Interior. The Order-in-Council creating Prince Albert National Park had just been signed, but there was no reference to it in the Department of the Interior yearly report dated to the end of fiscal year 31 March 1927.

69 Canada, Department of the Interior, *Annual Report* 1925. Report of C. MacFadyen, District Forest Inspector, Dominion Forests in Saskatchewan, 81.

70 Many of the advocates for National Park status were also members of local Fish and Game leagues. See Webb, "Legal Surveys"; Waiser, *Saskatchewan's Playground*.

71 *Canada Gazette*, 4 June 1927, Vol. 60, no. 49. Copy found in LAC, RG10, Volume 7766 File 27107-4 Pt. 1.

72 See Webb, "Legal Surveys"; see also SAB, Post-1930 settlement files, R 2004-220 S43.

73 Harris, *A Masterpiece in our Midst.*.

74 For maps of the original creation and later additions, see Waiser, *Saskatchewan's Playground*, 18, 23, 53. See also Shortt, "A Survey of the Human History of Prince Albert National Park," 112, 113. See also Harris, *Masterpiece in Our Midst*; *Prince Albert Daily Herald*, 11 July 1931, "New Tourist Highway to North Looms. Barnett expects 2,000 North Homestead Filings by September."

75 Mrs. Lydia Cook of Little Red River, Interview with Vicky Roberts, La Ronge Long Term Care Hospital, May 1997, in Roberts, ed., *Historical Events of the Woodland Cree*, 47.

76 For a lyrical example of this problem, see Campbell, *Halfbreed*. Campbell writes about her father's experience hunting within the park, and being sent to jail. See also Campbell, *Stories of the Road Allowance People*.

77 RG 10, Volume 7766 file 27107-4 Pt.1, Bishop of Saskatchewan George Exton Lloyd to Deputy Superintendent General of Indian Affairs Duncan Scott, 11 July 1927; W. Graham, Indian Commissioner to Secretary, Department of Indian Affairs, 8 July 1927; J.D. McLean, Assistant Deputy Secretary Indian Affairs to Canadian National Parks Branch, Department of the Interior, 15 July 1927.

78 Ibid., Lloyd to Scott, 11 July 1927.

79 Ibid., Commissioner J.B. Harkin to Duncan McLean, 21 July 1927.

80 LAC, RG10, Vol., 7766, File 27107-4 pt.1, Secretary, Indian Affairs to W.M. Graham , 25 July 1927; W.M. Graham to Secretary, Department of Indian Affairs, 5 August 1927.

81 See ibid., Harkin to Scott, 28 February 1928; Graham to Indian Affairs, memorandum, 8 March 1928; Mackenzie to Fairchild, 30 March 1928; Harkin to Scott, 28 November 1928; Scott to Harkin, 12 December 1928; Harkin to Scott, 27 December 1928.

82 For an overview of the boundary debates, see Waiser, *Saskatchewan's Playground*, 40–1, 103.

83 See *Prince Albert Daily Herald*, 2 August 1928; 9 July 1929; 5 July 1932; 21 July 1932.

84 See *Modern Voyageurs*, Department of the Interior, 1931. I viewed this movie courtesy of the Prince Albert National Park Archives, Waskesiu.

85 See "James Brown and Family," *Tweedsmuir*, 40–2.

86 See Prince Albert Historical Society, Bill Smiley Archives, H series H-515 for an advertisement of the Teepee Tea Room.

87 See file, "Handicrafts on Little Red, Montreal and Sturgeon," LAC, RG 10, Vol. 7553, File 41, 107-1, C14818.

88 See *Tweedsmuir*.

89 *Prince Albert Daily Herald*, 2 August 1928.

90 Canada, Department of the Interior, *Annual Report*, 1928. Report of the Commissioner J.B. Harkin, National Parks of Canada, 78.

91 For a superb look at the wilderness concept in Ontario and its impact on tourism, see Jasen, *Wild Things*.

92 For a discussion of mental maps, see Gould and White, *Mental Maps*.

93 Canada, Department of the Interior, *Natural Resources of the Prairie Provinces. A brief compilation respecting the development of Manitoba Saskatchewan and Alberta*, 1925.

94 *Prince Albert Daily Herald* 2 August 1928. Inspiring Messages from the Public. Message from W.J. Patterson.

95 Hunt, "Image as a Factor in Tourism Development," 1–7.

96 The "Lake Waskesiu Foxtrot" was also written in 1935. See Canada, Department of the Interior *Annual Report*, National Parks of Canada report, "Publicity," 1931–1936.

97 Several books offer biographies of Grey Owl and outline his impact on Prince Albert National Park and the environmental movement. In particular, see Waiser, *Saskatchewan's Playground*, Chapter 7; Shortt, "A Survey of the Human History of Prince Albert National Park"; Ruffo, *Grey Owl*; Hutchinson, *Grey Owl*; for a critical review of Belaney's self-identity as Indian, see Braz, "Modern Hiawatha."

98 Grey Owl, *Pilgrims of the Wild*, 281.

99 Waiser, *Saskatchewan's Playground*, 38–9.

100 Canada, Department of the Interior, *Annual Report*, National Parks of Canada, 1929.

101 Ibid., 26.

102 See Department of the Interior, *Annual Report*, National Parks of Canada, Report of the Commissioner J.B. Harkin, 1929.

103 Waiser, *Saskatchewan's Playground*, 42.

104 Saskatchewan, Department of the Environment, *A Study of Land and Water Use at Emma and Christopher Lakes* Final Report, March 1976, 44.

105 Canada, Department of the Interior, *Annual Report*, Canada Parks Reports, 1928–1935.

106 Canada, Department of the Interior, *Annual Report*, 1932. Prince Albert National Park report.

107 See advertisement, *Prince Albert Daily Herald*, 9 July 1929.

108 SAB, NR.1/1 Department of Natural Resources F-400-F/EL Forestry, Emma Lake, 1930, "Emma Lake Outing Club."

109 Saskatchewan, Department of the Environment, *A Study of Land and Water Use at Emma and Christopher Lakes*, March 1976, 45.

110 Canada, Department of the Interior, *Annual Report* 1932, Prince Albert National Park report.

111 See, for example, *Prince Albert Daily Herald* 3 July 1931; 5 August 1932; 2 July 1934.

112 Canada, Department of the Interior *Annual Report* 1922, Report of Commissioner J.B. Harkin, Canadian National Parks.

113 The Paddockwood board of trade formed in 1932, and operated throughout the Great Depression, disbanding in 1938. For its formation, see *Prince Albert Daily Herald*, 6 September 1932.

114 The honorary president of this board of trade was T.C. Davis, MLA for the Prince Albert region. The honorary vice president was W.W. Whelan, once a dominion lands agent and homestead inspector. Other members included merchants, real estate agents and postmasters, as well as local farmers who operated large threshing businesses or cordwood camps.

115 "Paddockwood: The Mixed Farming Paradise of Saskatchewan," found in the Walter Whelan Scrapbook, *Prince Albert Historical Society Bill Smiley Archives*, Prince Albert.

116 Ibid.

117 SAB, R249, Vol. 36, *Royal Commission on Immigration and Settlement (Saskatchewan)*, 1930. Evidence taken at Prince Albert, 26 April 1930. Testimony of Duncan McLeod.

118 Ibid.

119 See *Cordwood and Courage*, various family stories. For reference to the Muskeg Elks, see "McGowan, Sargent Hugh and Muriel," 355.

120 For an analysis on the concept of social capital, see Van Staveren and Knorringa, eds., *Beyond Social Capital*. For a Saskatchewan evaluation and case study of the concept in action, see Diaz and Nelson, "The Changing Prairie Social Landscape of Saskatchewan."

121 University of Saskatchewan Archives, RG 13, S.2, Year Books, Murray Point, 1936. Newspaper article, no name, no date, entitled "Kenderine Pictures are vivid stories of western progress."

122 Bell, "Augustus Kenderine," 13–19.

123 Excerpt from Memorial Tribute to Augustus Kenderine, given by University of Saskatchewan President J.S. Thompson, 5 August 1947. Quoted in Morrison, "Beginnings," 21.

124 Bell, "Augustus Kenderine," 13.

125 Ibid., 15.

126 *Prince Albert Daily Herald*, 24 July 1934. "Going North as the Holiday Maker Sees."

127 See *Prince Albert Daily Herald*, 7 August 1931.

128 For northern development in Saskatchewan post-1945, see Quiring, *Battling Parish Priests, Bootleggers and Fur Sharks*.

CHAPTER EIGHT: EVEN THE TURNIPS WERE EDIBLE

1   McGowan, "Gee and Haw," *Cordwood and Courage*, 634–5. For the McGowan story, see "McGowan, Sargent Hugh and Muriel," *Cordwood and Courage*, 354–7.

2   This number was conservatively calculated in Britnell, *Wheat Economy*, 202–3. Census material between 1930 and 1936 showed an increase of 9,438 farms in the parkland and forest zones. A further 2,000 homesteads were filed from 1935 to 1940. Britnell noted that the actual number of settlers who moved was "in excess of" 45,000 but that many of the resettlers could not be traced. The estimated number of 45,000 has been repeated by most researchers, including Fitzgerald, "Pioneer Settlement in Northern Saskatchewan"; Powell, "Northern Settlement"; and McDonald, "Soldier Settlement and Depression Settlement." McDonald points to Census records which indicate that forest fringe population in 1941 (excluding Prince Albert) "exceeded 80,000, just over half of whom had migrated north during the 1930s." R.A. Stutt produced an exhaustive study of the forest fringe in 1946 and argued that of those interviewed, nearly one-third had "migrated from the farming districts of southern Saskatchewan." One-third was an average: in the northwest (Meadow Lake and region) one half were migrants; in the northeast (Nipawin-Carrot River area) only one quarter were prairie migrants. See Stutt, *Land Settlement*, 4.

3   Paddockwood Museum. Paddockwood *Pow-Wow*, Diamond Jubilee edition, 1965, "Down Memory Lane."

4   Some of the most interesting texts include: Francis and Ganzevoort, eds., *The Dirty Thirties in Prairie Canada*; Gray, *Men Against the Desert* and *The Winter Years*; Thompson and Seager, *Canada, 1922–1939*; Struthers, *No Fault of the Their Own*; Grayson and Bliss, eds., *Wretched of Canada*. Numerous theses have been written on various aspects of the Depression in Saskatchewan, including Lawton, "Urban Relief in Saskatchewan"; Matheson, "Saskatchewan Relief Commission"; Bowen, "Forward to a Farm." For an overview of the decade, including the Great Trek migration, see Waiser, *Saskatchewan*, "Nothing of Everything." For a Great Plains interpretation of drought and dust storms, see Cunfer, *On the Great Plains*.

5   Both these quotes are taken from well-known book and article titles: Broadfoot, *Ten Lost Years*; "Our World Stopped and We Got Off," Chapter 1 of Gray, *Winter Years*.

6   See Wood, *Places of Last Resort*, endcover.

7   In particular, see Bowen, "Forward to a Farm"; Powell, "Northern Settlement"; McDonald, "Soldier Settlement and Depression Settlement"; and Wood, *Places of Last Resort*. Fitzgerald also examines some of the government schemes, but not in great detail. For a general overview of land settlement policies across the northern fringe, see England, *The Colonization of Western Canada* and "Land Settlement in Northern Areas."

8   See SAB, R-266, IV.40, Homestead Entries. "Saskatchewan Homestead Entries 1905 to 1943 by Land Agencies and Census Divisions."

9   There are numerous family histories in the Paddockwood history book, *Cordwood and Courage*, that explain how the family filed on the homestead land in the late 1920s but made the move north at a later date.

10   Until 1930, immigrants from outside Saskatchewan could still take first homesteads in northern Saskatchewan.

11   *Prince Albert Daily Herald*, 2 August 1928.

12   Piper, *Industrial Transformation*, 81.

13   A discussion of the Crown land transfer is found in Martin, *"Dominion Lands" Policy*. See also O'Bryne, "The 'Answer to the *Natural Resources* Question.'"

14   Bowen, "Forward to a Farm," 30.

15   See Powell, "Northern Settlement."

16   Bowen, "Forward to a Farm," 235–8.

17   Fitzgerald, "Pioneer Settlement," Chapters 5 and 6.

18   Interpretations vary regarding which years saw the greatest exodus. Some, like Fitzgerald, argue that the strongest migration years were 1932 and 1933; others suggest that northern migration peaked in

1934 and 1935. Britnell noted the highest population movement in 1931 and 1932. For an overview of this debate, see McDonald, "Soldier Settlement and Depression Settlement," footnote 55.

19   See Mrs. A.W. Bailey, "The Year We Moved," *Saskatchewan History,* Winter 1967. See also Fenske, *Riverlore.*

20   For an example, see *Western Producer,* 31 January 1932, "Five Hundred Horses Die over Winter."

21   Mrs. A.W. Bailey, "The Year We Moved."

22   Russell, "Subsistence, Diversification, and Staple Orientation," 15–28.

23   See the recreated Bennett Buggy at the Western Development Museum, Saskatoon. Quote from Wright, *Saskatchewan,* 225.

24   Fitzgerald, "Pioneer Settlement," 314–5.

25   Bill Grohn, interview with Merle Massie, September 2009. Grohn went with neighbours to cut feed and to pasture horses and cattle in central Manitoba. As well, he participated in the dominion "hired hand" program where farmhands earned five dollars per month. For an overview of this program, see Danysk, "No Help for the Farm Help."

26   Lila Sully, interview with Merle Massie, September 2009.

27   Interview, Edna Dobie with Merle Massie, November 2008. See also "Brook, Arthur John and Bertha," by Edna Dobie, *Cordwood and Courage,* 126–7. Dobie has written a memoir of these events with her sister, which is unpublished.

28   See *Cordwood and Courage,* "Blumer, Jack and Elsa," 100; "Craig, Frederick and Esther," 150.

29   Mrs. A.W. Bailey, "The Year We Moved."

30   Wright, *Saskatchewan,* 226.

31   "60 Families Move North From Farms. Stoughton District Land Abandoned as Feed Situation Becomes Serious." Special Dispatch to the *Regina Leader,* 30 August 1934.

32   SAB, MA.3.8, Local Improvement Districts Branch, Northern Settlers Re-Establishment Branch. Address given by G.J. Matte, Commissioner, Northern Settlers Re-Establishment Branch over Station CJRM on 31 January 1939.

33   Mather, "Trek to Meadow Lake," *Macleans,* 1 April 1932.

34   J. David Wood's book crosses too much territory and too much time. It does not concentrate on the Trek. In 2005, Peggy Durant self-published a children's book, *The Long Trek,* based on stories told by Depression refugees who went north. Although entertaining, it is not available in bookstores for a broader audience.

35   See Wright, *Saskatchewan;* Archer, *Saskatchewan: A History;* Waiser, *Saskatchewan.*

36   Gray, *Men Against the Desert,* 189.

37   Ibid., 190.

38   For an accurate analysis of population trends in Saskatchewan during the Great Depression, see Waiser, *Saskatchewan,* 302.

39   See McLeman et al., "GIS-based modeling of drought and historical population change on the Canadian Prairies."

40   See Anderson, "Population Trends," *Encyclopaedia of Saskatchewan,* 705–8.

41   SAB, MA.3.8, Local Improvement Districts Branch, Radio Address by Mr. Matte on the Northern Settlers Re-Establishment Branch, 31 January 1939.

42   For a discussion of the social shame of relief, and its impact on the human psyche, see Waiser, *Who Killed Jackie Bates?*

43   Many of these loans were eventually reduced or cancelled, which did much to improve farming conditions in the 1940s and 1950s across Saskatchewan. See Struthers, *No Fault of Their Own.* For an investigation of combined public and voluntary efforts, see Pitsula, "Mixed Social Economy of Unemployment Relief." In this interpretation, welfare comes from four sources: the state, the voluntary sector, the family, and the market, which all played a role.

44   Bowen, "Forward to a Farm," 34.

45 Ibid., 128.

46 After ten years, 20 percent remained on the land. See Bowen, "Forward to a Farm," 243–4. If two-thirds gained title to their homesteads but, after ten years, only 20 percent remained on their farms, over 40 percent of the land had been sold.

47 Prince Albert Historical Society, Bill Smiley Archives, "Paddockwood: The Mixed Farming Paradise of Saskatchewan," found in the Walter Whelan Scrapbook, oversize shelf. The pamphlet emphasized what dust-covered prairie citizens wanted most: trees for shelter and fuel, water, mixed farming, recreation, garden produce and a low cost of living.

48 Some northern municipalities did express concern with northern migration. The community of Medstead, for example, raised the issue at various meetings of the Saskatchewan Association of Rural Municipalities, confronting the provincial government and asking for guarantees that northern migrants would be supported by the provincial government and their municipality of origin, should they need relief, and not their new host community. *The Western Producer*, 28 February 1935. Soon after Medstead raised these concerns, northern relief fell under the auspices of the Northern Settlers Re-Establishment Branch.

49 "Down Memory Lane," Paddockwood Pow-Wow, Diamond Jubilee Edition, 1965.

50 "McGowan, Sargent Hugh and Muriel," *Cordwood and Courage*, 355.

51 Stutt and Van Vliet, "Economic Study of Land Settlement in Representative Pioneer Areas," 30.

52 See Ulmer, "Report on Unemployment and Relief in Western Canada in 1932," Chapter 3, "Whitton on Tour."

53 Stutt and Van Vliet, "Economic Study of Land Settlement in Representative Pioneer Areas," 36–40. See also Hope and Stutt, "Economic Study of Land Settlement in the Albertville-Garrick Area." The second report added, "There are some of these factors which cannot be measured statistically, but which are very important, such as the personal ambition, energy, and initiative of the settler," 27.

54 Regional, even microlocal, variations in northern settlement success and failure has skewed historical interpretation. The push to present a broad analysis of the Great Trek, combined with an over-reliance on provincial relief and resettlement information, has favoured stories of hardship and need over success. While some communities experienced tough conditions, others found long-term success. The north Prince Albert region experienced both, which makes it an ideal case study.

55 Stutt and Van Vliet, "Economic Study of Land Settlement in Representative Pioneer Areas," 36–41.

56 Fitzgerald, "Pioneer Settlement," 318. See Hope and Stutt, "Economic Study of Land Settlement in the Albertville-Garrick Area," 26.

57 Stutt and Van Vliet, "Economic Study of Land Settlement in Representative Pioneer Areas," 68.

58 The post-1930 settlement records showed that many quarters in the north Paddockwood district were homesteaded several times, particularly throughout the 1920s to early 1930s. Each homesteader might clear a few acres, put up buildings, build a fence, or dig a well. If they subsequently abandoned the land, they would be paid for any improvements made by the next homesteader. Sometimes, the homesteader who finally succeeded in gaining patent was building not only on their own efforts, but on the efforts of those who preceded them on the land.

59 McDonald, "Soldier Settlement and Depression Settlement," 44.

60 Powell, "Northern Settlement," 81.

61 Stutt and Van Vliet, "Economic Study of Land Settlement in Representative Pioneer Areas," 7, 68.

62 "Rambling Thoughts by a Prairie Immigrant," *Cordwood and Courage*, 636–637. Many loans from the Northern Settlers Re-Establishment Branch went to purchase horses.

63 SAB, R-183, I.290. Reports on individual townships in the north Prince Albert region, M.D. McCloskey.

64 See "McGowan, Sargent Hugh and Muriel."

65 SAB, S43, 2004-220, S10184, Post-1930 Settlement Records. Jas. Barnett, Inspector Dominion Lands, 4 July 1931 regarding NW ¼ 26 54 25 W 2. Eventually this quarter was successfully homesteaded and patented, but the land was taken over by the provincial government to create a community pasture in the 1960s.

66 The Austin family of Forest Gate is an example. See *Cordwood and Courage*, "Austin, Harold and Mary," "Austin, Lester and Rita." See also interviews, Merle Massie with Miriam (Austin) Swenson, November 2008 (MMPC); Merle Massie with Lester Austin, November 2008 (MMPC). Lester and Miriam, brother and sister, both noted in separate interviews that most of those who ended up at Hell's Gate soon moved south, to rent or purchase farms on better soil.

67 Stutt and Van Vliet, "Economic Study of Land Settlement in Representative Pioneer Areas," 28–9.

68 SAB, S43, 2004-220. In addition to not enough people, two men from the original school board were in jail.

69 Relief requirements were noticeable in the municipal files, the Northern Settlers Re-Establishment Branch files, LID #959 files at the RM of Paddockwood, and the notes of government inspectors and other branches in charge of relief efforts.

70 Powell, "Northern Settlement"; McDonald, "Soldier Settlement and Depression Settlement."

71 For stories of relief officers and their charges, see SAB, Municipal Affairs, Northern Settlers Re-Establishment Branch files.

72 *Regina Leader*, 17 October 1931.

73 Robert McLeman, "Climate-Related Human Migration: Enhancing our Understanding Through Use of Analogues," unpublished conference paper presented at Canadian Association of Geographers annual meeting, Prairie Summit 2010, Regina, 3 June 2010.

74 Fitzgerald, "Pioneer Settlement," 353.

75 Ibid., 354. The Hudson Bay region averaged just over five dollars per person per year; Bjorkdale and Carrot River less than two dollars per person per year. Stutt and Van Vliet noted that settlers in the northwestern districts of Saskatchewan received more aid; those in the northeastern areas, less. The average amount of aid per settler *family* totalled $630 dollars in the northwest, and only $235 in the northeast. These numbers were substantially higher than Fitzgerald's calculations, but still far less than the majority of prairie farmers or urban residents who required relief for many years.

76 Province of Saskatchewan, "A Submission By the Government of Saskatchewan to the Royal Commission on Dominion-Provincial Relations" (Canada, 1937), 185–7.

77 Fitzgerald, "Pioneer Settlement," 353.

78 Britnell, *Wheat Economy*, 207. Fitzgerald noted that the provincial government made Crown land *less* easy to obtain, increasing the size of forest reserves and screening purchasers to be sure they had enough capital to develop the land quickly. See Fitzgerald, "Pioneer Settlement," 321.

79 Britnell, *Wheat Economy*, 208.

80 SAB, R-261, File 26.5. Saskatchewan Department of Agriculture, Soldier Settlement branch. Soldier Settlement Board circular letter 24 June 1931.

81 SAB, R-5 F.H. Auld papers, Miscellaneous Correspondence no. 11, "The Problem of Saskatchewan," paper presented by J.G. Taggart, Minister of Agriculture and E.E. Eisenhauer, Irrigation Specialist, at the General Professional Meeting of the Engineering Institute of Canada at Ottawa, Ontario, 15 February 1939.

82 SAB, MA.3.8, Radio address, 31 January 1939.

83 McDonald, "Soldier Settlement and Depression Settlement," 5; Powell, "Northern Settlement," 95.

84 Fitzgerald, "Pioneer Settlement," 325.

85 Except for the original sixteen-dollar down payment. See ibid., 326–8.

86 Ibid., 328.

87 Stutt and Van Vliet, "Economic Study of Land Settlement in Representative Pioneer Areas," 59.

88 Most of the land ceded to the Land Utilization Board was, in fact, marginal prairie land. It was turned over to the PFRA and eventually converted to pasture. See SAB, "The Problem of Saskatchewan."

89 Powell, "Northern Settlement," 96.

90 A farmer required more cleared grey soil to make a viable farm than on black or transitional soil. Grey soil also needed adequate fertilization. Stutt and Van Vliet claimed, however, that government

investment in land clearing would pay off, as farmers could easily carry the debt load caused by land clearing. Stutt and Van Vliet, "Economic Study of Land Settlement," 68. Costs for land clearing had declined throughout the 1930s. As mechanization increased, cost per acre for clearing and breaking decreased from fifteen to ten dollars per acre of heavy bush. See Hope and Stutt, "Economic Study of Land Settlement," 25. Increased mechanization and decreased costs helped post-Depression northern farmers clear acreage quickly, making northern farms viable.

91 Stutt and Van Vliet calculated that of the northern families interviewed in 1941, an average of one-third had received re-establishment funds. On a microlocal level, these numbers broke down even further. In the brand new communities such as Goodsoil-Pierceland, 70 percent received re-establishment assistance. Settlers in older communities such as Carrot River or the soldier settlement community of Carragana required less, from 5 to 15 percent taking loans. See Stutt and Van Vliet, "Economic Study of Land Settlement in Representative Pioneer Areas," 59–60. In the north Prince Albert region, re-establishment loans could be found primarily in the most northerly districts, around Emma and Christopher Lake, Beaton, Forest Gate and Moose Lake school districts. See SAB, Municipal Affairs fonds, MA 3.31, Northern Settlers Re-Establishment Board files. See also Gilbert and McLeman, "Household Access to Capital."

92 "Paddockwood: The Mixed Farming Paradise of Saskatchewan."

93 SAB, RC 236, File C67, box 12, Royal Commission on Agriculture and Rural Life, Community Brief, Paddockwood.

94 Fitzgerald, "Pioneer Settlement," 410.

95 "McGowan, Sargent Hugh and Muriel." Interestingly, their son Sargent Ernest became a prolific and highly successful hunter, fisherman, and trapper.

96 Stutt, "Land Settlement," 13.

97 For an overview of the rise of commercial fishing on the northern lakes, see Seymour, "Geographical Study of the Commercial Fishing Industry in Northern Saskatchewan." See also Piper, *Industrial Transformation*.

98 See "Wiberg, Ernest and Jean," in *Cordwood and Courage*, 508–9.

99 Sigfusson, *Sigfusson's Roads*, 49.

100 See, for example, "Arne Jacobson and family," *Tweedsmuir*, 85–90; the Merrell family, *Cordwood and Courage*, 369–70; Bryce Dunn's memoirs, "Yesteryears Reflections"; "Daley, Fred and Thelma," *Cordwood and Courage*, 167–8.

101 *Prince Albert Daily Herald,* 7 August 1931; 14 August 1931.

102 "Arne Jacobsen and family," *Tweedsmuir*, 85–90.

103 Rees, *New and Naked Land,* 95–6.

104 Ibid., 96–9.

105 Howard Andrews, who grew up north of Paddockwood, shot and skinned squirrels. See *Fur, Fish, and Forest*, "Andrews, Howard and Ileen," 120. Dunn, "Yesteryears Reflections," 24–8.

106 See "Hayes, Paul and Dolly," in *Fish, Fur, and Forest*, 180–2.

107 Fitzgerald, "Pioneer Settlement," 436–7.

108 Saskatchewan Environment and Resource Management, Wildlife Technical Report Number 5, "A Century of Fur Harvesting in Saskatchewan," 1995, 32.

109 Fitzgerald, "Pioneer Settlement," 439, 439a.

110 Karras, *North to Cree Lake* and *Face the North Wind.*

111 Grey Owl, *Men of the Last Frontier*, 26.

112 Quiring, *Battling Parish Priests, Bootleggers and Fur Sharks*, 101. White trappers' disregard for northern resources was reiterated and strengthened by Tough, *As Their Natural Resources Fail*. Both concede that northern trapping became popular following World War I, and increased throughout the 1920s. It was not a specifically Depression phenomenon, but part of a general push north.

113 A fascinating series of articles by H. Clifford Dunfield in the *Western Producer* throughout the spring, summer, and fall of 1971 is a spectacular, if underutilized, source for First Nations history along the

forest fringe and north to the Churchill River Basin. Titled "The Fur Forest of Saskatchewan," Dunfield provided a window into fur conservation and ecology, First Nations views and economics, as well as stories, anecdotes, characters, and incidents from the western Churchill basin.

114 For an important examination of human-set forest fires by prospectors in northern Saskatchewan throughout the 1920s and 1930s, and their impact on First Nations, see Gulig, "'Determined to Burn off the Entire Country.'"

115 See "A Century of Fur Harvesting in Saskatchewan," 25.

116 SAB, MA 3.7, Northern Settlers Re-Establishment fonds.

117 Trapping licences were introduced in Saskatchewan in 1920. By 1922, over 8000 licences were issued; in 1928, over 12,000. These numbers moderated in the 1930s, from a low of 2600 in 1932 to a high of 10,400 licences in 1936. Indeed, overall there were fewer licences purchased in the 1930s (71,965 between 1920 and 1929 and 66,839 between 1930 and 1939). In some cases, people trapped without licences, if they could not afford to purchase one. Many traders would take furs without asking to see a licence. However, the overall drop in licences could suggest that pressure from white trappers was perhaps *less* than previously charged. If so, the role of environmental stress on fur stocks should be re-examined. See "A Century of Fur Harvesting in Saskatchewan," trapper licence sales 1920–1940, 17, 26. See also *Fur, Fish, and Forest* and "Yesteryears Reflections." It should be noted that trapping generally increased in popularity throughout the twentieth century. During the 1970s, 124,000 trapping licences were issued; in the 1980s, over 155,000—but the overall population of Saskatchewan was about the same as it was in the 1930s.

118 The lake, originally called Pelican Lake for its tremendous pelican population, was not part of the park's original boundaries. When the boundaries were extended north in 1929, most of Lavallée Lake fell within the expanded park. See Waiser, *Saskatchewan's Playground*, 104. Because the lake was so remote, and only occasional canoeists found their way to the lake, Lavallée was not, at first, pressured to move.

119 Fitzgerald, "Pioneer Settlement," 338.

120 For an overview of the settlement at Fish Lake and its people, see *Tweedsmuir*, 93–100.

121 For an overview of Métis history in Saskatchewan, see Préfontaine, "Métis Communities," *Encyclopaedia of Saskatchewan*; Campbell, *Stories of the Road Allowance People*. Two excellent documentaries include "Jim Settee: The Way Home" and "The Story of the Crescent Lake Metis."

122 First Nations historian John Tobias declared that drought trekkers went north to "live like the Métis." Private communication, June 2008.

123 Interestingly, one writer for the Tweedsmuir local history book thought that Billy Bear "must have been a white man" because he owned a farm. See "James Brown and Family," *Tweedsmuir*, 41. For other aspects of Billy Bear's life, see the files of Indian Affairs, particularly LAC, RG 10, Vol. 7766.

124 "History of Little Red River Reserve," as told by Angus Merasty, *Saskatchewan Indian* 3, 6 (June 1972): 10. By the 1970s, Merasty claimed, leased agricultural land brought $75,000 annually to Lac La Ronge, and likely a proportionate amount to the Montreal Lake band. By 2008, the land leases represented a significant portion of band income. Palmer Hanson rented and broke Little Red River reserve land, as did many of his neighbours in the Spruce Home and Northside districts. Interview, Palmer and Frances Hanson with Merle Massie, summer 2007.

125 For the individual family histories, see *Cordwood and Courage*, "Bentz, John and Dagmar," "McGowan, Sargent and Muriel," "Goplen, Axel and Betty," "Wiberg, Ernest and Jean," "Wiberg, Clarence and Lorna," and "Wiberg, Allan and Clara." The Norman McGowan history is found in *As Far As the Eye Can See*.

126 Bowen, "Forward to a Farm," 226.

127 Archer, *Saskatchewan*, 240.

128 Mrs. Bailey and her family went north in 1937. See "The Year We Moved." See also Fenske, *Riverlore*.

129 Fitzgerald, "Pioneer Settlement," 350.

130 *Census of the Prairie Provinces 1946 Volume I.* Population by census subdivisions, nos. 519, 520, and 521.

131 Fitzgerald, "Pioneer Settlement," 352.

132 The Prince Albert census district population dropped from 89,036 in 1941 to 83,776 in 1946 and 81,160 in 1951. Its population in 1931 was 83,703. See *Census of the Prairie Provinces*, 1946. North Battleford census district dropped from 53,212 in 1941 to 45,211 in 1951. Nipawin dropped from 65,166 in 1941 to 61,615 in 1951.

133 *Census of Canada*, 1951.

134 McDonald, "Soldier Settlement and Depression Settlement," 35.

135 Wood, *Places of Last Resort*, 182.

136 *Census of Canada*, 1951.

137 An overview of farm changes during the 1940s is found in Andal, *Changes in the Farms*.

138 Northern farms continued to operate as livestock and mixed farms; on the prairies, farms closer to urban centres began to specialize. Many that had been mixed farms became exclusive dairy farms. Others remained grain farms. See Andal, *Changes in the Farms*, 6.

139 Income on the farms in the northern areas exceeded that on farms in the west central area in 1947. See Andal, *Changes in the Farms*, 35.

140 SAB, RC 236, C67, Box 12, Royal Commission on Agriculture and Rural Life. Community brief, Paddockwood, 4. See "Kirychuk, Emil and Polly" in *Cordwood and Courage*, 309–10. More of the newly patented land was sold to returned soldiers, such as Allan and Clarence Wiberg and John Bentz.

141 The Red Cross Outpost Hospital closed its doors in 1949. Better roads to Prince Albert and a shortage of nursing staff, however, contributed more to its closure than did local population statistics. See Massie, "Ruth Dulmage Shewchuk."

142 Province of Saskatchewan, *Royal Commission on Agriculture and Rural Life*, "Movement of Farm People."

143 *Prince Albert Daily Herald*, 29 April 1966, "Paddockwood Homesteads First Taken Up in 1911."

144 The community pasture project along the northern parkland/forest fringe (other projects included Hafford and Fairholme, for example), was a late offshoot of the community pasture projects initiated by the Prairie Farm Rehabilitation Administration during the 1930s in the drought regions. See Abramson, *A Study of the Effects of Displacement on Farmers*.

145 Other reasons included the closing of the local school; Moose Lake's situation at the edge of the forest (there was no agricultural development further north); the creation of highway Number Two which replaced the Montreal Lake Trail; and the need for additional pasture land to support the stock base of north Paddockwood farmers.

146 See Abramson, *Effects of Displacement on Farmers*, 74.

147 *Regina Leader*, 17 October 1931. The journalist was probably W.J. Mather, who published a similar article, with similar phrasing, in *Maclean's* magazine, 1 April 1932.

148 See Bennett and Kohl, *Settling the Canadian and American West*.

149 "Rambling Thoughts by a Prairie Immigrant," *Cordwood and Courage*, 637.

CONCLUSION: SOUTH OF THE NORTH, NORTH OF THE SOUTH

1 Usher, "The North: One Land, Two Ways of Life," 483.

2 Coates and Morrison, *Forgotten North*.

3 Merasty, "History of Little Red River Reserve," 10.

4 "The Claxton Family," in *Tweedsmuir*, 52.

5 See Quiring, *CCF Colonialism*; Bone, "Saskatchewan's Forgotten North."

BIBLIOGRAPHY

UNPUBLISHED SOURCES

Dunn, Margaret. Diary. From the collection of Bryce Dunn, Paddockwood. Copy in Merle Massie Private Collection (MMPC).

McGowan, Sargent Ernest. "The Key Is in the Horse," unpublished manuscript, c. 2001–02. MMPC.

———. "Under the Raven's Nest," unpublished manuscript, 2005. MMPC.

INTERVIEWS BY THE AUTHOR

Andrews, Howard. Candle Lake, 10 November 2008.

Austin, Lester. Paddockwood, 11 November 2008.

Dobie, Edna. Prince Albert, 12 November 2008.

Dunn, Bryce. Paddockwood, 5 July 2006, 11 August 2007.

Elliott, Charlie. Paddockwood, 10 November 2008.

Hansen, Palmer and Frances. Spruce Home, 11 August 2007.

Swenson, Miriam. Prince Albert, 12 November 2008.

Wiberg, Clara. Prince Albert, 12 November 2008.

Wiberg, Jean. Prince Albert, 12 November 2008.

ARCHIVAL COLLECTIONS

Library and Archives Canada

Canadian Film Board, V1 2008-12-0004. *Freighting in Northern Canada.*

Canadian National Railways fonds RG 30. Graphic material.

Indian Affairs files, RG 10, vol. 2656, file 9092; vol. 3601, file 1754; vol. 7766, file 27107-4 part 2; vol. 3815, file 56622; C12112, vol. 7839, file 30107-4; vol. 7553, file 41, 107-1, C14818.

Parks Canada fonds, vol. 1726, microfilm reel T-11266. "Vidal's Point Park, History and Establishment."

Saskatchewan Archives Board

A 241. Manuscript Division. Reminiscences of Skuli Bachman.

A 281. Christina Bateman fonds. "Northern Saskatchewan Holiday." Our Legacy website, http://scaa.
sk.ca/ourlegacy, database ID 27383.

AG 2-7. Department of Agriculture files. General file. Application for Free Shipment of Settler's Effects.

B11 10. Richmond Mayson fonds.

B11 13. Department of Agriculture. Prince Albert Board of Trade.

Cummins Map Company, map Sask. 258, 1922 and 1930.

F375 S2005-15. Lucy Margaret Baker fonds.

MA 3.31. Municipal Affairs fonds. Northern Settlers Re-Establishment Branch files.

MA 3.8. Local Improvement Districts Branch, Northern Settlers Re-Establishment Branch.

Matte, G.J., Commissioner, Northern Settlers Re-Establishment Branch. Address over Station CJRM, 31
January 1939.

Microfilm S.183. Records of Premier William Martin. Soldier Settlement files.

Morton Manuscript Collection. S-A32, vol. IX. Historical Geography.

Morton Manuscript Collection. Mss C555/2/10a. "Prince Albert: Europe's Easiest Way"; Prince Albert
Board of Trade, 1910; 10b, "Prince Albert, Saskatchewan: The Ideal Spot for the British Settler"; 10c,
"Prince Albert, Saskatchewan: The Easiest Way," c. 1911; 10d, "Prince Albert Investments: Issued
Monthly in the Interests of Prince Albert and Vicinity," November 1911.

MS W586. Whelan, W.W. "Echoes of Yesterday." Unpublished manuscript. NR 1/1. Department of
Natural Resources, F-400-F/EL Forestry, Emma Lake, 1930. "Emma Lake Outing Club."

NR 5, B.12.9. Crown Timber Agency files.

Ra 220 102; Ra 200 b 20; Ra 400 2a. Department of Railways files.

R-A1384. Interview. Albert Russell. Prince Albert. 12 July 1978.

R-A1387. Interview. Stuart I. Dawley. Prince Albert. 7 July 1978.

R-A1388. Interview. Albert Davey. Prince Albert. 17 July 1978.

R-A1389. Interview. Axel Olson. Prince Albert. 14 July 1978.

R-A1390. Interview. Mrs. Thomas Harvey. Prince Albert. 27 October 1978.

R-A1393. Interview. Dave Giesbrecht. Prince Albert. N.d.

R-A1396. Interview. Bill Cheyney. N.d.

R-A1397. Interview. Harold Read. N.d.

R-A1398. Interview. Mary Read. N.d.

R-A4535. Photograph by William James.

R-1385, R-1386. Interview. Odias Cartier. 12 July 1978.

R-9218. Interview. Irene Johns. 7 February 1984.

R-A92222. Interview. France Nolan. Prince Albert. 4 July 1983.

RC 236, file C67, box 12. Royal Commission on Agriculture and Rural Life. Community Brief, Paddockwood.

R-5. F.H. Auld papers. Miscellaneous Correspondence no. 11, "The Problem of Saskatchewan." Paper
presented by J.G. Taggart, Minister of Agriculture, and E.E. Eisenhauer, Irrigation Specialist, at the
General Professional Meeting of the Engineering Institute of Canada, Ottawa, 15 February 1939.

R-73. Richmond A. Mayson fonds.

R-183 I.352; R-183 I.290. Department of the Interior, Dominion Lands Branch fonds.

R-249. Royal Commission on Immigration and Settlement. Vol. 35, 87-103; vol. 36.

R-261, file 26.5. Saskatchewan Department of Agriculture, Soldier Settlement branch.

R-266.1; R-266 no. 1644; R-266.IV.40. Department of Agriculture fonds. "Homestead Entries 1905 to 1943 by Land Agencies and Census Divisions."

Saskatchewan School District Jubilee Histories. "Alingly School District Jubilee History," 1955.

S43 R2004-220. Post-1930 settlement files, homestead records.

S-Q80, S2000-51. Webb, John. "Forward: Legal Surveys of Prince Albert National Park, Waskesiu, Saskatchewan." Unpublished document.

University of Saskatchewan Archives

Davis Family fonds, f373.

Homemakers Clubs of Saskatchewan fonds, 2109, boxes 14 and 15. "Paddockwood Red Cross Outpost Hospital Record of Patients 1920–1947"; "A History of the Paddockwood Homemakers Club," c. 1980; "History [of] Prince Albert District Homemakers"; "Paddockwood"; "Monthly Highlights of Paddockwood Homemakers Club," c. 1982.

RG 13 S.2. Year Books, Murray Point, 1936.

Prince Albert Historical Society (Bill Smiley Archives)

File 76-58. Lockhart-Smith, C.J. "Indians of Montreal Lake."

File 694b. Soldier Settlement documents.

File 705b. Dice, Richard. "Alingly and Surrounding Districts."

H series H-515. Teepee Tea Room.

Local history fonds, Buckland. "From Ox-Team to Combine: Local History of Buckland District."

Surveyor's maps. Township maps. Department of the Interior.

Timber maps. Shelf 18.

Walter Whelan scrapbook. Oversize shelf 29.

Paddockwood Museum

Elk Range Community Club records.

Paddockwood *Pow-Wow,* diamond jubilee edition, 1965. "Down Memory Lane."

"Paddockwood: The Mixed Farming Paradise of Saskatchewan."

Reminiscences of Orlin Elliott.

Prince Albert National Park Archives, Waskesiu

Department of the Interior. *Modern Voyageurs,* 1931. Silent movie.

"HBC Post at Red Deer Lake, Saskatchewan," 24 March 1969 (historical material on Red Deer Post compiled by HBC Archives, Winnipeg).

Lumby Production Company. *Giants of Their Time: The Lumberjack,*" c. 1970s.

Glenbow Archives

Canadian Red Cross Society, Alberta-North West Territories Division fonds. M8228 Series 6a-24; 6b-226. Photograph collection.

Friends of Prince Albert National Park, Waskesiu

Department of the Interior, Sturgeon Lake Forest Reserve map c. 1925.

LOCAL HISTORY BOOKS

Archer, J.H., and the Lake Katepwa Historical Society. *Lake Katepwa: Memories of Yesterday with Notes for Today.* Fort Qu'Appelle, SK: Lake Katepwa Historical Society, 1984.

As Far as the Eye Can See: Weyburn RM 67. Weyburn RM 67 History Book Committee. Regina: Focus Publishing, 1986.

Atkinson, Rita, ed. *The History of Lakeland, Paddockwood, and Tweedsmuir: Progress in Harmony with Nature.* RM of Lakeland, 2005.

Buckland's Heritage. Buckland History Book Committee. North Battleford: Turner-Warwick Printers, 1980.

Cordwood and Courage. Paddockwood and District History Book Committee. Altona, MB: Friesen Printers, 1982.

Department of Natural Resources. *Resource Tales and Trails.* Regina: Print West Communications, 1994.

DiLella, Anna-Marie, in collaboration with the settlers of Dore Lake. *A Look at the Past: A History of Dore Lake, Saskatchewan.* Dore Lake Historical Society. Altona, MB: Friesen Printers, 1983.

Dunn, Bryce. "Yesteryears Reflections: A Pictorial and Written History of Times Past Seen through the Eyes of a Boy Who Lived Those Times to the Fullest." Self-published, n.d.

Footprints of Our Pioneers: Briarlea, Crutwell, Holbein, Nibet, Rozilee, Wild Rose. Wild Rose and Area History Book Committee. Altona, MB: Friesen Printers, 1990.

From Bush to Grain: A History of Albertville, Meath Park, and District. Meath Park History Committee. Altona, MB: Friesen Printers, 1984.

Fur, Fish, and Forest: A Candle Lake Legacy. Lake History Book Committee. Altona, MB: Friesen Printers, 1991.

Lavigne, Solange. *Kaleidoscope: Many Cultures—One Faith.* Muenster, SK: St. Peter's Press, 1990.

Our Harvest of Memories. Shell River North History Committee. Altona, MB: Friesen Printers, 1983.

Prince Albert Outing Club, Round Lake, Saskatchewan, 1905 to 1990. Prince Albert: Prince Albert Outing Club, 1990.

Tweedsmuir: Community and Courage. Tweedsmuir History Committee. Prince Albert: Campbell Printing, 2006.

FILM DOCUMENTARIES

Corrigal, Jeanne. *Jim Settee: The Way Home.* Saskatoon: Inner Nature Productions, 2009.

The Story of the Crescent Lake Métis: Our Life on the Road Allowance. Saskatoon: Gabriel Dumont Institute, 2002.

NEWSPAPER SOURCES

Globe and Mail

London Times

Prince Albert Advocate

Prince Albert Daily Herald

Prince Albert Times

Regina Leader

Regina Leader-Post

Regina Post

Regina Times

Saskatchewan Farmer

Saskatchewan Times

Saskatoon Star-Phoenix

Western Producer

GOVERNMENT SOURCES

Canada

The Canada Gazette 60, 49 (4 June 1927).

Census of the Prairie Provinces 1946, Volume I: Population. Ottawa: Minister of Trade and Commerce, Census Division, 1946.

Department of the Interior. *Annual Reports,* 1920–39.

———. Lands Branch. *Annual Reports,* 1920–30.

———. *Natural Resources of the Prairie Provinces: A Brief Compilation Respecting the Development of Manitoba, Saskatchewan, and Alberta,* 1925.

Environment Canada, Lands Directorate. "The Agriculture-Forest Interface: An Overview of Land Use Change," by Michael Fox and Sandra Macenko, Working Paper 38, 1985.

House of Commons. *Sessional Papers,* 1894, vol. 27, no. 11, app. 10, "Annual Report of the Department of Marine and Fisheries."

———. *Sessional Papers,* 1897, vol. XLII, no. 12.

———. *Sessional Papers,* 1909, vol. 25, 8–9, Edward VII A.

Senate. *Debates,* 1907.

Soldier Settlement Board. "Ninth Report of the Soldier Settlement of Canada," 1931.

"Soldier Settlement on the Land." Report of the Soldier Settlement Board, 31 March 1921.

Statutes of Canada, 13–14 Geo. V, c. 44.

Saskatchewan

Andal, M.E. *Changes in the Farms of West Central and Northern Saskatchewan, 1942–43 to 1947.* Ottawa: Department of Agriculture, Marketing Service Extension Division, 1951.

Department of Agriculture. *Annual Report,* 1909.

———. *Saskatchewan* (booklet), 1909.

Department of the Environment. *A Study of Land and Water Use at Emma and Christopher Lakes,* final report, March 1976.

Information Services Corporation (ISC). Dominion Land Grants, RM of Paddockwood No. 520.

Province of Saskatchewan. *Report of the Royal Commission of Inquiry into Farming Conditions,* 1921.

———. Royal Commission on Agriculture and Rural Life. *Movement of Farm People.* Regina: Queen's Printer, 1957.

———. *Sessional Papers,* 1925.

———. "A Submission by the Government of Saskatchewan to the Royal Commission on Dominion-Provincial Relations," 1937.

Saskatchewan Archives Office. "Index to Material Relating to Saskatchewan Indian Reserves in Annual Reports of Department of Indian Affairs 1900–1973."

Saskatchewan Environment and Resource Management. "A Century of Fur Harvesting in Saskatchewan," Wildlife Technical Report 5, 1995.

INTERNET SOURCES

Atlas of Canada. http://atlas.nrcan.gc.ca.

Canada Land Inventory. http://www.geostrategis.com/c_cli-prince-albert.htm.

Canadian Geographic. http://www.canadiangeographic.ca/mapping/historical_maps.

Forest Fringe. http://www.snoriderswest.com.

"Freight Swing Era." http://www.jkcc.com/brfreight.html.

Historic Treaties. http://www.ainc-inac.gc.ca.

Indian Claims Commission. http://www.indianclaims.ca.

Land Use and Land Cover Change program of the United States Global Change Research Program. http://www.usgcrp.gov/usgcrp/ProgramElements/land.htm.

Network in Canadian History & Environment (NiCHE). http://niche-canada.org/.

Saskatchewan borders. http://www.rootsweb.ancestry.com/evolution.boundaries.

Saskatchewan municipalities. http://www.municipal.gov.sk.ca.

Soils of Saskatchewan. http://www.soilsofsask.ca.

The Soldier Settlement Act. http://laws.justice.gc.ca/S-12.8/text.html.

CANADIAN INSTITUTE FOR HISTORICAL MICROREPRODUCTIONS (CIHM)

Lorne Agricultural Society, Prince Albert. "Prince Albert and the North Saskatchewan: A Guide to the 'Fertile Belt' Now Being Opened Up by Railway from Regina to Prince Albert, the Central City and Capital of Saskatchewan." Printed by the *Prince Albert Times.* CIHM 29478.

Mitchell, Peter. "The West and North-West: Notes on a Holiday Trip: Reliable Information for Immigrants, with Maps, etc." CIHM 11139.

"Prince Albert District Saskatchewan," c. 1891. CIHM 30434.

"Yukon via Prince Albert" (pamphlet), c. 1898. CIHM 15253.

SECONDARY SOURCES (BOOKS, PERIODICALS, AND REPORTS)

Abel, Kerry. *Changing Places: History, Community, and Identity in Northeastern Ontario.* Montreal: McGill-Queen's University Press, 2006.

———. "History and the Provincial Norths: An Ontario Example." In *Northern Visions: New Perspectives on the North in Canadian History,* edited by Kerry Abel and Ken Coates, 127–40. Peterborough: Broadview Press, 2001.

Abel, Kerry, and Ken Coates, eds. *Northern Visions: New Perspectives on the North in Canadian History.* Peterborough: Broadview Press, 2001.

Abrams, Gary. *Prince Albert: The First Century 1866–1966.* Saskatoon: Modern Press, 1966.

Abramson, Jane. *A Study of the Effects of Displacement on Farmers Whose Land Was Purchased for Two Community Pastures in Saskatchewan.* An ARDA research report. Saskatoon: Centre for Community Studies, 1965.

Amato, Joseph. *Rethinking Home: A Case for Writing Local History.* Berkeley: University of California Press, 2002.

Andal, M.E. *Changes in the Farms of West Central and Northern Saskatchewan, 1942–3 to 1947.* Ottawa: Department of Agriculture, 1951.

Anderson, Alan. "Population Trends." In *Encyclopedia of Saskatchewan.* Regina: Canadian Plains Research Center, 2005.

Ankli, Robert, H. Dan Helsberg, and John Herd Thompson. "The Adoption of the Gasoline Tractor in Western Canada." In *Canadian Papers in Rural History,* vol. 2, ed. by Donald H. Akenson, 9–40. Gananoque: Langdale Press, 1980.

Ankli, Robert, and Wendy Millar. "Ontario Agriculture in Transition: The Switch from Wheat to Cheese." *Journal of Economic History* 42, 1 (1982): 207–15.

Apostle, Alisa. "Canada, Vacations Unlimited: The Canadian Government Tourism Industry, 1934–1959." PhD diss., Queen's University, 2003.

Archer, John. *Saskatchewan: A History.* Saskatoon: Western Producer Prairie Books, 1980.

Arthur, George. "The North American Plains Bison: A Brief History." *Prairie Forum* 9, 2 (1984): 281–90.

Ashton, E.J. "Soldier Land Settlement in Canada." *Quarterly Journal of Economics* 39, 3 (1925): 488–98.

Atwood, Margaret. *Strange Things: The Malevolent North in Canadian Literature.* Oxford: Clarendon Press, 1995.

———. *Survival: A Thematic Guide to Canadian Literature.* Toronto: Anansi Press, 1972.

Augustus, Camie. "The Scrip Solution: The North West Métis Scrip Policy, 1885–1887." MA thesis, University of Calgary, 2006.

Avery, Donald. *Dangerous Foreigners: European Immigrant Workers and Labour Radicalism in Canada, 1896–1932.* Toronto: McClelland and Stewart, 1979.

Bailey, Mrs. A.W. "The Year We Moved." *Saskatchewan History* 20 (1967): 19-31.

Baker, William M. "The Miners and the Mediator: The 1906 Lethbridge Strike and Mackenzie King." *Labour/Le Travail* 11 (1983): 89–117.

———. "The Miners and the Mounties: The Royal North West Mounted Police and the 1906 Lethbridge Strike." *Labour/Le Travail* 27 (1991): 55–96.

———. "So What's the Importance of the Lethbridge Strike of 1906? Local History and the Issue of Significance." *Prairie Forum* 12, 2 (1987): 295–300.

Ballantine, Archie. "Recollections and Reminiscences: Steamboating on the Saskatchewan." *Saskatchewan History* 18, 3 (1965): 99–114.

Ballantyne, P., et al. *Aski-Puko: The Land Alone.* Prepared for the Federation of Saskatchewan Indians, 1976.

Bamforth, Douglas. "Historical Documents and Bison Ecology on the Great Plains." *Plains Anthropologist* 32 (1987): 1–16.

Barris, T. *Fire Canoe: Prairie Steamboat Days Revisited.* Toronto: McClelland and Stewart, 1977.

Bateman, Rebecca. "Talking with the Plow: Agricultural Policy and Indian Farming in the Canadian and U.S. Prairies." *Canadian Journal of Native Studies* 16, 2 (1996): 1–32.

Beal, Bob. "Treaty Six." In *Encyclopedia of Saskatchewan.* Regina: Canadian Plains Research Center, 2005.

Beal, Bob, and R.C. Macleod. *Prairie Fire.* Toronto: McClelland and Stewart, 1985.

Beames, John. *Gateway.* London: Ernest Benn Limited,1933.

Bell, Keith. "Augustus Kenderine: Representing the Northern Saskatchewan Landscape." In *Augustus Kenderine 1870–1947,* 13-19. Saskatoon: Kenderine Gallery, University of Saskatchewan, 1991.

Belyea, Barbara, ed. *A Year Inland: The Journal of a Hudson's Bay Company Winterer.* Waterloo: Wilfrid Laurier University Press, 2000.

Bickle, Ian. *Turmoil and Triumph: The Controversial Railway to Hudson Bay.* Calgary: Detselig Enterprises, 1995.

Binnema, Theodore. *Common and Contested Ground: A Human and Environmental History of the Northwestern Plains.* Norman: University of Oklahoma Press, 2001.

Bird, Ralph. *Ecology of the Aspen Parkland of Western Canada, in Relation to Land Use.* Ottawa: Research Branch, Department of Agriculture, 1961.

Black, Norman Fergus. *A History of Saskatchewan and the Old North West.* Regina: North West Historical Company, 1913.

Bone, R.M. "Saskatchewan's Forgotten North: 1905 to 2005." In *Perspectives of Saskatchewan,* edited by Jene M. Porter, 13–36. Winnipeg: University of Manitoba Press, 2009.

Bowen, Dawn. "Forward to a Farm: The Back-to-the-Land Movement as a Relief Initiative in Saskatchewan during the Great Depression." PhD diss., Queen's University, 1998.

Bowes, Gordon, ed. *Peace River Chronicles*. Vancouver: Prescott Publishing Company, 1963.

Bowman, Isaiah. *The Pioneer Fringe*. New York: American Geographical Society, Special Publication 13, 1931.

———. "The Pioneering Process." *Science,* New Series 75, 1951 (1932): 521–28.

———. "Planning in Pioneer Settlement." *Annals of the Association of American Geographers* 22, 2 (1932): 93–107.

———. "The Scientific Study of Settlement." *Geographical Review* 16, 4 (1926): 647–53.

Bowman, Isaiah, et al. *Pioneer Settlement: Co-Operative Studies by Twenty-Six Authors*. New York: American Geographical Society, 1932.

Bradford, Tolly. "'Home Away from Home': Old Swan, James Bird, and the Edmonton District, 1795–1815." *Prairie Forum* 29, 1 (2004): 25–44.

Braz, A. "The Modern Hiawatha: Grey Owl's Construction of His Aboriginal Self." In *Auto/biography in Canada: Critical Directions*. Waterloo: Wilfrid Laurier University Press, 2005.

Breen, David H. *The Canadian Prairie West and the Ranching Frontier 1874–1924*. Toronto: University of Toronto Press, 1983.

Britnell, G.E. *The Wheat Economy*. Toronto: University of Toronto Press, 1939.

Broadfoot, Barry. *Ten Lost Years: 1929–1939*. Canada: Doubleday/Paperjacks, 1975.

Brooks, John A. *Strange Hunters: Life and Adventures in Northern Saskatchewan during the 1920s and 30s*. Port Alberni, BC: Coast Printers, 1982.

Buckley, Helen. *From Wooden Ploughs to Welfare: Why Indian Policy Failed in the Prairie Provinces*. Montreal: McGill-Queen's University Press, 1992.

Bumsted, J.M. *The Peoples of Canada: A Post-Confederation History*. Toronto: Oxford University Press, 1992.

Burpee, Lawrence, ed. *An Adventurer from Hudson Bay: Journal of Matthew Cocking, from York Factory to the Blackfeet Country, 1772–73*. Toronto: Transactions of the Royal Society of Canada, Section II, 1908.

Burtman, Phillip Joseph. *Towards Sustainable Management of the Boreal Forest*. Ottawa: National Research Council of Canada, 2003.

Byers, Elizabeth. *Lucy Margaret Baker: A Biographical Sketch of the First Missionary of Our Canadian Presbyterian Church to the North-West Indians*. Toronto: Women's Missionary Society of the Presbyterian Church of Canada, 1920.

Campbell, Celina, et al. "Bison Extirpation May Have Caused Aspen Expansion in Western Canada." *Ecography* 17, 4 (1994): 360–62.

Campbell, Maria. *Halfbreed*. Toronto: McClelland and Stewart, 1973.

———. *Stories of the Road Allowance People*. Penticton, BC: Theytus Books, 1995.

Carnegie, James, the Earl of Southesk. *Saskatchewan and the Rocky Mountains: A Diary and Narrative of Travel, Sport, and Adventure in 1859 and 1860*. Edinburgh: Edmonston and Douglas, 1875.

Carter, Sarah. "An Infamous Proposal: Prairie Indian Reserve Land and Soldier Settlement after World War I." *Manitoba History* 37 (1999): 9–21.

———. "'Daughters of British Blood' or 'Hordes of Men of Alien Race:' The Homesteads-for-Women Campaign in Western Canada," *Great Plains Quarterly* (2009): Paper 1267.

———. *Lost Harvests: Prairie Indian Reserve Farmers and Government Policy*. Montreal: McGill-Queen's University Press, 1990.

Cavanaugh, Catherine. "'No Place for a Woman': Engendering Western Canadian Settlement." *Western Historical Quarterly* 28 (1997): 493–518.

Chambers, Ernest. *The Unexploited West: A Compilation of All the Authentic Information Available at the Present Time as to the Natural Resources of the Unexploited Regions of Northern Canada*. Ottawa: n.p., 1914.

Champ, Joan. "Difficult to Make Hay": Early Attempt at Agriculture on the Montreal Lake Indian Reserve." *Saskatchewan History* 47, 1 (1995): 27–35.

Chapman, Ethel. "For the Soldier Settler's Family." *MacLean's*, 1920.

Cherwinski, Joe. "Cold Comfort: The Brutal Winter of 1906–07 and the Defining of the Prairie Regional Identity." Paper presented at the Canadian Historical Association annual meeting, Toronto, May 2002.

———. "The Rise and Incomplete Fall of a Contemporary Legend: Frozen Englishmen in the Canadian Prairies during the Winter of 1906–07." *Canadian Ethnic Studies/Etudes ethniques au Canada* 30, 3 (1999): 20–43.

Church, G.C. "Dominion Government Aid to the Dairy Industry in Western Canada, 1890–1906." *Saskatchewan History* 16, 2 (1963): 41–58.

Clark, S. Delbert. "Settlement in Saskatchewan with Special Reference to the Influence of Dry Farming." MA thesis, University of Saskatchewan, 1931.

Clow, R. "Bison Ecology: Brule and Yankton Winter Hunting, and the Starving Winter of 1832–33." *Great Plains Quarterly* 15 (1995): 259–70.

Coates, Colin M. "Like 'The Thames towards Putney': The Appropriation of Landscape in Lower Canada." *Canadian Historical Review* 74, 3 (1993): 317–43.

Coates, Ken, and William Morrison. *The Forgotten North: A History of Canada's Provincial Norths.* Toronto: James Lorimer and Company, 1992.

———. "The New North in Canadian History and Historiography." *History Compass* 6, 2 (2008): 639–58.

Code, Paget. "Les Autres Métis." MA thesis, University of Saskatchewan, 2006.

Colpitts, George. *Game in the Garden: A Human History of Wildlife in Western Canada.* Vancouver: UBC Press, 2002.

———. "'Victuals to Put into Our Mouths': Environmental Perspectives on Fur Trade Provisioning Activities at Cumberland House, 1775–1782." *Prairie Forum* 22, 1 (1997): 1–20.

Coupland, Robert T., and T. Christopher Brayshaw. "The Fescue Grassland in Saskatchewan." *Ecology* 34, 2 (1953): 386–405.

Cronon, William. *Changes in the Land: Indians, Colonists, and the Ecology of New England.* Rev. ed. New York: Hill and Wang, 2003.

———. "A Place for Stories: Nature, History, and Narrative." *Journal of American History* 78, 4 (1992): 1347–76.

Cross, Michael. Introduction. In *The Frontier Thesis and the Canadas: The Debate on the Impact of the Canadian Environment.* Issues in Canadian History. Toronto: Copp Clark, 1970.

Cunfer, Geoff. *On the Great Plains: Agriculture and Environment.* College Station: Texas A&M University Press, 2005.

Danysk, Cecelia. "No Help for the Farm Help: The Farm Employment Plans of the 1930s in Prairie Canada." *Prairie Forum* 19, 2 (1994): 231–51.

Daschuk, James. "A Dry Oasis: The Canadian Plains in Late Prehistory." *Prairie Forum* 34, 1 (2009): 1–29.

Dawson, Bruce. "Better than a Few Squirrels: The Greater Production Campaign on the First Nations Reserves of the Canadian Prairies." MA thesis, University of Saskatchewan, 2001.

———. "The Roots of Agriculture: A Historiographical Review of First Nations Agriculture and Government Indian Policy." *Prairie Forum* 28, 1 (2003): 99–115.

Dawson, Michael. "Taking the 'D' out of Depression: The Promise of Tourism in British Columbia, 1935–1939." *BC Studies* 132 (2001): 31–59.

den Otter, A.A. *Civilizing the West: The Gaits and the Development of Western Canada.* Edmonton: University of Alberta Press, 1982.

Diaz, Polo, and Mark Nelson. "The Changing Prairie Social Landscape of Saskatchewan: The Social Capital of Rural Communities." *Prairie Forum* 30, 1 (2005): 43–54.

Dobak, William. "Killing the Canadian Buffalo, 1821–1881." *Western Historical Quarterly* 27 (1996): 33–52.

Drake, Brian. "Waving 'A Bough of Challenge': Forestry on the Kansas Grasslands, 1868–1915." *Great Plains Quarterly* 23, 2 (1984): 156–58.

Dunfield, H. Clifford. "The Fur Forest of Saskatchewan." *Western Producer,* March-October 1971.

Durant, Peggy. *The Long Trek.* Self-published, 2005.

Dyck, Lyle. *Farmers 'Making Good': The Development of the Abernethy District, Saskatchewan 1880–1920.* Ottawa: Canadian Parks Service, 1989; Calgary: University of Calgary Press, 2008.

Elias, Peter. *The Dakota of the Canadian Northwest: Lessons for Survival.* Winnipeg: University of Manitoba Press, 1988.

Elliott, Jayne. "Blurring the Boundaries of Space: Shaping Nursing Lives at the Red Cross Outposts in Ontario, 1922–1945." *Canadian Bulletin of Medical History* 21, 2 (2004): 303–25.

———. "(Re)constructing the Identity of a Red Cross Outpost Nurse: The Letters of Louise de Kiriline, 1927–1936." In *Place and Practice in Canadian Nursing History,* edited by Jayne Elliott, Meryn Stuart, and Cynthia Toman, 136–52. Vancouver: UBC Press, 2008.

Elliott, Jayne, Dianne Dodd, and Nicole Rousseau. "Outpost Nursing in Canada." In *On All Frontiers: Four Centuries of Nursing in Canada,* edited by Christina Bates, Dianne Dodd, and Nicole Rousseau, 139–52. Ottawa: Canadian Museum of Civilization and University of Ottawa Press, 2005.

Elofson, Warren. *Cowboys, Gentlemen, and Cattle Thieves: Ranching on the Western Frontier.* Montreal: McGill-Queen's University Press, 2000.

England, Robert. *The Colonization of Western Canada: A Study of Contemporary Land Settlement 1896–1934.* London: P.S. King and Son, 1995.

———. "Land Settlement in Northern Areas of Western Canada 1925–1935." *Canadian Journal of Economics and Political Science* 1, 4 (1935): 578–87.

Ens, Gerhard. *Homeland to Hinterland: The Changing Worlds of the Red River Métis in the Nineteenth Century.* Toronto: University of Toronto Press, 1996.

Epp, H.T. "Way of the Migrant Herds: Dual Dispersion Strategy among Bison." *Plains Anthropologist* 33, 121 (1988): 309–20.

Erasmus, Peter. *Buffalo Days and Nights* (as told to Henry Thompson). Calgary: Fifth House Publishers, 1999.

Fedorowich, Kent. *Unfit for Heroes: Reconstruction and Soldier Settlement in the Empire between the Wars.* Manchester: Manchester University Press, 1995.

Felske, Lorry, and Beverly Rasporich. *Challenging Frontiers: The Canadian West.* Calgary: University of Calgary Press, 2004.

Fenske, Harold. *Riverlore: The Headwaters of the Assiniboine Will Always Be Home.* Self-published, 2002.

Fitzgerald, Denis Patrick. "Pioneer Settlement in Northern Saskatchewan." PhD diss., University of Minnesota, 1966.

Flanagan, Thomas. *1885 Reconsidered: Riel and the Rebellion.* Saskatoon: Western Producer Prairie Books, 1983.

Fleming, H.A. *Canada's Arctic Outlet: A History of the Hudson Bay Railway.* Berkeley: University of California Press, 1957.

Flores, Dan. "Bison Ecology and Bison Diplomacy: The Southern Plains from 1800 to 1850." *Journal of American History* 78, 2 (1991): 465–85.

———. "Place: An Argument for Bioregional History." *Environmental History Review* 18, 4 (1994): 1–18.

Foster, John, Dick Harrison, and I.S. MacLaren, eds. *Buffalo.* Edmonton: University of Alberta Press, 1992.

Fowke, V.C. *The National Policy and the Wheat Economy.* Toronto: University of Toronto Press, 1957.

Francis, R. Douglas. *Images of the West: Changing Perceptions of the Prairies, 1690–1960.* Saskatoon: Western Producer Prairie Books, 1989.

Francis, R.D. and H. Ganzevoort, eds. *The Dirty Thirties in Prairie Canada*. BC Geographical Series 26. Vancouver: Tantalus Research, 1980.

Friesen, Gerald. "Defining the Prairies: or, why the prairies don't exist" in *Toward Defining the Prairies: Region, Culture, and History* edited by Robert Wardhaugh, 13–28. Winnipeg: University of Manitoba Press, 2001.

————. *The Canadian Prairies: A History*. Toronto: University of Toronto Press, 1984.

————. *River Road: Essays on Manitoba and Prairie History*. Winnipeg: University of Manitoba Press, 1996.

Fung, Ka-iu, ed. *Atlas of Saskatchewan*. Saskatoon: University of Saskatchewan, 1999.

Gilbert, Genevieve, and Robert McLeman. "Household Access to Capital and Its Effects on Drought Adaptation and Migration: A Case Study of Rural Alberta in the 1930s." *Population and Environment* 32, 1 (2010): 3–26.

Gillespie, Greg. "The Imperial Embrace: British Sportsmen and the Appropriation of Landscape in Nineteenth Century Canada." PhD diss., University of Western Ontario, 2001.

Goode, P. *A Historical/Cultural/Natural Resource Study of the Prince Albert Model Forest Region*. Report submitted to the Prince Albert Model Forest Association. Saskatoon: Sentar Consultants, 1995.

Goode, Peter, Joan Champ, and Leslie Amundson. *The Montreal Lake Region: Its History and Geography*. Report submitted to the Prince Albert Model Forest Association. Saskatoon: Sentar Consultants, 1996.

Gould, Peter, and Rodney White. *Mental Maps*. New York: Penguin Books, 1974.

Granatstein, J.L. *Who Killed Canadian History?* Toronto: HarperCollins, 1998.

Gray, James. *Men against the Desert*. Saskatoon: Western Producer Prairie Books, 1967.

————. *The Winter Years*. Toronto: Macmillan, 1966.

Grayson, L.M., and M. Bliss, eds. *The Wretched of Canada: Letters to R.B. Bennett*. Toronto: University of Toronto Press, 1971.

Green, Larry. " 'The House in Buffalo Country': Hudson House on the North Saskatchewan River, 1778–1787." *Saskatchewan History* 56, 1 (2004): 30–39.

Grey Owl. *The Men of the Last Frontier*. 1931; reprinted, Toronto: Macmillan, 1989.

————. *Pilgrims of the Wild*. Toronto: Macmillan, 1935; First Laurentian Library edition 1978.

————. *Tales of an Empty Cabin*. Toronto: Key Porter Books, 2005.

Gulig, Tony. "'Determined to Burn Off the Entire Country': Prospectors, Caribou, and the Denesuliné in Northern Saskatchewan, 1900–1940." *American Indian Quarterly* 26, 3 (2002): 335–59.

————. "Sizing up the Catch: Native-Newcomer Resource Competition in the Early Years of Saskatchewan's Northern Commercial Fishery," *Saskatchewan History* 47, 2 (1995): 3-11.

Haig, Bruce, ed. *A Look at Peter Fidler's Journal: Journal of a Journey over Land from Buckingham House to the Rocky Mountains in 1792 and 1793*. Lethbridge: HRC Limited Edition Series, 1991.

Hak, Gordon. "Prairie Capital, Prairie Markets, and Prairie Labour: The Forest Industry in the Prince George District, British Columbia, 1910–1930." *Prairie Forum* 14, 11 (1989): 9–22.

Hargreaves, Mary. *Dry Farming in the Northern Great Plains, 1900–1925*. Cambridge, MA: Harvard University Press, 1957.

Harris, Herbert. *Book of Memories and a History of the Porcupine Soldier Settlement and Adjacent Areas Situated in North-Eastern Saskatchewan Canada 1919–1967*. Porcupine Plain: Shand Agricultural Society, 1967.

Harris, James M. *A Masterpiece in Our Midst: A Review of a Stanley Thompson Masterpiece: Waskesiu Golf Course 1935–2010*. Altona, MB: Friesens, 2010.

Hawkes, John. *The Story of Saskatchewan and Its People*. Chicago: S.J. Clarke, 1924.

Hayball, Gwen. "Historic Lobsticks and Others." *Canadian Geographical Journal* 86, 2 (1973): 62–66.

Hays, Samuel. *Conservation and the Gospel of Efficiency: The Progressive Conservation Movement, 1890–1920*. Pittsburgh: University of Pittsburgh Press, 1999.

Hedges, James B. *Building the Canadian West: The Land and Colonization Policies of the Canadian Pacific Railway.* Toronto: Macmillan, 1939.

Higham, Carol, and Robert Thacker, eds. *One West, Two Myths: A Comparative Reader.* Calgary: University of Calgary Press, 2004.

———. *One West, Two Myths II: Essays on Comparison.* Calgary: University of Calgary Press, 2006.

Hind, Henry Youle. *Narrative of the Canadian Red River Exploring Expedition of 1857 and of the Assinniboine and Saskatchewan Exploring Expedition of 1858.* London: Longman, Green, Longman and Roberts, 1860.

Holzkam, Tim, Victor Lytwyn, and Leo Waisberg. "Rainy River Sturgeon: An Ojibway Resource in the Fur Trade." *Canadian Geographer* 32, 3 (1988): 194–205.

Hope, E.C., and R.A. Stutt. "An Economic Study of Land Settlement in the Albertville-Garrick Area of Northern Saskatchewan, 1941." Dominion of Canada, Department of Agriculture Multilith Report, January 1944.

Howard, Joseph Kinsey. *Montana: High, Wide, and Handsome.* Lincoln: University of Nebraska Press, 2003.

Howlett, Michael. "The Forest Industry on the Prairies: Opportunities and Constraints for Future Development." *Prairie Forum* 14, 2 (1989): 233–57.

Hunt, John D. "Image as a Factor in Tourism Development." *Journal of Travel Research* 13, 1 (1975): 1–7.

Hutchinson, G. *Grey Owl: The Incredible Story of Archie Belaney 1888–1938.* Brede: Hastings, 1985.

Hyde, Anny. "From Stagecoach to Packard Twin Six: Yosemite and the Changing Face of Tourism, 1880–1930." *California History* 69, 2 (1990): 154–69.

Isenberg, Andrew. *The Destruction of the Bison: An Environmental History, 1750–1920.* Cambridge, UK: Cambridge University Press, 2000.

Ivanochko, Bob. "Steamboats." In *Encyclopedia of Saskatchewan.* Regina: Canadian Plains Research Center, 2005.

Jasen, Patricia. *Wild Things: Nature, Culture, and Tourism in Ontario 1790–1914.* Toronto: University of Toronto Press, 1995.

Johnson, Charles W. "Relative Decline of Wheat in the Prairie Provinces of Canada." *Economic Geography* 24, 3 (1948): 209–16.

Johnson, Edward, and Kiyoko Miyanishi, eds. *Forest Fires: Behavior and Ecological Effects.* Toronto: Academic Press, 2001.

Jones, David. *Empire of Dust: Settling and Abandoning the Prairie Dry Belt.* Calgary: University of Calgary Press, 2002.

———. *"We'll all be buried down here": The Prairie Dryland Disaster 1917–1926.* Calgary: Historical Society of Alberta, 1986.

Kabzems, A., A.L. Kosowan, and W.C. Harris. *Mixedwood Section in an Ecological Perspective.* Technical Bulletin 8. Regina: Forestry Branch, Department of Tourism and Renewable Resources, 1976.

Kammen, Carol, ed. *The Pursuit of Local History: Readings on Theory and Practice.* Walnut Creek, CA: Altamira Press, 1996.

Kammen, Carol, and Norma Prendergast, eds. *Encyclopedia of Local History.* Walnut Creek, CA: Altamira Press, 2000.

Karras, A.L. *Face the North Wind.* Calgary: Fifth House, 2005.

———. *North to Cree Lake.* Calgary: Fifth House, 2003.

Keighley, Sydney Augustus. *Trader, Tripper, Trapper: The Life of a Bay Man.* Winnipeg: Watson and Dwyer Publishing, 1989.

Kelly, L.V. *The Range Men: The Story of the Ranchers and Indians of Alberta.* Toronto: W. Briggs, 1913.

Kemp, H.M.S. *Northern Trader.* Toronto: Ryerson Press, 1956.

Kennedy, Allan. "Reminiscences of a Lumberjack." *Saskatchewan History* 19, 1 (1966): 24–34.

Kirby, C.L. *Growth and Yield of White Spruce-Aspen Stands in Saskatchewan.* Forestry Branch Technical Bulletin 4. Regina: Department of Natural Resources, 1962.

Kitzan, Chris. "The Fighting Bishop: George Exton Lloyd and the Immigration Debate." MA thesis, University of Saskatchewan, 1996.

———. "Preaching Purity in the Promised Land: George Exton Lloyd and the Immigration Debate." In *The Prairie West as Promised Land,* edited by R. Douglas Francis and Chris Kitzan, 291–312. Calgary: University of Calgary Press, 2007.

Klaus, J.F. "Early Trails to Carlton House," *The Beaver* 297 (Autumn 1966): 32–9.

Kupsch, W.O, and S.A. Hanson, eds. *Gold and other stories as told to Berry Richards.* Regina: Saskatchewan Mining Association, 1986.

Lawton, Alma. "Urban Relief in Saskatchewan during the Years of the Depression, 1930–1939." MA thesis, University of Saskatchewan, 1969.

Lehr, John. "Government Coercion in the Settlement of Ukrainian Immigrants in Western Canada." *Prairie Forum* 8, 2 (1983): 179–94.

———. "The Rural Settlement Behavior of Ukrainian Pioneers in Western Canada, 1891–1914." In *Western Canada Research in Geography,* edited by B.M. Barr, 51–66. Vancouver: Tantalus Research, 1975.

Leonard, David, and Victoria Lemieux. *A Fostered Dream: The Lure of the Peace River Country.* Calgary: Detselig Enterprises, 1992.

Lewis, G. Malcolm. *Cartographic Encounters: Perspectives on Native American Mapmaking and Map Use.* Chicago: University of Chicago Press, 1998.

———. "The Recognition and Delimitation of the Northern Interior Grasslands during the Eighteenth Century." In *Images of the Plains: The Role of Human Nature in Settlement,* edited by Brian Boulet and Merlin P. Lawson, 23–44. Lincoln: University of Nebraska Press, 1975.

Lewis, Henry, and Theresa Ferguson. "Yards, Corridors, and Mosaics: How to Burn a Boreal Forest." *Human Ecology* 16, 1 (1988): 57–77.

Loo, Tina. *States of Nature: Conserving Canada's Wildlife in the Twentieth Century.* Vancouver: UBC Press, 2006.

Louter, David. *Windshield Wilderness: Cars, Roads, and Nature in Washington's National Parks.* Seattle: University of Washington Press, 2006.

Lower, A.R.M. *The North American Assault on the Canadian Forest.* Toronto: Ryerson Press, 1938.

Lower, A.R.M., and Harold Innis. *Settlement and the Forest Frontier in Eastern Canada* and *Settlement and the Mining Frontier.* Vol. 9 of *Canadian Frontiers of Settlement,* edited by W.A. Mackintosh and W.L.G. Jeorg. Toronto: Macmillan, 1936.

Macarthur, D.A. "Immigration and Colonization in Canada, 1900–1930." In *Pioneer Settlement: Co-Operative Studies by Twenty-Six Authors.* No editor: 57–63. New York: American Geographical Society 1932.

MacEwan, Grant. *The Battle for the Bay.* Saskatoon: Western Producer Prairie Books, 1975.

———. *Between the Red and the Rockies.* Toronto: University of Toronto Press, 1952.

Mackay, J.A. "The journal of the Reverend J. A. Mackay, Stanley Mission, 1870–72," *Saskatchewan History,* 16 (1963): 95–113.

MacLaren, I.S. "The Influence of Eighteenth-Century British Landscape Aesthetics on Narrative and Pictorial Responses to the British North American North and West, 1769–1872." PhD diss., University of Western Ontario, 1983.

———. "The Limits of the Picturesque in British North America." *Journal of Garden History* 5, 1 (1985): 97–111.

Macoun, John. *Manitoba and the Great North-West: The Field for Investment; the Home of the Emigrant.* Guelph: World Publishing Company, 1882.

Malainey, M. "The Reconstruction and Testing of Subsistence and Settlement Strategies for the Plains, Parkland, and Southern Boreal Forest." PhD diss., University of Manitoba, 1997.

Malainey, M.E., R. Przybylski, and B.L. Sherriff. "One Person's Food: How and Why Fish Avoidance May Affect the Settlement and Subsistence Patterns of Hunter-Gatherers." *American Antiquity* 66, 1 (2001): 141–61.

Malainey, M.E., and B.L. Sherriff. "Adjusting Our Perspectives: Historical and Archaeological Evidence of Winter on the Plains of Western Canada." *Plains Anthropology* 41 (1996): 333–57.

Mandelbaum, David. *The Plains Cree: An Ethnographic, Historical, and Comparative Study.* Regina: Canadian Plains Research Center, 1979.

Marchildon, Greg. "History of the Special Areas of Alberta: Institutional Adaptation to Climate Change." Paper presented at the Canadian Association of Geographers, Prairie Summit conference, Regina, 4 June 2010.

Martin, Chester. *"Dominion Lands" Policy.* Edited by Lewis H. Thomas. Carleton Library No. 69. Toronto: McClelland and Stewart Limited, 1973.

Martin, Phyllis. *Red Cross Nurse on the Bay Line.* Self-published, n.d.

Massie, Merle. "Red Cross Outpost Hospitals." In *Encyclopedia of Saskatchewan.* Regina: Canadian Plains Research Center, 2005.

———. "Ruth Shewchuk: A Red Cross Outpost Nurse." *Saskatchewan History* 56, 2 (2004): 35–44.

———. "Scribes of Stories, Tellers of Tales: The Phenomenon of Community History in Saskatchewan." MA thesis, University of Saskatchewan, 1997.

———. "Trapping and Trapline Life," in *kā-kē-pē-isi-nakatamākawihahk Our Legacy: Essays.* Edited by Cheryl Avery and Darlene Fichter. Saskatoon: University of Saskatchewan, 2008: 143–168.

———. "When You're Not from the Prairie: Place History in the Forest Fringe of Saskatchewan." *Journal of Canadian Studies* 44, 2 (2010): 171–93.

Mather, W.J. "Trek to Meadow Lake." *Maclean's,* 1 April 1932. See also *Regina Leader* 17 October 1931.

Matheson, D.G. "The Saskatchewan Relief Commission 1931–1934." MA thesis, University of Saskatchewan, 1974.

Mavor, James. "The Economic Results of the Specialist Production and Marketing of Wheat." *Political Science Quarterly* 26, 4 (1911): 659–75.

McDermott, George. "Frontiers of Settlement in the Great Clay Belt, Ontario and Quebec." *Annals of the Association of American Geographers* 51, 3 (1961): 261–73.

McDonald, John. "Soldier Settlement and Depression Settlement in the Forest Fringe of Saskatchewan." *Prairie Forum* 6, 1 (1981): 35–55.

McGowan, Don C. *Grassland Settlers: The Swift Current Region during the Era of the Ranching Frontier.* Regina: Canadian Plains Research Center, 1975.

McInnis, Marvin. "The Changing Structure of Canadian Agriculture, 1867–1897." *Journal of Economic History* 42, 1 (1982): 191–98.

McIntyre, Tobi. "Canada's Incendiary Past." http://www.canadiangeographic.ca/magazine/ja03/indepth/timeline.asp.

McKay, Ian. "The Liberal Order Framework": A Prospectus for a Reconnaissance of Canadian History," *Canadian Historical Review,* 81, 4 (2000): 616–78.

McLeman, Robert. "Climate-Related Human Migration: Enhancing Our Understanding through Use of Analogues." Paper presented at the Canadian Association of Geographers annual meeting, Prairie Summit conference, Regina, 3 June 2010.

McLeman, R., S. Herold, Z. Reljic, M. Sawada, and D. McKenney. "GIS-Based Modeling of Drought and Historical Population Change on the Canadian Prairies." *Journal of Historical Geography* 36, 1 (2010): 43–56.

McLeman, R., and B. Smit. "Migration as an Adaptation to Climate Change." *Climatic Change* 76, 1–2 (2006): 31–53.

McMan, C.J. "Trade Unionism in District 18, 1900–1925: A Case Study." MBA thesis, University of Alberta, 1969.

McManus, Curt. *Happyland: A History of the "Dirty Thirties" in Saskatchewan, 1947–1937.* Calgary: University of Calgary Press, 2011.

McNeill, J.R., and Verena Winiwarter, eds. *Soils and Societies: Perspectives from Environmental History.* Isle of Harris, UK: White Horse Press, 2006.

McOwan, "The Great Northland," *Prince Albert Daily Herald* 14 January 1919.

McPhillips, H.T. *McPhillips' Saskatchewan Directory.* Prince Albert, NWT: The Author, 1888.

Merasty, Angus. "History of Little Red River," *Saskatchewan Indian* 3, 6 (June 1972): 10–12.

Meyer, David. *The Red Earth Crees, 1860–1960.* Canadian Ethnology Service, Paper 100, 1985.

———. "Waterfowl in Cree Ritual—the Goose Dance." In *Proceedings of the Second Congress of the Canadian Ethnology Society, Vol. 2,* edited by Jim Freedman and Jerome H. Barkow, 437. Mercury Series, Ethnology Service Paper 28. Ottawa: National Museum of Man, 1975.

Meyer, David, Alwynn Beaudoin, and Leslie J. Amundsen. "Human Ecology of the Canadian Prairie Ecozone ca. 9000BP: The Paleo-Indian Period" in *Human Ecology of the Canadian Prairie Ecozone 11,000 to 300BP,* edited by B.A. Nicholson, 5–54. Regina: Canadian Plains Research Center Press, 2011.

Meyer, David, and Henry T. Epp. "North-South Interaction in the Late Prehistory of Central Saskatchewan." *Plains Anthropologist* 35, 132 (1995): 321–42.

———. "The Pegogamaw Cree and Their Ancestors: History and Archaeology in the Saskatchewan Forks Region." *Plains Anthropologist* 51, 199 (2006): 303–24.

———. "'So Fine and Pleasant, beyond Description': The Lands and Lives of the Pegogamaw Crees." *Plains Anthropologist* 49, 191 (2004): 217–52.

Meyer, David, and Paul Thistle. "Saskatchewan River Rendezvous Centres and Trading Posts: Continuity in a Cree Social Geography." *Ethnohistory* 42, 3 (1995): 403–44.

Miller, Gertrude LeRoy. *Mustard Plasters and Handcars: Through the Eyes of a Red Cross Outpost Hospital Nurse.* Toronto: Natural Heritage Books, 2000.

Miller, J.R. *Compact, Contract, Covenant: Aboriginal Treaty-making in Canada.* Toronto: University of Toronto Press, 2009.

———. *Shingwauk's Vision: A History of Native Residential Schools.* Toronto: University of Toronto Press, 1996.

Mochoruk, Jim. *Formidable Heritage: Manitoba's North and the Cost of Development 1870 to 1930.* Winnipeg: University of Manitoba Press, 2004.

Montgomery, L.M. *Rilla of Ingleside.* 1920; reprinted, Toronto: McClelland and Stewart, 1973.

———. *The Selected Journals of L.M. Montgomery Volume I: 1889–1910.* Edited by Mary Rubio and Elizabeth Waterston. Toronto: Oxford University Press, 1985.

Moodie, D.W., and A.J. Ray. "Buffalo Migrations in the Canadian Plains." *Plains Anthropologist* 21, 71 (1976): 45–52.

Moodie, D.W. and Barry Kaye, "Indian Agriculture in the Fur Trade Northwest," *Prairie Forum* 11, 2 (1986): 171-83.

Morgan, E.C. "The Bell Farm." *Saskatchewan History* 19, 2 (1966): 41–60.

———. "Soldier Settlement in the Prairie Provinces." *Saskatchewan History* 21, 2 (1968): 41–55.

Morgan, R.G. "Bison Movement Patterns on the Canadian Plains: An Ecological Analysis." *Plains Anthropologist* 25, 88 (1980): 143–60.

Morrison, Ann K. "Beginnings: The Murray Point Summer School of Art 1936–1955." In *The Flat Side of the Landscape: The Emma Lake Artists' Workshops.* Saskatoon: Mendel Art Gallery, 1989.

Morton, A.S. *A History of the Canadian West to 1870–1871.* 2nd ed. Toronto: University of Toronto Press, 1973.

Morton, A.S., ed. *The Journal of Duncan McGillivray of the North West Company at Fort George on the Saskatchewan, 1794–1795.* Toronto: Macmillan, 1929.

Morton, Desmond, and Glenn Wright. *Winning the Second Battle: Canadian Veterans and the Return to Civilian Life 1915–1930.* Toronto: University of Toronto Press, 1987.

Muldrew, Jean. *Useful Hints on ... Home Management.* Ottawa: Soldier Settlement Board, 1930.

Murchie, R.W., William Allen, and J.F. Booth. *Agricultural Progress on the Prairie Frontier.* Vol. 5 of *Canadian Frontiers of Settlement.* Toronto: Macmillan, 1936.

Murton, James. *Creating a Modern Countryside: Liberalism and Land Resettlement in British Columbia.* Vancouver: UBC Press, 2007.

Nesmith, Tom. "The Philosophy of Agriculture: The Promise of the Intellect in Ontario Farming, 1835–1914." PhD diss., Carleton University, 1988.

Nestor, Rob. "Almighty Voice," in *Encyclopedia of Saskatchewan.* Regina: Canadian Plains Research Center, 2005: 54.

Nisbet, James. *Home and Foreign Record of the Canada Presbyterian Church,* 13, 4 (April 1874): 103–106.

Novosel, Tom. "Pulp Fictions: The CCF Government and the Promise of a Pulp Industry in Saskatchewan, 1944–1964." MA thesis, University of Saskatchewan, 2007.

O'Bryne, Nicole. "The 'Answer to the *Natural Resources* Question': A Historical Analysis of the *Natural Resources Transfer* Agreements." MA thesis, McGill University, 2006.

Odum, E.P. *Fundamentals of Ecology.* 3rd ed. Philadelphia: W.B. Saunders, 1971.

Ommer, Rosemary E., and Nancy J. Turner. "Informal Rural Economies in History." *Labour/Le Travail* 53 (2004): 127–57.

Osborne, Brian, and Susan Wurtele. "The Other Railway: Canadian National's Department of Colonization and Agriculture." *Prairie Forum* 20, 2 (1995): 231–53.

Owram, Doug. "Narrow Circles: The Historiography of Recent Canadian Historiography." *National History: A Canadian Journal of Enquiry and Opinion* 1, 1 (1997): 5–21.

———. *Promise of Eden: The Canadian Expansionist Movement and the Idea of the West, 1856–1900.* Toronto: University of Toronto Press, 1980.

Palliser, John. *The Journals, Detailed Reports, and Observations Relative to the Exploration.* London: G.E. Eyre and W. Spottiswoode, 1863.

Pannekoek, Frits. *A Snug Little Flock: The Social Origins of the Riel Resistance of 1869–70.* Winnipeg: Watson and Dwyer Publishing, 1991.

Parker, C.W. *Who's Who and why: A Biographical Dictionary of Notable Men and Women of Western Canada Volume 2.* Toronto: Canadian Press Association Limited, 1912.

Parr, Joy. *The Gender of Breadwinners: Women, Men, and Change in Two Industrial Towns, 1880–1950.* Toronto: University of Toronto Press, 1990.

Peel, Bruce. *Steamboats on the Saskatchewan.* Saskatoon: Western Producer Prairie Books, 1972.

Pickwell, F.C. "Saskatoon and the North." *Saturday Night,* 16 April 1927.

Piper, Liza. *The Industrial Transformation of Subarctic Canada.* Vancouver: UBC Press, 2009.

Piper, Liza, and John Sandlos, "A Broken Frontier: Ecological Imperialism in the Canadian North." *Environmental History* 12, 4 (2007): 759–95.

Pitsula, James. "The Mixed Social Economy of Unemployment Relief in Regina during the 1930s." *Journal of the Canadian Historical Association* 15, 1 (2004): 97–122.

Podruchny, Caroline. *Making the Voyageur World: Travelers and Traders in the North American Fur Trade.* Lincoln: University of Nebraska Press, 2006.

Powell, T.J.D. "Northern Settlement, 1929–1935." *Saskatchewan History* 30, 3 (1977): 81–98.

Pratt, A.M., and John Archer. *The Hudson's Bay Route.* Published under the joint auspices of the governments of Manitoba and Saskatchewan, 1953.

Pratt, Mary Louise. *Imperial Eyes: Travel Writing and Transculturation.* New York: Routledge, 1992.

Préfontaine, Darren. "Métis Communities." In *Encyclopaedia of Saskatchewan.* Regina: Canadian Plains Research Center, 2005.

The Publications of the Hudson's Bay Record Society. Cumberland and Hudson House Journals, 1775–82, Second Series, 1779–82. London: Hudson's Bay Record Society, 1952.

Pyne, Stephen. *Awful Splendour: A Fire History of Canada.* Vancouver: UBC Press, 2007.

Quiring, David. *CCF Colonialism in Northern Saskatchewan: Battling Parish Priests, Bootleggers, and Fur Sharks.* Vancouver: UBC Press, 2004.

Rasmussen, Linda, Lorna Rasmussen, Candace Savage, and Anne Wheeler. *A Harvest Yet to Reap: A History of Prairie Women.* Toronto: Canadian Women's Educational Press, 1976.

Ray, Arthur J. *Indians in the Fur Trade: Their Role as Hunters, Trappers, and Middlemen in the Lands Southwest of Hudson Bay, 1660–1870.* Toronto: University of Toronto Press, 1974.

———. *The Canadian Fur Trade in the Industrial Age.* Toronto: University of Toronto Press, 1990.

———. "The Northern Great Plains: Pantry of the Northwestern Fur Trade, 1774–1885." *Prairie Forum* 9, 2 (1984): 263–80.

Ray, Arthur J., Jim Miller, and Frank Tough. *Bounty and Benevolence: A History of Saskatchewan Treaties.* Montreal: McGill-Queen's University Press, 2000.

Rees, Ronald. *New and Naked Land: Making the Prairies Home.* Saskatoon: Western Producer Prairie Books, 1988.

Regehr, T.D. *The Canadian Northern Railway: Pioneer Road of the Northern Prairies, 1895–1918.* Toronto: Macmillan, 1976.

Rhoades, Robert E. "Archaeological Use and Abuse of Ecological Concepts and Studies: The Ecotone Example." *American Antiquity* 43, 4 (1978): 608–14.

Richards, J. Howard. *Saskatchewan: A Geographical Appraisal Part 1, the Setting: Land Use, Agriculture and Forest.* Saskatoon: University of Saskatchewan: Division of Extension and Community Relations, 1981.

Roberts, Vicky, ed. *Historical Events of the Woodland Cree.* La Ronge, SK: Lac La Ronge Indian Band, 1997.

Roe, Frank Gilbert. "The Alberta Wet Cycle of 1899–1903: A Climatic Interlude." *Agricultural History* 28, 3 (1954): 112–20.

———. *The North American Buffalo.* Toronto: University of Toronto Press, 1951.

Rogers, Edward S. "The Dugout Canoe in Ontario." *American Antiquity* 30, 4 (1965): 454–59.

Rollings-Magnusson, Sandra. "Canada's Most Wanted: Pioneer Women on the Western Prairies." *Canadian Review of Sociology and Anthropology* 37, 2 (2000): 223–38.

———. "Necessary for Survival: Women and Children's Labour on Prairie Homesteads, 1871–1911." *Prairie Forum* 29, 2 (2004): 227–43.

Rothman, Hal K. *Devil's Bargains: Tourism in the Twentieth-Century American West.* Lawrence: University of Kansas Press, 1998.

Ruffo, Armand Garnet. *Grey Owl: The Mystery of Archie Belaney.* Regina: Coteau Books, 1997.

Russell, Dale. *Eighteenth-Century Western Cree and Their Neighbours.* Archaeological Survey of Canada, Mercury Series Paper 143, Canadian Museum of Civilization, 1991.

Russell, Peter. "The Far-from-Dry Debates: Dry Farming on the Canadian Prairies and the American Great Plains." *Agricultural History* 81, 4 (2007): 493–521.

———. "Subsistence, Diversification, and Staple Orientations on Saskatchewan Farms: Parklands vs. Prairie, 1911–1926." *Saskatchewan History* 57 (2005): 15–28.

Ryan, Simon. *The Cartographic Eye.* Cambridge, UK: Cambridge University Press, 1996.

Sanderson, Marie. "Drought in the Canadian Northwest." *Geographical Review* 38, 2 (1948): 289–99.

Sandwell, Ruth. *Contesting Rural Space: Land Policy and the Practices of Resettlement on Saltspring Island 1859-1891* Montreal: McGill-Queen's University Press, 2005.

———. "Notes toward a history of rural Canada" in *Social transformation in rural Canada: Community, Cultures, and Collective Action,* edited by John R. Parkins and Maureen G. Reed, 21–42. Vancouver: UBC Press, 2012.

———."Rural Reconstruction: Towards a New Synthesis in Canadian History." *Histoire sociale/Social History* 27, 53 (1994): 1–32.

Schobert, Harold H. *Energy and Society: An Introduction.* London: Taylor and Francis, 2002.

Schultz, J.A. "Canadian Attitudes toward Empire Settlement, 1919–1930." *Journal of Imperial and Commonwealth History* 1, 2 (1973): 237–51.

Seager, A. "A Proletariat in Wild Rose Country: The Alberta Miners, 1905–1945." PhD diss., York University, 1982.

Seymour, Gary Ronald. "A Geographical Study of the Commercial Fishing Industry in Northern Saskatchewan: An Example of Resource Development." MA thesis, University of Saskatchewan, 1971.

Shapiro, Aaron. "Up North on Vacation: Tourism and Resorts in Wisconsin's North Woods." *Wisconsin Magazine of History* 89, 4 (2006): 2–13.

Shilliday, Jim. *Canada's Wheat King: The Life and Times of Seager Wheeler.* Regina: Canadian Plains Research Center, 2007.

Shortt, James. *A Survey of the Human History of Prince Albert National Park, 1887–1945.* Parks Canada Manuscript Report Number 239, 1977.

Sigfusson, Svein. *Sigfusson's Roads.* Winnipeg: J. Gordon Shillingford Publishing, 2003.

Silverman, Eliane Leslau. *The Last Best West: Women on the Alberta Frontier 1880–1930.* Montreal: Eden Press, 1984.

Silversides, Brock. *Gateway to the North: A Pictorial History of Prince Albert.* Saskatoon: Western Producer Prairie Books, 1989.

Smiley, Bill. "The Forest Industry in Prince Albert to 1918." Updated in 2007 by Carmen Bellehumeur and the 2007 Tour Guide Team. Unpublished manuscript, Prince Albert Historical Society.

Smith, Neil. "Political Geographers of the Past. Isaiah Bowman: Political Geography and Geopolitics." *Political Geography Quarterly* 3, 1 (1984): 69–76.

Spafford, Paul et al. "The Amazing Adventures of Christina and Nan: Christina Henry's trip diary with annotations." *Saskatchewan History* 63, 2 (2011): 14-33.

Spector, David. *Agriculture on the Prairies.* History and Archaeology Circular 65. Ottawa: Parks Canada and Environment Canada, National Historic Parks and Sites Branch, 1983.

Sprague, D.N., with Thomas R. Berger. *Canada and the Métis, 1869-1885.* Waterloo: Wilfrid Laurier University Press, 1988.

Stanley, G.F.G. *The Birth of Western Canada: A History of the Riel Rebellions.* Toronto: University of Toronto Press, 1961.

———. "The Western Canadian Mystique." In *Prairie Perspectives: Papers of the Western Canadian Studies Conference,* edited by David P. Gagan, 6-29. Toronto: Holt, Rinehart and Winston, 1970.

"Stanley Notes." *The Beaver,* 1, 6 (1921): 29.

Stegner, Wallace. *Wolf Willow: A History, a Story, and a Memory of the Last Plains Frontier.* Toronto: Macmillan, 1955.

Stonechild, Blair, and Bill Waiser. *Loyal till Death: Indians in the Northwest Rebellion.* Saskatoon: Fifth House, 1997.

Strong, W.L., and L.V. Hills. "Late-Glacial and Holocene Palaeovegetation Zonal Reconstruction for Central and North-Central North America." *Journal of Biogeography* 32 (2005): 1043–62.

Strong-Boag, Veronica. "Pulling in Double Harness or Hauling a Double Load: Women, Work, and Feminism on the Canadian Prairie." *Journal of Canadian Studies* 21, 3 (1986): 32–50.

Struthers, James. *No Fault of Their Own: Unemployment and the Canadian Welfare State, 1914–1941.* Toronto: University of Toronto Press, 1983.

Stunden Bower, Shannon. *Wet Prairie: People, Land, and Water in Agricultural Manitoba.* Vancouver: UBC Press, 2011.

Stutt, R.A. *Land Settlement in Northern Pioneer Areas of Saskatchewan.* Reprinted from *Agricultural Institute Review,* Agricultural Institute of Canada, January 1946.

Stutt, R.A., and H. Van Vliet. "An Economic Study of Land Settlement in Representative Pioneer Areas of Northern Saskatchewan." Technical Bulletin 52. Ottawa: Department of Agriculture, Marketing Service, Economics Division,1945.

Sundberg, Sara Brooks. "Farm Women on the Canadian Prairie Frontier: The Helpmate Image." In *Rethinking Canada: The Promise of Women's History,* edited by Veronica Strong-Boag and Vicki Fellman, 95-106. Toronto: Copp Clark Pittman, 1986.

Sutter, Paul. *Driven Wild: How the Fight against Automobiles Launched the Modern Wilderness Movement.* Seattle: University of Washington Press, 2002.

Taché, Archbishop A.A. *Sketch of the North West of North America.* Translated from the French by Captain D.R. Cameron, Royal Artillery. Montreal: John Lovell, 1870.

Thompson, Christian. "Sturgeon Lake First Nation." In *Encyclopedia of Saskatchewan.* Regina: Canadian Plains Research Center, 2005.

Thompson, E.P. *Customs in Common: Studies in Traditional Popular Culture.* New York: New Press, 1991.

———. *The Making of the English Working Class.* London: V. Gollancz, 1980.

Thompson, J.H. *The Harvests of War—the Prairie West, 1914–1918.* Toronto: McClelland and Stewart, 1992.

———. "'Permanently Wasteful But Immediately Profitable': Prairie Agriculture and the Great War." In *Canadian Historical Association Historical Papers,* 193–206. Ottawa: Canadian Historical Association, 1976.

Thompson, John Herd, and Ian MacPherson. "How You Gonna Get 'em Back to the Farm? Writing the Rural/Agricultural History of the Prairie West." Paper presented at the Western Canadian Studies Conference, University of Saskatchewan, 23 October 1987.

Thompson, J.H., with A. Seager. *Canada, 1922–1939: Decades of Discord.* Toronto: McClelland and Stewart, 1985.

Thompson, Sharon. "Life on the Edge: The Cultural Value of Disappearing Sites." http://crm.cr.nps.gov/archive/20-4/20-4-18.pdf.

Thorpe, Jeffery. "Models of Succession in the Southern Boreal Forest." Prince Albert Model Forest Association report, January 1996.

Tough, Frank. *"As Their Natural Resources Fail": Native Peoples and the Economic History of Northern Manitoba, 1870–1930.* Vancouver: UBC Press, 1996.

Turkell, William. *The Archive of Place: Unearthing the Pasts of the Chilcotin Plateau.* Vancouver: UBC Press, 2007.

Turner, Frederick Jackson. "The Significance of the Frontier in American History." In *The Frontier in American History.* New York: Holt and Company, 1920.

Turner, Nancy J., Iain J. Davidson-Hunt, and Michael O'Flaherty. "Living on the Edge: Ecological and Cultural Edges as Sources of Diversity for Social-Ecological Resilience." *Human Ecology* 31, 3 (2003): 439–61.

Tyman, John Langton. *By Section, Township, and Range: Studies in Prairie Settlement.* Brandon: Assiniboine Historical Society, 1972.

Ulmer, Catherine Mary. "The Report on Unemployment and Relief in Western Canada in 1932: Charlotte Whitton, R.B. Bennett, and the Federal Response to Relief." MA thesis, University of Victoria, 2009.

Urry, John. *The Tourist Gaze.* London: Sage, 2002.

Usher, Peter J. "The North: One Land, Two Ways of Life," in *Heartland and Hinterland: A Geography of Canada,* second edition. Edited by L.D. McCann, 483–529. Scarborough: Prentice-Hall, 1987.

Vanderhill, B.G. "Observations on the Pioneer Fringe in Western Canada." *Journal of Geography* 57, 9 (1958): 431–40.

———. "The Passing of the Pioneer Fringe in Western Canada." *Geographical Review* 72, 2 (1982): 200–17.

Van Staveren, Irene, and B. Knorringa, eds. *Beyond Social Capital: A Critical Approach.* London: Routledge, 2008.

Vickers, J.R. "Seasonal Round Problems on the Alberta Plains." *Canadian Journal of Archaeology* 15 (1991): 55–72.

Vickers, J. Rod, and Trevor Peck. "Islands in a Sea of Grass: The Significance of Wood in Winter Campsite Selection on the Northwestern Plains." In *Archaeology on the Edge: New Perspectives from the Northern Plains,* edited by Brian Kooyman and Jane Kelley, 95–124. Calgary: University of Calgary Press, 2004.

The Voice of the People: Reminiscences of Prince Albert Settlement's Early Citizens. Prince Albert: Prince Albert Historical Society, 1984.

Voisey, Paul. "A Mix Up over Mixed Farming: The Curious History of the Agricultural Diversification Movement in a Single Crop Area of Southern Alberta." In *Building beyond the Homestead: Rural History on the Prairies,* edited by David C. Jones and Ian MacPherson, 179–206. Calgary: University of Calgary Press, 1985.

———. "Rural Local History and the Prairie West." In *The Prairie West: Historical Readings,* 2nd ed., edited by R. Douglas Francis and Howard Palmer, 497–510. Edmonton: University of Alberta Press, 1992.

———. *Vulcan: The Making of a Prairie Community.* Toronto: University of Toronto Press, 1988.

Waiser, Bill. *Who Killed Jackie Bates? Murder and Mercy during the Great Depression.* Calgary: Fifth House, 2008.

———. "Mackay, John Alexander." http://www.biographi.ca.

———. *The New Northwest: The Photographs of the Frank Crean Expeditions.* Saskatoon: Fifth House, 1993.

———. *Saskatchewan: A New History.* Calgary: Fifth House, 2005.

———. *Saskatchewan's Playground: A History of Prince Albert National Park.* Saskatoon: Fifth House, 1989.

———. "A Willing Scapegoat: John Macoun and the Route of the CPR." *Prairie Forum* 10, 1 (1985): 65–81.

Ward, Tony. "The Origins of the Canadian Wheat Boom, 1880–1910." *Canadian Journal of Economics* 27, 4 (1994): 865–83.

Weir, J.M.H. "The Fire Frequency and Age Mosaic of a Mixed Wood Boreal Forest." MSc thesis, University of Calgary, 1996.

Weir, J.M.H., and E.A. Johnson. "Effects of Escaped Settlement Fires and Logging on Forest Composition in the Mixedwood Boreal Forest." *Canadian Journal of Forest Resources* 28 (1998): 459–67.

Wetherell, Donald, and Irene Kmet. *Alberta's North: A History, 1890–1950.* Edmonton: Canadian Circumpolar Institute Press, University of Alberta Press, and Alberta Community Development, 2000.

White, Richard. *Land Use, Environment, and Social Change: The Shaping of Island Country, Washington.* Seattle: University of Washington Press, 1980.

———. *The Middle Ground: Indians, Empires, and Republics in the Great Lakes Region, 1650–1815.* Cambridge, UK: Cambridge University Press, 1991.

Wilder, Laura Ingalls. *Farmer Boy.* 1933; reprinted, New York: HarperCollins, 1994.

———. *The First Four Years.* New York: HarperCollins, 1971.

Williams, C.M. (Red). "Always the Bridesmaid: The Development of the Saskatchewan Beef Production System," part 1. *Saskatchewan History* 42, 3 (1989): 106–18.

Wishart, David. "Preliminary Thoughts on Region and Period." Center for Great Plains Studies. http://www.unl.edu/plains/about/thoughts.shtml.

Wood, J. David. *Places of Last Resort: The Expansion of the Farm Frontier into the Boreal Forest in Canada, c. 1910–1940*. Montreal: McGill-Queen's University Press, 2006.

Wright, Jim. *Saskatchewan: The History of a Province*. Toronto: McClelland and Stewart, 1955.

Wrobel, David, and Michael Steiner, eds. *Many Wests: Place, Culture, and Regional Identity*. Lincoln: University Press of Kansas, 1997.

Zaslow, Morris. *The Northward Expansion of Canada*. Toronto: McClelland and Stewart, 1988.

————. *The Opening of the Canadian North 1870–1914*. Toronto: McClelland and Stewart, 1971.

INDEX

167–69; environmental impact of, 85–87,
89–90; and First Nations, 58, 59, 64, 80–85,
91; importance of railway to, 110; and Sturgeon River Forest Reserve, 87–88

Lundlie, O.M., 194

M

MacFadyen, C., 196

Mackay, John A., 60, 63, 106, 157

Mackenzie, Alexander, 49

Macoun, John, 68, 69, 97, 280n121

Mather, W.J., 224

Matte, G.J., 223–24, 239

Mayor, James, 96

McCloskey, M.D., 144, 146, 147, 148, 189–90,
233

McGillivray, Duncan, 48

McGowan, Mabel, 249

McGowan, Muriel, 213, 228, 233, 242, 248

McGowan, Norman, 249

McGowan, Sargent, 213, 228, 242, 248

McKay, Nan, 176, 184–86, 189

McOwan, A., 154

Meadow Lake, 236

mechanization, 152, 240, 242–43, 251, 260

Medstead, 296n48

Melfort, 137

Métis, 53, 160, 247–48

Milligan, Silas, 84

mining, 171–74, 217–18

Mistawasis, 55

Mitchell, Hillyard, 157, 158–59

mixed farming: as choice of bored wheat farmers,
129–30; combined with ranching, 114,
146–47; and cordwood economy, 169–71;
during Depression, 214, 228–29; economics
of, 155; and edge theory, 121–22, 153, 228;
as government's mode of agriculture, 125–26,
148, 209; and Home Branch, 140–43; and
Land Settlement Act, 218–19; land sold back
to government, 251–52, 260–61; mechanization of, 152; movement for, 97–101, 154–55,
258; in north Prince Albert region, 93, 103,
104–5, 107–9, 111–13, 114, 115–22, 152,
230–34; and off-farm opportunities, 160,
164–65, 167–69, 174–75; and resilience, 92,

97, 121; and second homestead applications,
216–17; and soldier settlement, 134–38,
148–49, 258–59; as subsistence farming,
252–53; why it failed to gain converts,
100–102

Modern Voyageurs, 201, 204, 247

Montgomery, Lucy Maud, 177, 181, 184, 212

Montreal Lake, 157–61, 184–87

Montreal Lake Reserve, 200–201

Montreal Lake Trail, 256–57

Montreal River, 173

Moore, William, 69–70, 73, 178, 289n9

Moose Lake, 233–34, 251–52

Morse, C.H., 87

Motherwell, W. R., 97

Muldrew, Jean, 142

Murray, Walter, 210

Murray Point Art School, 210–11

N

National Parks Branch, 194–206

Neis, George, 212, 244

New Northwest, 111

Newnham, J.A., 89–90

Nisbet, James, 56

Nisbet Provincial Forest, 31, 32

north Prince Albert region: abundance of, 47,
48; adhesions to Treaty 6, 59–62; area of,
17–18, 19; climate, 35–36; conditions today,
253, 260; cordwood economy of, 169–71;
creation of NSRB, 239–40; Cree inhabitants
of, 44–48, 51–53; crop failure of 1937, 250;
ecological history, 28–30, 36; as ecotone, 254;
and fur trade, 48, 53; as haying and ranching country, 127, 146–47; immigration to,
102–3, 125, 151–52; importance of fire to,
28–29, 30–31; and mixed farming, 93, 103,
104–5, 107–9, 111–13, 114, 115–22, 152,
230–34; need of bridge over N. Saskatchewan, 110–11; occupational sources during
Depression, 240–46; out-migration from,
250–51; physiography, 31–35; prehistory
of, 27–28; promoted for its beauty, 177–78,
180–81; rail service to, 110–11, 145–46; receives southern migrants, 126, 127–29, 147,
151, 174, 213–16; resource development,
217–18; second homestead applications,
216–17; and soldier settlement, 119, 123–25,